BLOODY CROSS

1

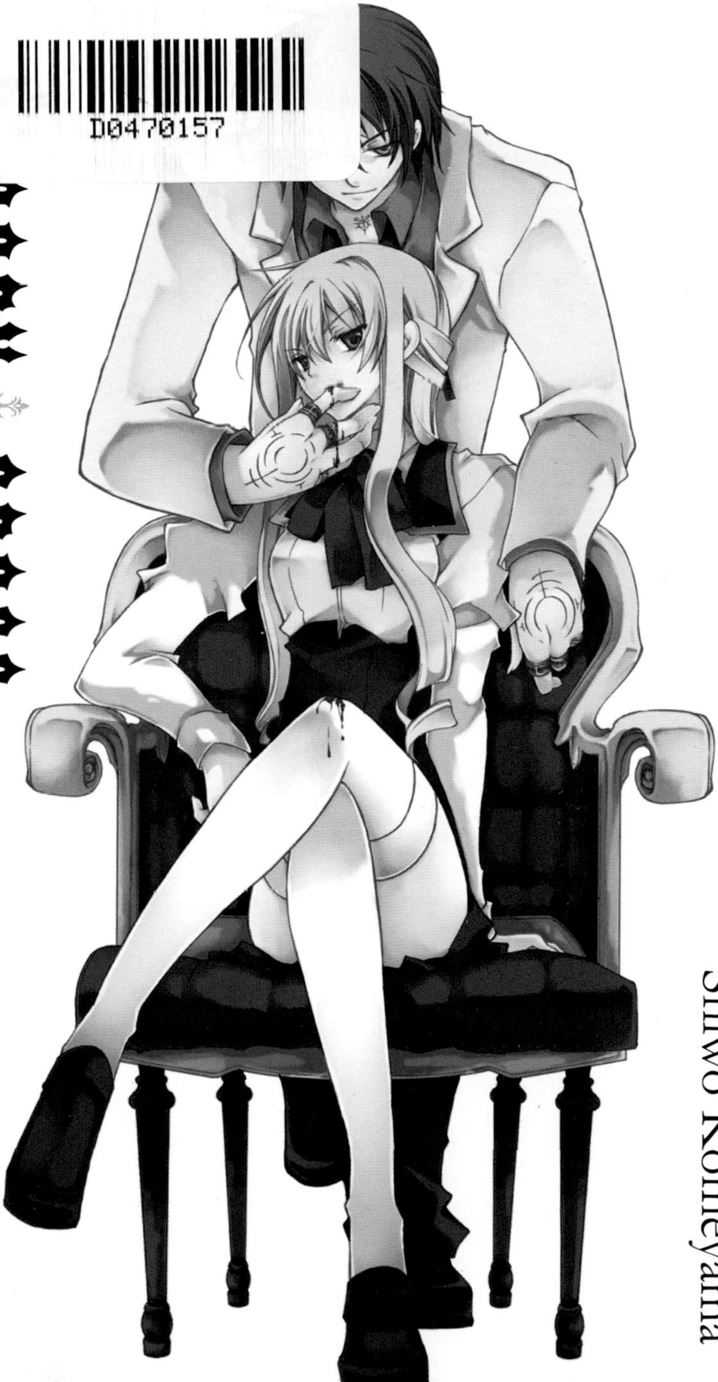

Shiwo Komeyama

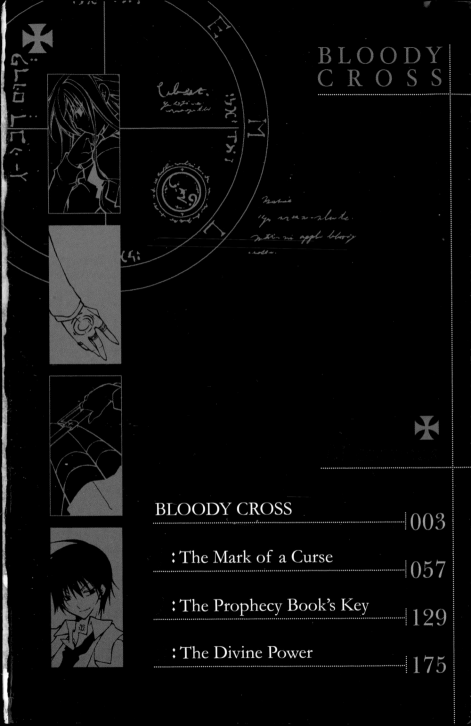

BLOODY CROSS

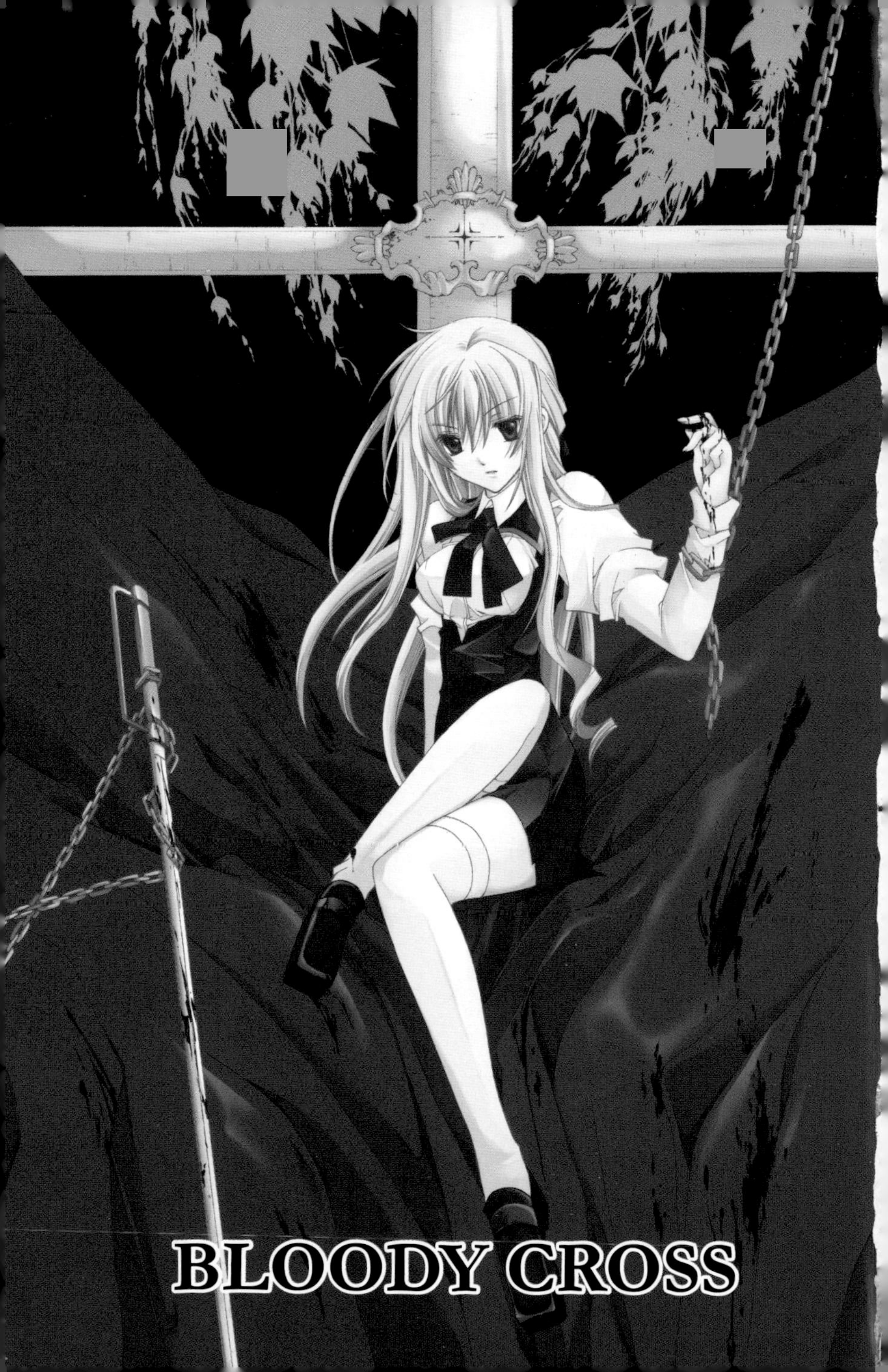
BLOODY CROSS

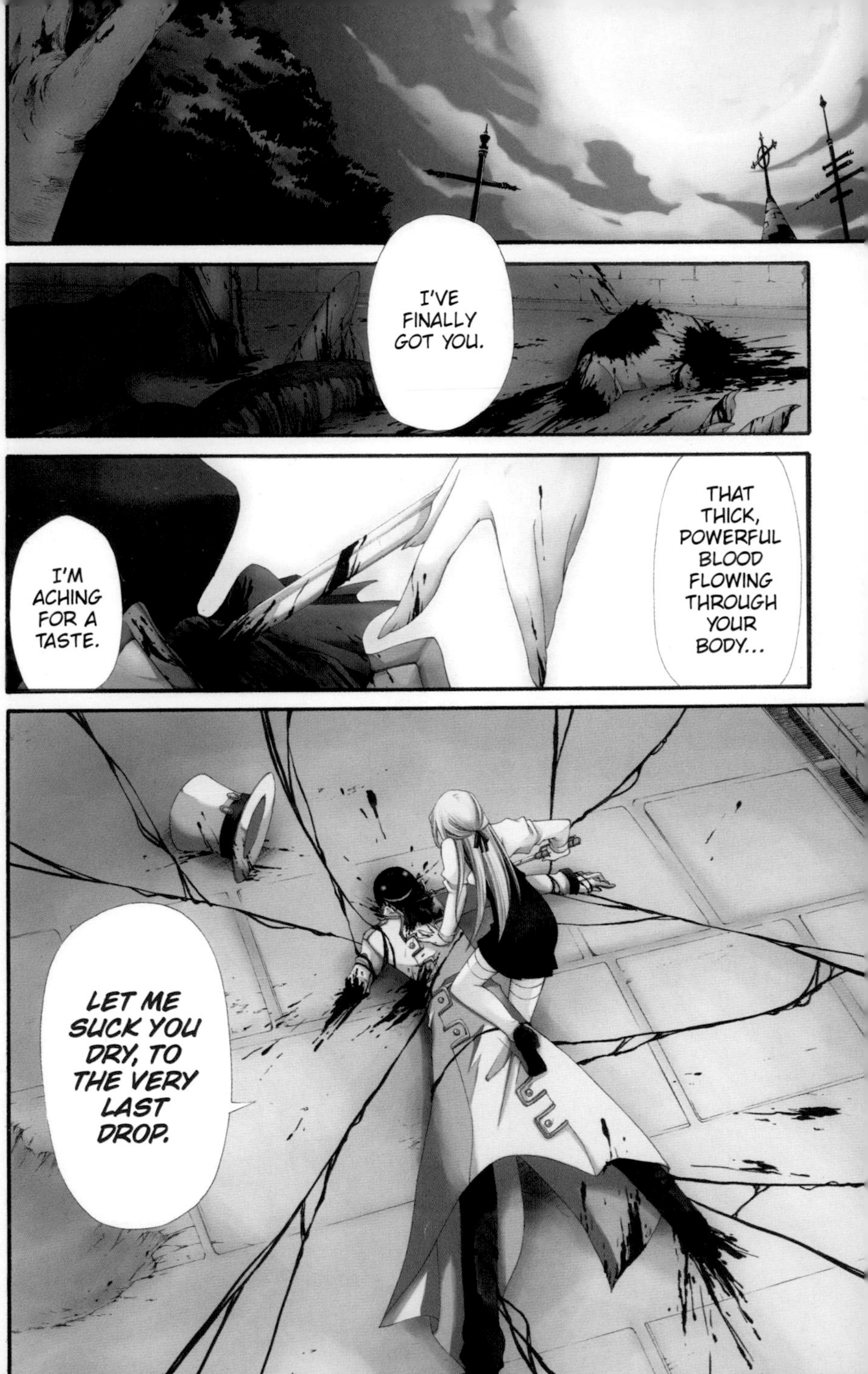
I'VE FINALLY GOT YOU.
THAT THICK, POWERFUL BLOOD FLOWING THROUGH YOUR BODY...
I'M ACHING FOR A TASTE.
LET ME SUCK YOU DRY, TO THE VERY LAST DROP.

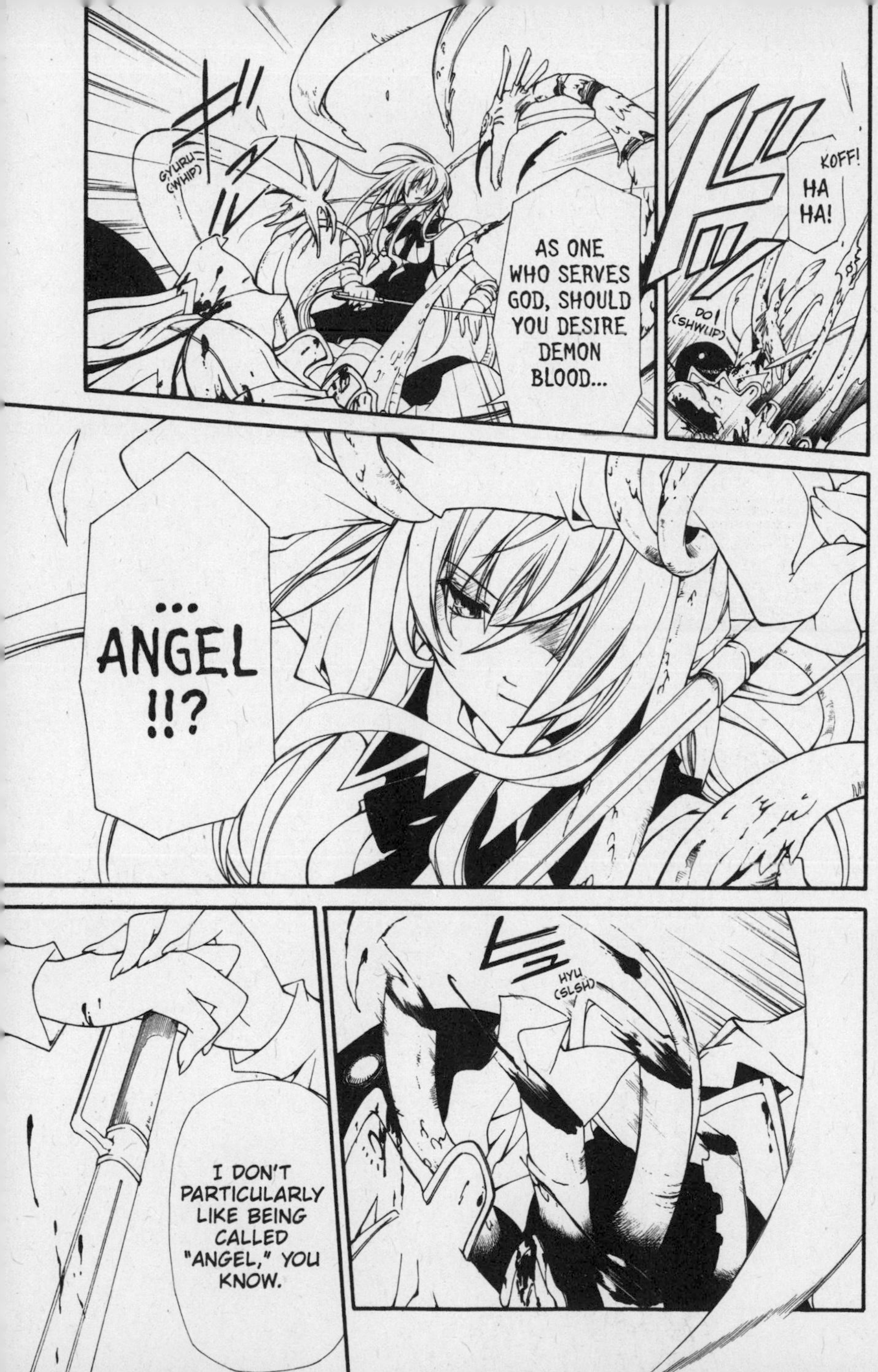
KOFF!
HA HA!
DO (SHWLIP)
GYURU (WHIP)
AS ONE WHO SERVES GOD, SHOULD YOU DESIRE DEMON BLOOD...
...ANGEL!!?
HYU (SLSH)
I DON'T PARTICULARLY LIKE BEING CALLED "ANGEL," YOU KNOW.

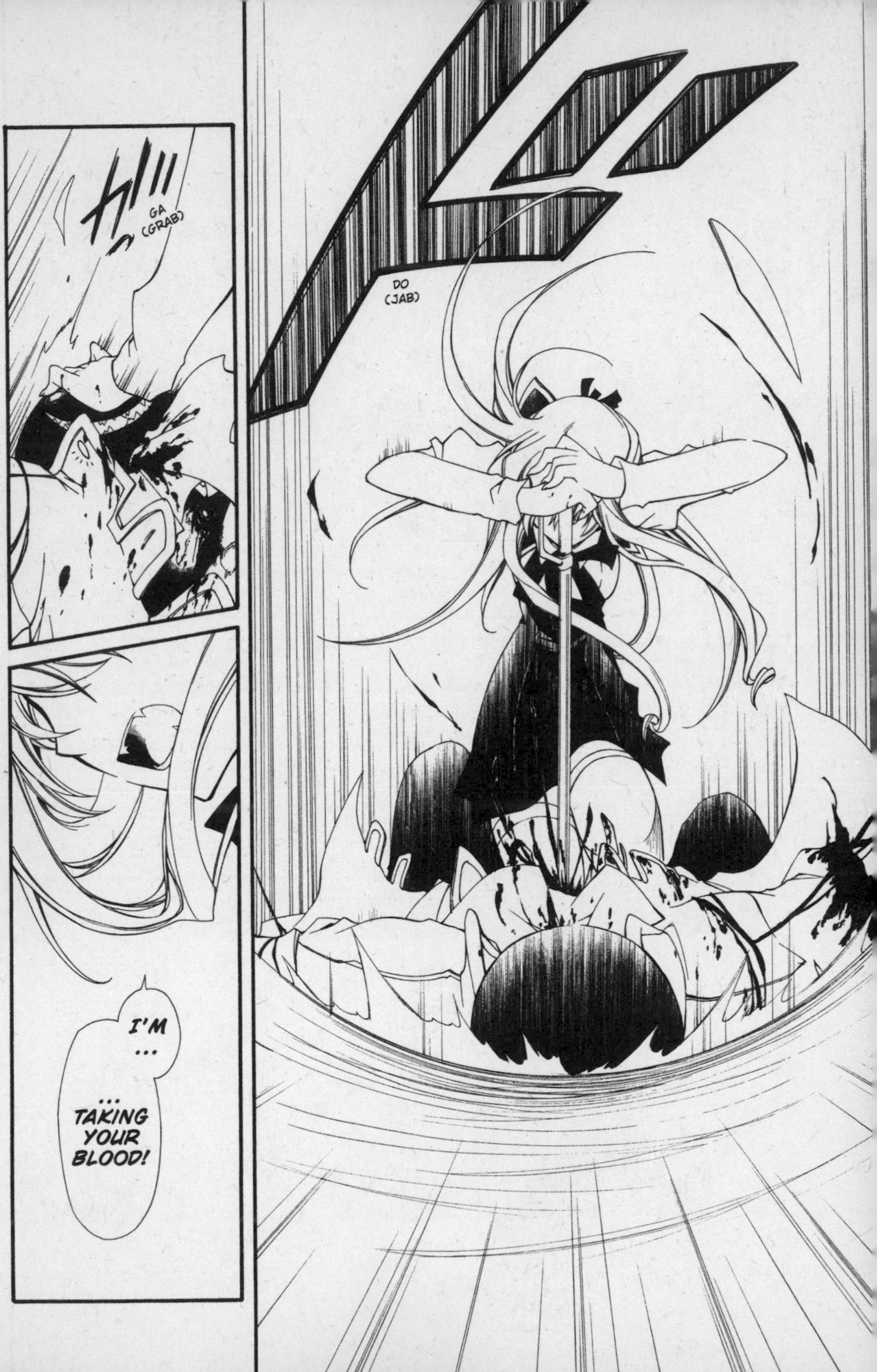
DO
(JAB)
ガ!!
GA
(GRAB)
I'M ...
... TAKING YOUR BLOOD!

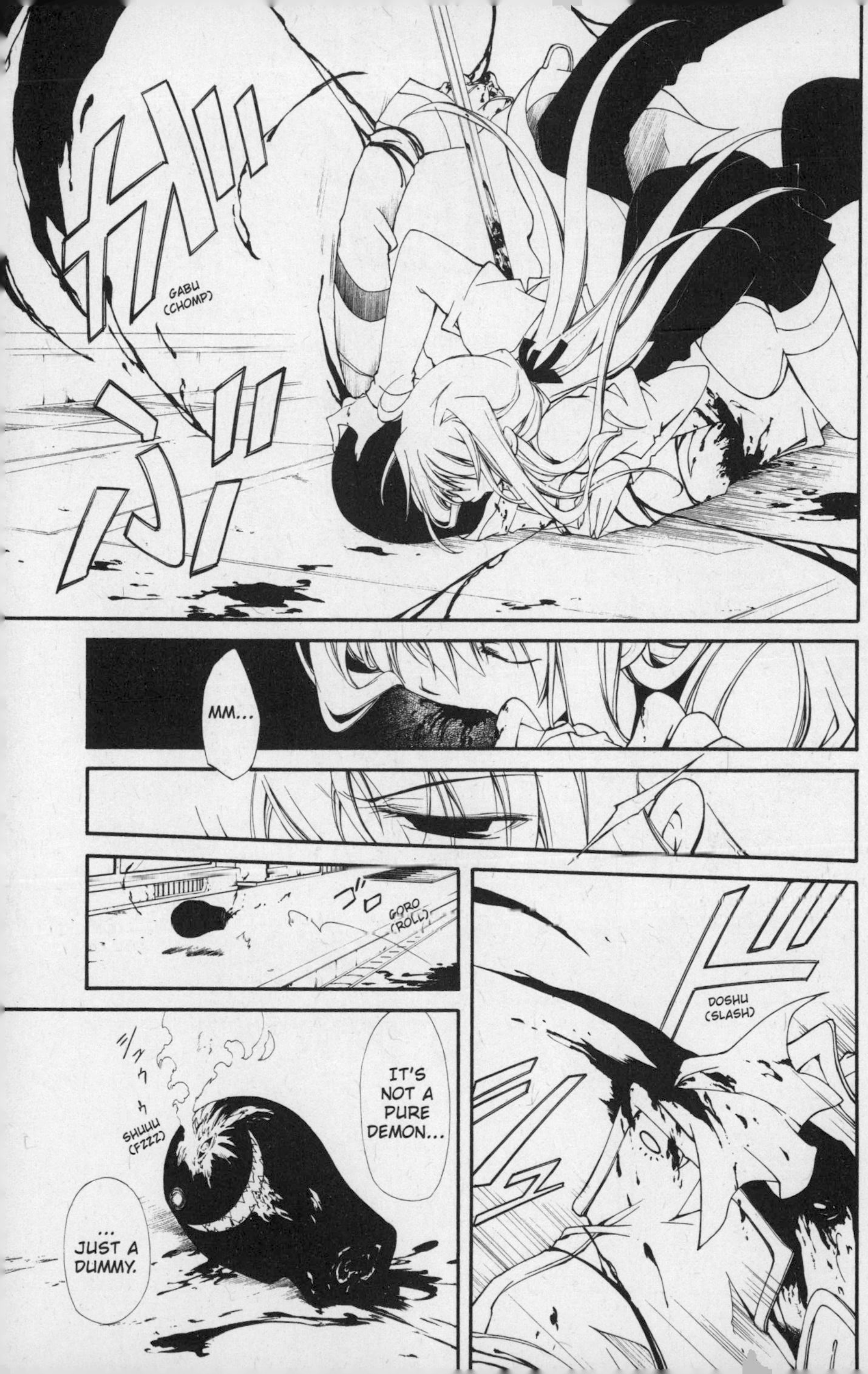
GABU (CHOMP)
MM...
DOSHU (SLASH)
GORO (ROLL)
IT'S NOT A PURE DEMON...
SHUUU (FZZZ)
... JUST A DUMMY.

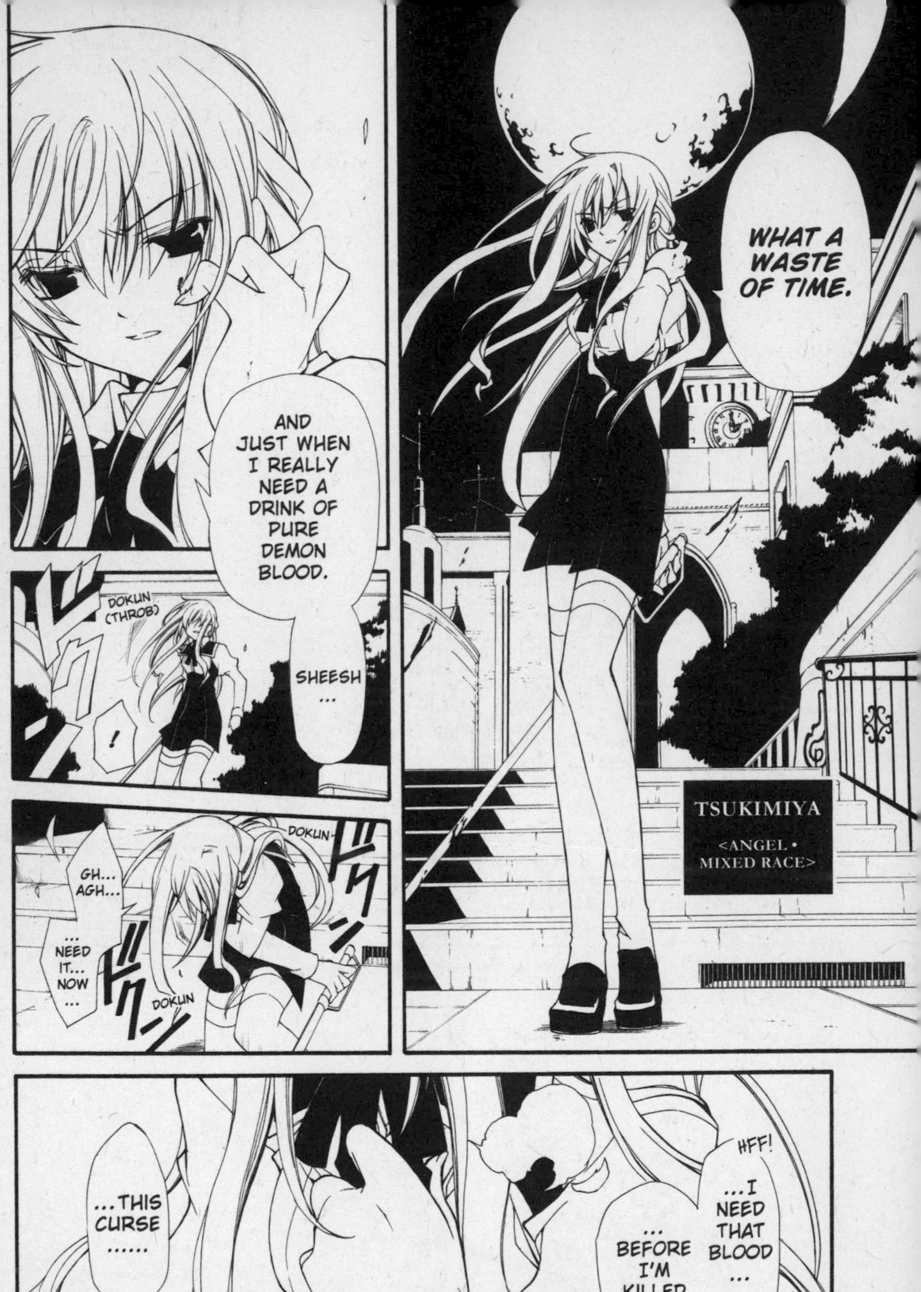
WHAT A WASTE OF TIME.
TSUKIMIYA
<ANGEL • MIXED RACE>
AND JUST WHEN I REALLY NEED A DRINK OF PURE DEMON BLOOD.
SHEESH ...
DOKUN (THROB)
!
DOKUN
GH... AGH...
... NEED IT... NOW ...
DOKUN
HFF!
...I NEED THAT BLOOD ...
... BEFORE I'M KILLED BY...
...THIS CURSE ......

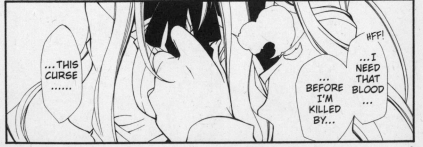

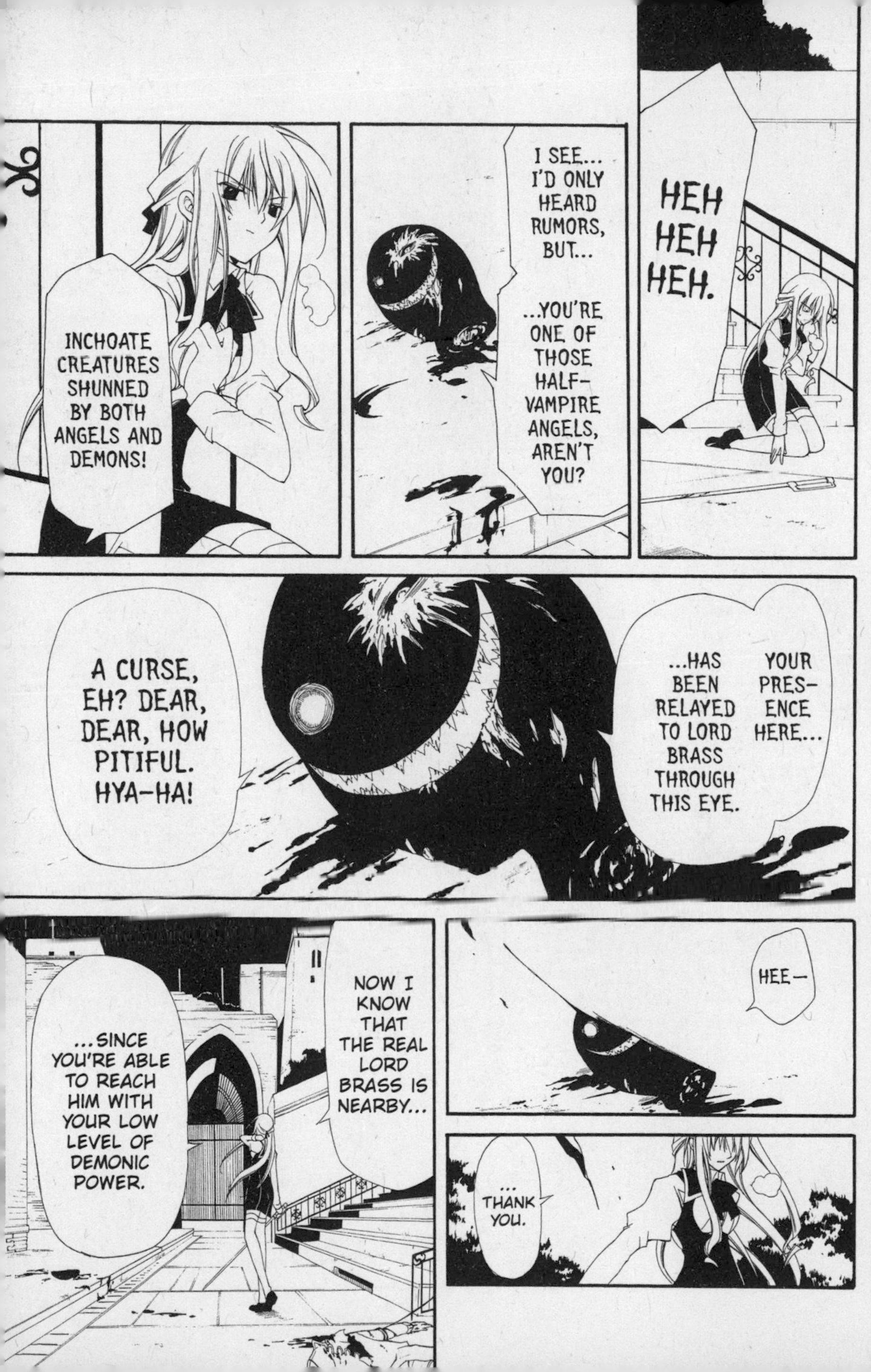
HEH HEH HEH.
I SEE... I'D ONLY HEARD RUMORS, BUT...
...YOU'RE ONE OF THOSE HALF-VAMPIRE ANGELS, AREN'T YOU?
INCHOATE CREATURES SHUNNED BY BOTH ANGELS AND DEMONS!
YOUR PRES-ENCE HERE...
...HAS BEEN RELAYED TO LORD BRASS THROUGH THIS EYE.
A CURSE, EH? DEAR, DEAR, HOW PITIFUL. HYA-HA!
HEE—
...THANK YOU.
NOW I KNOW THAT THE REAL LORD BRASS IS NEARBY...
...SINCE YOU'RE ABLE TO REACH HIM WITH YOUR LOW LEVEL OF DEMONIC POWER.

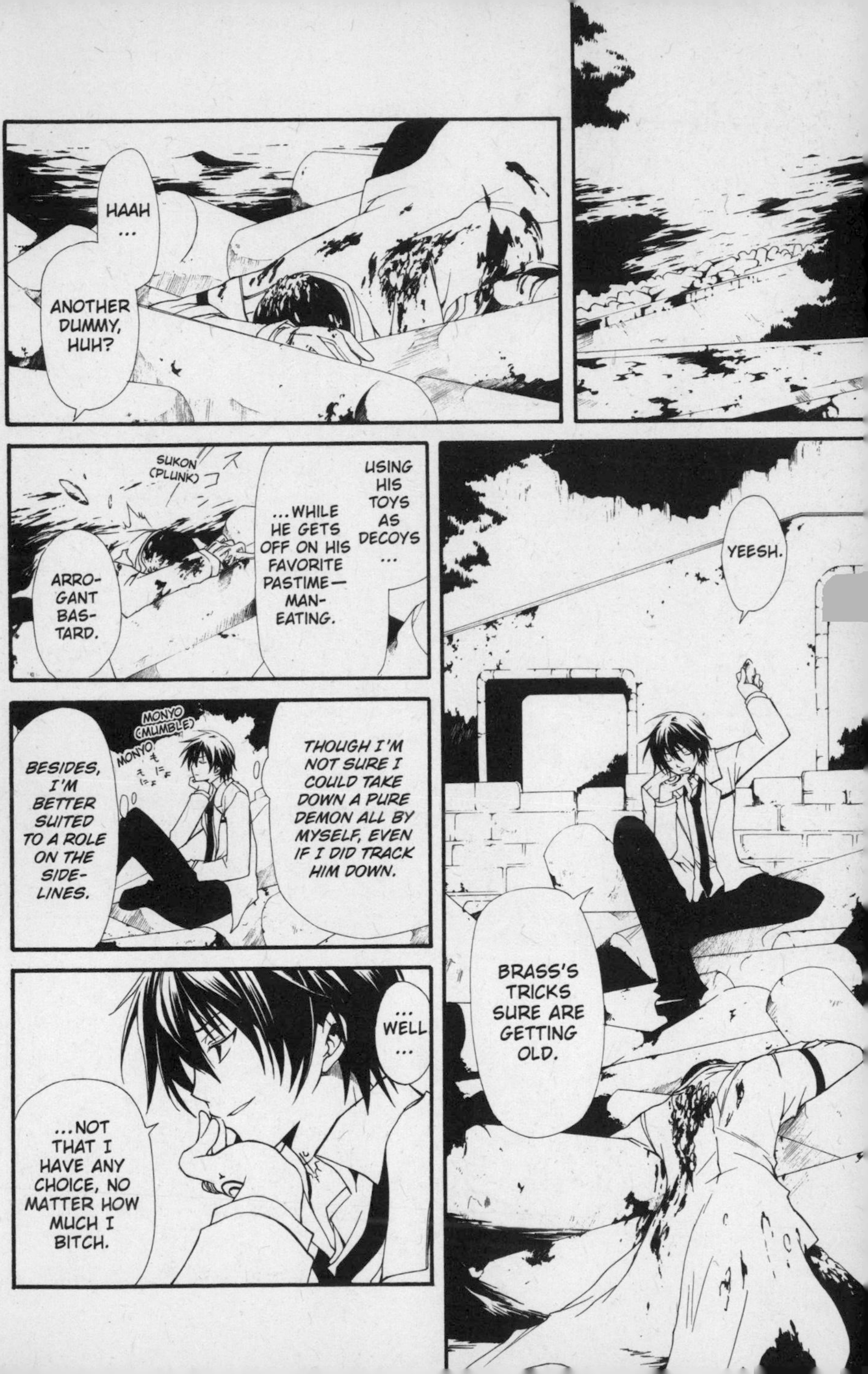
HAAH ...
ANOTHER DUMMY, HUH?
YEESH.
BRASS'S TRICKS SURE ARE GETTING OLD.
USING HIS TOYS AS DECOYS ...
...WHILE HE GETS OFF ON HIS FAVORITE PASTIME—MAN-EATING.
SUKON (PLUNK)
ARRO-GANT BAS-TARD.
THOUGH I'M NOT SURE I COULD TAKE DOWN A PURE DEMON ALL BY MYSELF, EVEN IF I DID TRACK HIM DOWN.
MONYO (MUMBLE)
MONYO
BESIDES, I'M BETTER SUITED TO A ROLE ON THE SIDE-LINES.
... WELL ...
...NOT THAT I HAVE ANY CHOICE, NO MATTER HOW MUCH I BITCH.

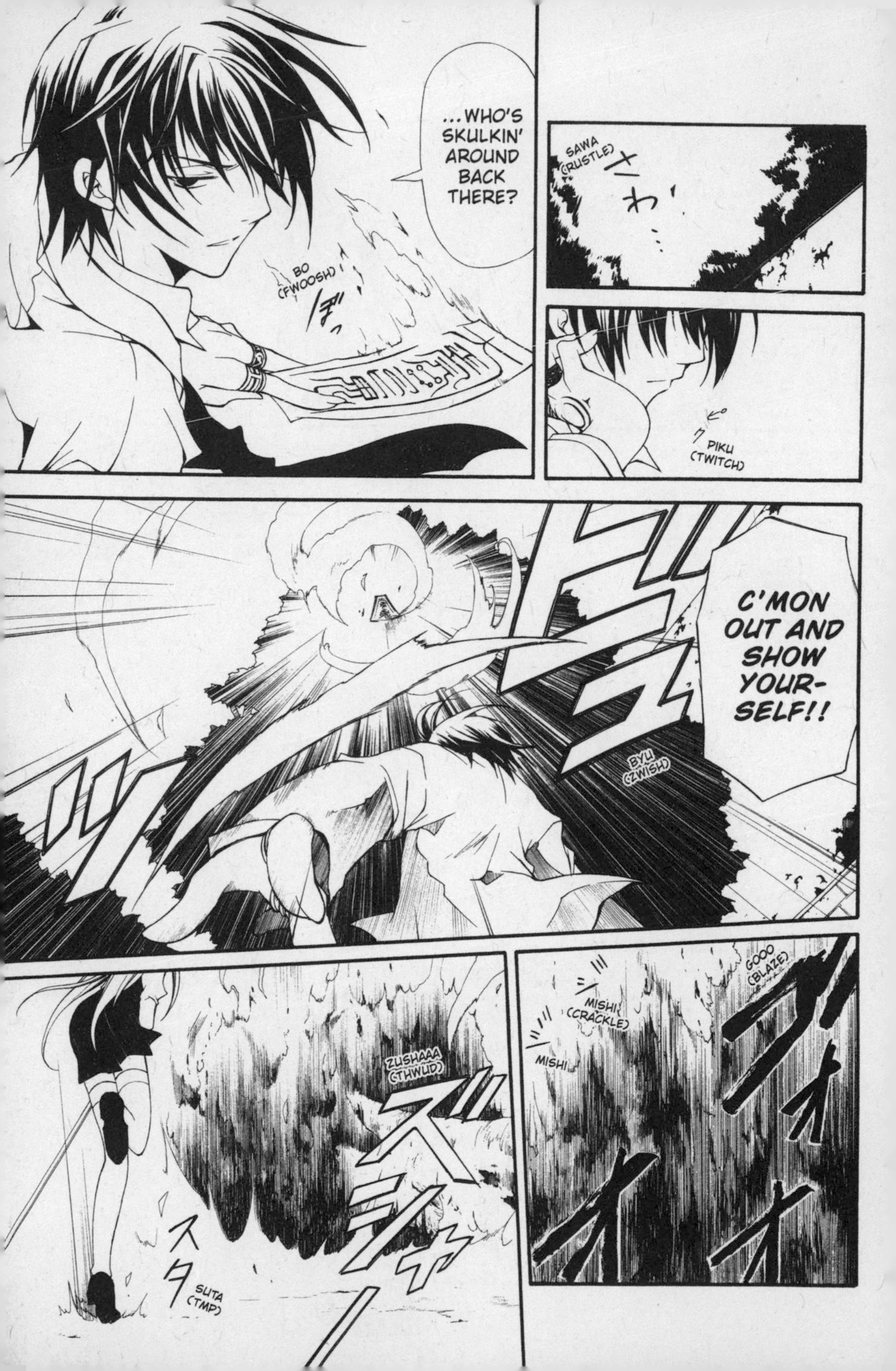
SAWA (RUSTLE)
さわ
PIKU (TWITCH)
ピク
...WHO'S SKULKIN' AROUND BACK THERE?
BO (FWOOSH)
ぼっ
BYU (ZWISH)
C'MON OUT AND SHOW YOUR-SELF!!
GOOO (BLAZE)
MISHI (CRACKLE)
MISHI
ZUSHAAA (THWUD)
SUTA (TMP)
スタ

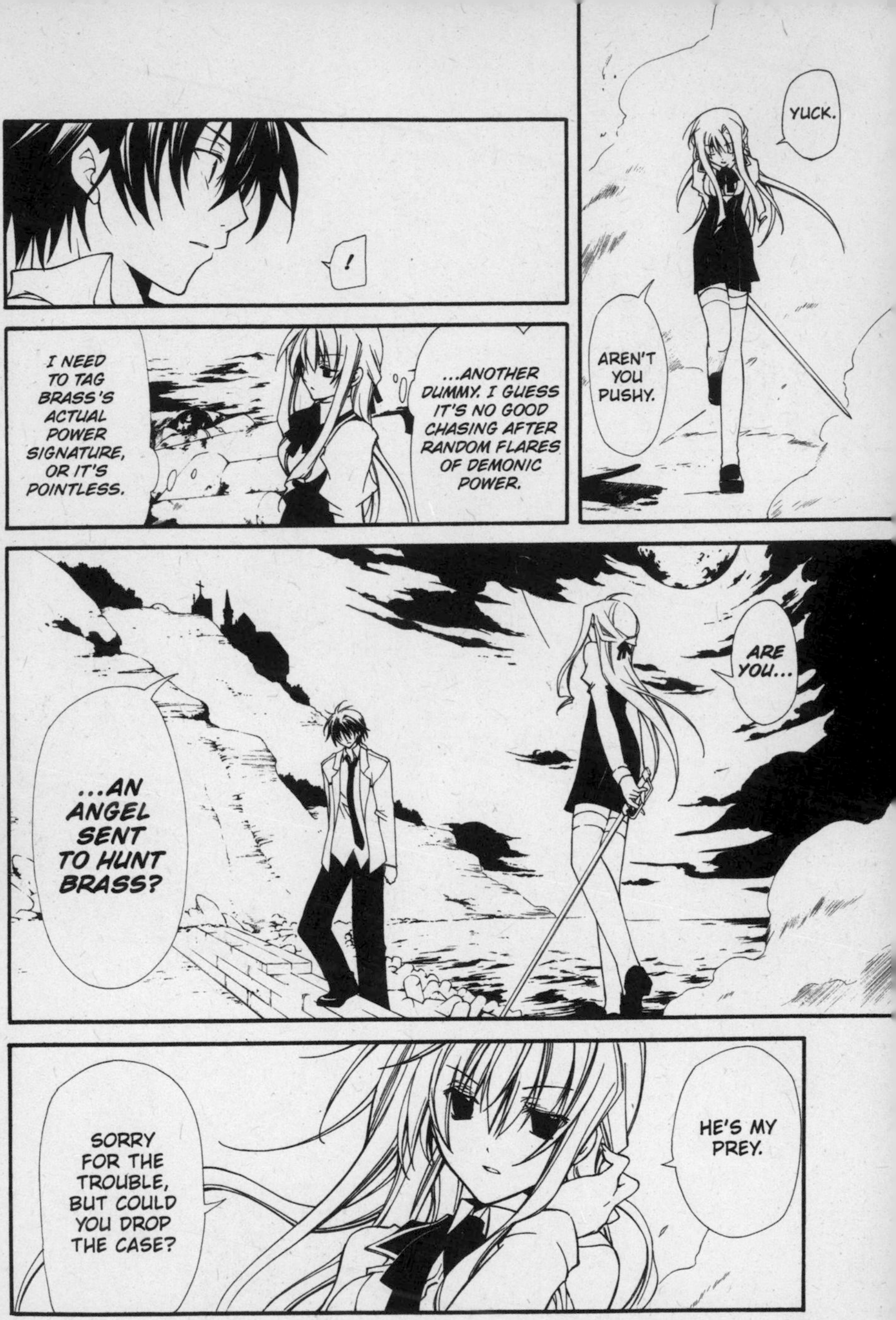
YUCK.
AREN'T YOU PUSHY.
!
...ANOTHER DUMMY. I GUESS IT'S NO GOOD CHASING AFTER RANDOM FLARES OF DEMONIC POWER.
I NEED TO TAG BRASS'S ACTUAL POWER SIGNATURE, OR IT'S POINTLESS.
ARE YOU...
...AN ANGEL SENT TO HUNT BRASS?
HE'S MY PREY.
SORRY FOR THE TROUBLE, BUT COULD YOU DROP THE CASE?

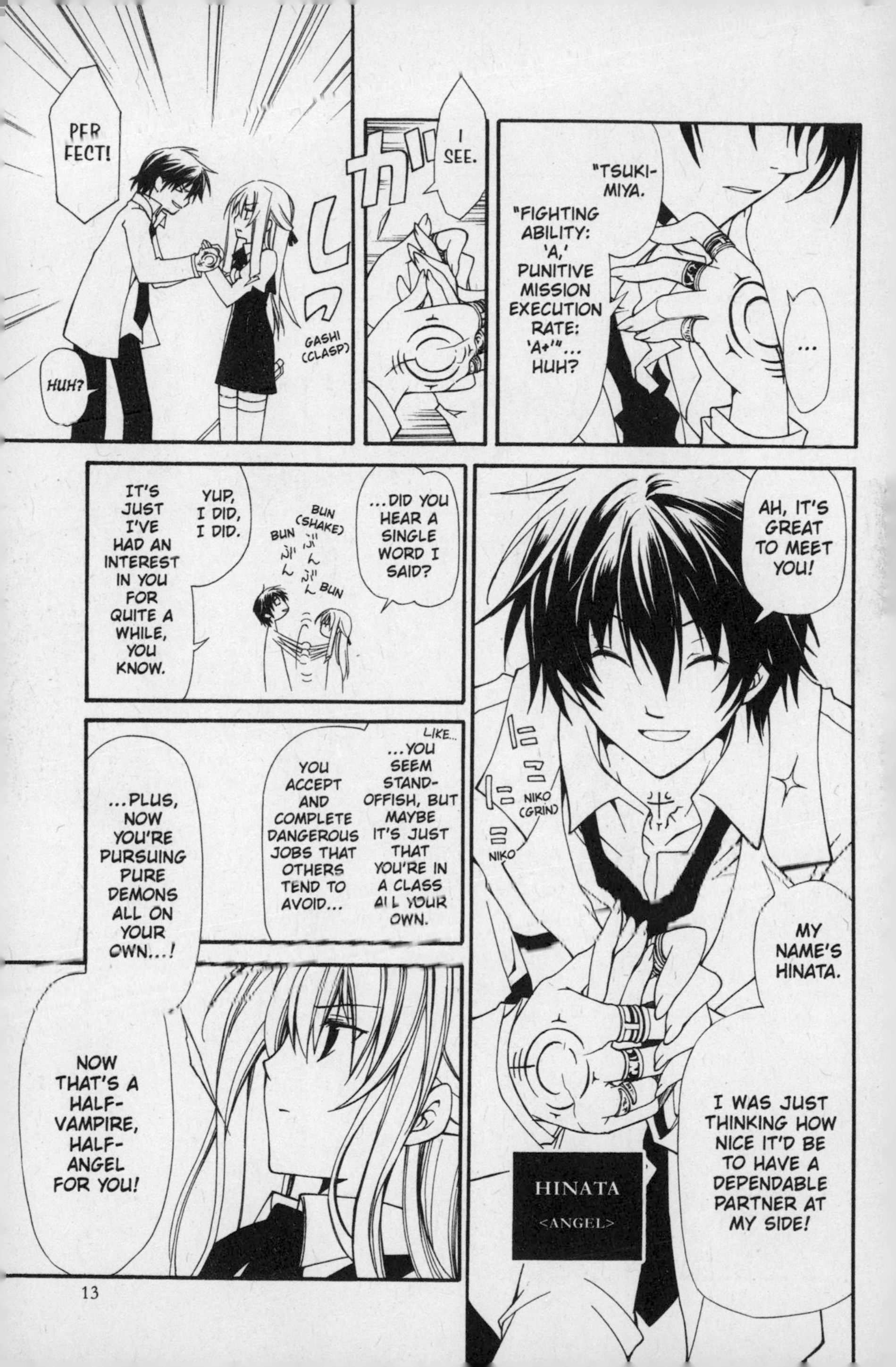
"TSUKIMIYA. "FIGHTING ABILITY: 'A,' PUNITIVE MISSION EXECUTION RATE: 'A+'"... HUH?
...
I SEE.
GASHI (CLASP)
PERFECT!
HUH?
AH, IT'S GREAT TO MEET YOU!
NIKO (GRIN)
NIKO
MY NAME'S HINATA.
I WAS JUST THINKING HOW NICE IT'D BE TO HAVE A DEPENDABLE PARTNER AT MY SIDE!
HINATA
<ANGEL>
...DID YOU HEAR A SINGLE WORD I SAID?
BUN (SHAKE) BUN BUN
YUP, I DID, I DID.
IT'S JUST I'VE HAD AN INTEREST IN YOU FOR QUITE A WHILE, YOU KNOW.
LIKE... ...YOU SEEM STANDOFFISH, BUT MAYBE IT'S JUST THAT YOU'RE IN A CLASS ALL YOUR OWN.
YOU ACCEPT AND COMPLETE DANGEROUS JOBS THAT OTHERS TEND TO AVOID...
...PLUS, NOW YOU'RE PURSUING PURE DEMONS ALL ON YOUR OWN...!
NOW THAT'S A HALF-VAMPIRE, HALF-ANGEL FOR YOU!

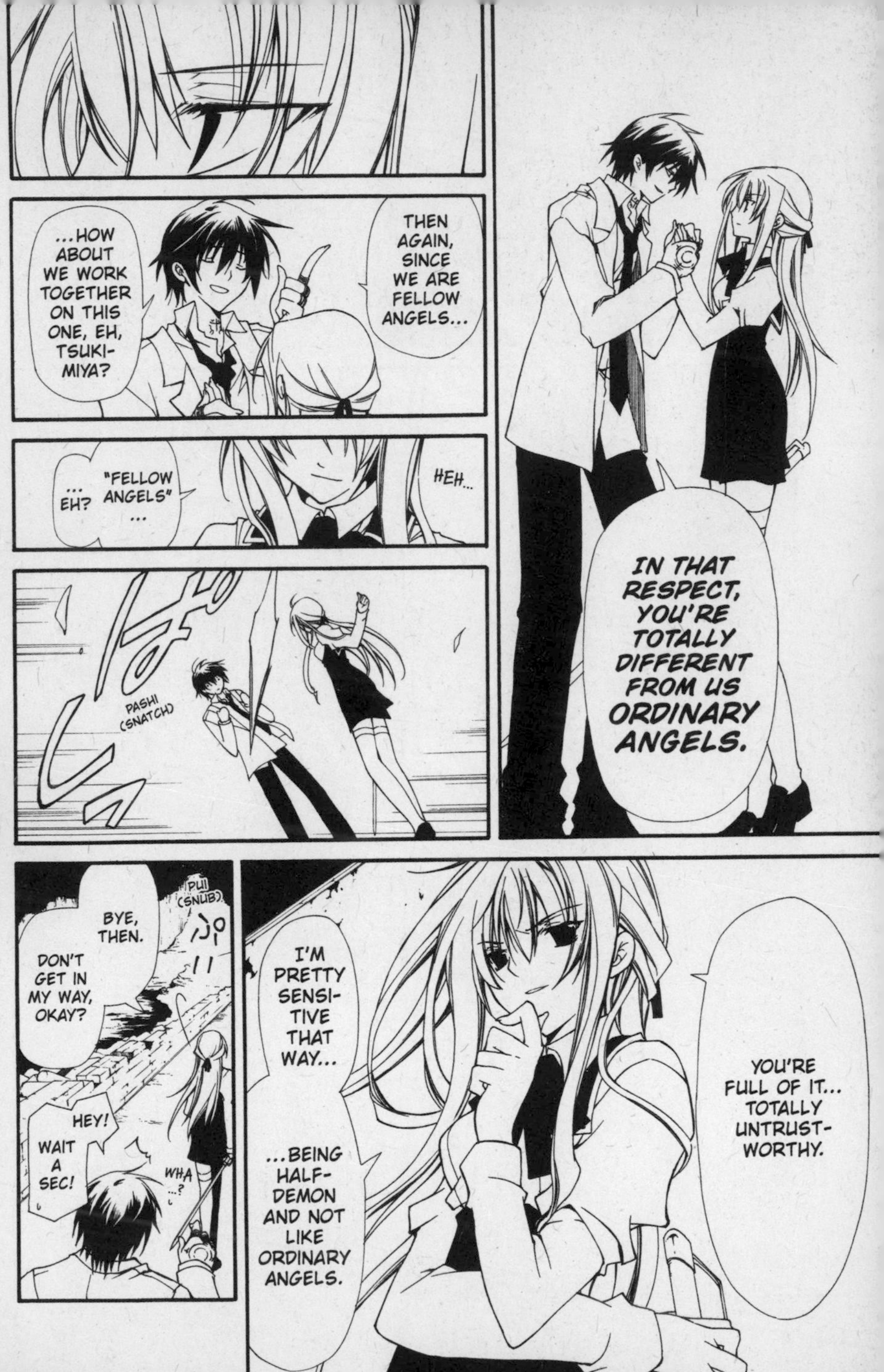
IN THAT RESPECT, YOU'RE TOTALLY DIFFERENT FROM US ORDINARY ANGELS.
THEN AGAIN, SINCE WE ARE FELLOW ANGELS...
...HOW ABOUT WE WORK TOGETHER ON THIS ONE, EH, TSUKI-MIYA?
HEH...
"FELLOW ANGELS"...
...EH?
PASHI (SNATCH)
YOU'RE FULL OF IT... TOTALLY UNTRUST-WORTHY.
I'M PRETTY SENSI-TIVE THAT WAY...
...BEING HALF-DEMON AND NOT LIKE ORDINARY ANGELS.
PUI (SNUB)
BYE, THEN.
DON'T GET IN MY WAY, OKAY?
WHA...?
HEY! WAIT A SEC!

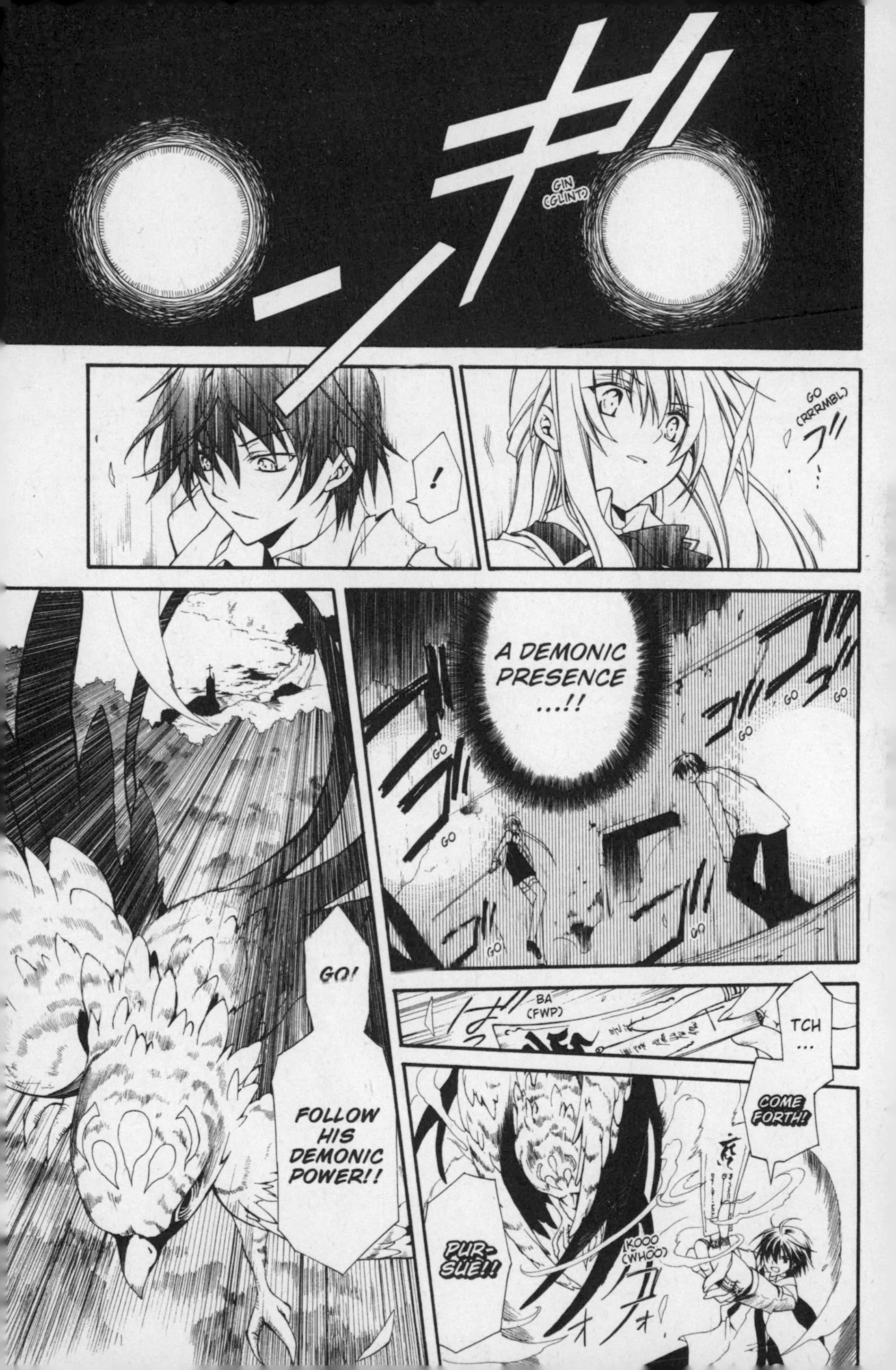
GIN (GLINT)
GO (RRRMBL)
!
A DEMONIC PRESENCE ...!!
GO GO GO GO GO GO GO
BA (FWP)
TCH ...
COME FORTH!
KOOO (WHOO)
PUR-SUE!!
GO!
FOLLOW HIS DEMONIC POWER!!

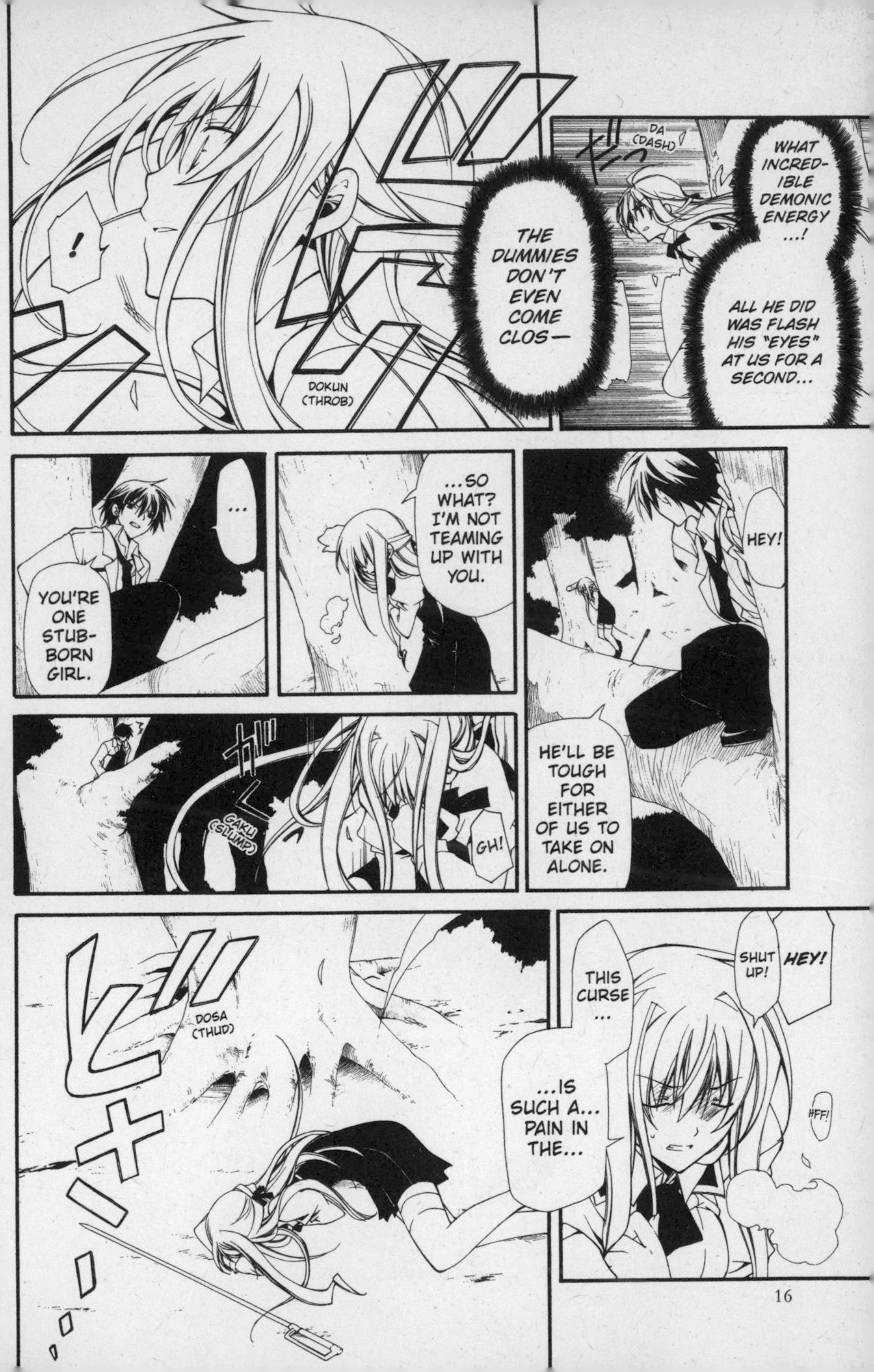
DA (DASH)
WHAT INCREDIBLE DEMONIC ENERGY...!
ALL HE DID WAS FLASH HIS "EYES" AT US FOR A SECOND...
!
THE DUMMIES DON'T EVEN COME CLOS—
DOKUN (THROB)
HEY!
HE'LL BE TOUGH FOR EITHER OF US TO TAKE ON ALONE.
...SO WHAT? I'M NOT TEAMING UP WITH YOU.
...
YOU'RE ONE STUBBORN GIRL.
GAKU (SLUMP)
GH!
HEY!
SHUT UP!
THIS CURSE...
...IS SUCH A... PAIN IN THE...
HFF!
DOSA (THUD)

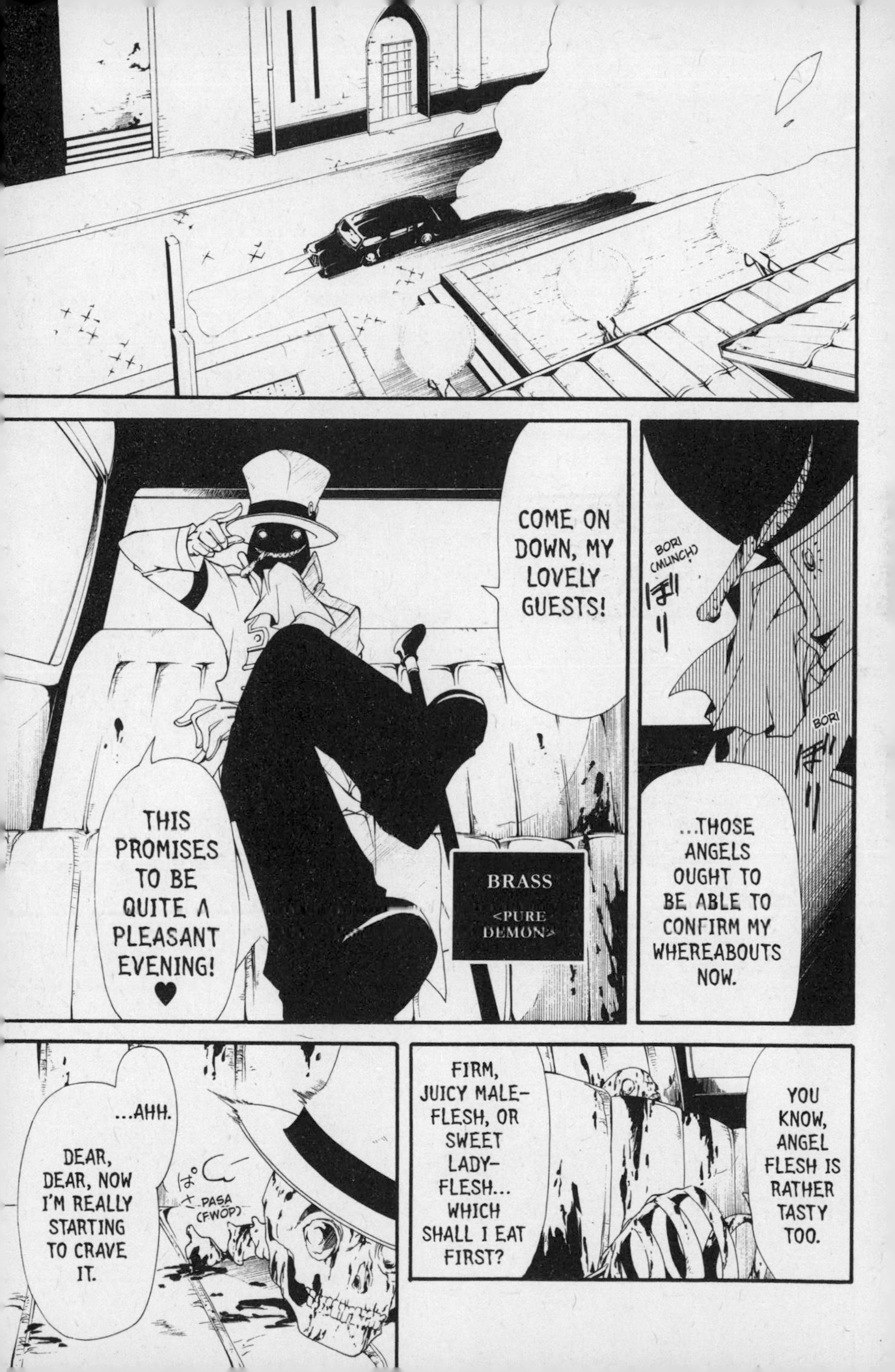
ぼり
BORI (MUNCH)
ぼり
BORI
...THOSE ANGELS OUGHT TO BE ABLE TO CONFIRM MY WHEREABOUTS NOW.
COME ON DOWN, MY LOVELY GUESTS!
BRASS
<PURE DEMON>
THIS PROMISES TO BE QUITE A PLEASANT EVENING! ♥
YOU KNOW, ANGEL FLESH IS RATHER TASTY TOO.
FIRM, JUICY MALE-FLESH, OR SWEET LADY-FLESH... WHICH SHALL I EAT FIRST?
...AHH.
DEAR, DEAR, NOW I'M REALLY STARTING TO CRAVE IT.
ぱさ
PASA (F-WOP)

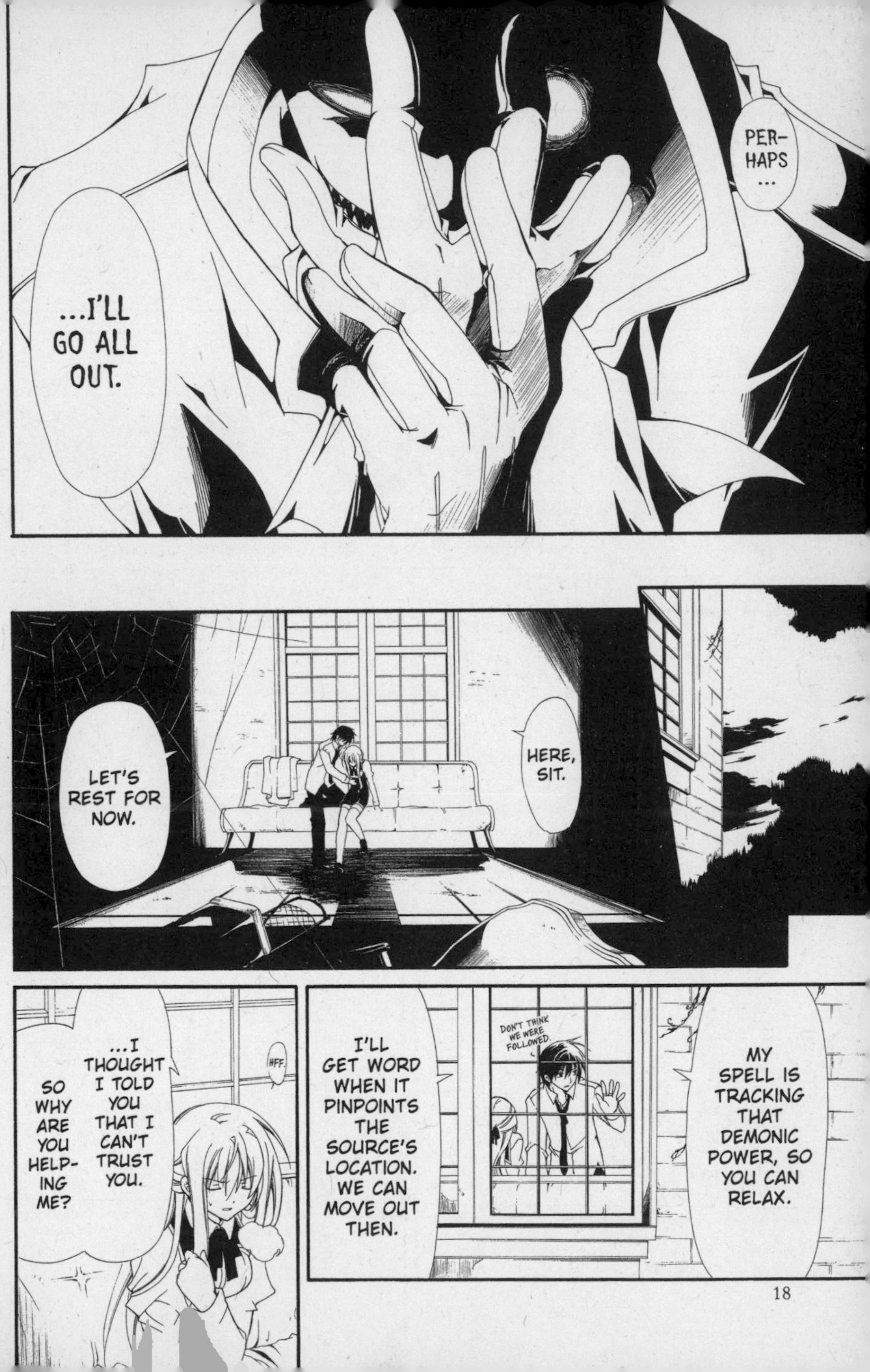
PER-HAPS...
...I'LL GO ALL OUT.
HERE, SIT.
LET'S REST FOR NOW.
MY SPELL IS TRACKING THAT DEMONIC POWER, SO YOU CAN RELAX.
DON'T THINK WE WERE FOLLOWED.
I'LL GET WORD WHEN IT PINPOINTS THE SOURCE'S LOCATION. WE CAN MOVE OUT THEN.
HFF.
...I THOUGHT I TOLD YOU THAT I CAN'T TRUST YOU.
SO WHY ARE YOU HELPING ME?

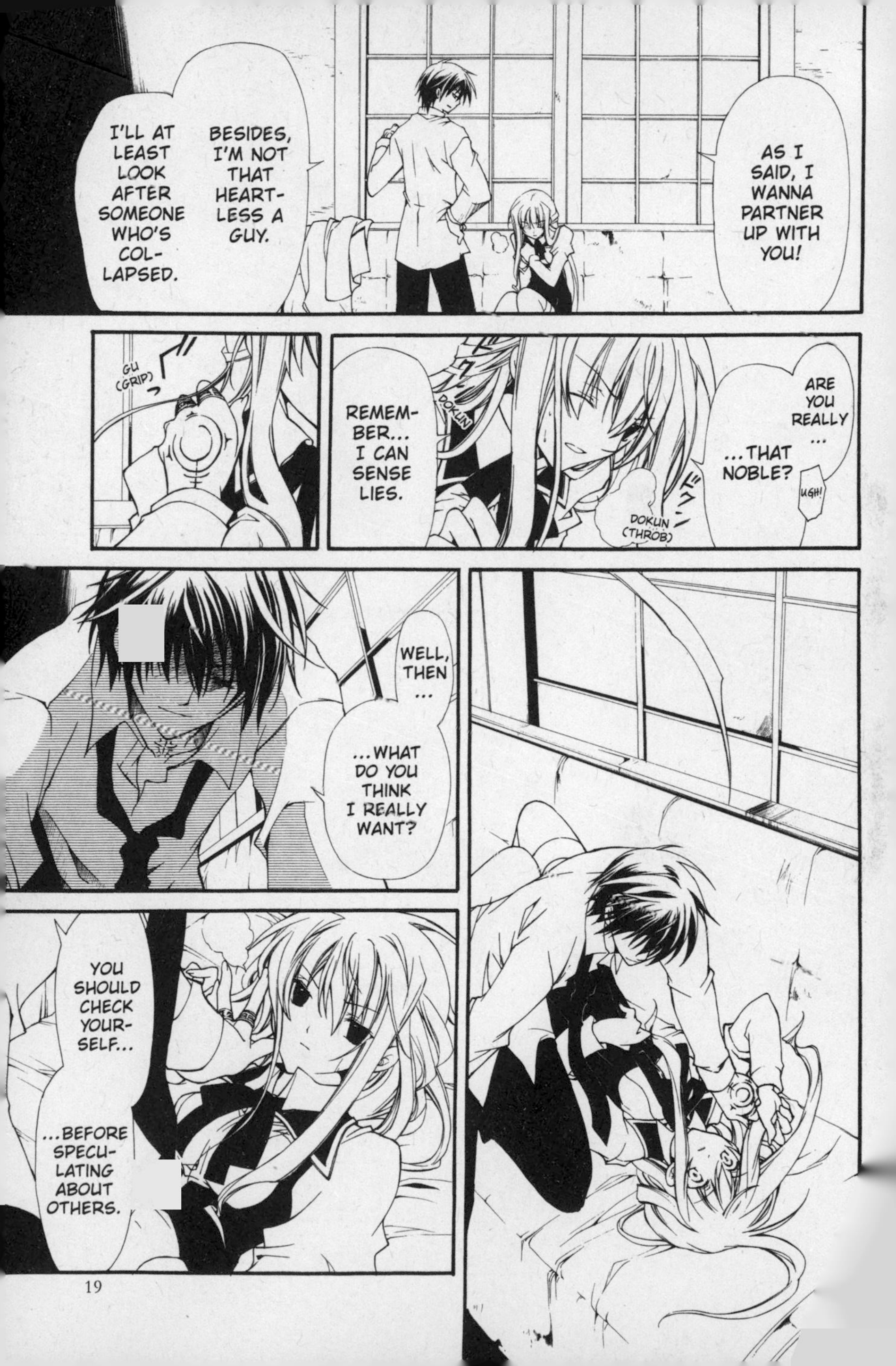

AS I SAID, I WANNA PARTNER UP WITH YOU!
BESIDES, I'M NOT THAT HEART-LESS A GUY.
I'LL AT LEAST LOOK AFTER SOMEONE WHO'S COL-LAPSED.
ARE YOU REALLY...
...THAT NOBLE?
UGH!
DOKUN (THROB)
DOKUN
REMEMBER... I CAN SENSE LIES.
GU (GRIP)
WELL, THEN...
...WHAT DO YOU THINK I REALLY WANT?
YOU SHOULD CHECK YOURSELF...
...BEFORE SPECULATING ABOUT OTHERS.

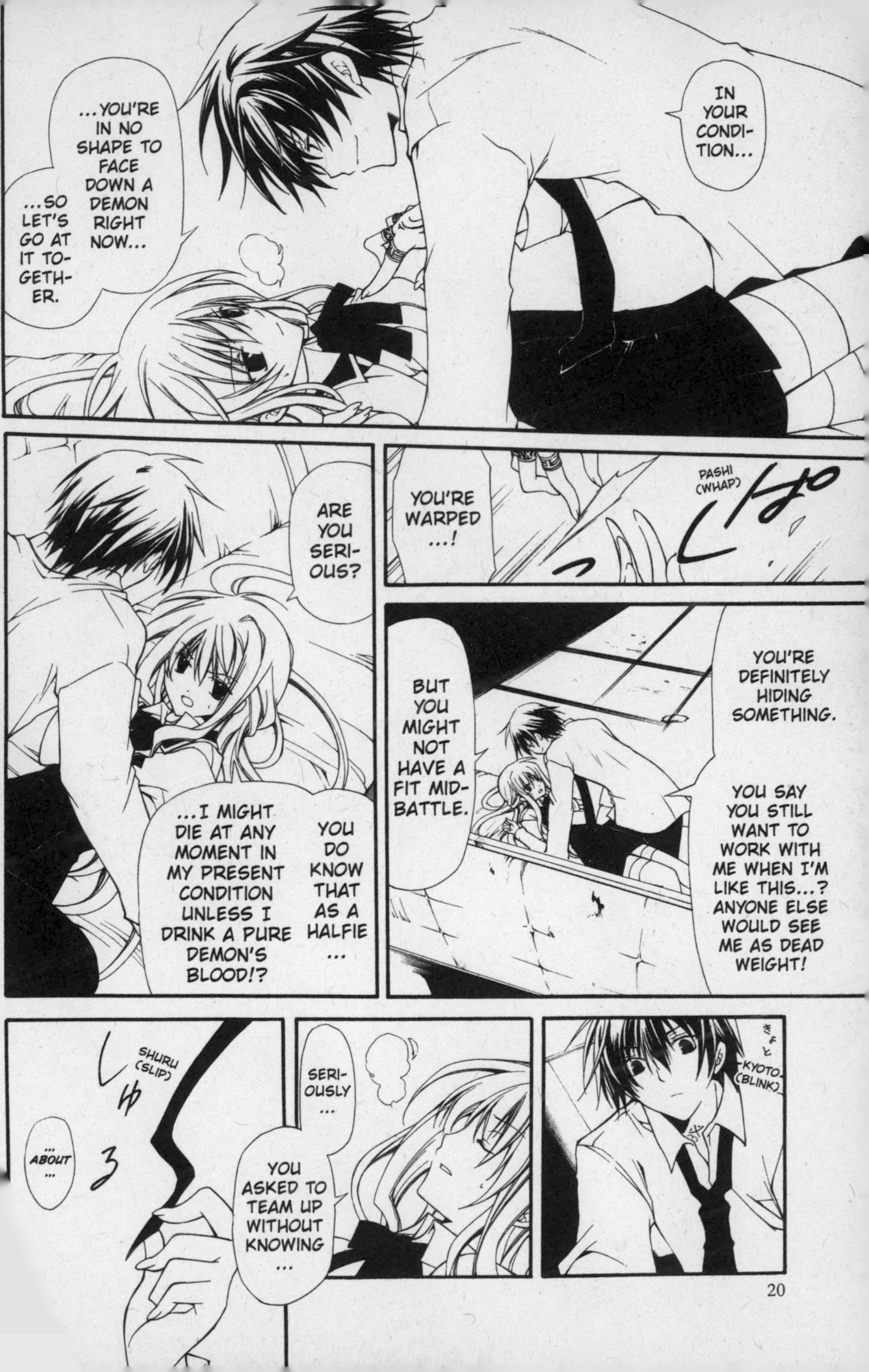
IN YOUR CONDITION...
...YOU'RE IN NO SHAPE TO FACE DOWN A DEMON RIGHT NOW...
...SO LET'S GO AT IT TOGETHER.
PASHI (WHAP)
ぱしっ
YOU'RE WARPED ...!
YOU'RE DEFINITELY HIDING SOMETHING.
YOU SAY YOU STILL WANT TO WORK WITH ME WHEN I'M LIKE THIS...? ANYONE ELSE WOULD SEE ME AS DEAD WEIGHT!
BUT YOU MIGHT NOT HAVE A FIT MID-BATTLE.
ARE YOU SERIOUS?
YOU DO KNOW THAT AS A HALFIE ...
...I MIGHT DIE AT ANY MOMENT IN MY PRESENT CONDITION UNLESS I DRINK A PURE DEMON'S BLOOD!?
きょと
KYOTO (BLINK)
SERIOUSLY ...
YOU ASKED TO TEAM UP WITHOUT KNOWING ...
SHURU (SLIP)
しゅる
...ABOUT...

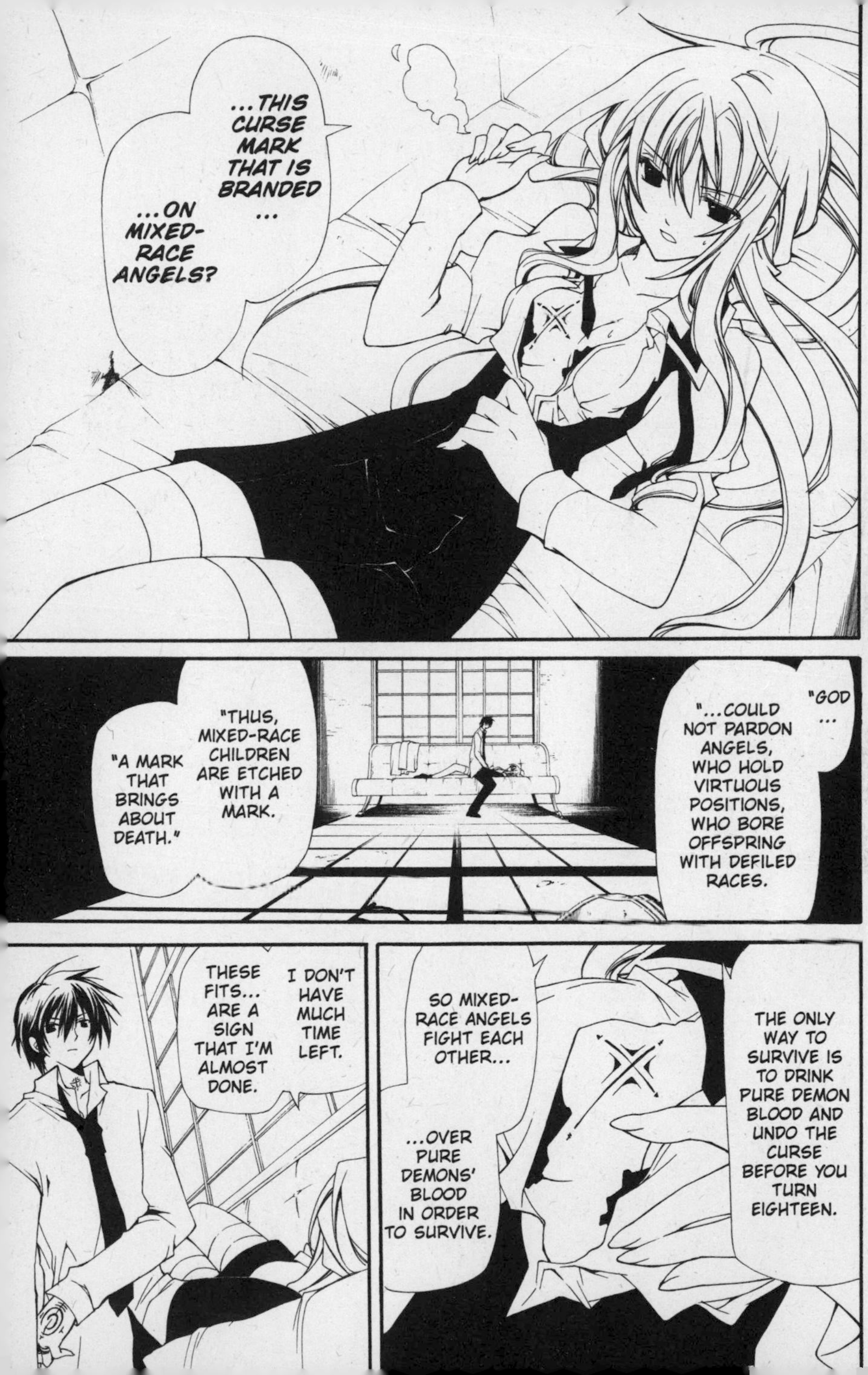
...THIS CURSE MARK THAT IS BRANDED ...
...ON MIXED-RACE ANGELS?
"GOD ...
"...COULD NOT PARDON ANGELS, WHO HOLD VIRTUOUS POSITIONS, WHO BORE OFFSPRING WITH DEFILED RACES.
"THUS, MIXED-RACE CHILDREN ARE ETCHED WITH A MARK.
"A MARK THAT BRINGS ABOUT DEATH."
THE ONLY WAY TO SURVIVE IS TO DRINK PURE DEMON BLOOD AND UNDO THE CURSE BEFORE YOU TURN EIGHTEEN.
SO MIXED-RACE ANGELS FIGHT EACH OTHER...
...OVER PURE DEMONS' BLOOD IN ORDER TO SURVIVE.
I DON'T HAVE MUCH TIME LEFT.
THESE FITS... ARE A SIGN THAT I'M ALMOST DONE.

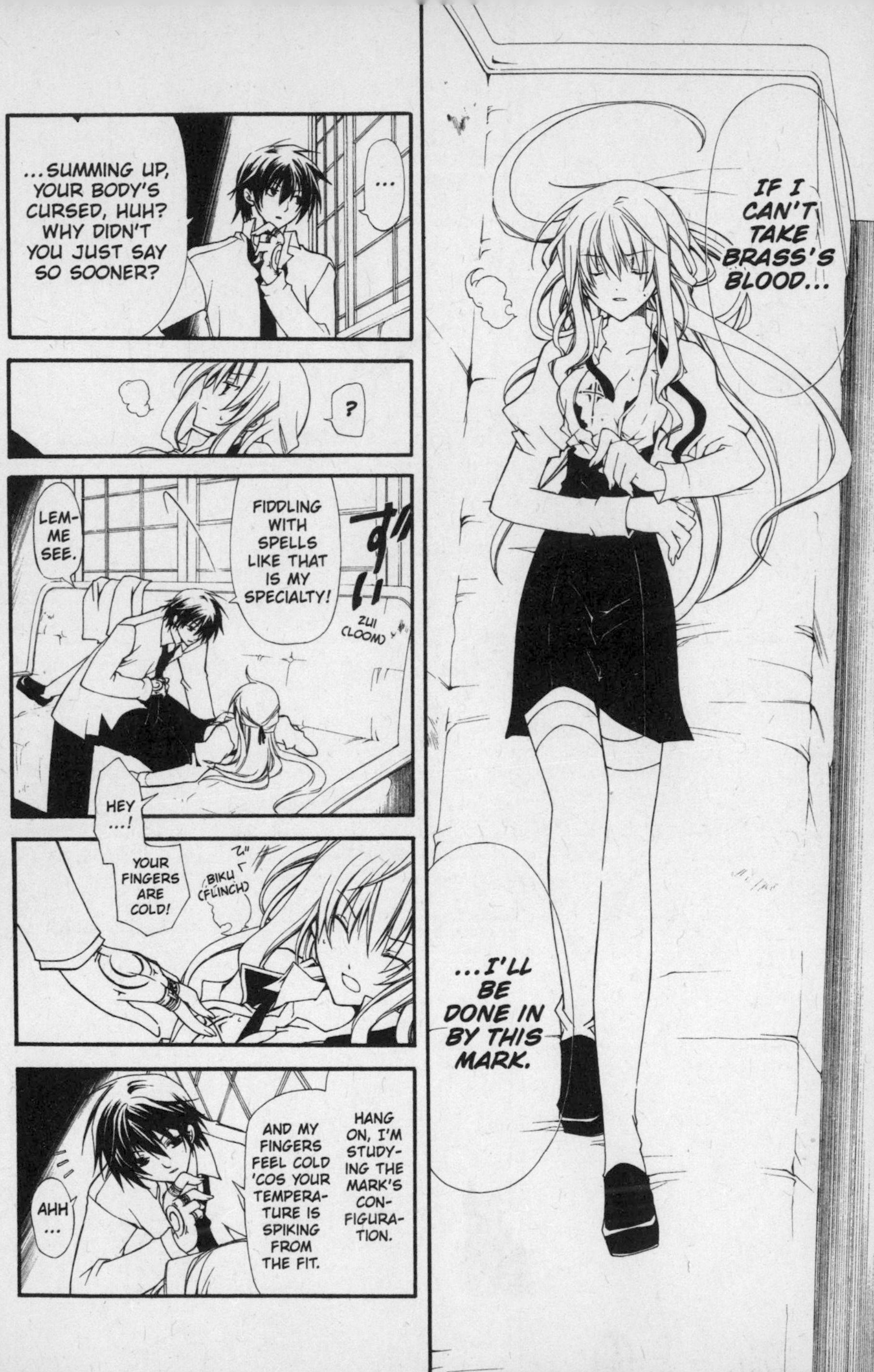
IF I CAN'T TAKE BRASS'S BLOOD...
...I'LL BE DONE IN BY THIS MARK.
...
...SUMMING UP, YOUR BODY'S CURSED, HUH? WHY DIDN'T YOU JUST SAY SO SOONER?
?
ZUI (LOOM)
FIDDLING WITH SPELLS LIKE THAT IS MY SPECIALTY!
LEM-ME SEE.
BIKU (FLINCH)
HEY ...!
YOUR FINGERS ARE COLD!
HANG ON, I'M STUDY-ING THE MARK'S CON-FIGURA-TION.
AND MY FINGERS FEEL COLD 'COS YOUR TEMPERA-TURE IS SPIKING FROM THE FIT.
AHH ...

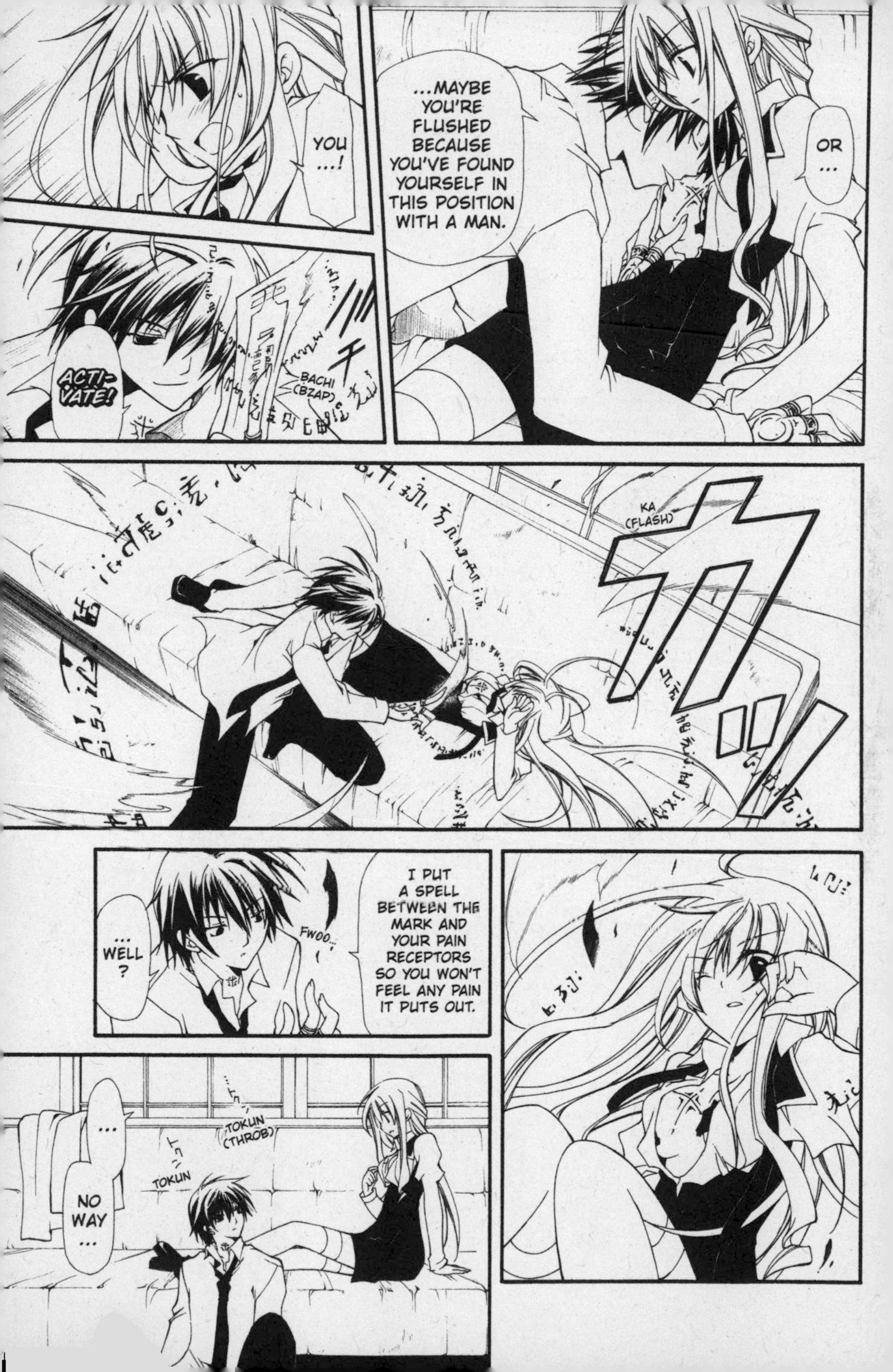
OR ...
...MAYBE YOU'RE FLUSHED BECAUSE YOU'VE FOUND YOURSELF IN THIS POSITION WITH A MAN.
YOU ...!
ACTI-VATE!
BACHI (BZAP)
KA (FLASH)
I PUT A SPELL BETWEEN THE MARK AND YOUR PAIN RECEPTORS SO YOU WON'T FEEL ANY PAIN IT PUTS OUT.
FWOO...
... WELL ?
TOKUN (THROB)
TOKUN
...
NO WAY ...

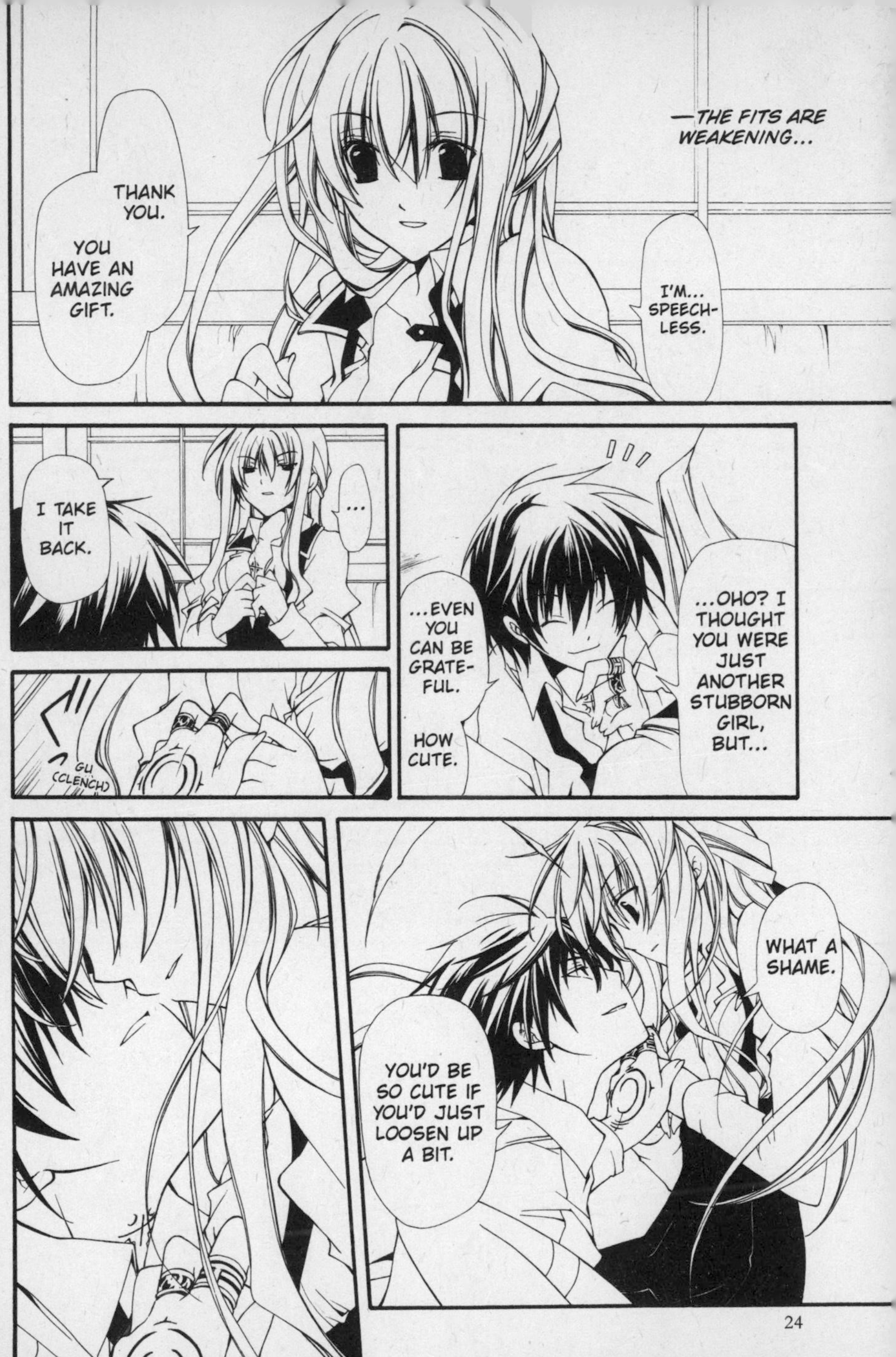
—THE FITS ARE WEAKENING…
I'M… SPEECHLESS.
THANK YOU.
YOU HAVE AN AMAZING GIFT.
…OHO? I THOUGHT YOU WERE JUST ANOTHER STUBBORN GIRL, BUT…
…EVEN YOU CAN BE GRATEFUL.
HOW CUTE.
…
I TAKE IT BACK.
GU (CLENCH)
WHAT A SHAME.
YOU'D BE SO CUTE IF YOU'D JUST LOOSEN UP A BIT.

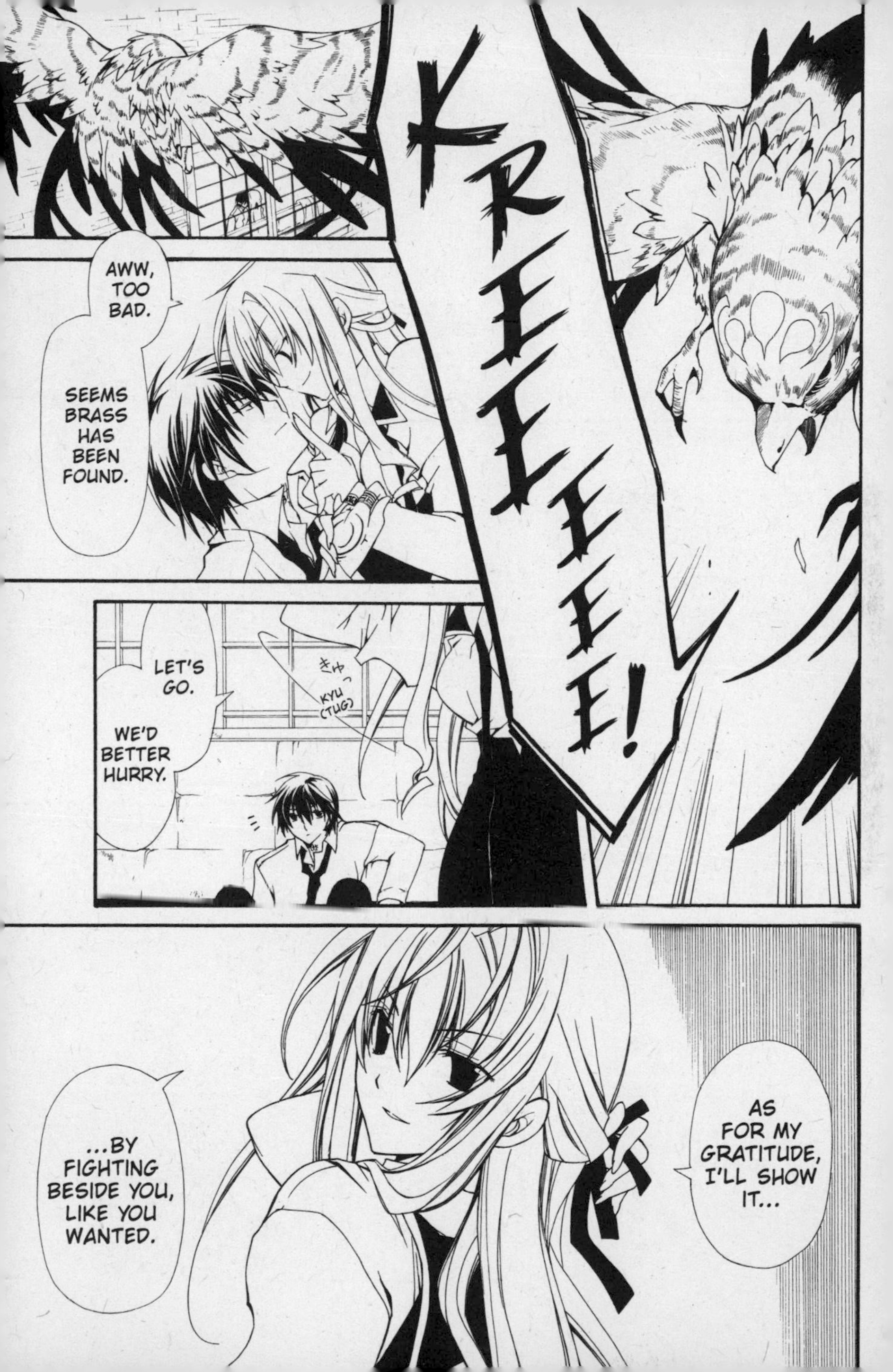
KREEEEEE!
AWW, TOO BAD.
SEEMS BRASS HAS BEEN FOUND.
LET'S GO.
きゅっ
KYU (TUG)
WE'D BETTER HURRY.
AS FOR MY GRATITUDE, I'LL SHOW IT...
...BY FIGHTING BESIDE YOU, LIKE YOU WANTED.

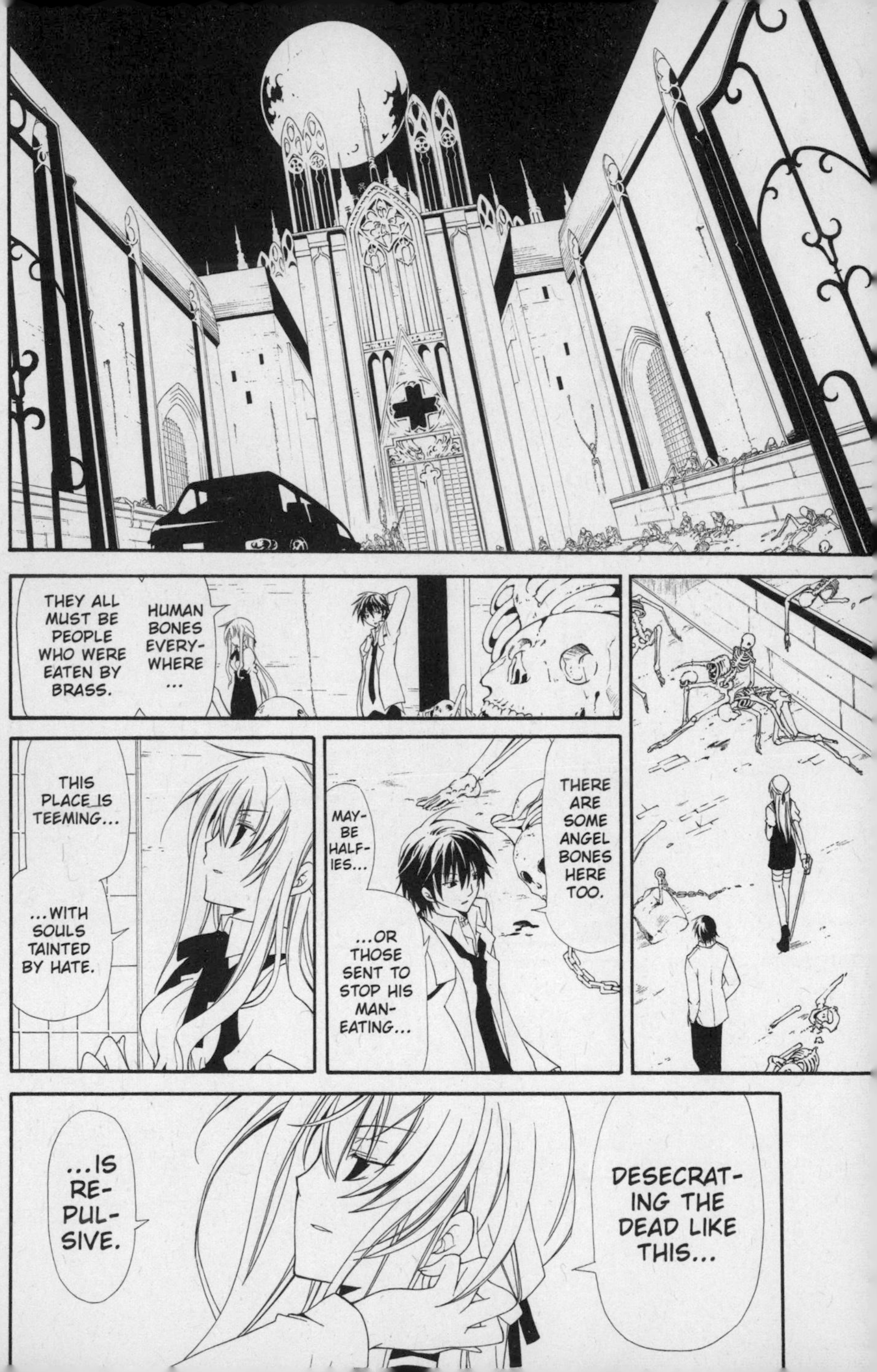
HUMAN BONES EVERYWHERE...
THEY ALL MUST BE PEOPLE WHO WERE EATEN BY BRASS.
THERE ARE SOME ANGEL BONES HERE TOO.
MAYBE HALFIES...
...OR THOSE SENT TO STOP HIS MAN-EATING...
THIS PLACE IS TEEMING...
...WITH SOULS TAINTED BY HATE.
DESECRATING THE DEAD LIKE THIS...
...IS REPULSIVE.

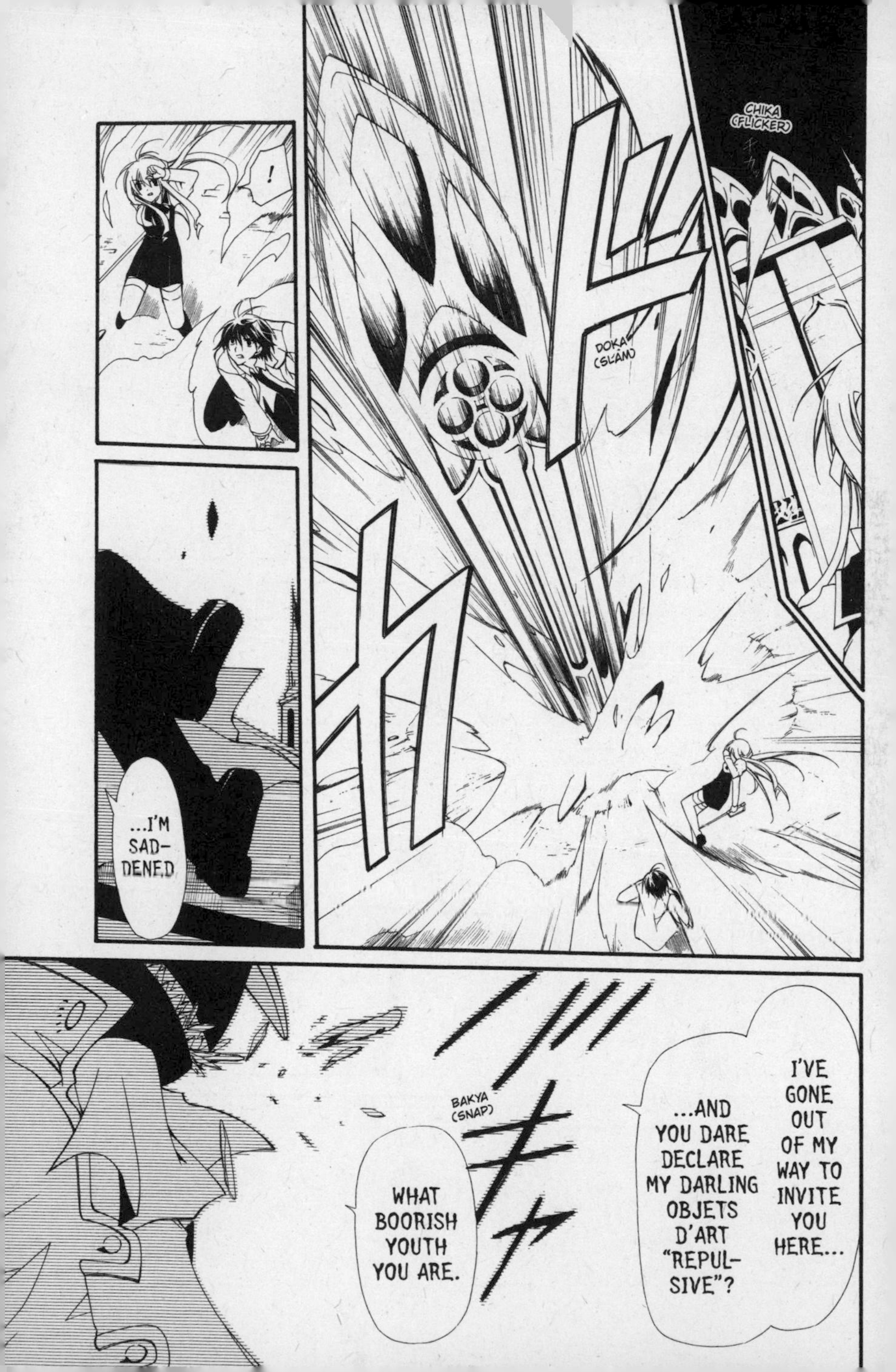
CHIKA (FLICKER)
DOKA (SLAM)
!
...I'M SAD-DENED
I'VE GONE OUT OF MY WAY TO INVITE YOU HERE...
...AND YOU DARE DECLARE MY DARLING OBJETS D'ART "REPUL-SIVE"?
BAKYA (SNAP)
WHAT BOORISH YOUTH YOU ARE.

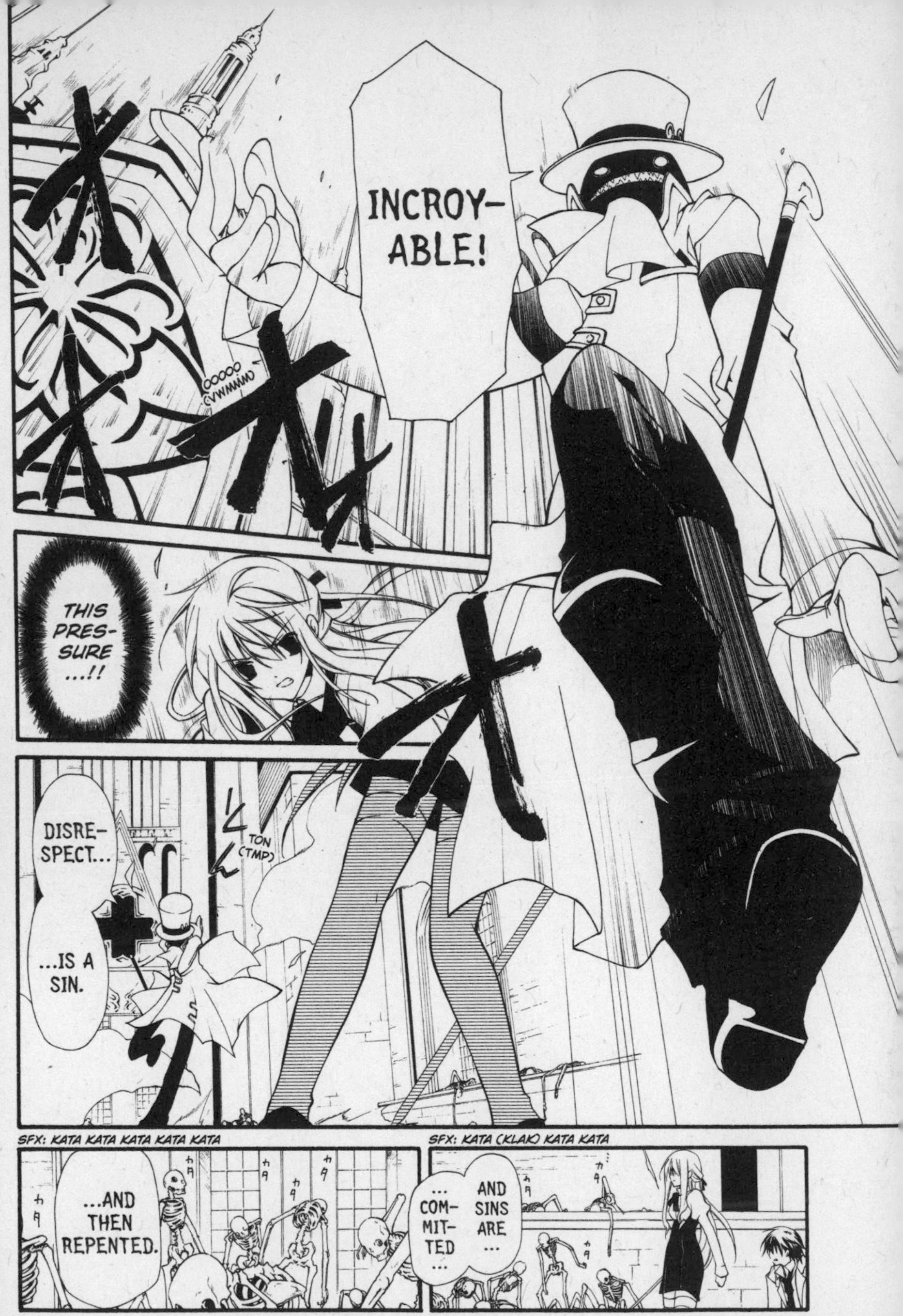
INCROY-ABLE!
OOOOO (VWMMM)
THIS PRES-SURE ...!!
TON (TMP)
DISRE-SPECT...
...IS A SIN.
SFX: KATA (KLAK) KATA KATA
AND SINS ARE ...
... COM-MIT-TED ...
SFX: KATA KATA KATA KATA KATA
...AND THEN REPENTED.

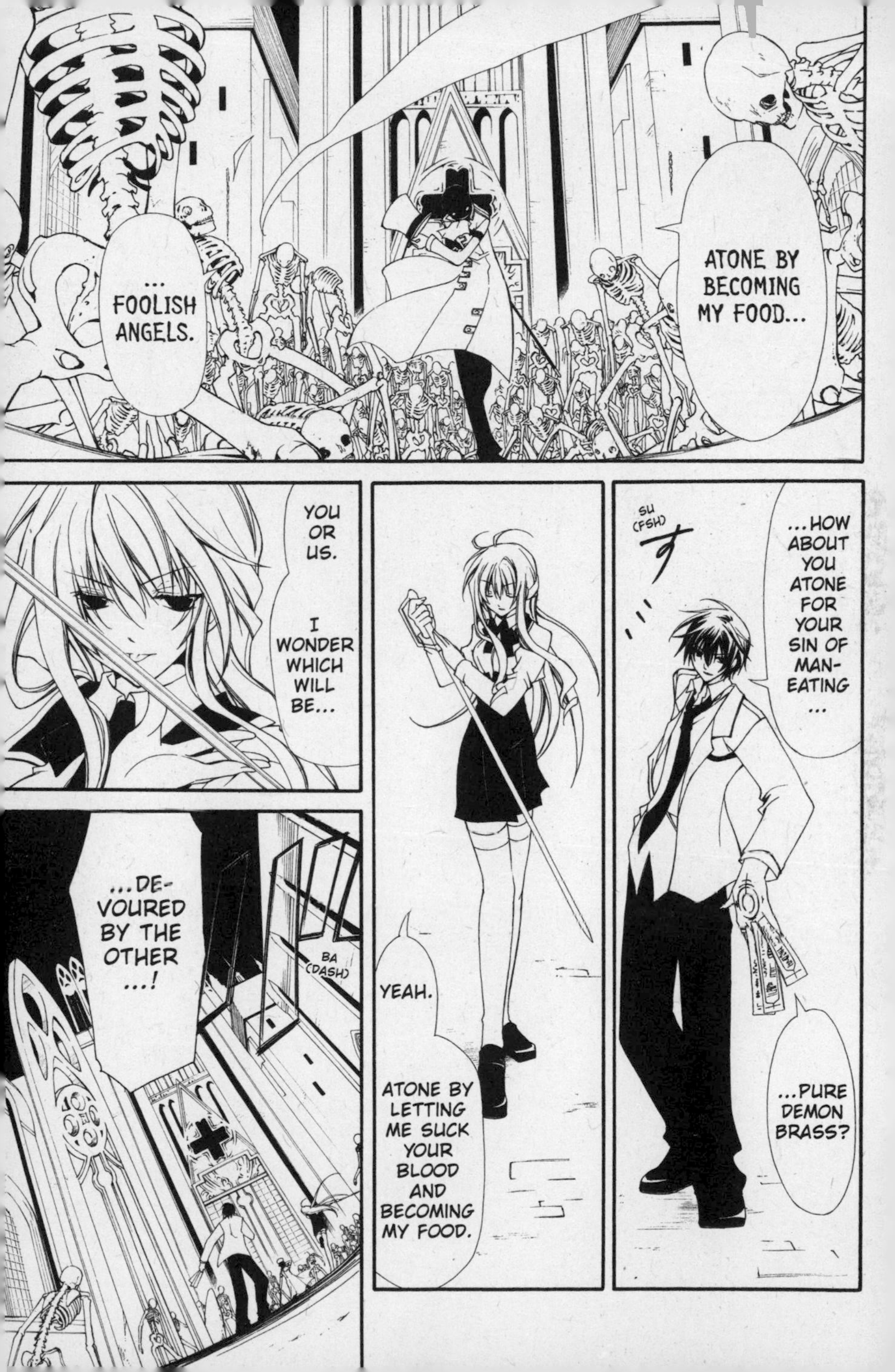
ATONE BY BECOMING MY FOOD...
...FOOLISH ANGELS.
す
SU (FSH)
...HOW ABOUT YOU ATONE FOR YOUR SIN OF MAN-EATING...
...PURE DEMON BRASS?
YEAH.
ATONE BY LETTING ME SUCK YOUR BLOOD AND BECOMING MY FOOD.
YOU OR US.
I WONDER WHICH WILL BE...
...DE-VOURED BY THE OTHER...!
BA (DASH)

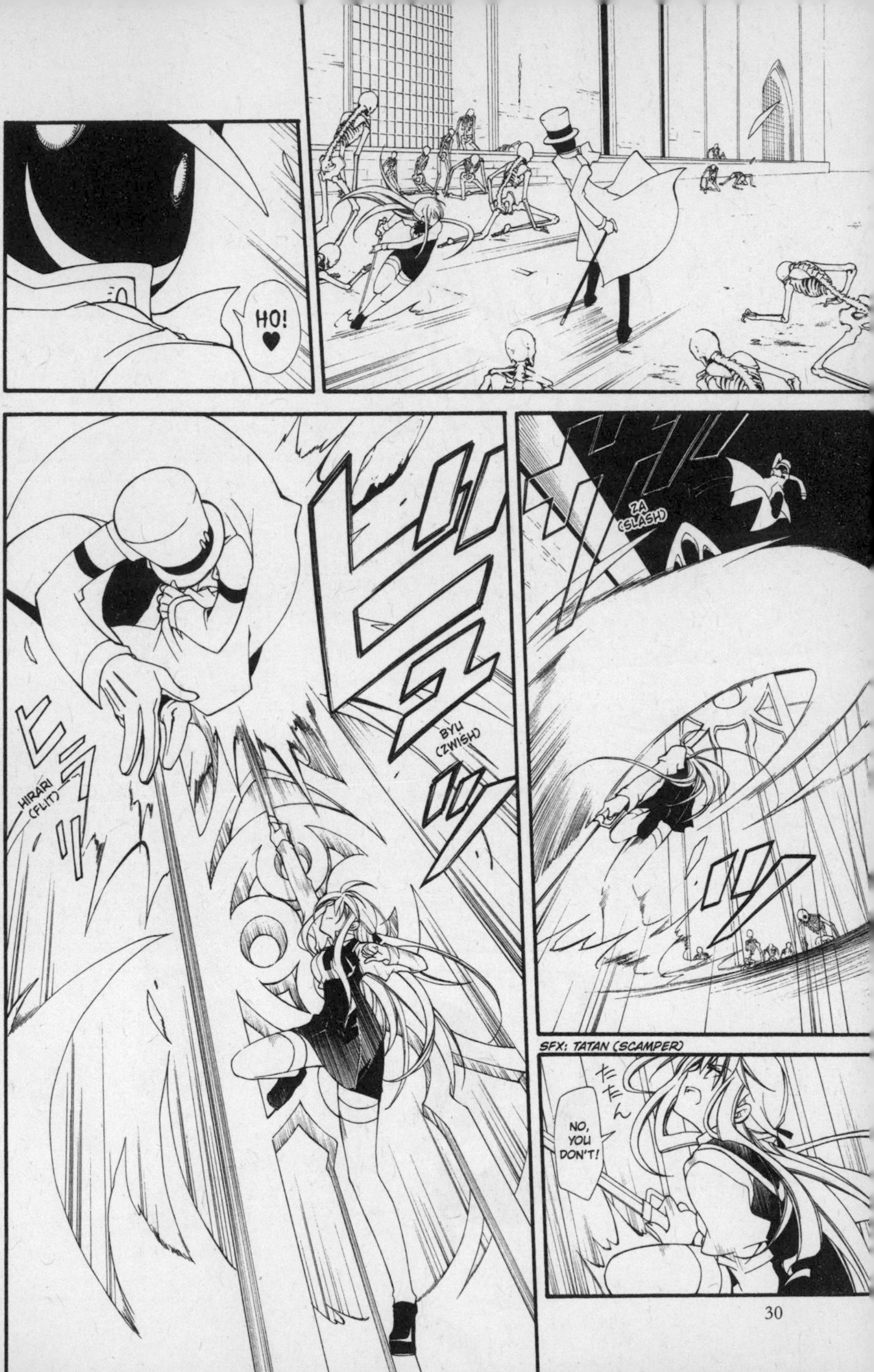
HO! ♥
ZA (SLASH)
SFX: TATAN (SCAMPER)
たたん
NO, YOU DON'T!
BYU (ZWISH)
HIRARI (FLIT)

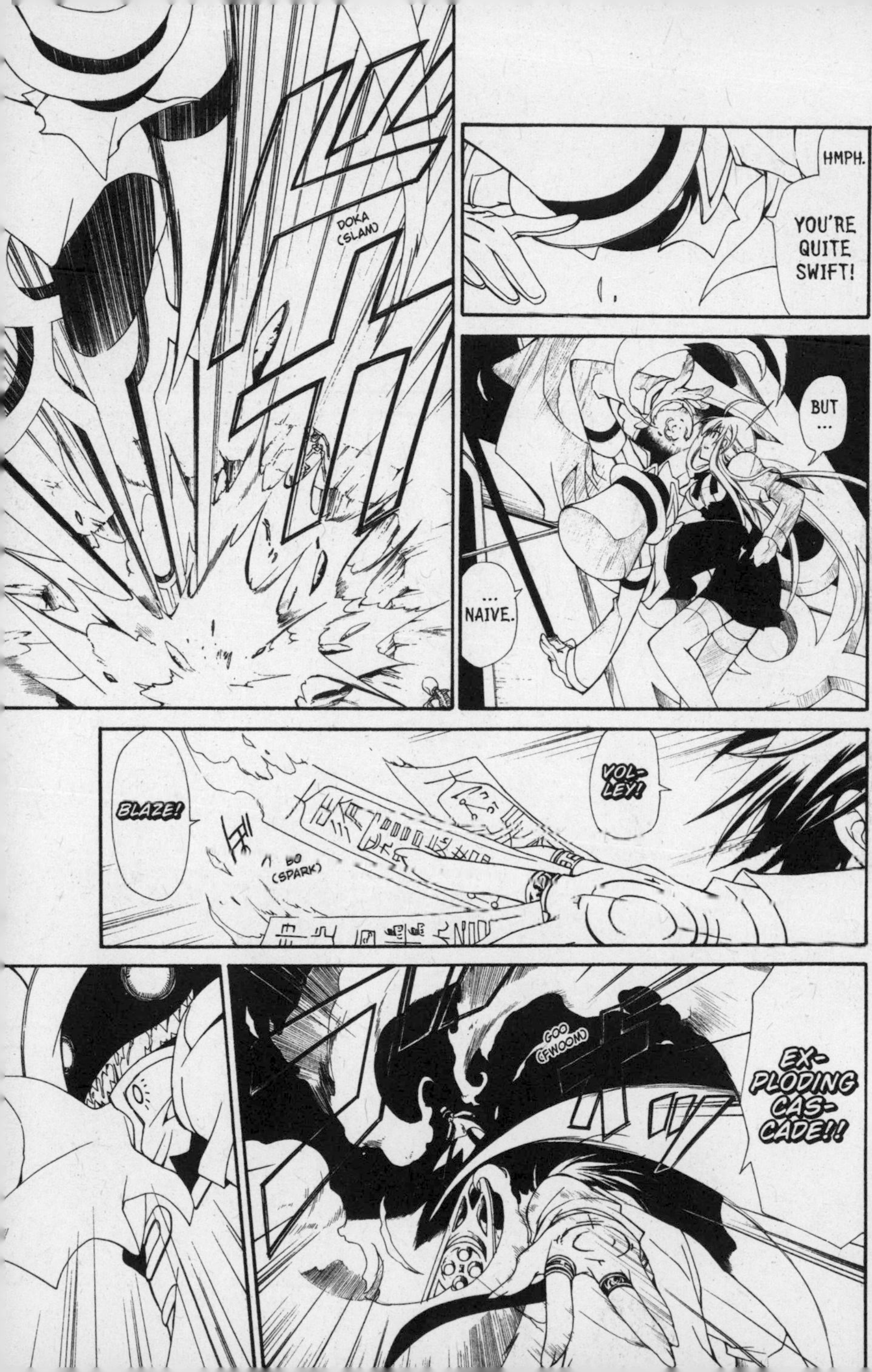
HMPH.
YOU'RE QUITE SWIFT!
BUT...
...NAIVE.
DOKA (SLAM)
VOL-LEY!
BLAZE!
BO (SPARK)
EX-PLODING CAS-CADE!!
GOO (FWOOM)

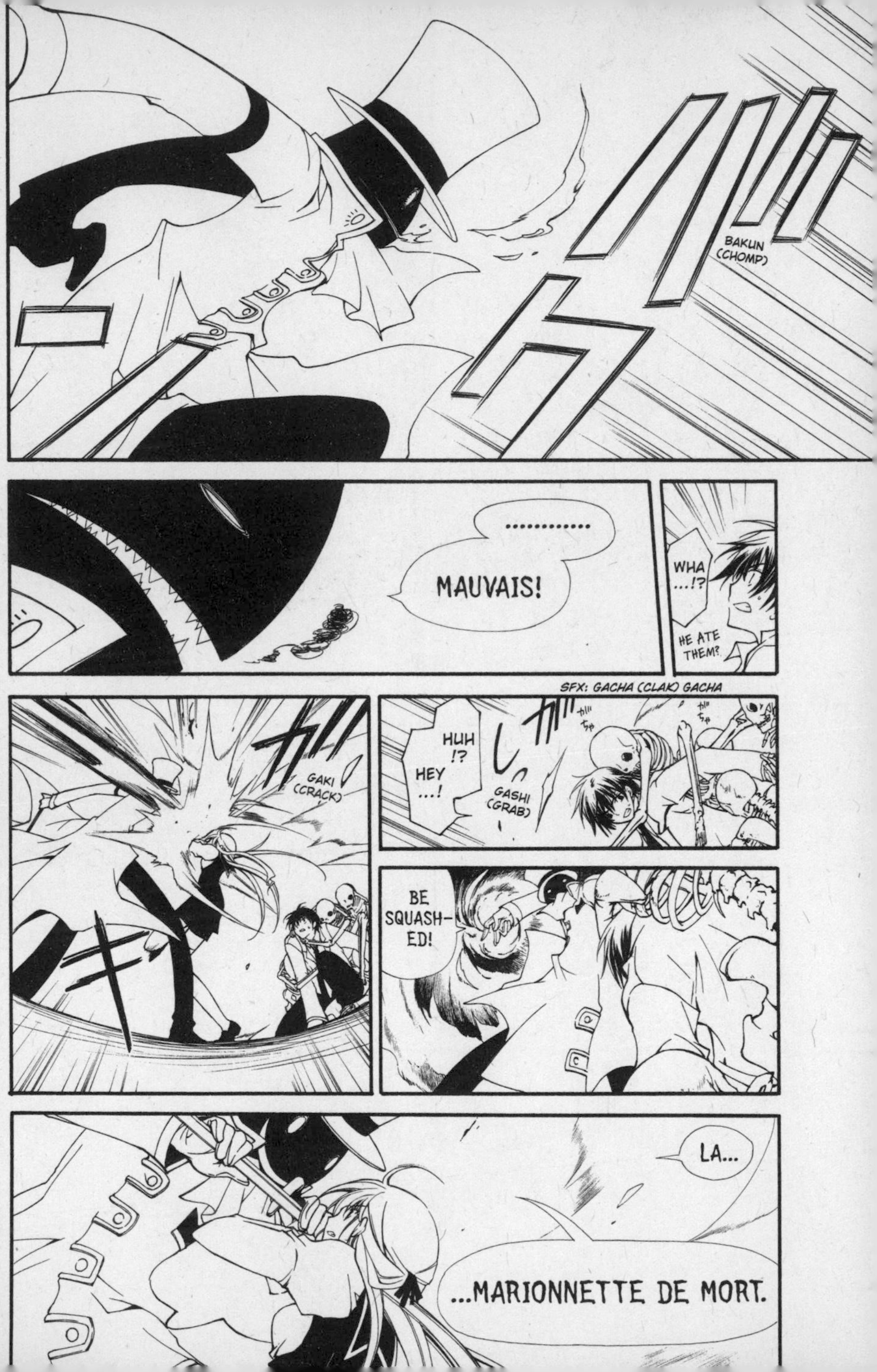
BAKUN (CHOMP)
WHA ...!?
HE ATE THEM?
....
MAUVAIS!
SFX: GACHA (CLAK) GACHA
HUH !? HEY ...!
GASHI (GRAB)
BE SQUASH-ED!
GAKI (CRACK)
LA...
...MARIONNETTE DE MORT.

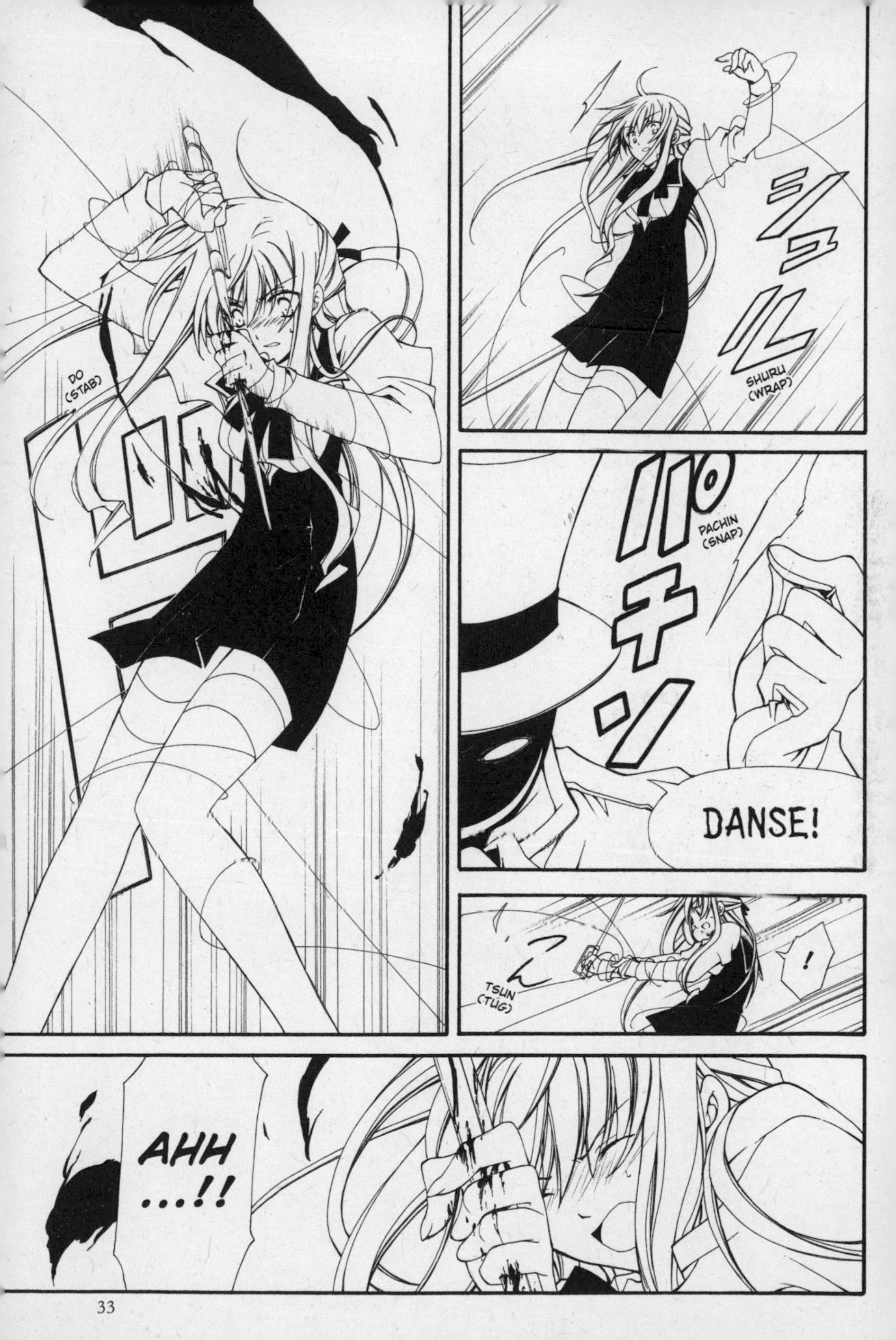
シュル
SHURU (WRAP)
パチン
PACHIN (SNAP)
DANSE!
TSUN (TUG)
!
DO (STAB)
AHH ...!!

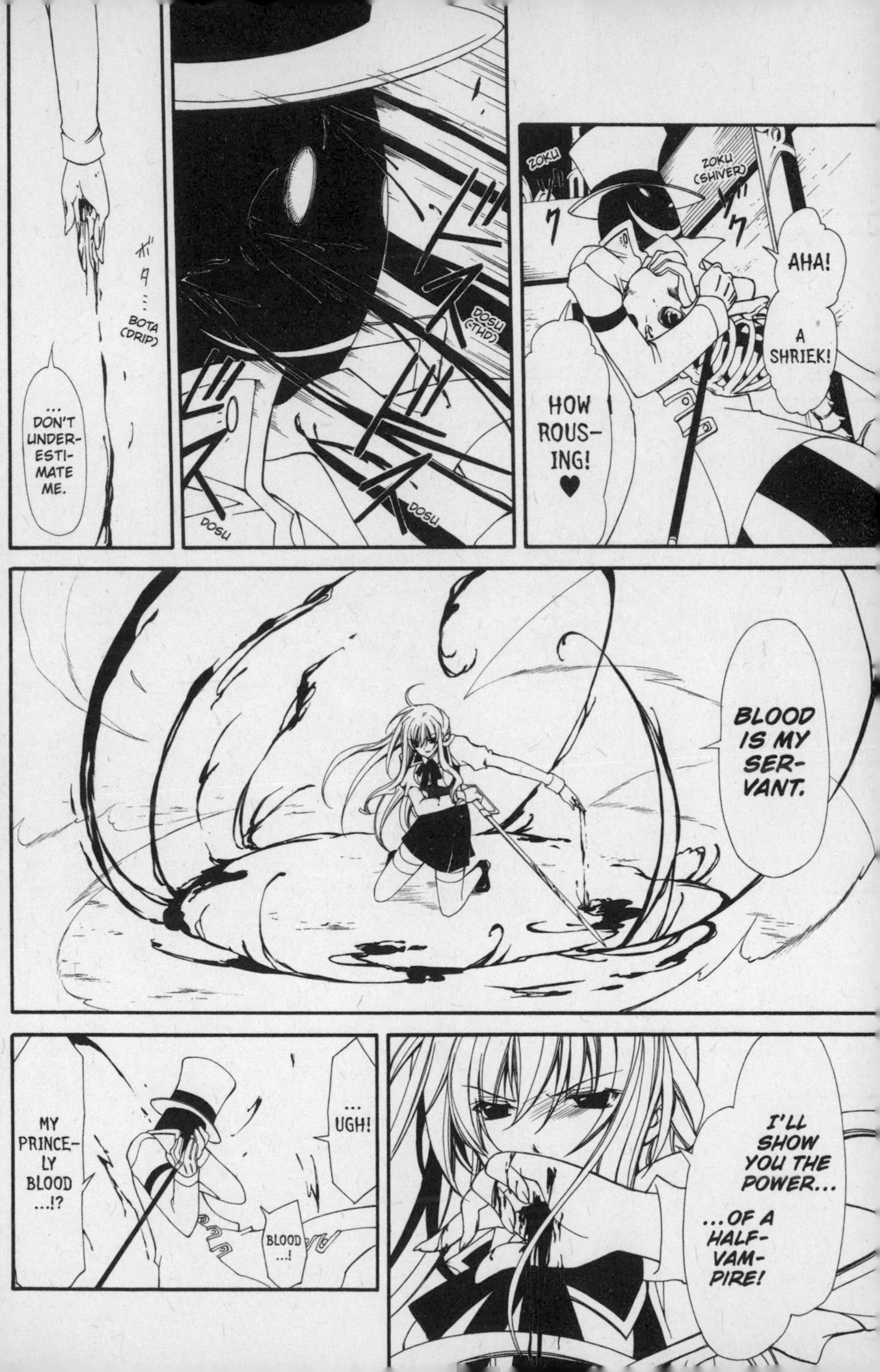
ZOKU
ZOKU (SHIVER)
AHA!
A SHRIEK!
HOW ROUSING! ♥
DOSU (THD)
DOSU
DOSU
BOTA (DRIP)
...DON'T UNDERESTIMATE ME.
BLOOD IS MY SERVANT.
I'LL SHOW YOU THE POWER...
...OF A HALF-VAMPIRE!
...UGH!
MY PRINCELY BLOOD...!?
BLOOD...!

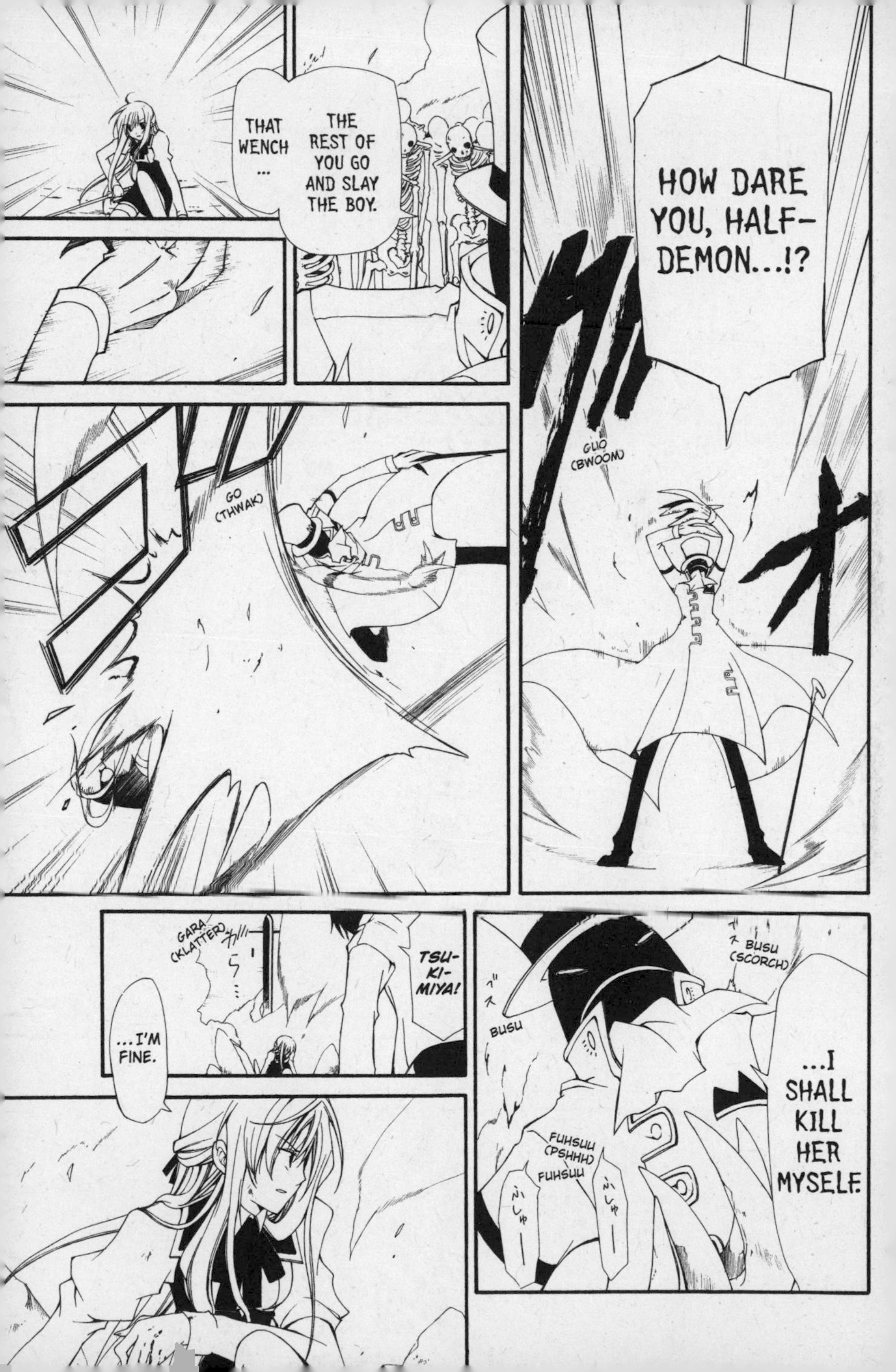
HOW DARE YOU, HALF-DEMON...!?
GUO (BWOOM)
THAT WENCH ... THE REST OF YOU GO AND SLAY THE BOY.
GO (THWAK)
BUSU (SCORCH)
BUSU
...I SHALL KILL HER MYSELF.
FUHSUU (PSHHH)
FUHSUU
TSUKIMIYA!
GARA (KLATTER)
...I'M FINE.

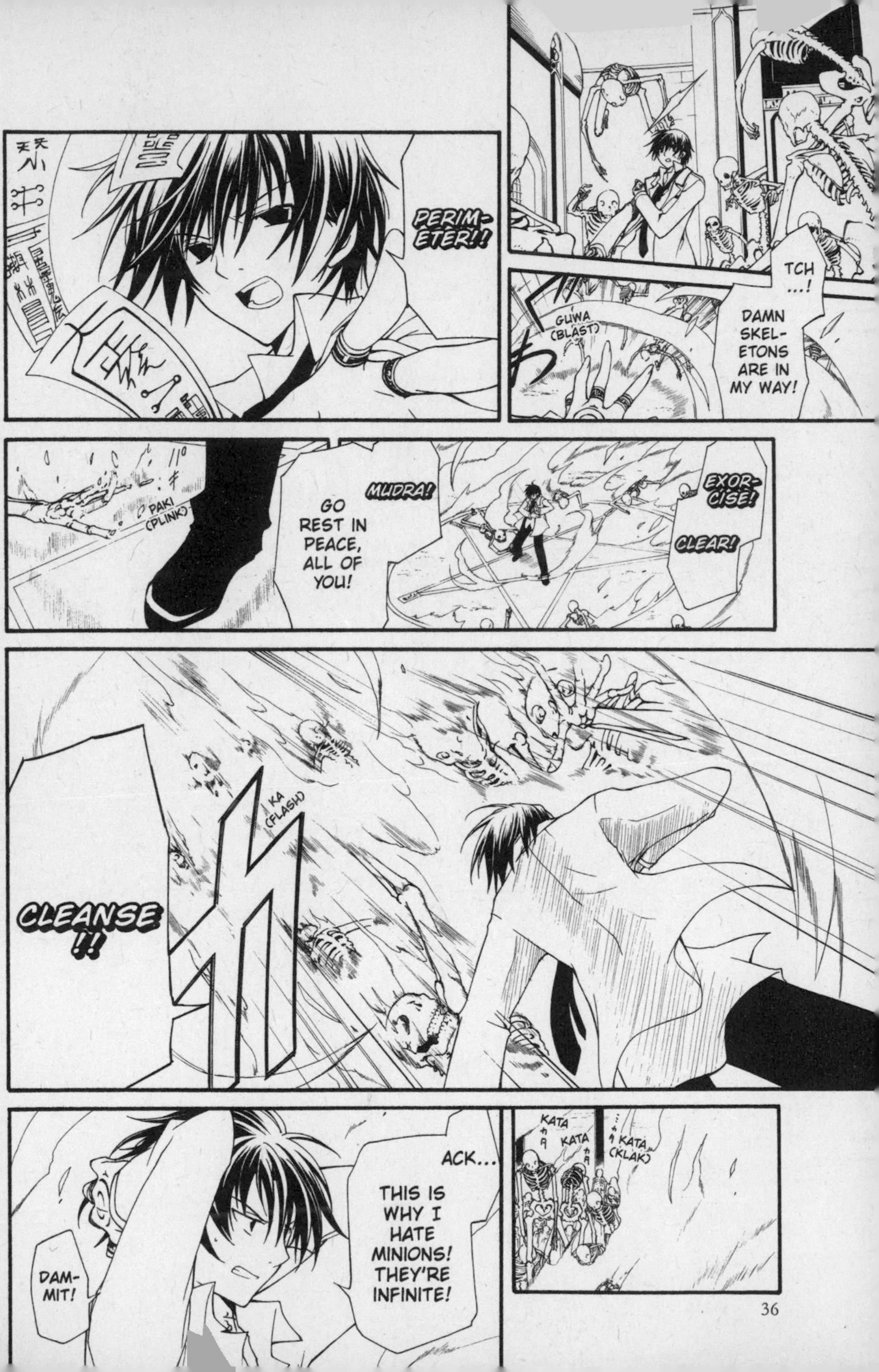
TCH ...!
DAMN SKELETONS ARE IN MY WAY!
GUWA (BLAST)
PERIMETER!!
EXORCISE!
CLEAR!
MUDRA!
GO REST IN PEACE, ALL OF YOU!
PAKI (PLINK)
KA (FLASH)
CLEANSE!!
KATA KATA KATA (KLAK)
ACK...
THIS IS WHY I HATE MINIONS! THEY'RE INFINITE!
DAMMIT!

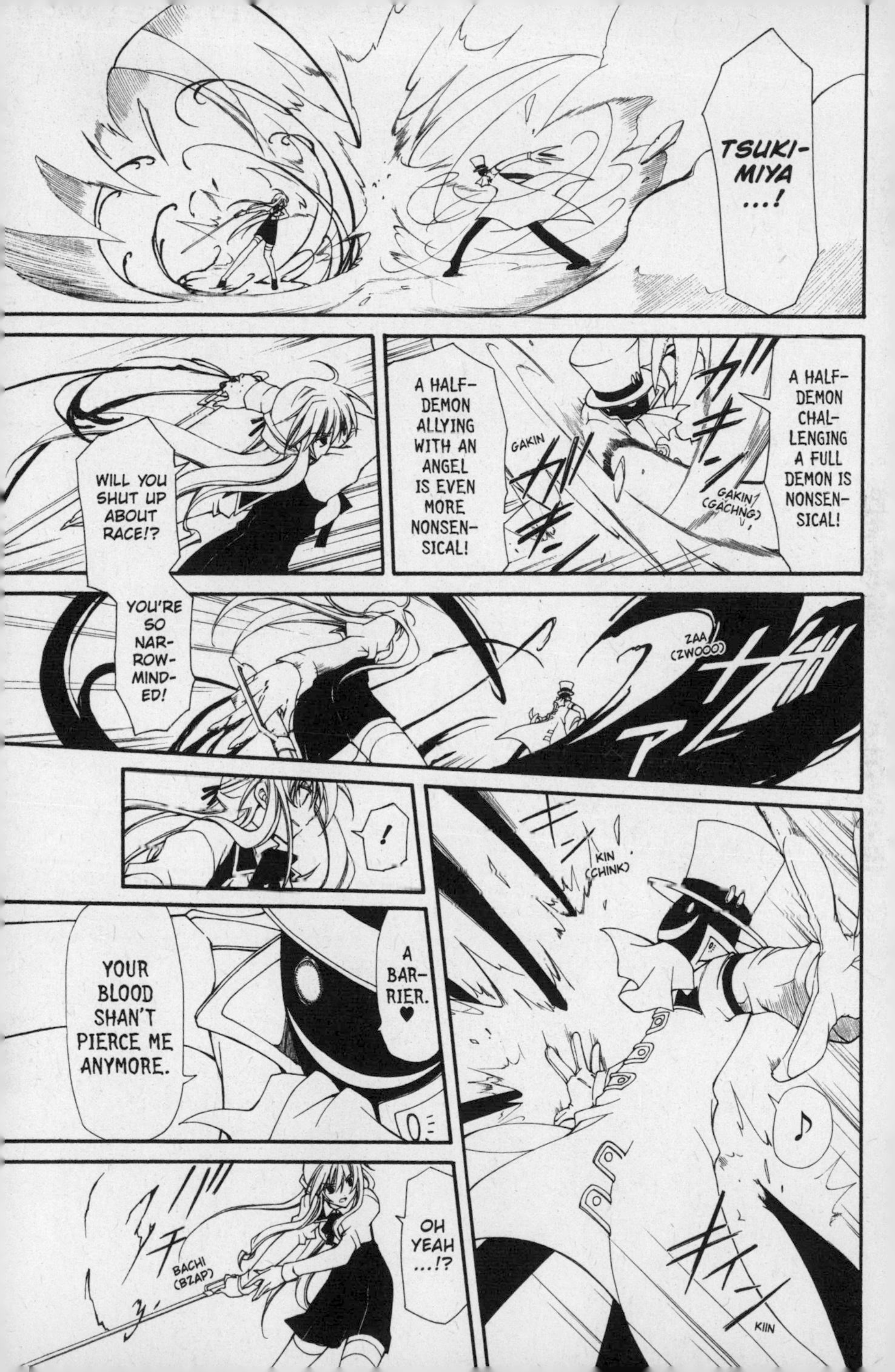

TSUKI-MIYA ...!
A HALF-DEMON CHALLENGING A FULL DEMON IS NONSENSICAL!
GAKIN (GACHNG)
GAKIN
A HALF-DEMON ALLYING WITH AN ANGEL IS EVEN MORE NONSENSICAL!
WILL YOU SHUT UP ABOUT RACE!?
ZAA (ZWOOO)
YOU'RE SO NARROW-MINDED!
KIN (CHINK)
♪
KIIN
!
A BARRIER. ♥
YOUR BLOOD SHAN'T PIERCE ME ANYMORE.
OH YEAH ...!?
BACHI (BZAP)

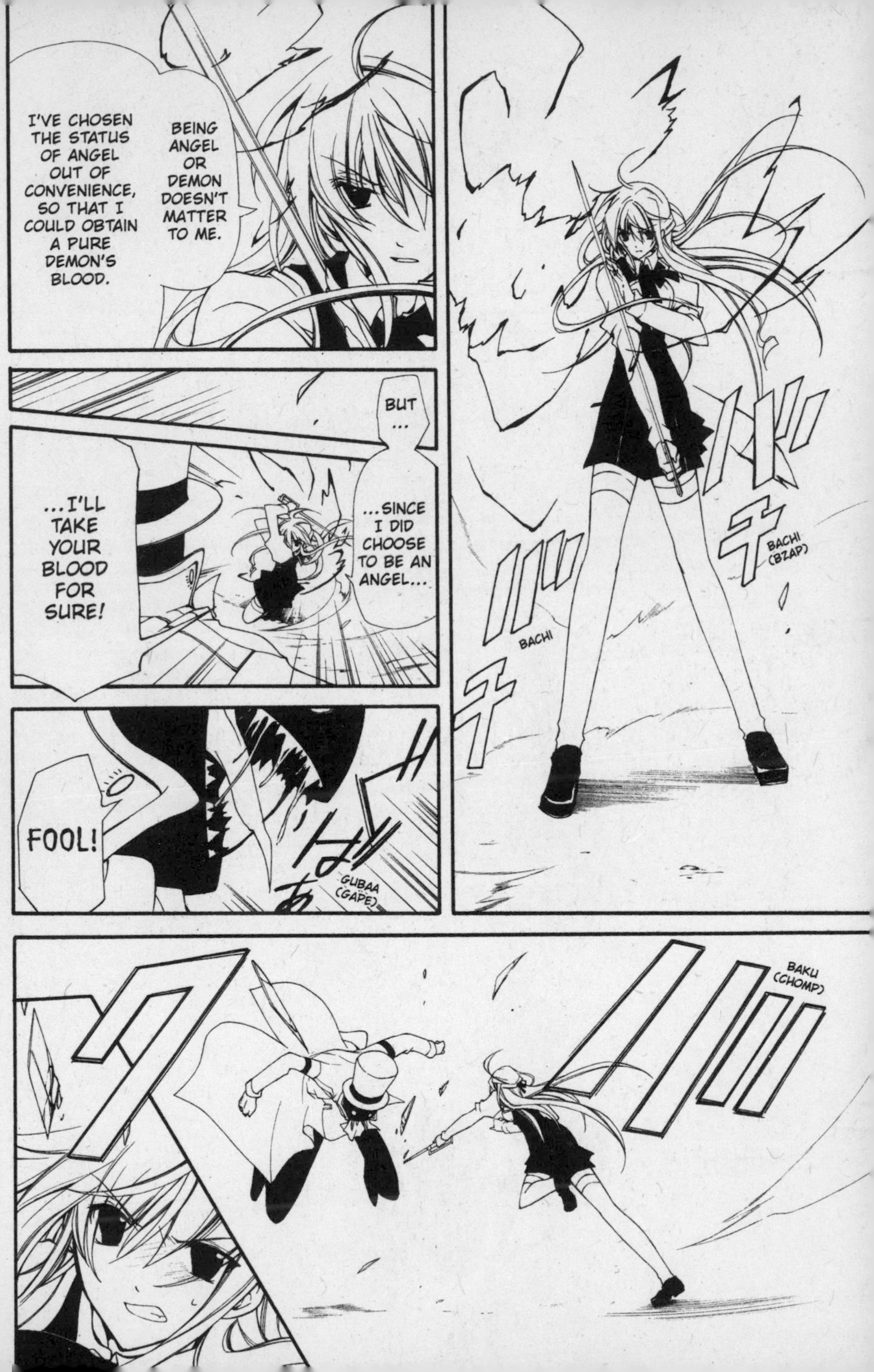
BACHI (BZAP)
BACHI
BEING ANGEL OR DEMON DOESN'T MATTER TO ME.
I'VE CHOSEN THE STATUS OF ANGEL OUT OF CONVENIENCE, SO THAT I COULD OBTAIN A PURE DEMON'S BLOOD.
BUT...
...SINCE I DID CHOOSE TO BE AN ANGEL...
...I'LL TAKE YOUR BLOOD FOR SURE!
GUBAA (GAPE)
FOOL!
BAKU (CHOMP)

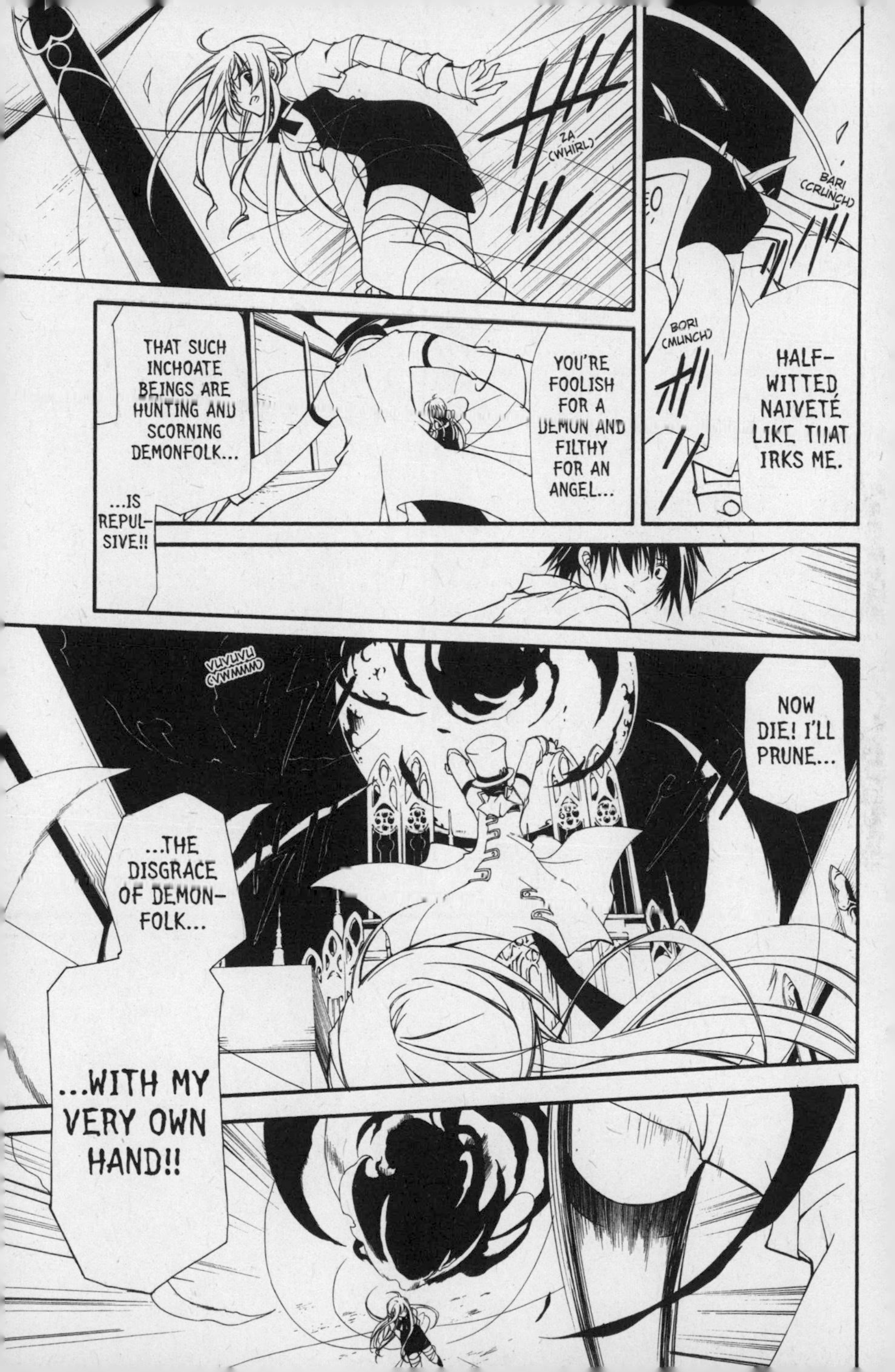
BARI (CRUNCH)
ZA (WHIRL)
BORI (MUNCH)
HALF-WITTED NAIVETÉ LIKE THAT IRKS ME.
YOU'RE FOOLISH FOR A DEMON AND FILTHY FOR AN ANGEL...
THAT SUCH INCHOATE BEINGS ARE HUNTING AND SCORNING DEMONFOLK...
...IS REPULSIVE!!
VUVUVU (VWMMM)
NOW DIE! I'LL PRUNE...
...THE DISGRACE OF DEMONFOLK...
...WITH MY VERY OWN HAND!!

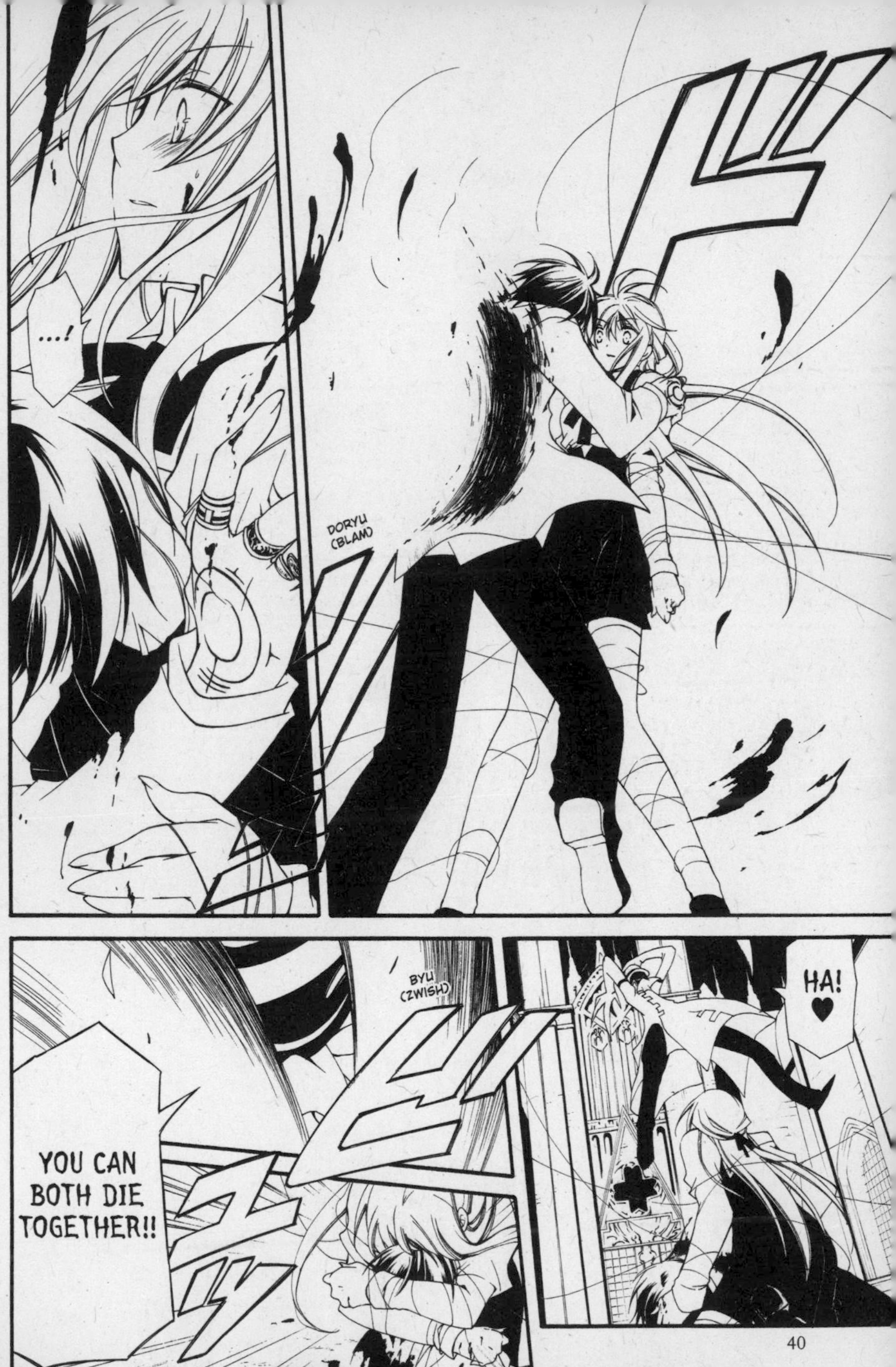
DORYU (BLAM)
...!
HA! ♥
BYU (ZWISH)
YOU CAN BOTH DIE TOGETHER!!

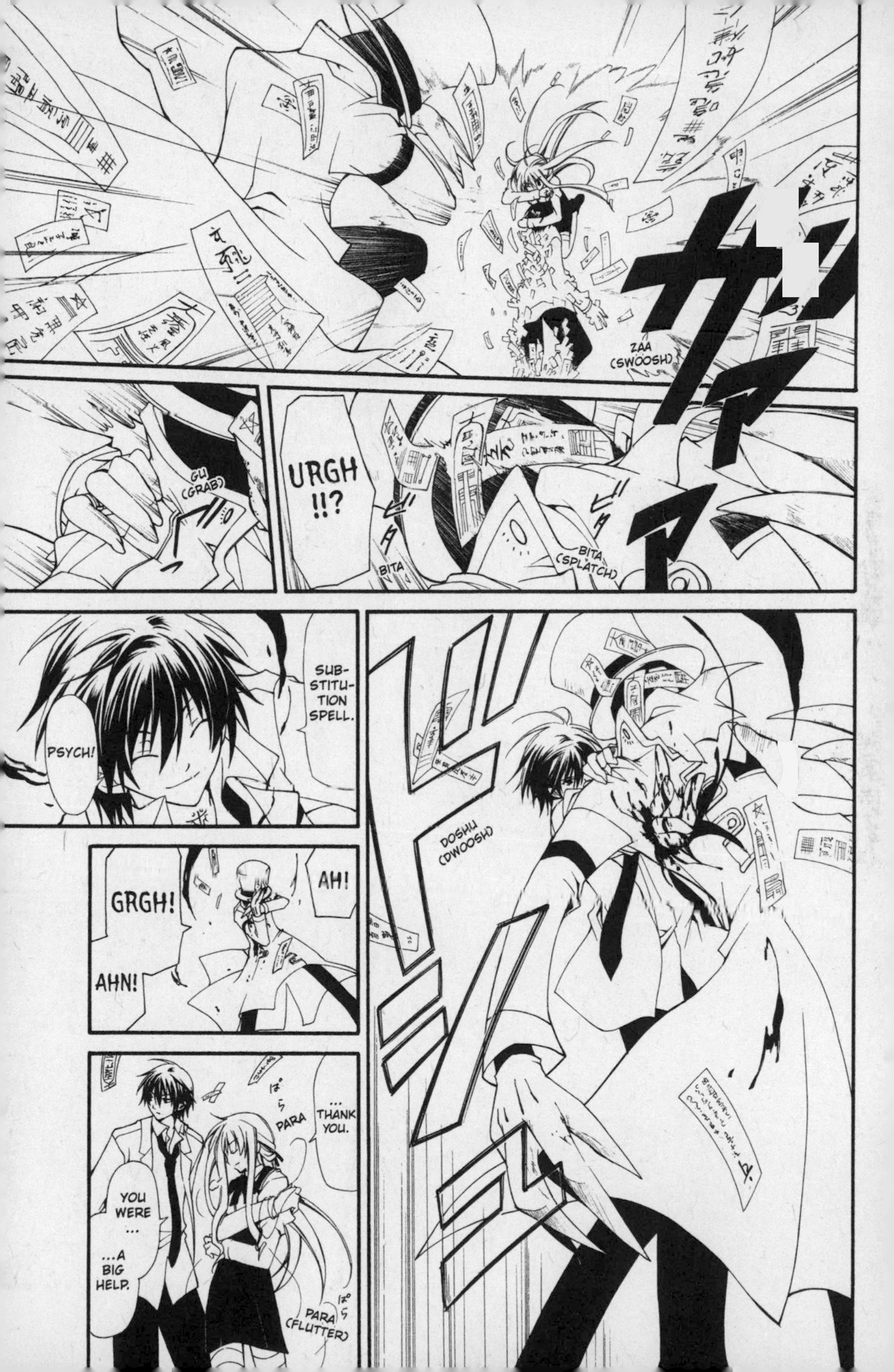
ZAA (SWOOSH)
URGH!!?
BITA (SPLATCH)
BITA
GU (GRAB)
DOSHU (DWOOSH)
SUB-STITU-TION SPELL.
PSYCH!
AH!
GRGH!
AHN!
... THANK YOU.
ぱら PARA
YOU WERE ...
...A BIG HELP.
ぱら PARA (FLUTTER)

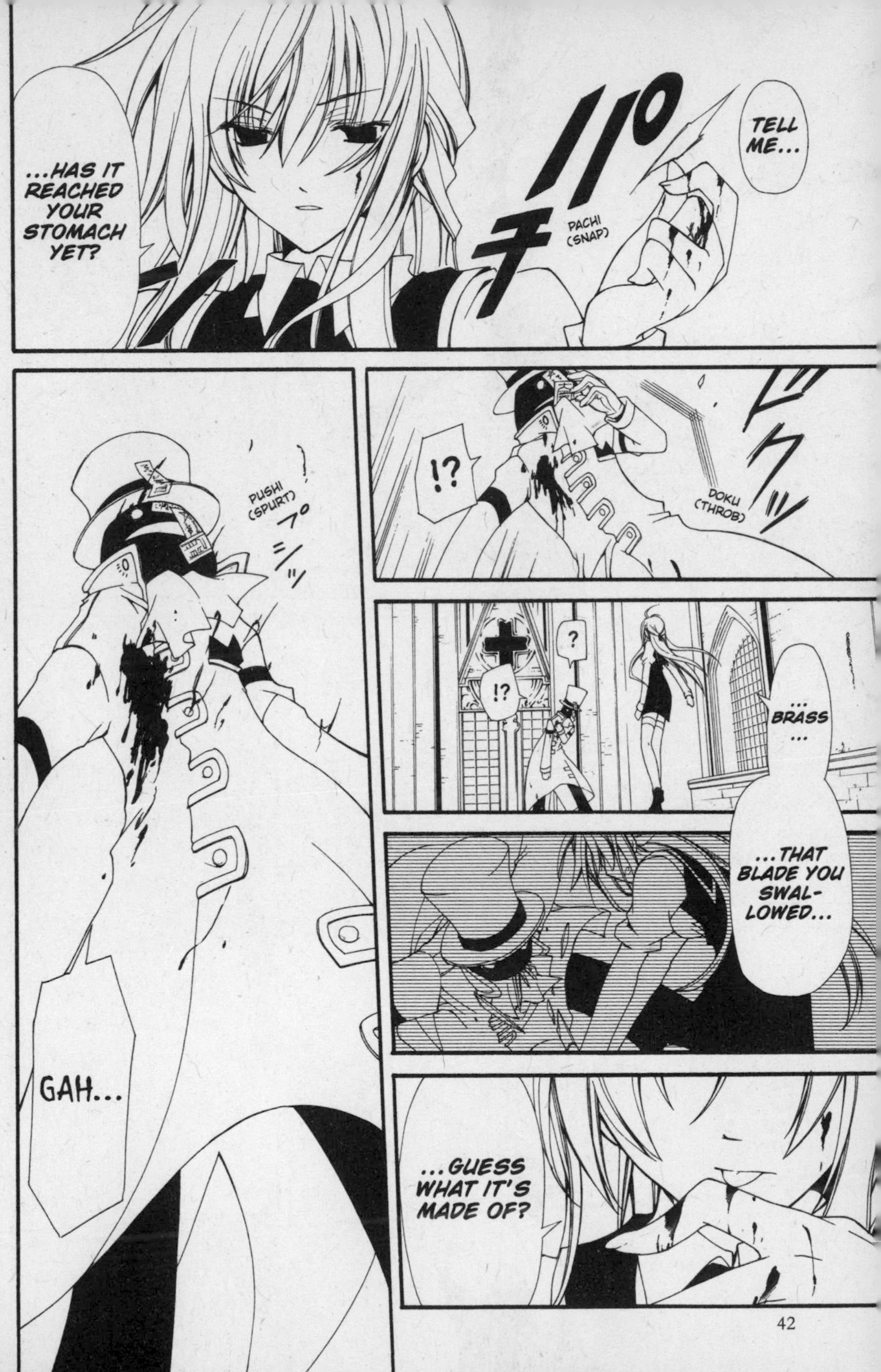
TELL ME...
PACHI (SNAP)
...HAS IT REACHED YOUR STOMACH YET?
DOKU (THROB)
!?
?
!?
...BRASS...
...THAT BLADE YOU SWAL-LOWED...
...GUESS WHAT IT'S MADE OF?
PUSHI (SPURT)
GAH...

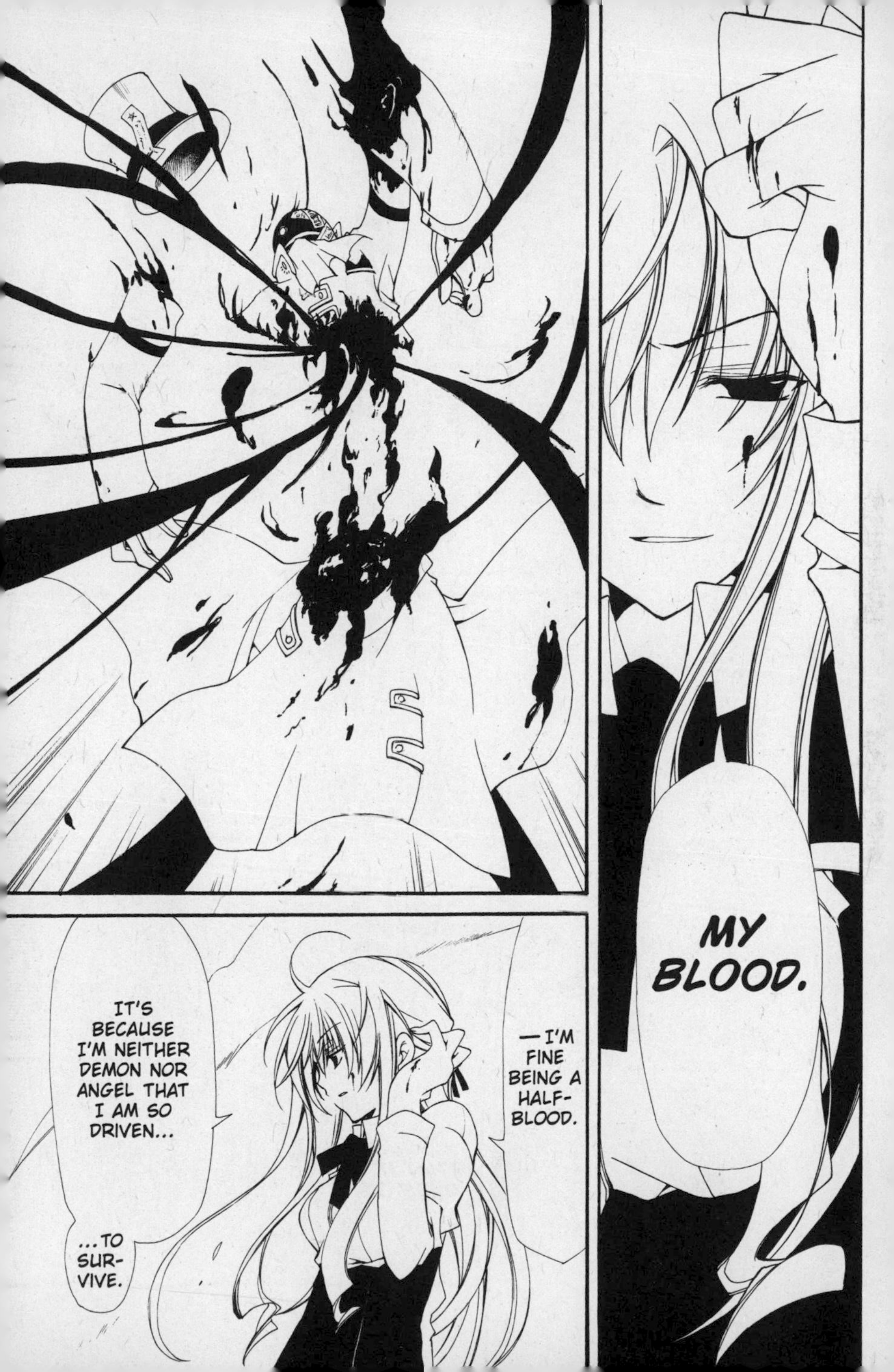
MY BLOOD.
—I'M FINE BEING A HALF-BLOOD.
IT'S BECAUSE I'M NEITHER DEMON NOR ANGEL THAT I AM SO DRIVEN...
...TO SURVIVE.

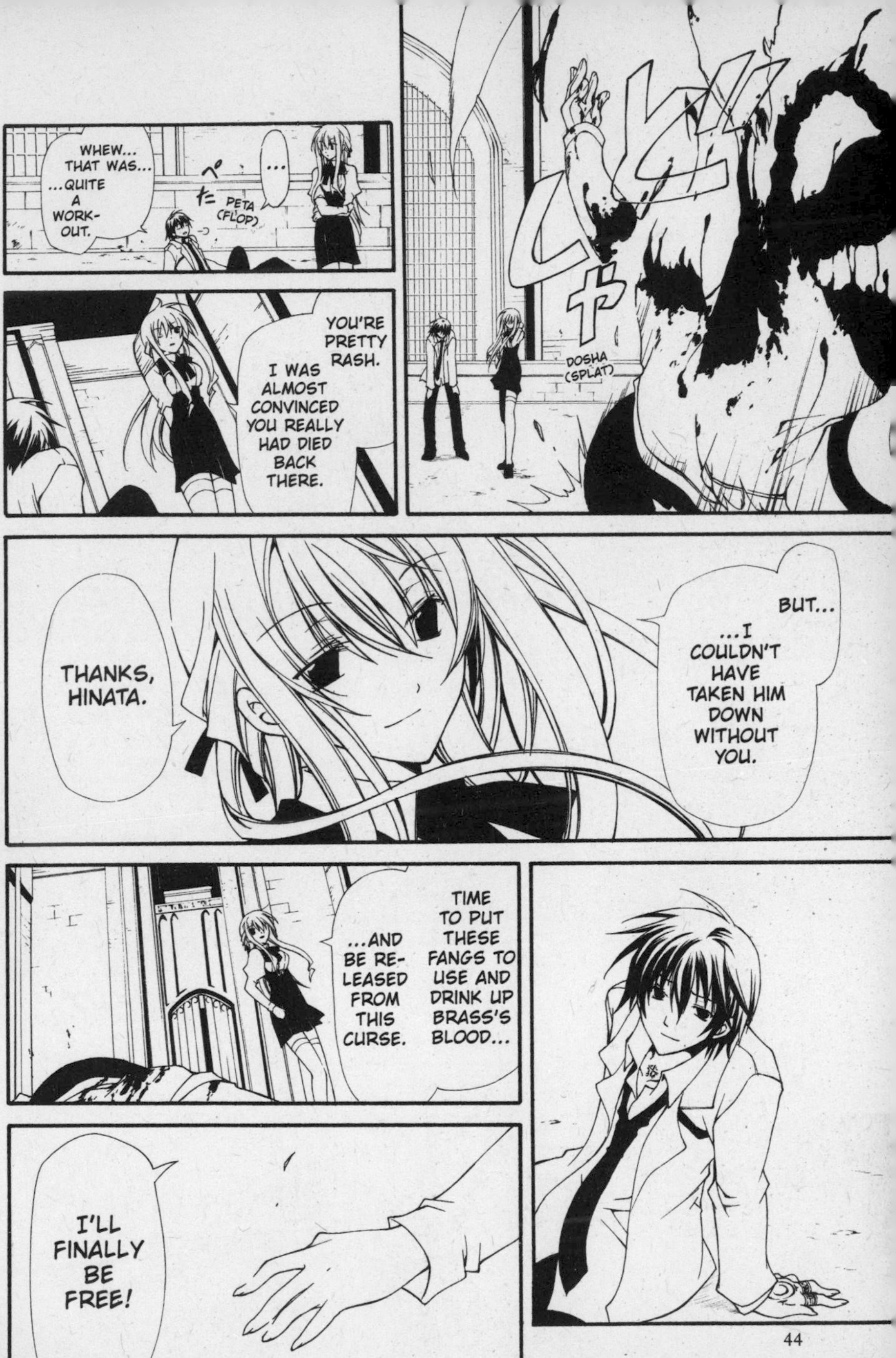
DOSHA (SPLAT)
...
PETA (FLOP)
WHEW... THAT WAS... ...QUITE A WORK-OUT.
YOU'RE PRETTY RASH. I WAS ALMOST CONVINCED YOU REALLY HAD DIED BACK THERE.
BUT... ...I COULDN'T HAVE TAKEN HIM DOWN WITHOUT YOU.
THANKS, HINATA.
TIME TO PUT THESE FANGS TO USE AND DRINK UP BRASS'S BLOOD...
...AND BE RE-LEASED FROM THIS CURSE.
I'LL FINALLY BE FREE!

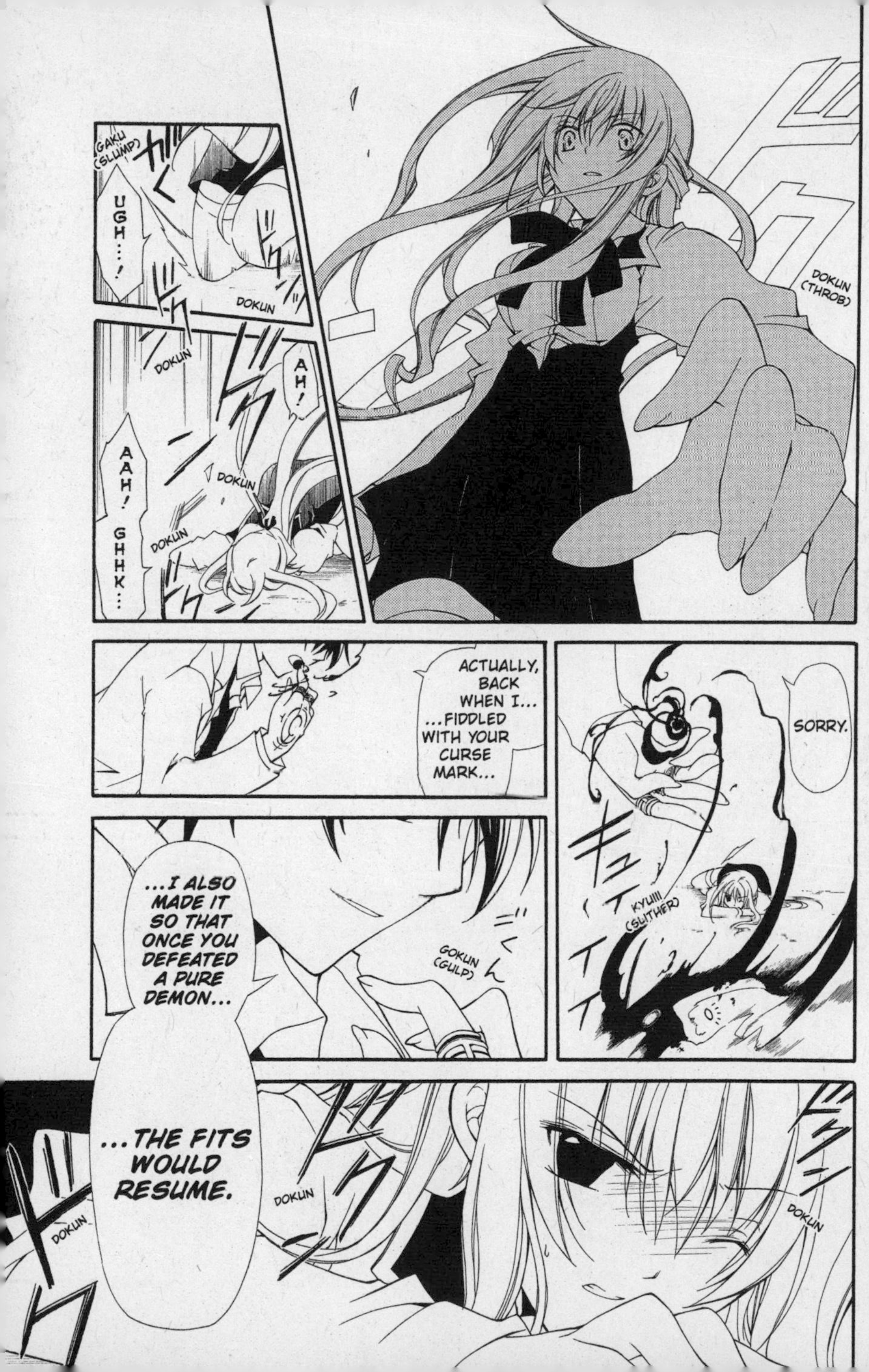
DOKUN (THROB)
DOKUN
UGH...!
GAKU (SLUMP)
AH!
DOKUN
DOKUN
DOKUN
AAH! GHHK...
SORRY.
KYUIII (SLITHER)
ACTUALLY, BACK WHEN I... ...FIDDLED WITH YOUR CURSE MARK...
GOKUN (GULP)
...I ALSO MADE IT SO THAT ONCE YOU DEFEATED A PURE DEMON...
DOKUN
DOKUN
...THE FITS WOULD RESUME.
DOKUN

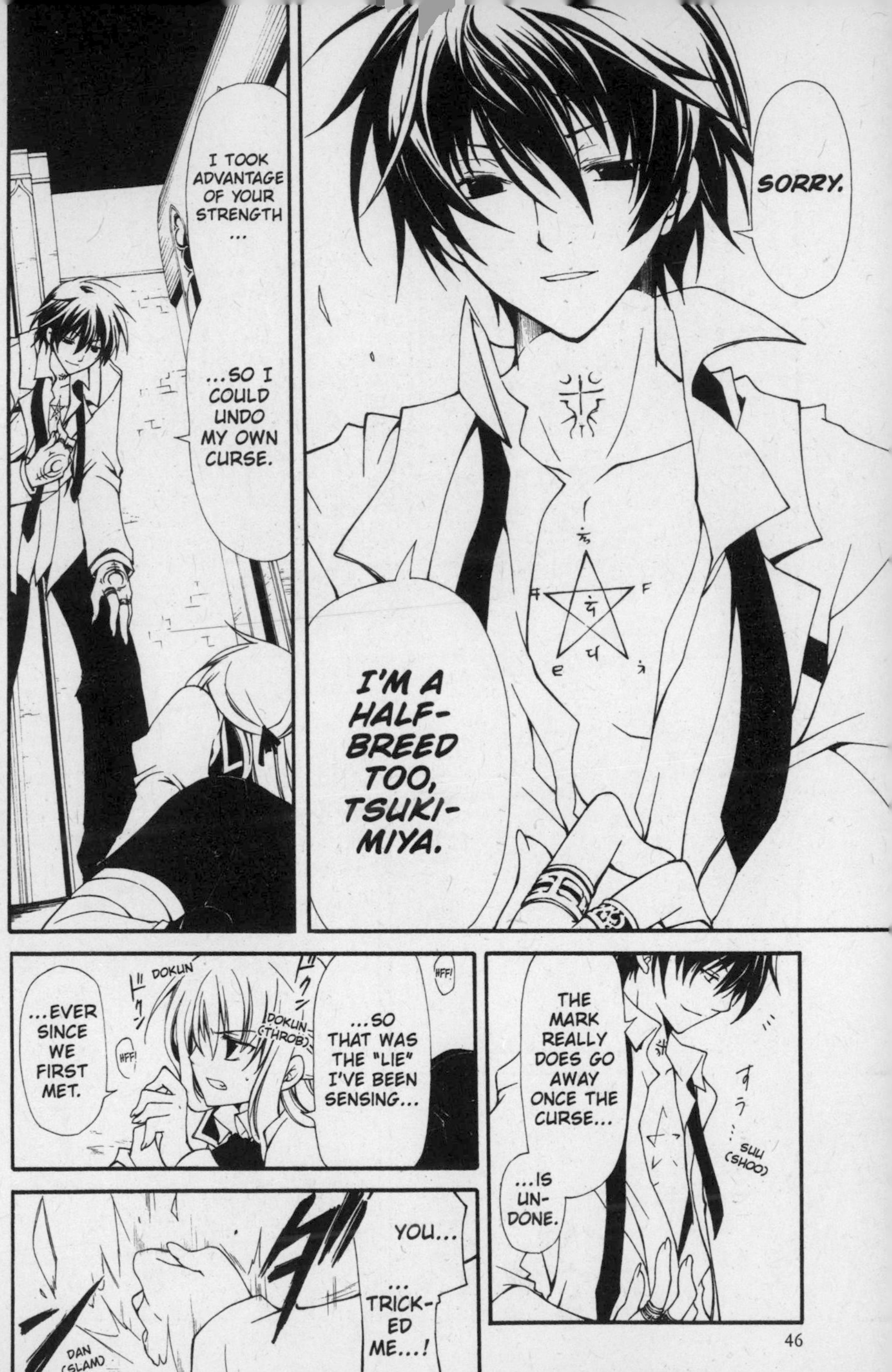

SORRY.
I'M A HALF-BREED TOO, TSUKIMIYA.
I TOOK ADVANTAGE OF YOUR STRENGTH...
...SO I COULD UNDO MY OWN CURSE.
THE MARK REALLY DOES GO AWAY ONCE THE CURSE...
...IS UN-DONE.
すっ
SUU (SHOO)
HFF!
...SO THAT WAS THE "LIE" I'VE BEEN SENSING...
DOKUN (THROB)
ドクン
DOKUN
HFF!
...EVER SINCE WE FIRST MET.
YOU...
...TRICK-ED ME...!
DAN (SLAM)

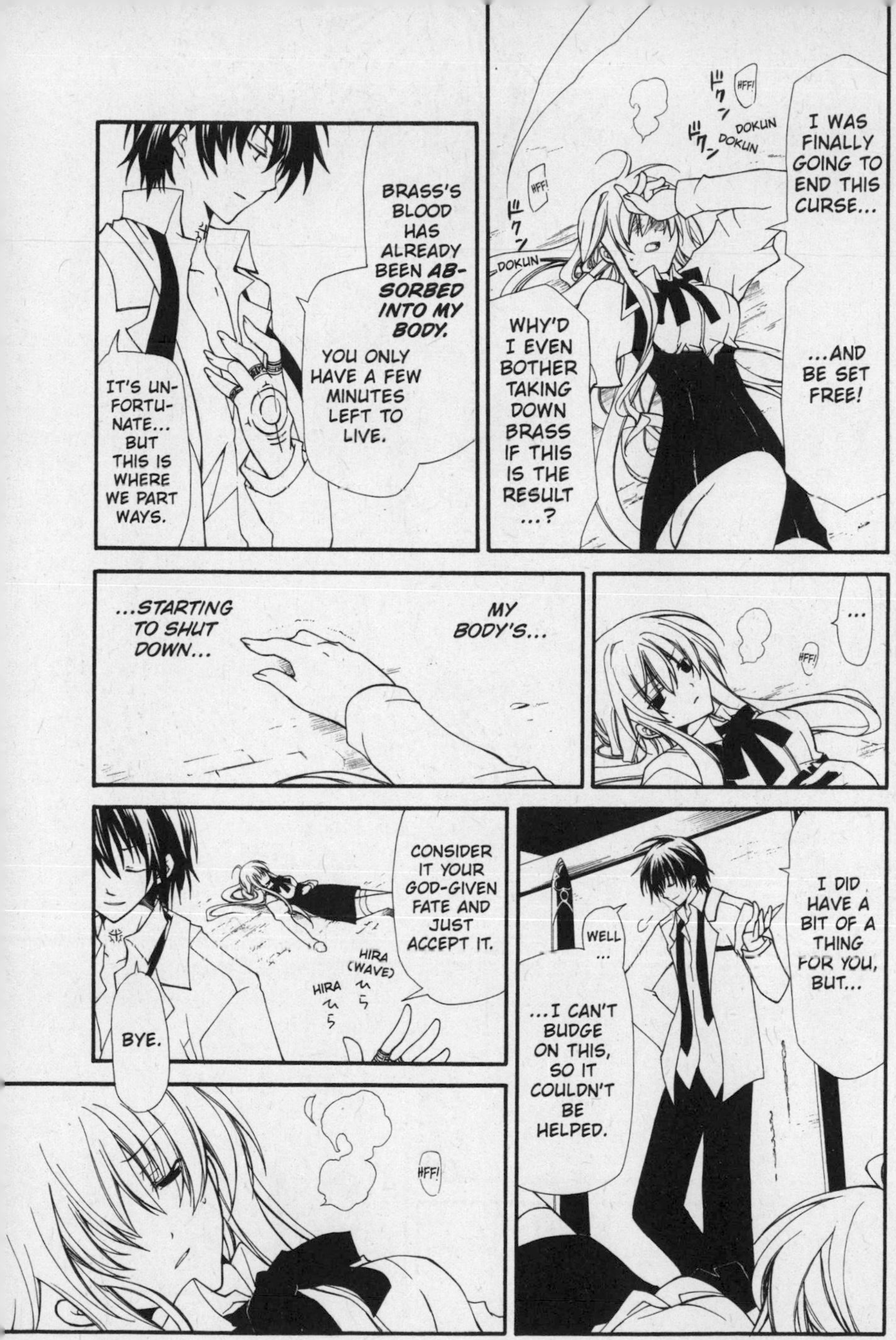

HFF!
ドクン DOKUN
ドクン DOKUN
I WAS FINALLY GOING TO END THIS CURSE...
...AND BE SET FREE!
HFF!
ドクン DOKUN
WHY'D I EVEN BOTHER TAKING DOWN BRASS IF THIS IS THE RESULT ...?
BRASS'S BLOOD HAS ALREADY BEEN ABSORBED INTO MY BODY.
YOU ONLY HAVE A FEW MINUTES LEFT TO LIVE.
IT'S UNFORTUNATE... BUT THIS IS WHERE WE PART WAYS.
...
HFF!
MY BODY'S...
...STARTING TO SHUT DOWN...
I DID HAVE A BIT OF A THING FOR YOU, BUT...
WELL...
...I CAN'T BUDGE ON THIS, SO IT COULDN'T BE HELPED.
CONSIDER IT YOUR GOD-GIVEN FATE AND JUST ACCEPT IT.
HIRA (WAVE)
HIRA
BYE.
HFF!

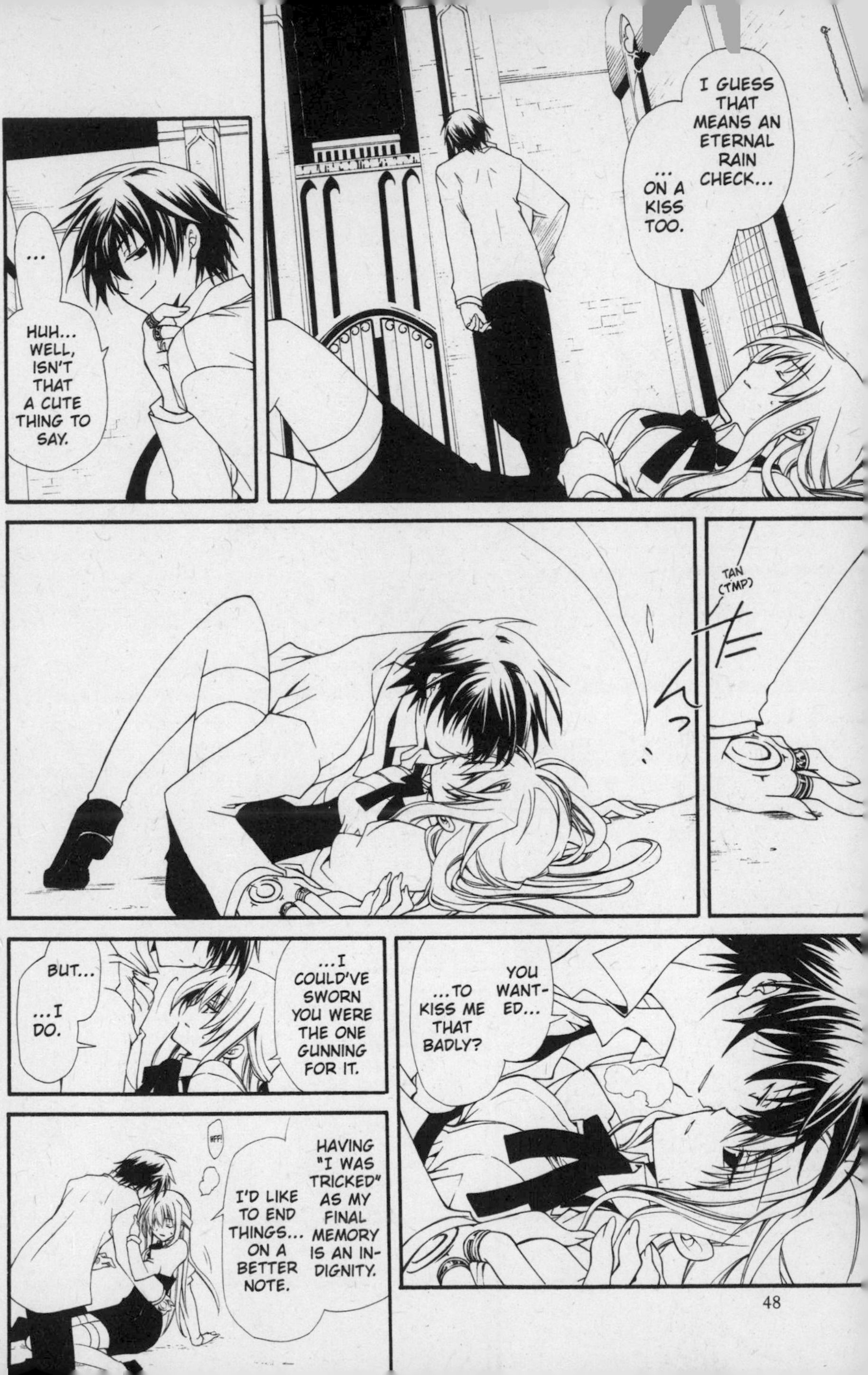
I GUESS THAT MEANS AN ETERNAL RAIN CHECK...
...ON A KISS TOO.
...
HUH... WELL, ISN'T THAT A CUTE THING TO SAY.
TAN (TMP)
YOU WANT-ED...
...TO KISS ME THAT BADLY?
...I COULD'VE SWORN YOU WERE THE ONE GUNNING FOR IT.
BUT...
...I DO.
HAVING "I WAS TRICKED" AS MY FINAL MEMORY IS AN IN-DIGNITY.
I'D LIKE TO END THINGS... ON A BETTER NOTE.

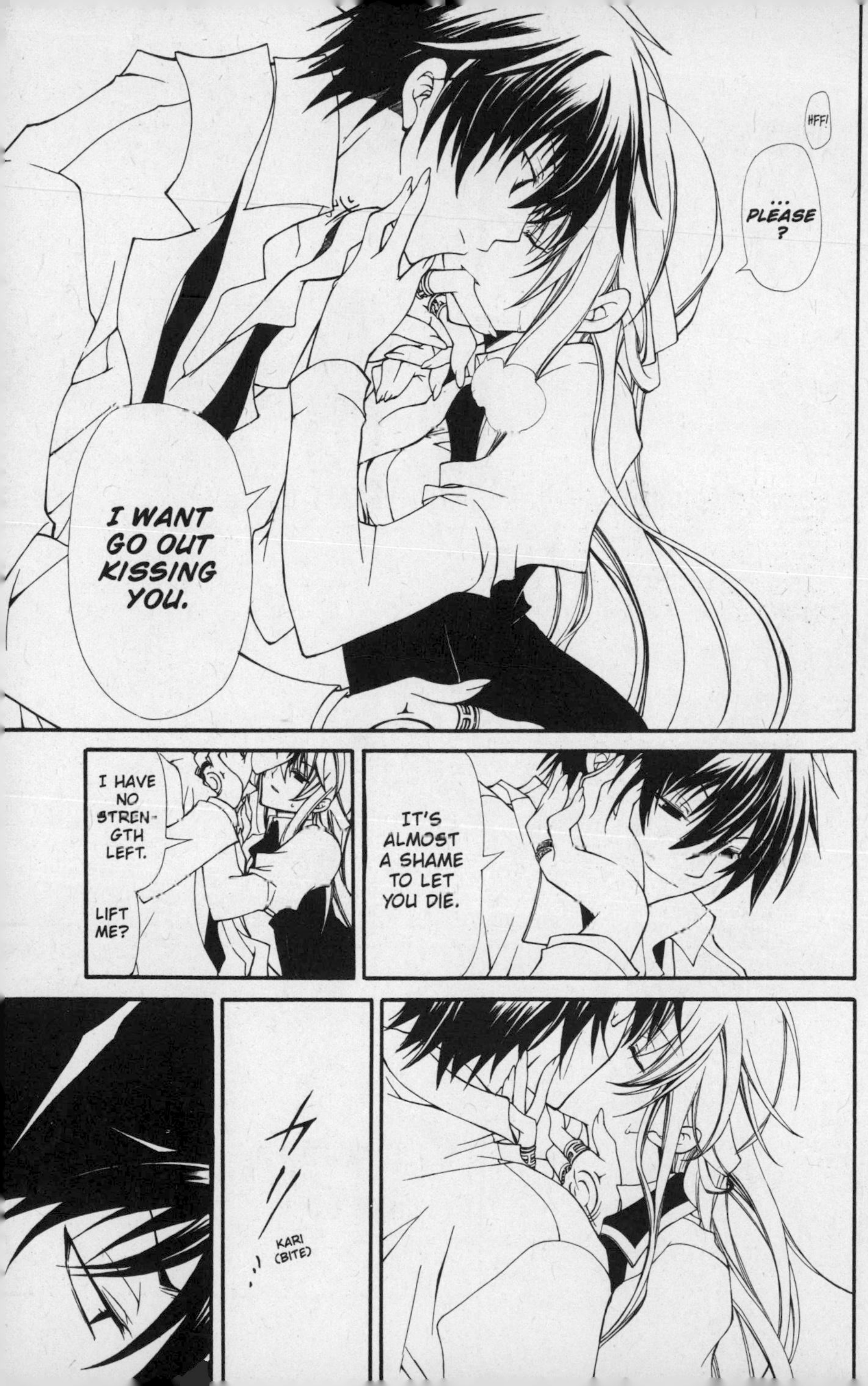
HFF!
...PLEASE?
I WANT GO OUT KISSING YOU.
IT'S ALMOST A SHAME TO LET YOU DIE.
I HAVE NO STREN-GTH LEFT.
LIFT ME?
KARI (BITE)

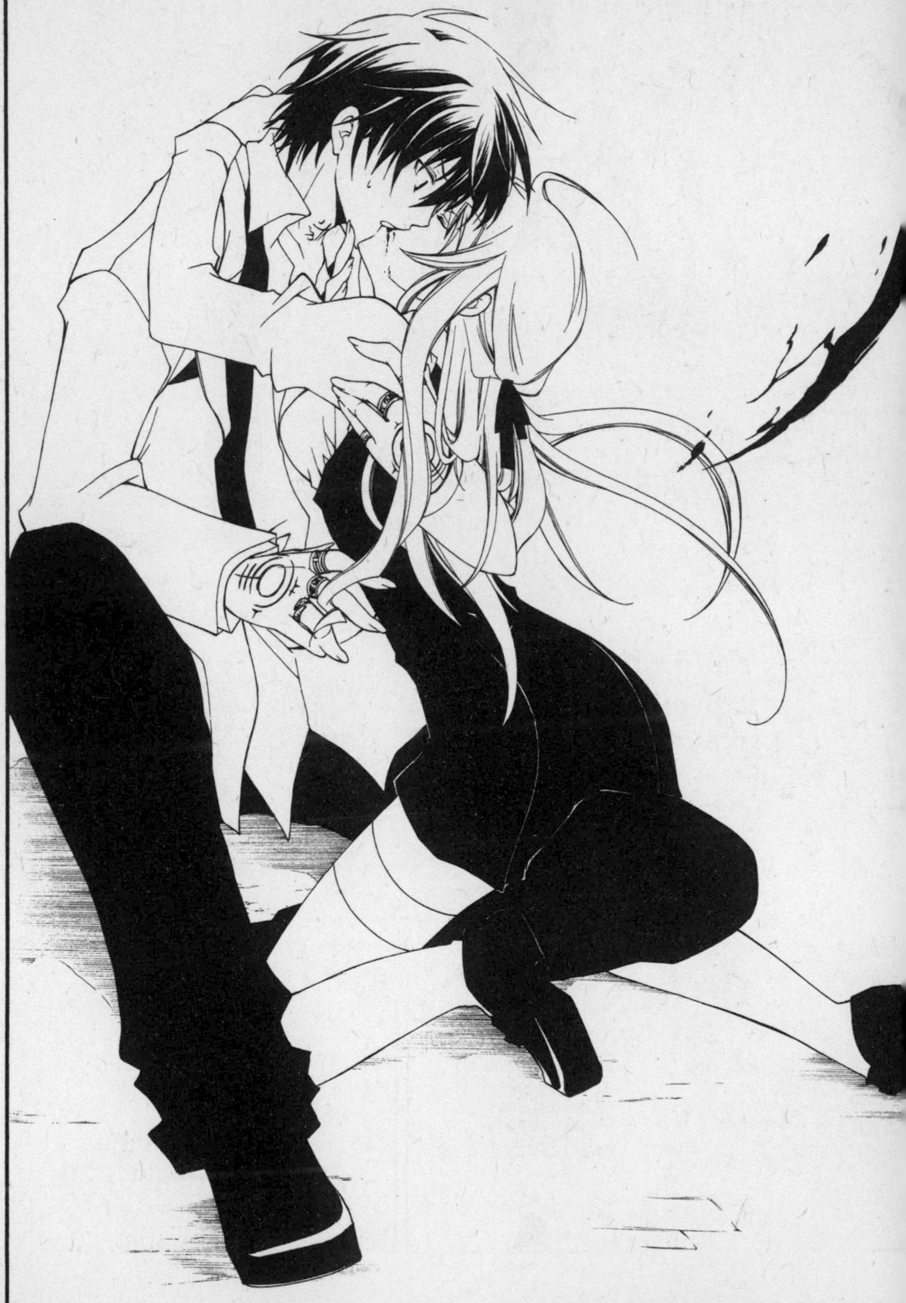

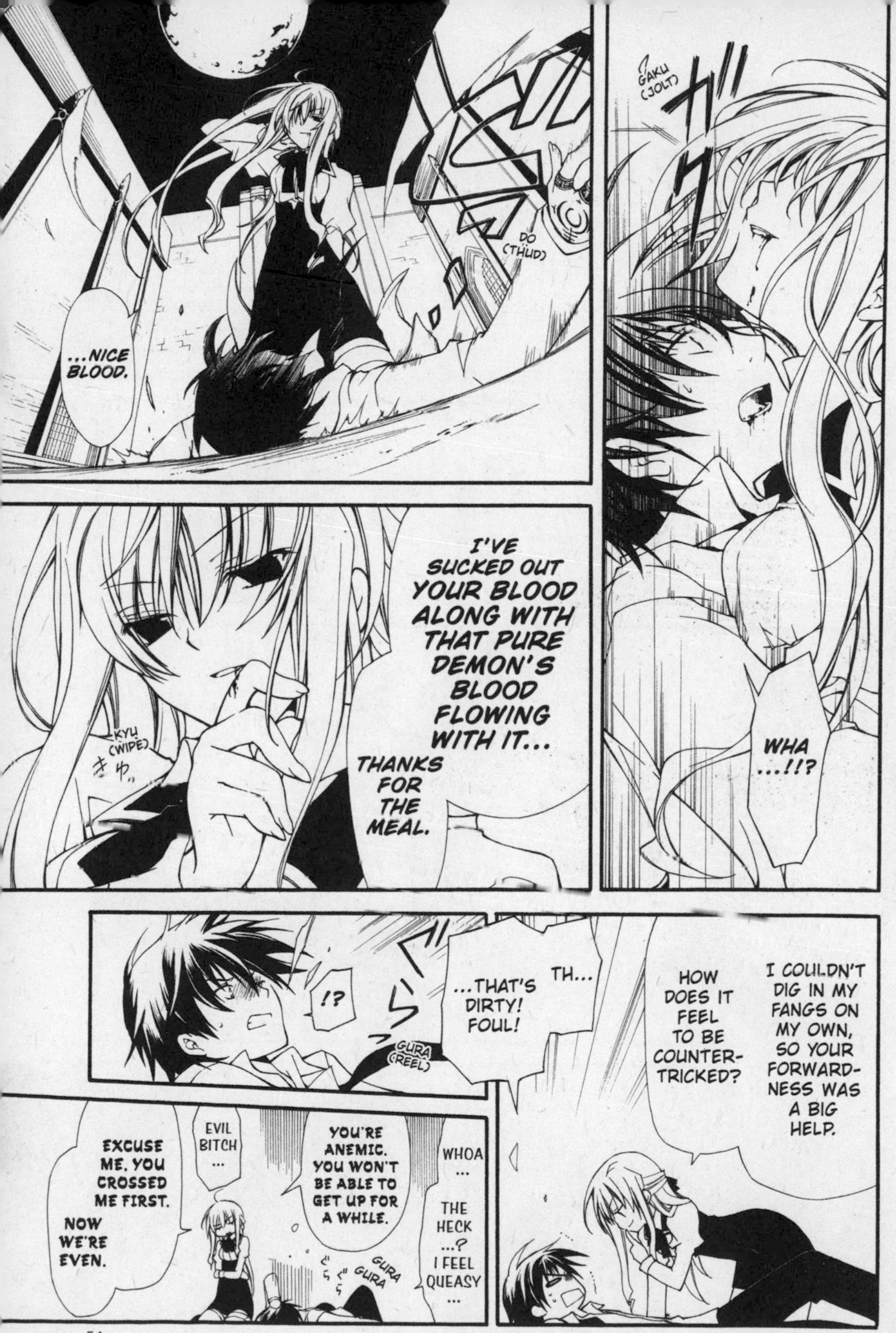
GAKU (JOLT)
WHA ...!!?
DO (THUD)
...NICE BLOOD.
I'VE SUCKED OUT YOUR BLOOD ALONG WITH THAT PURE DEMON'S BLOOD FLOWING WITH IT...
THANKS FOR THE MEAL.
KYU (WIPE)
I COULDN'T DIG IN MY FANGS ON MY OWN, SO YOUR FORWARDNESS WAS A BIG HELP.
HOW DOES IT FEEL TO BE COUNTER-TRICKED?
TH...
...THAT'S DIRTY! FOUL!
!?
GURA (REEL)
WHOA ... THE HECK ...? I FEEL QUEASY ...
YOU'RE ANEMIC. YOU WON'T BE ABLE TO GET UP FOR A WHILE.
GURA GURA
EVIL BITCH ...
EXCUSE ME, YOU CROSSED ME FIRST.
NOW WE'RE EVEN.

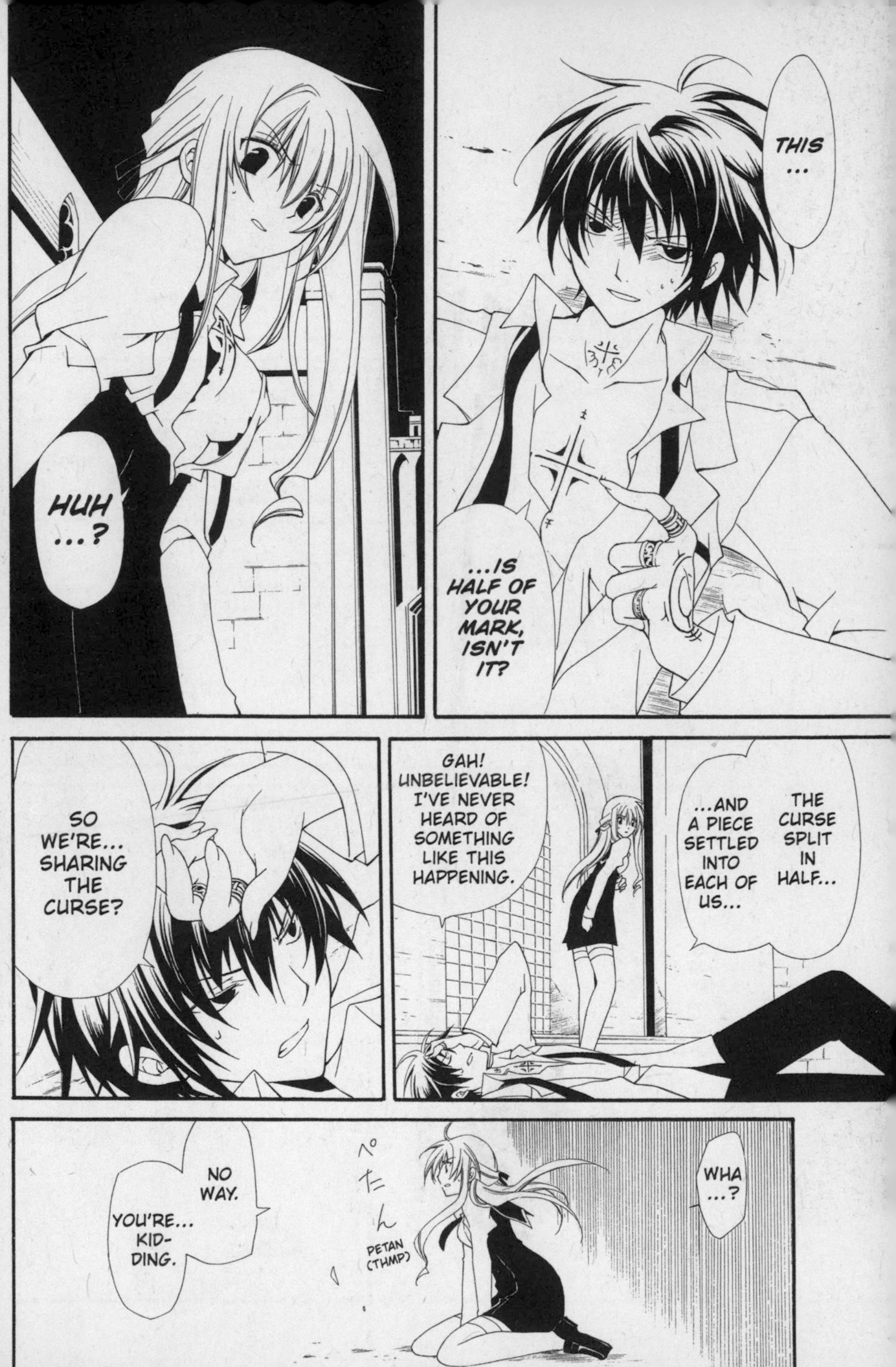
THIS ...
...IS HALF OF YOUR MARK, ISN'T IT?
HUH ...?
THE CURSE SPLIT IN HALF...
...AND A PIECE SETTLED INTO EACH OF US...
GAH! UNBELIEVABLE! I'VE NEVER HEARD OF SOMETHING LIKE THIS HAPPENING.
SO WE'RE... SHARING THE CURSE?
WHA ...?
ぺたん
PETAN (THMP)
NO WAY.
YOU'RE... KID-DING.

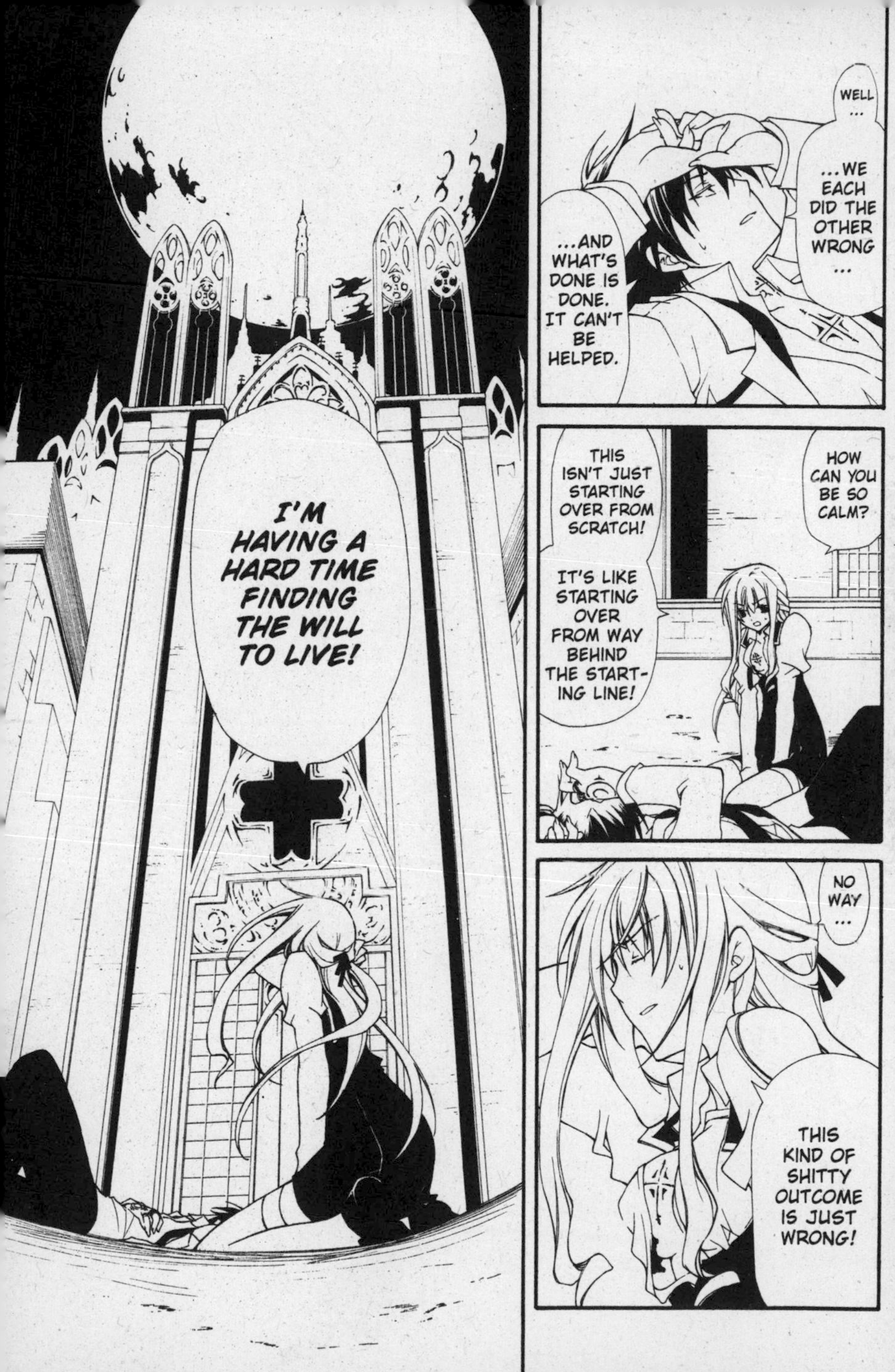
WELL ...
...WE EACH DID THE OTHER WRONG ...
...AND WHAT'S DONE IS DONE. IT CAN'T BE HELPED.
HOW CAN YOU BE SO CALM?
THIS ISN'T JUST STARTING OVER FROM SCRATCH!
IT'S LIKE STARTING OVER FROM WAY BEHIND THE START-ING LINE!
NO WAY ...
THIS KIND OF SHITTY OUTCOME IS JUST WRONG!
I'M HAVING A HARD TIME FINDING THE WILL TO LIVE!

BLOODY CROSS

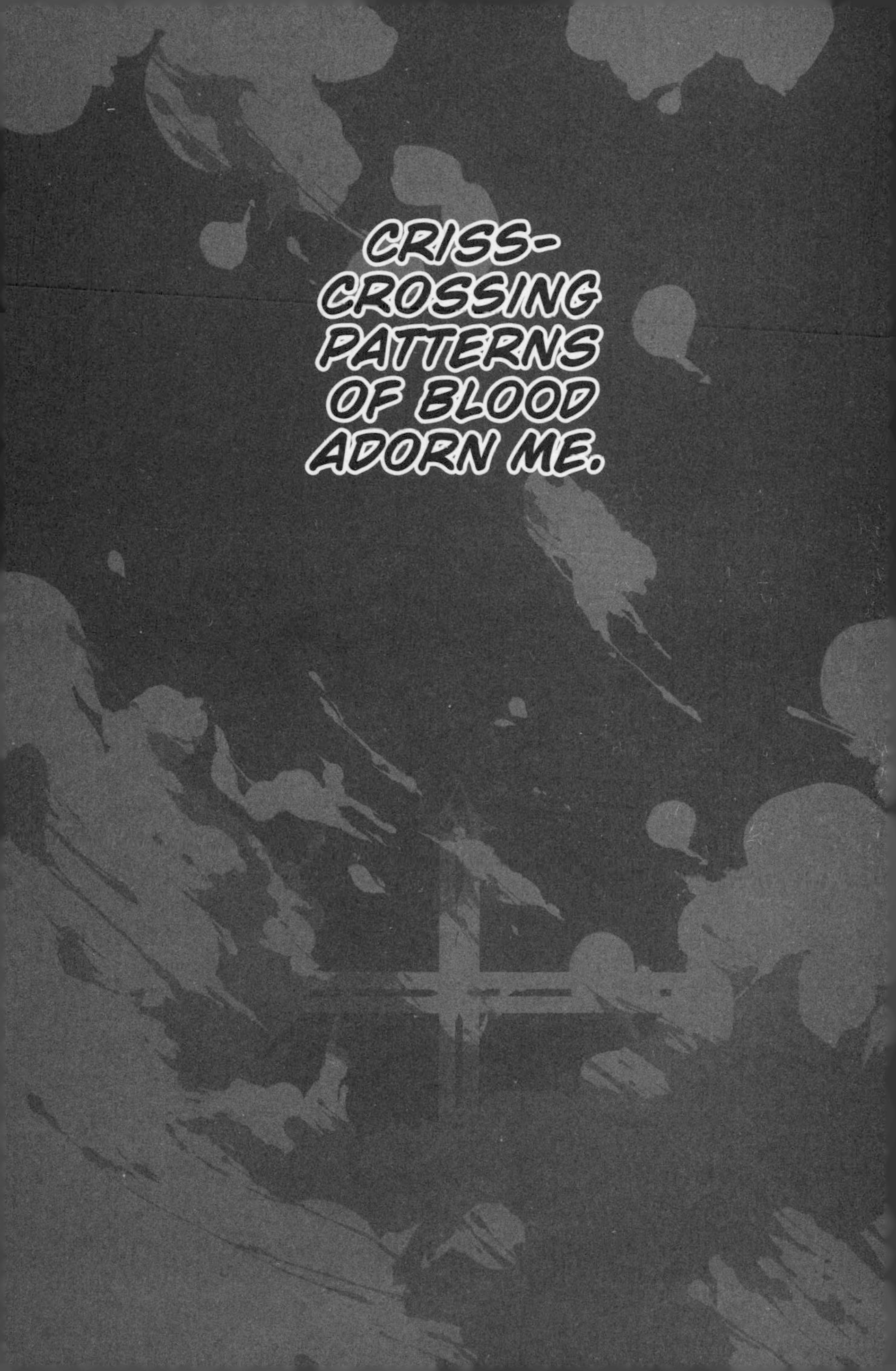
CRISS-CROSSING PATTERNS OF BLOOD ADORN ME.

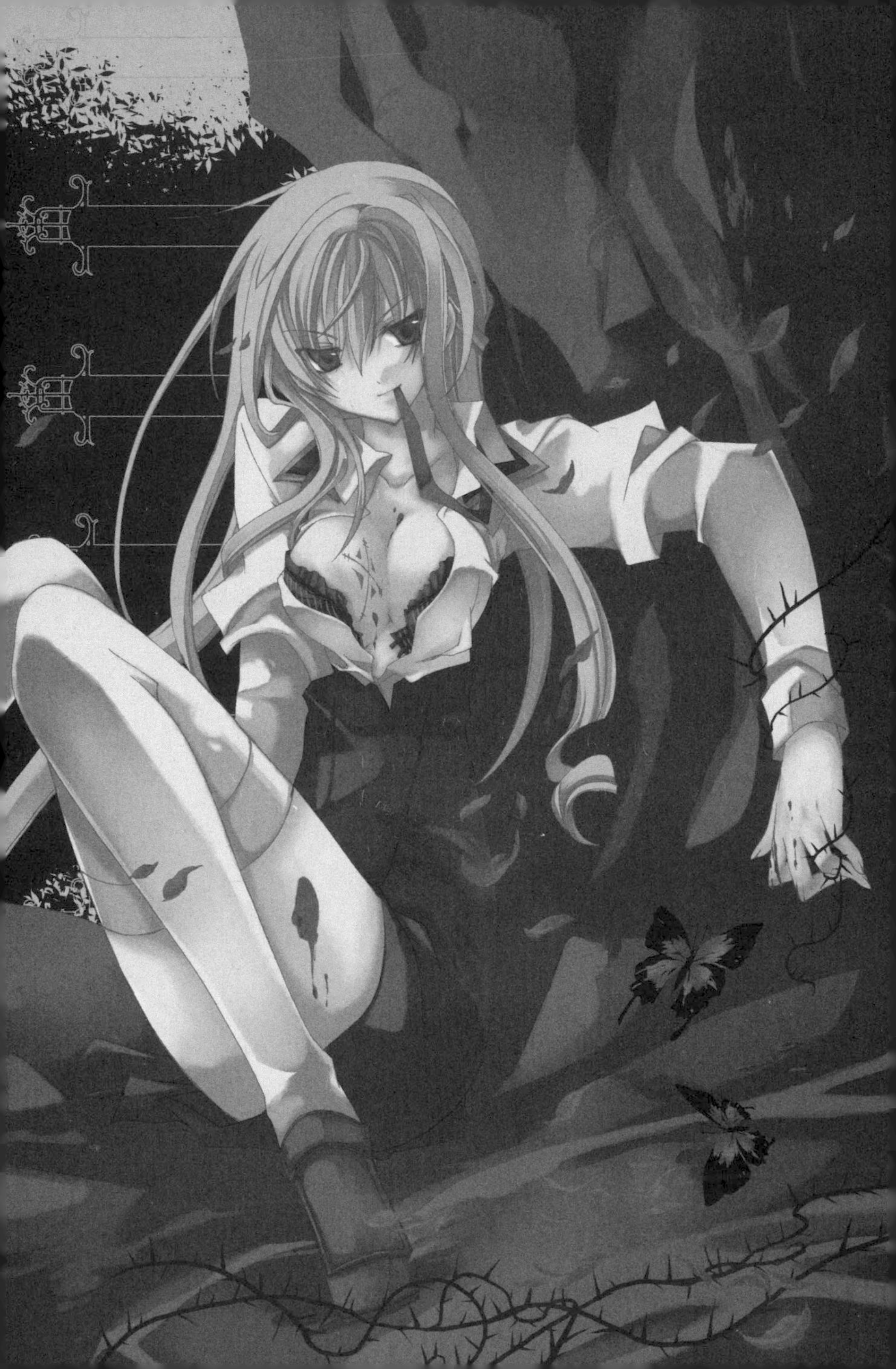

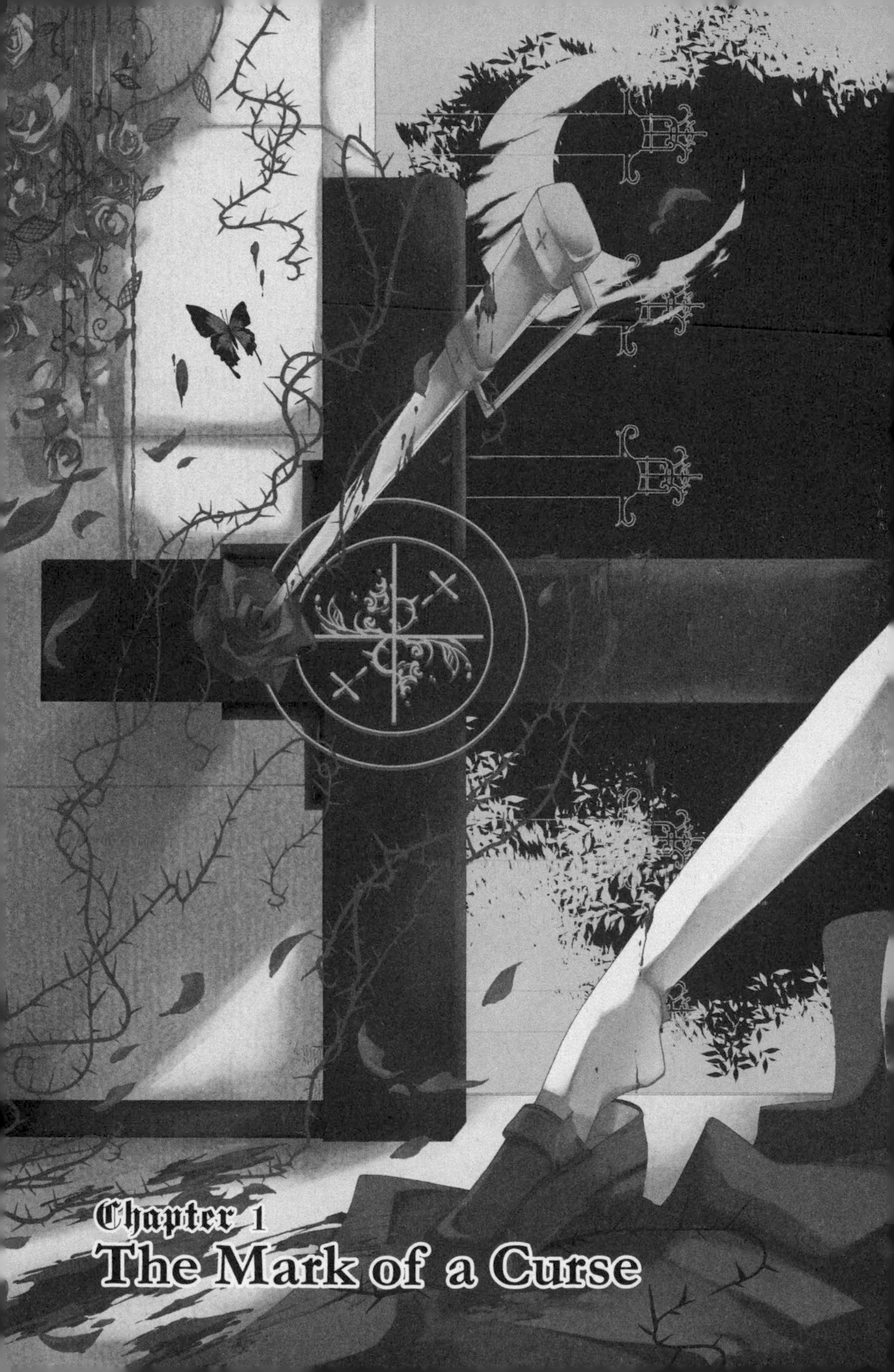

Chapter 1
The Mark of a Curse

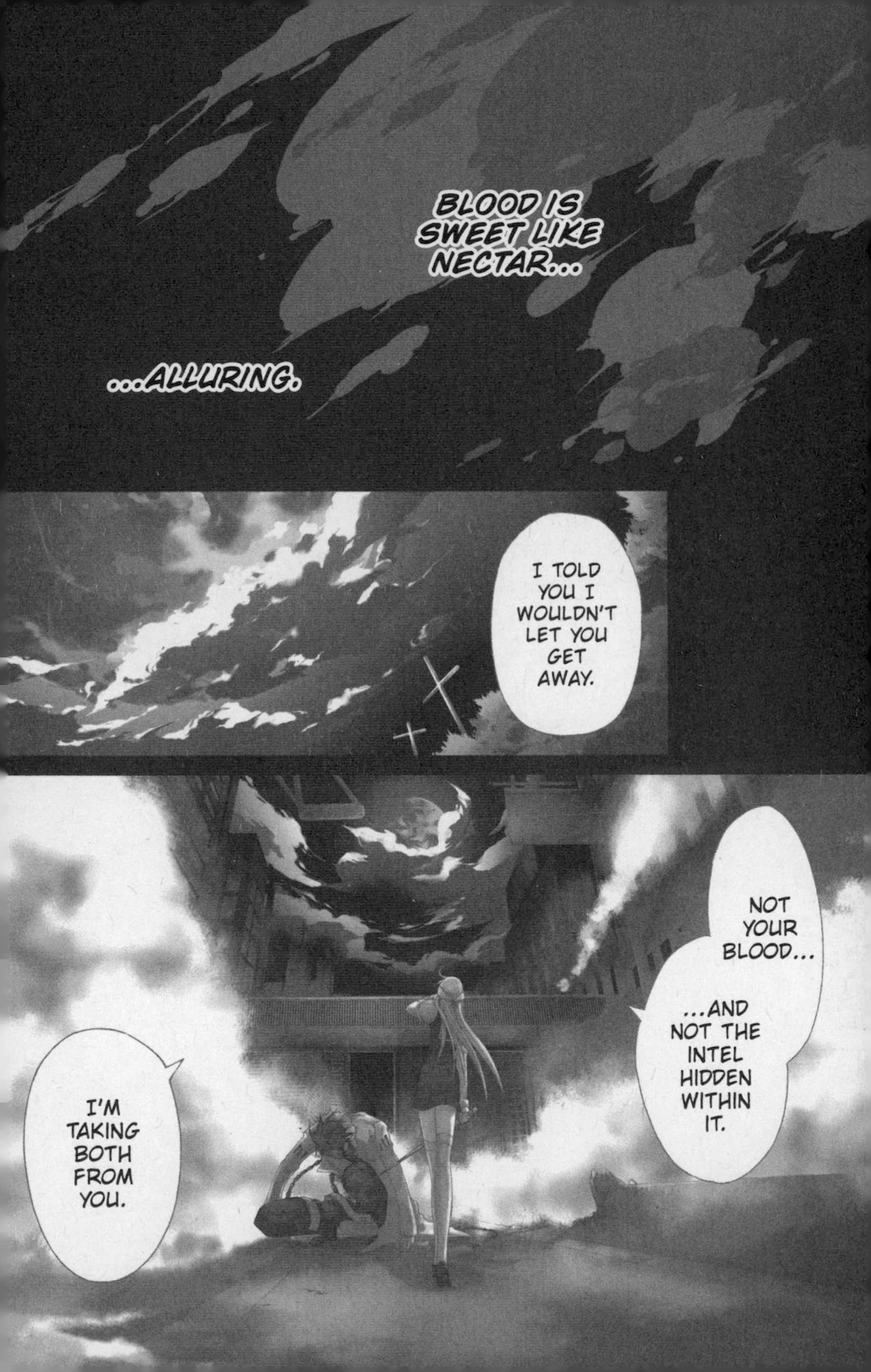
BLOOD IS SWEET LIKE NECTAR...
...ALLURING.
I TOLD YOU I WOULDN'T LET YOU GET AWAY.
NOT YOUR BLOOD...
...AND NOT THE INTEL HIDDEN WITHIN IT.
I'M TAKING BOTH FROM YOU.

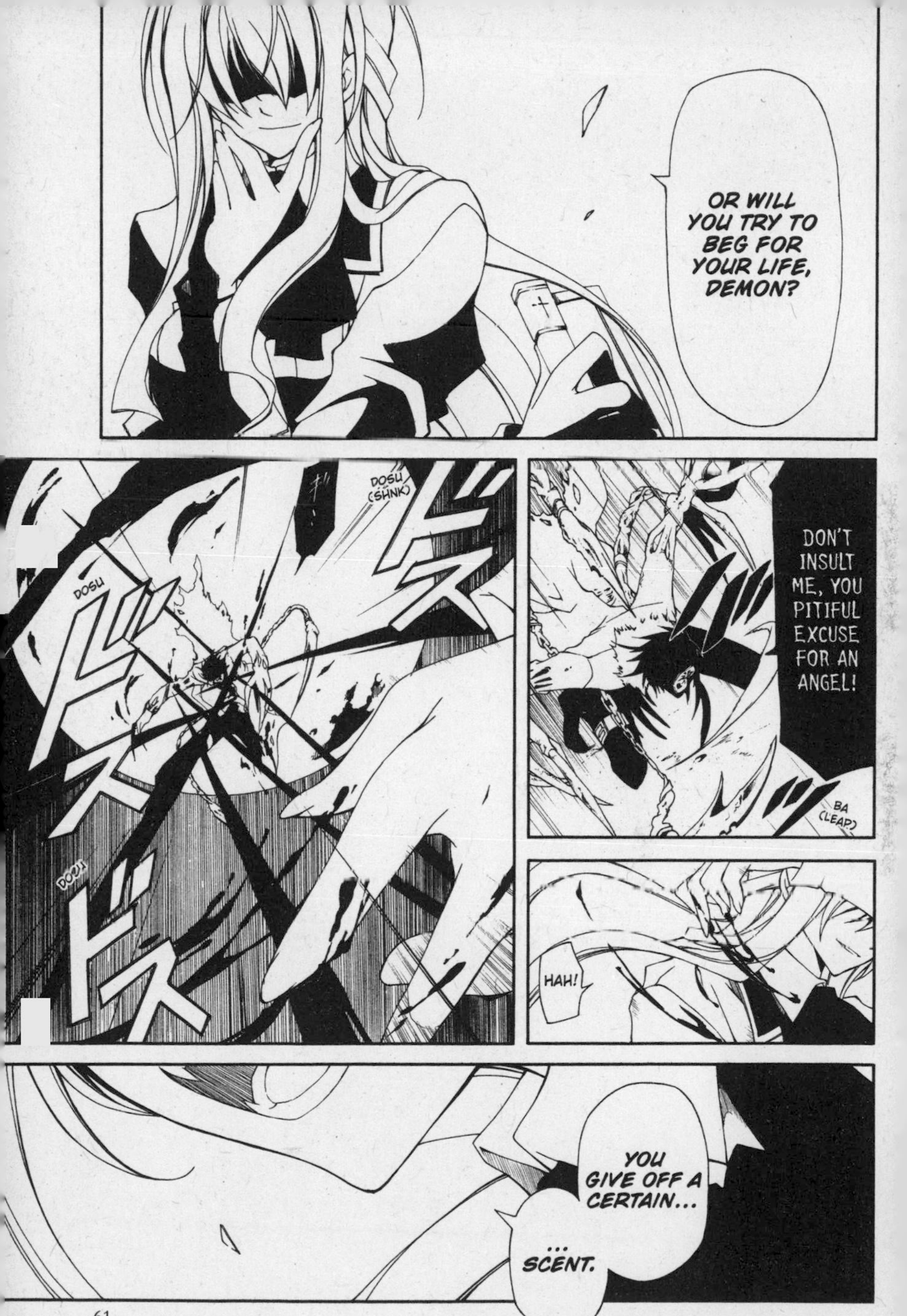
OR WILL YOU TRY TO BEG FOR YOUR LIFE, DEMON?
DON'T INSULT ME, YOU PITIFUL EXCUSE FOR AN ANGEL!
BA (LEAP)
HAH!
DOSU (SHNK)
DOSU
DOSU
YOU GIVE OFF A CERTAIN...
... SCËNT.

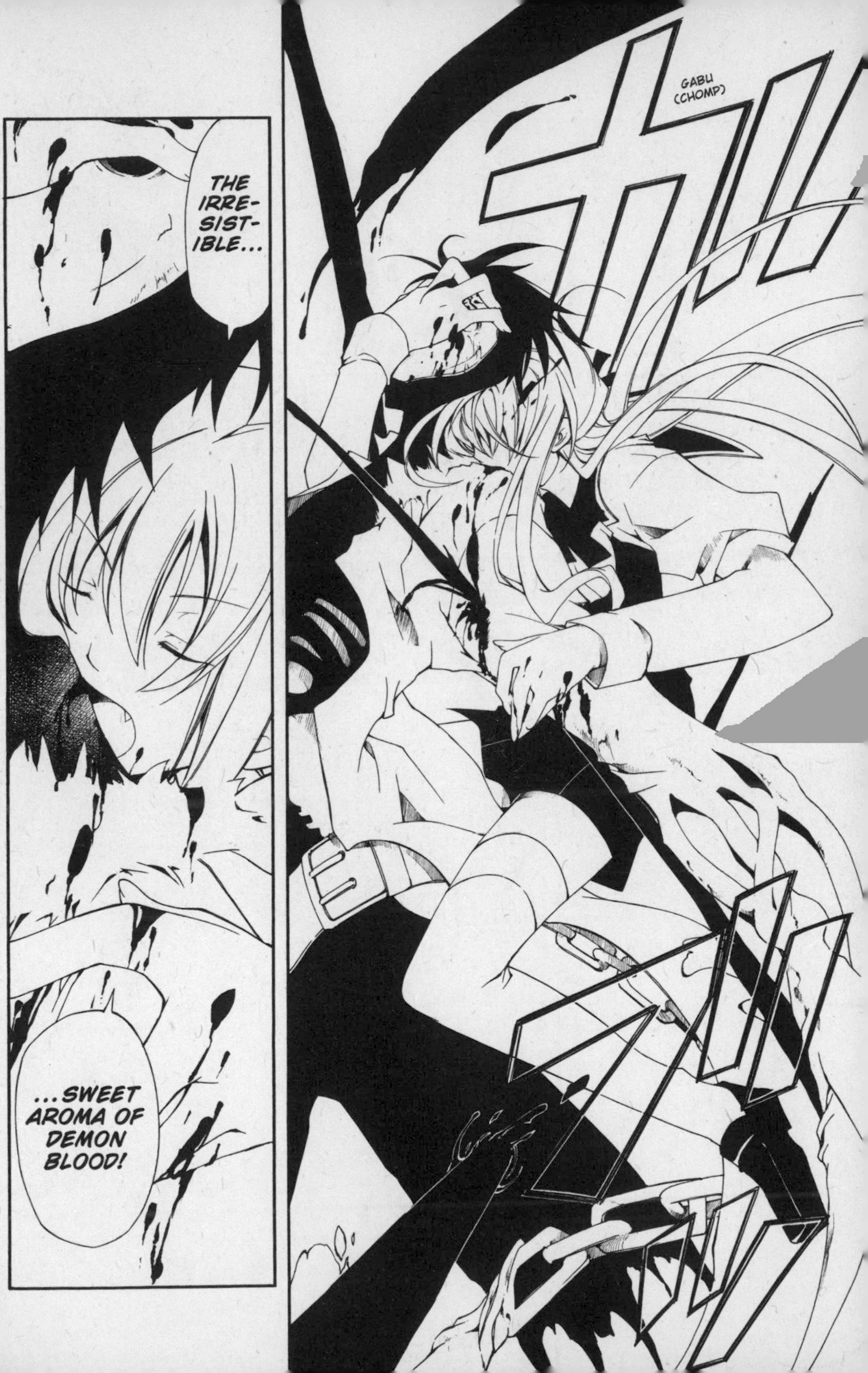
GABU (CHOMP)
THE IRRE-SIST-IBLE...
...SWEET AROMA OF DEMON BLOOD!

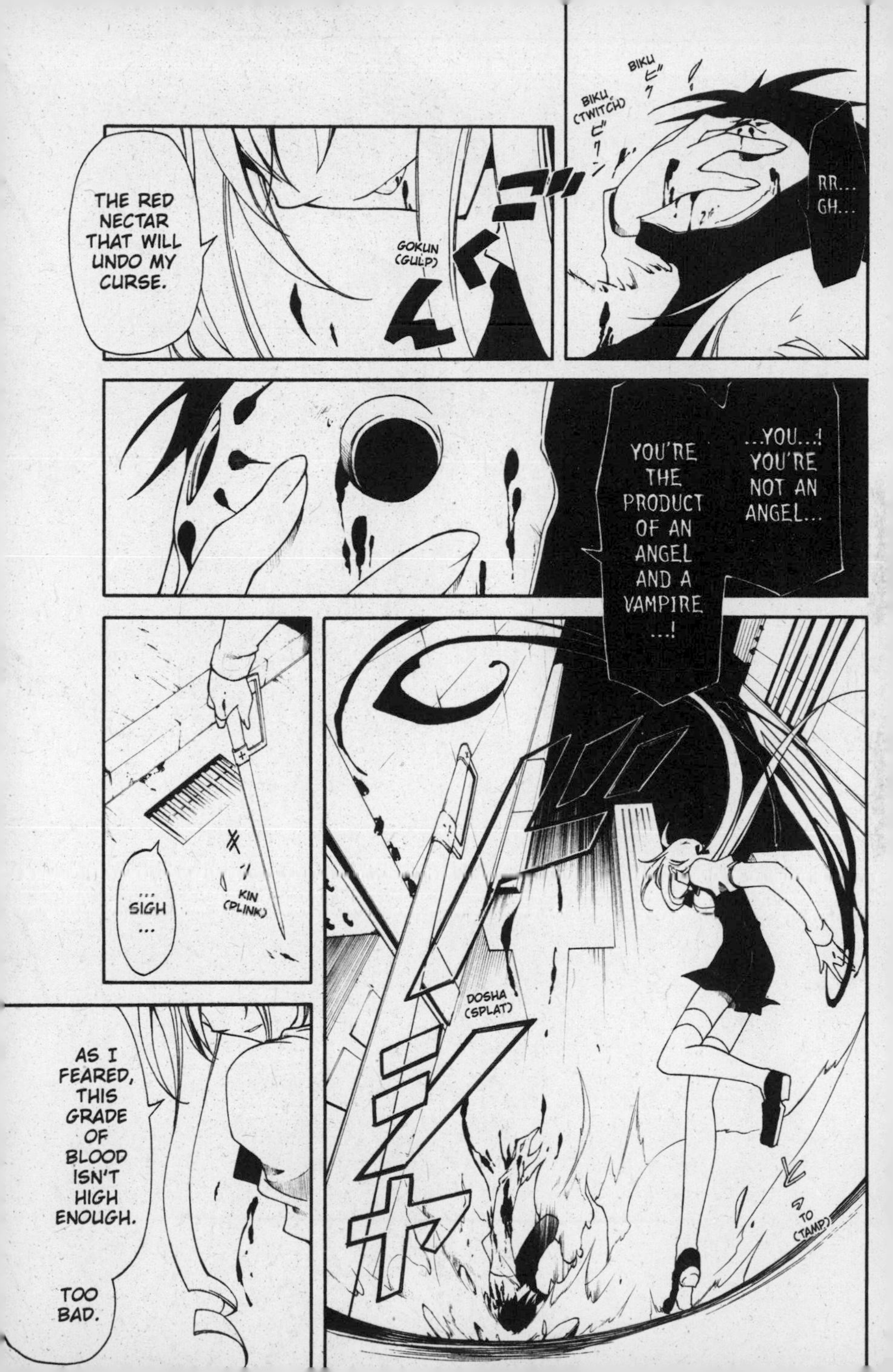
BIKU (TWITCH)
BIKU
RR... GH...
GOKUN (GULP)
THE RED NECTAR THAT WILL UNDO MY CURSE.
...YOU...! YOU'RE NOT AN ANGEL...
YOU'RE THE PRODUCT OF AN ANGEL AND A VAMPIRE ...!
DOSHA (SPLAT)
TO (TAMP)
KIN (PLINK)
...SIGH...
AS I FEARED, THIS GRADE OF BLOOD ISN'T HIGH ENOUGH.
TOO BAD.

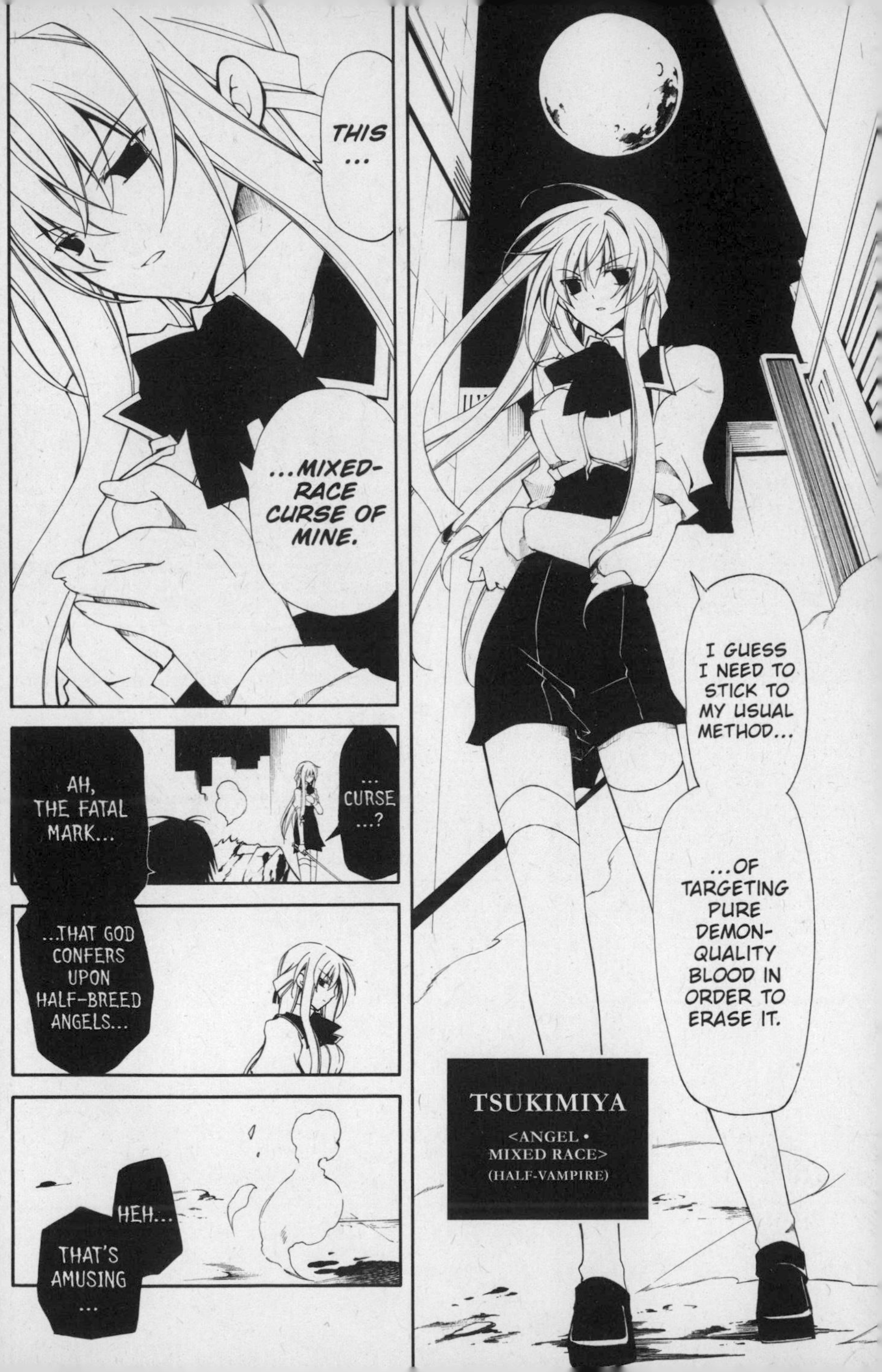
I GUESS I NEED TO STICK TO MY USUAL METHOD...
...OF TARGETING PURE DEMON-QUALITY BLOOD IN ORDER TO ERASE IT.
TSUKIMIYA
<ANGEL • MIXED RACE>
(HALF-VAMPIRE)
THIS...
...MIXED-RACE CURSE OF MINE.
...CURSE...?
AH, THE FATAL MARK...
...THAT GOD CONFERS UPON HALF-BREED ANGELS...
HEH...
THAT'S AMUSING...

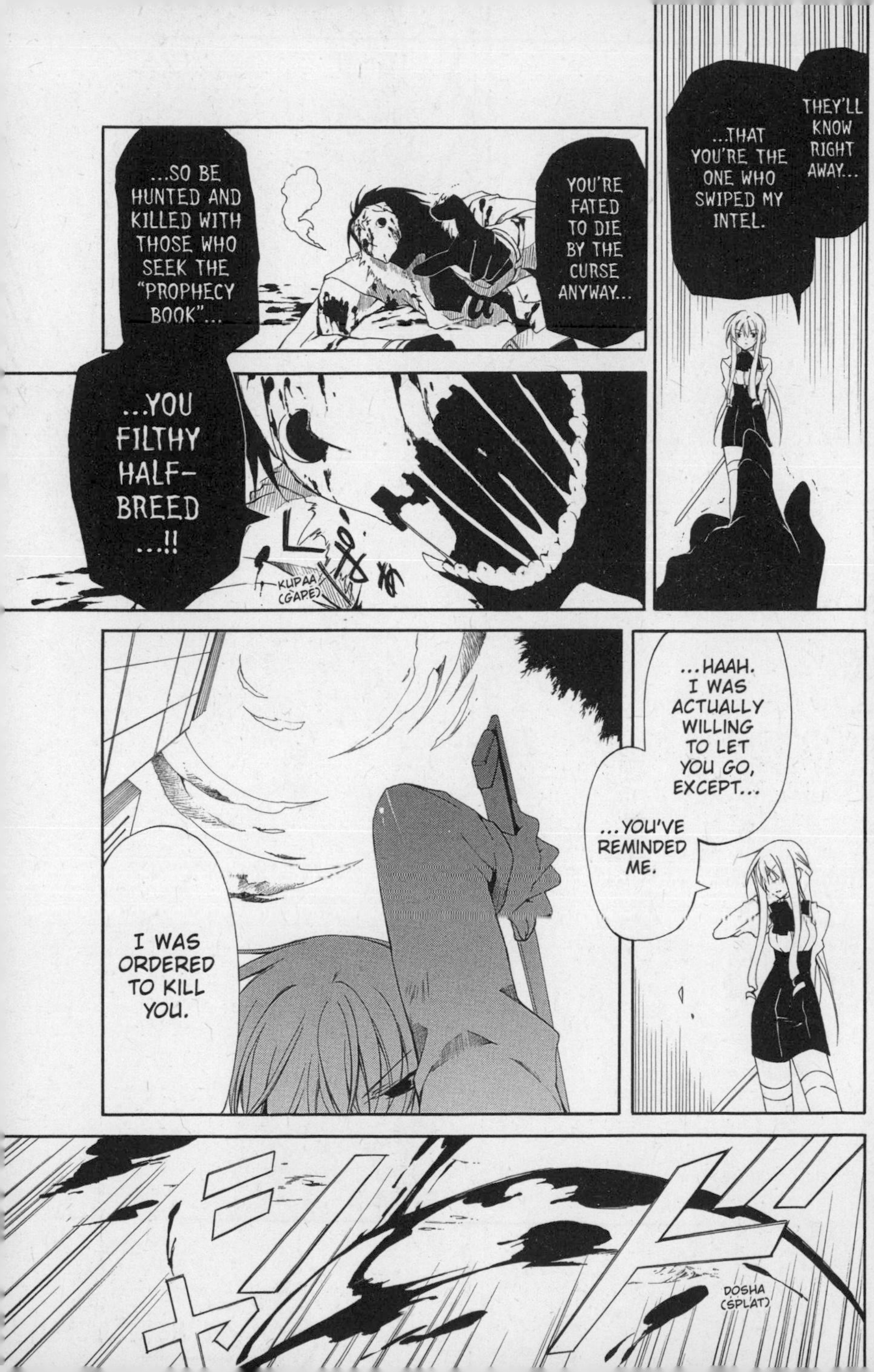
THEY'LL KNOW RIGHT AWAY...
...THAT YOU'RE THE ONE WHO SWIPED MY INTEL.
YOU'RE FATED TO DIE BY THE CURSE ANYWAY...
...SO BE HUNTED AND KILLED WITH THOSE WHO SEEK THE "PROPHECY BOOK"...
...YOU FILTHY HALF-BREED ...!!
KUPAA (GAPE)
...HAAH. I WAS ACTUALLY WILLING TO LET YOU GO, EXCEPT...
...YOU'VE REMINDED ME.
I WAS ORDERED TO KILL YOU.
DOSHA (SPLAT)

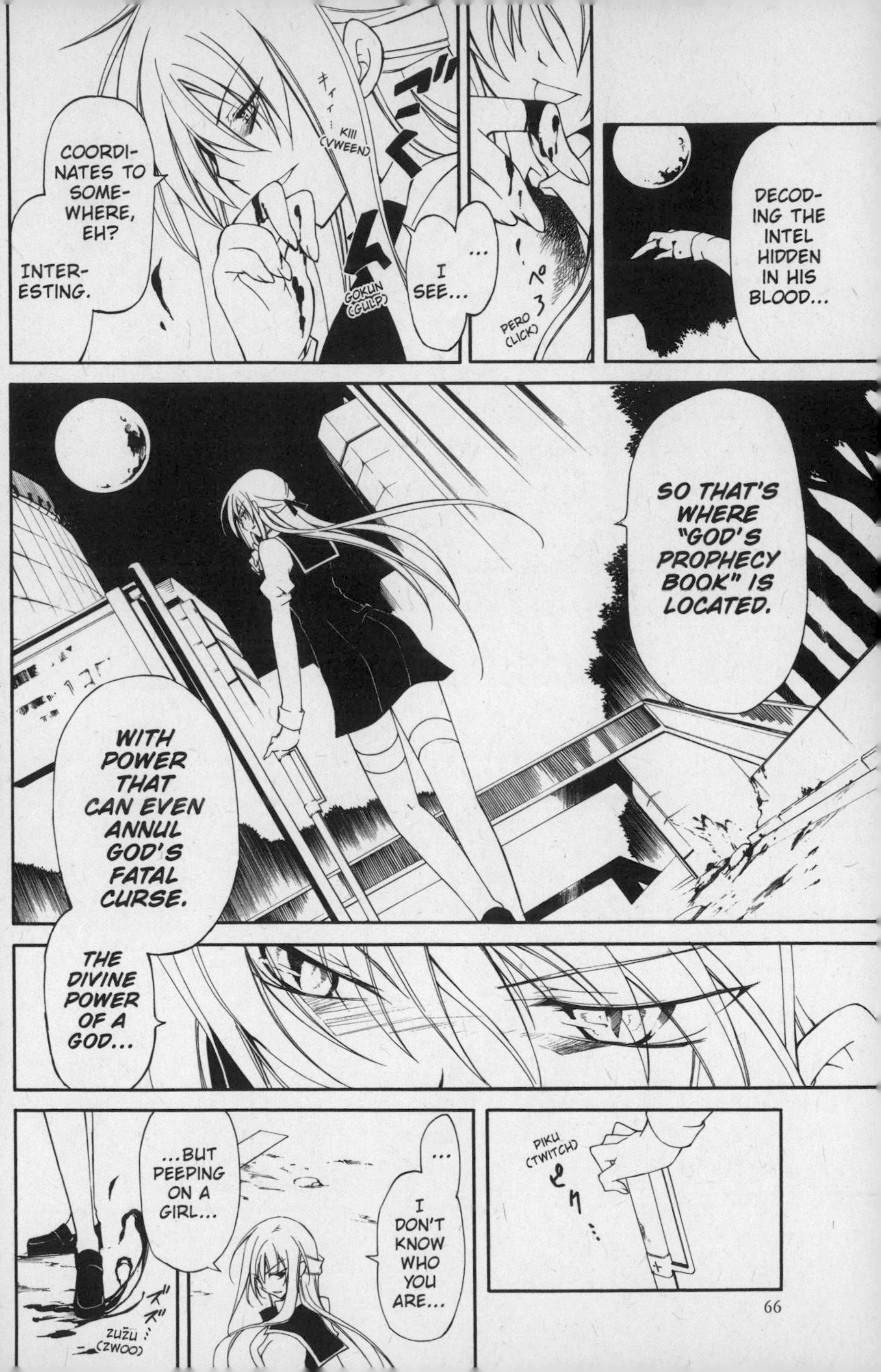
DECODING THE INTEL HIDDEN IN HIS BLOOD...
...
I SEE...
PERO (LICK)
KIII (VWEEN)
GOKUN (GULP)
COORDINATES TO SOMEWHERE, EH?
INTERESTING.
SO THAT'S WHERE "GOD'S PROPHECY BOOK" IS LOCATED.
WITH POWER THAT CAN EVEN ANNUL GOD'S FATAL CURSE.
THE DIVINE POWER OF A GOD...
PIKU (TWITCH)
...
I DON'T KNOW WHO YOU ARE...
...BUT PEEPING ON A GIRL...
ZUZU (ZWOO)

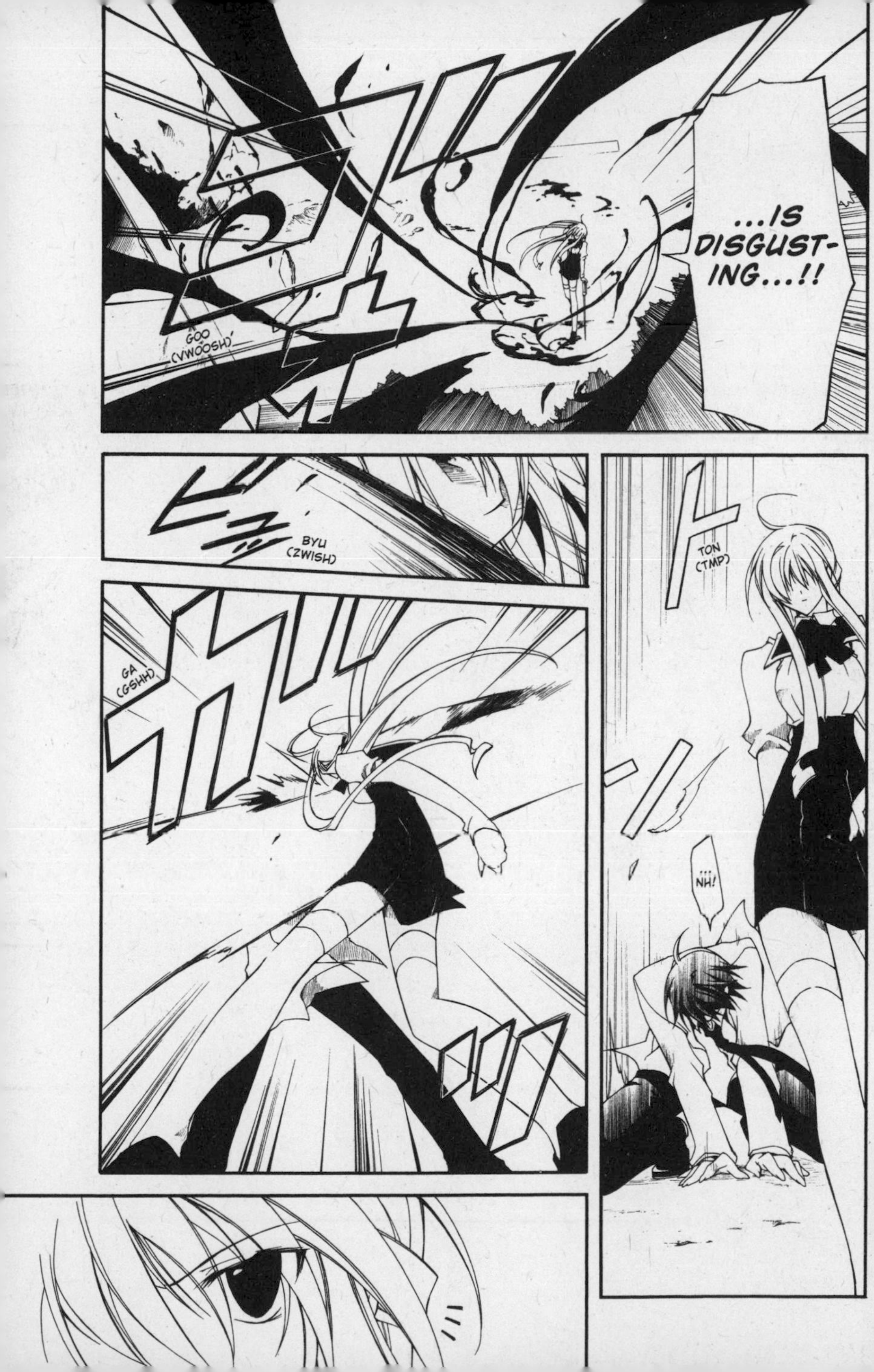
...IS DISGUST-ING...!!
GOO (VWOOSH)
TON (TMP)
...NH!
BYU (ZWISH)
GA (GSHH)

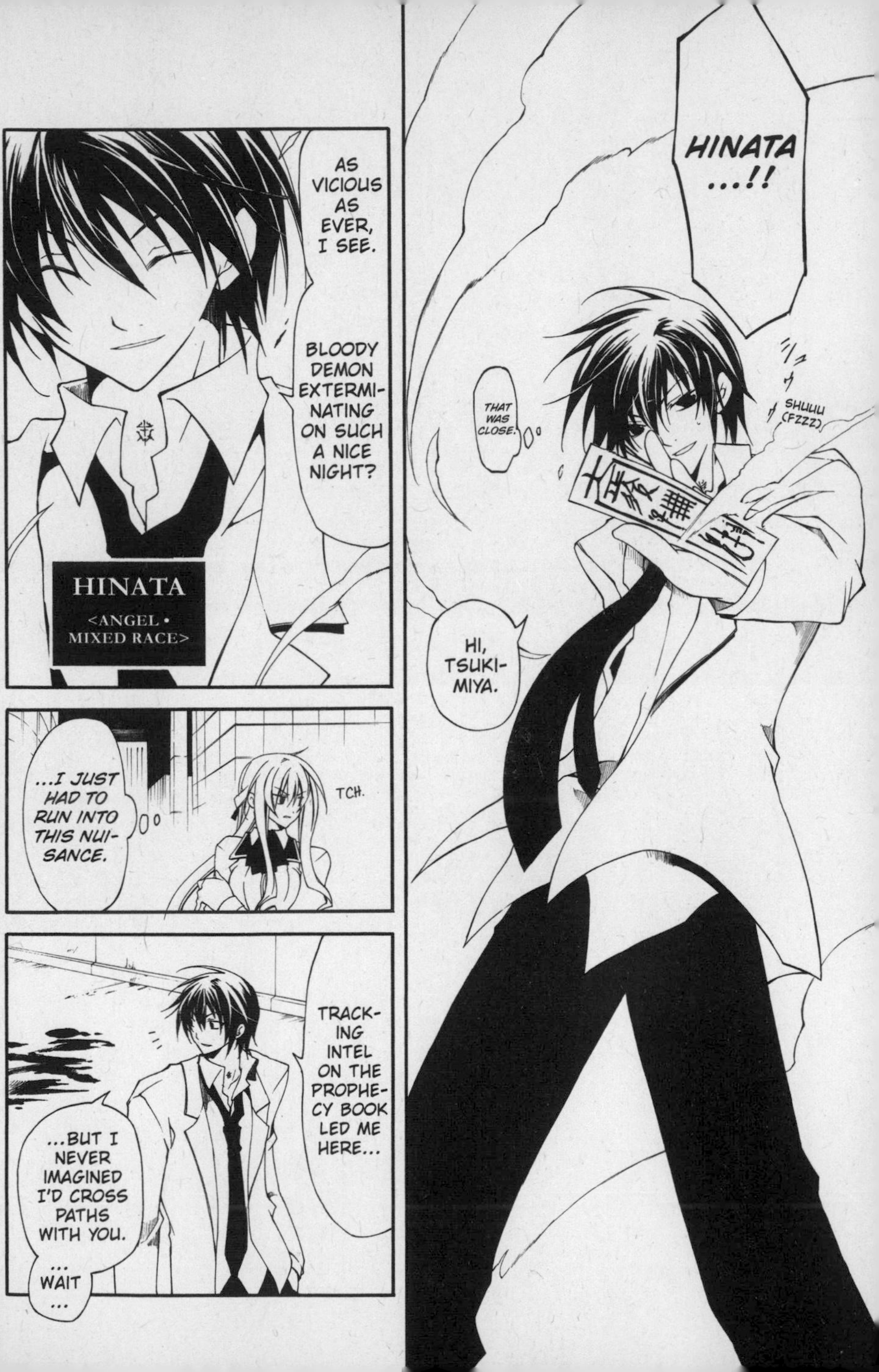
HINATA ...!!
SHUUU (FZZZ)
THAT WAS CLOSE.
HI, TSUKIMIYA.
AS VICIOUS AS EVER, I SEE.
BLOODY DEMON EXTERMINATING ON SUCH A NICE NIGHT?
HINATA
<ANGEL • MIXED RACE>
TCH.
...I JUST HAD TO RUN INTO THIS NUISANCE.
TRACKING INTEL ON THE PROPHECY BOOK LED ME HERE...
...BUT I NEVER IMAGINED I'D CROSS PATHS WITH YOU.
... WAIT ...

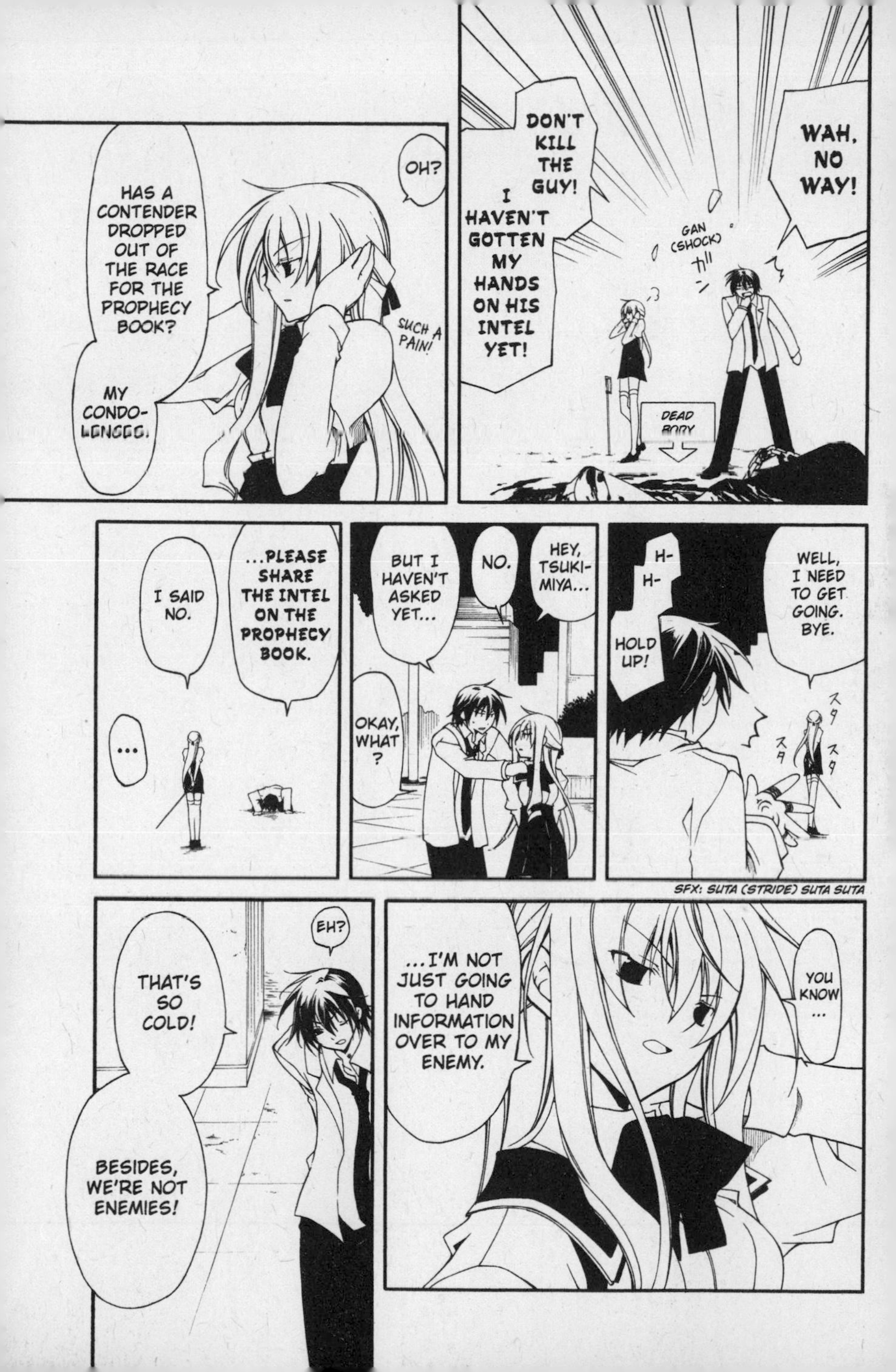
WAH, NO WAY!
DON'T KILL THE GUY! I HAVEN'T GOTTEN MY HANDS ON HIS INTEL YET!
GAN (SHOCK)
ガ
DEAD BODY
OH?
HAS A CONTENDER DROPPED OUT OF THE RACE FOR THE PROPHECY BOOK?
SUCH A PAIN!
MY CONDO-LENCES.
WELL, I NEED TO GET GOING. BYE.
スタ
スタ
スタ
H- H- HOLD UP!
HEY, TSUKI-MIYA...
NO.
BUT I HAVEN'T ASKED YET...
OKAY, WHAT?
...PLEASE SHARE THE INTEL ON THE PROPHECY BOOK.
I SAID NO.
...
SFX: SUTA (STRIDE) SUTA SUTA
YOU KNOW...
...I'M NOT JUST GOING TO HAND INFORMATION OVER TO MY ENEMY.
EH?
THAT'S SO COLD!
BESIDES, WE'RE NOT ENEMIES!

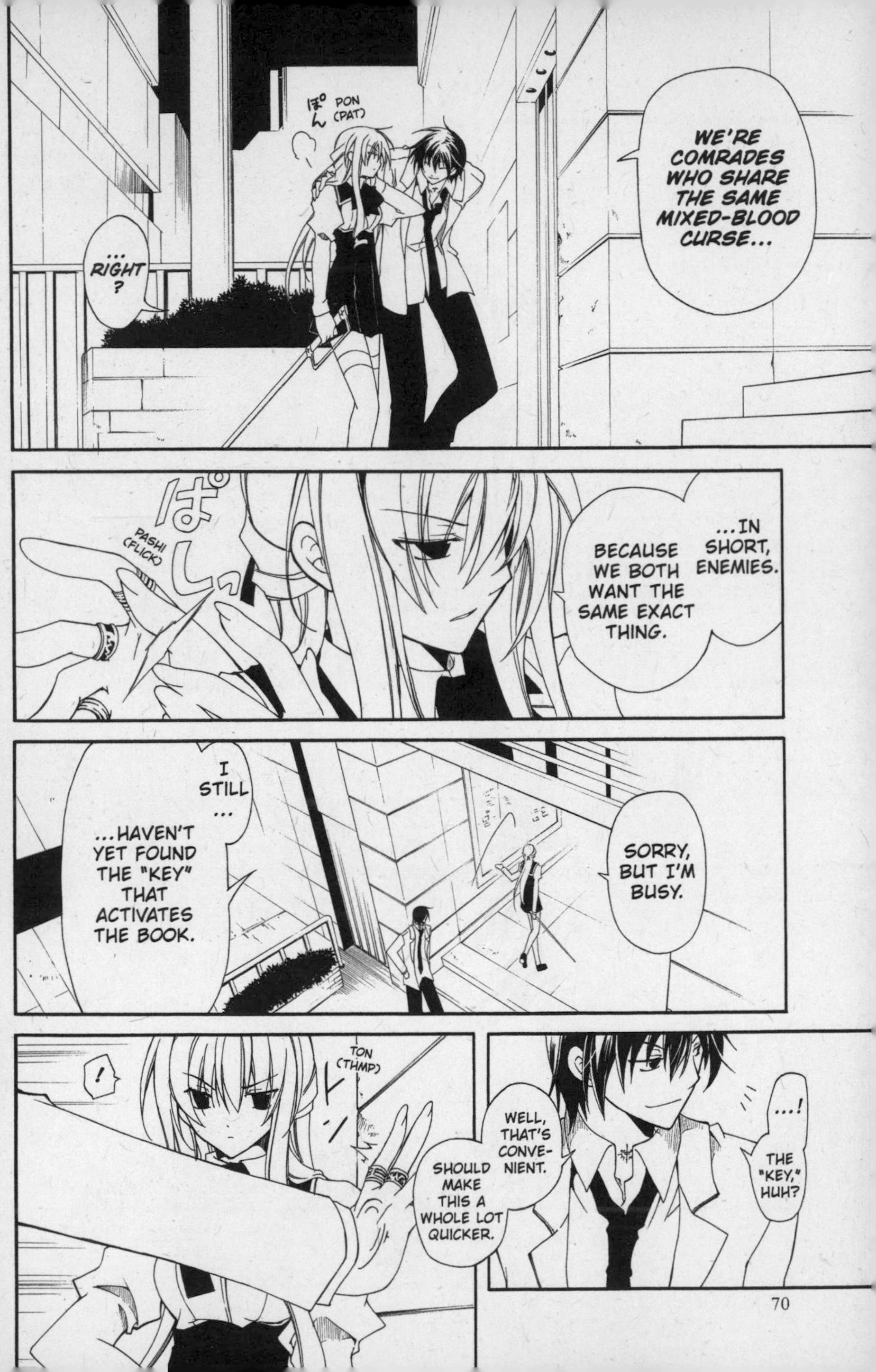
WE'RE COMRADES WHO SHARE THE SAME MIXED-BLOOD CURSE...
ぽん PON (PAT)
...RIGHT?
...IN SHORT, ENEMIES.
BECAUSE WE BOTH WANT THE SAME EXACT THING.
ぱしっ PASHI (FLICK)
SORRY, BUT I'M BUSY.
I STILL...
...HAVEN'T YET FOUND THE "KEY" THAT ACTIVATES THE BOOK.
...!
THE "KEY," HUH?
WELL, THAT'S CONVE-NIENT.
SHOULD MAKE THIS A WHOLE LOT QUICKER.
TON (THMP)
!

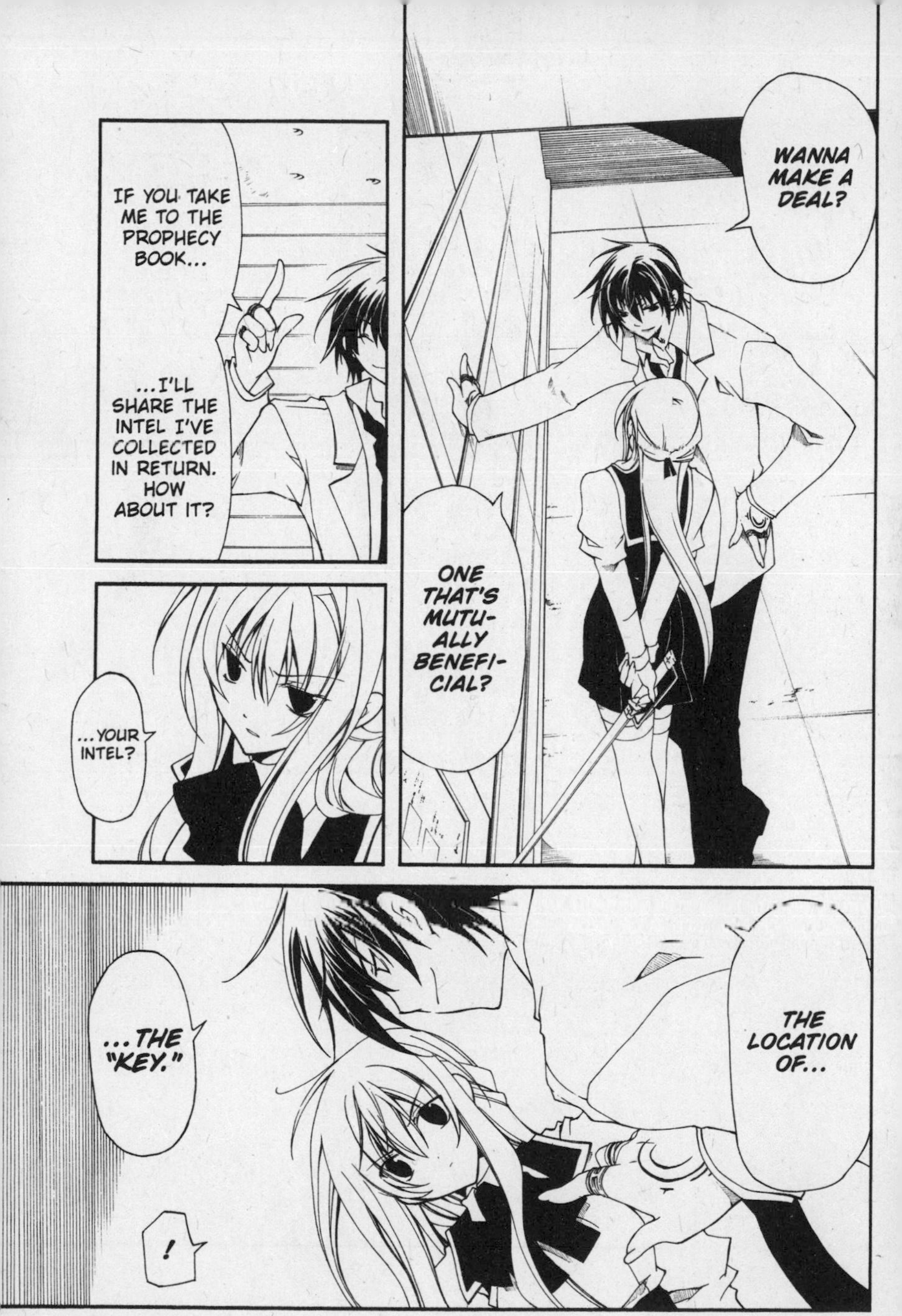
WANNA MAKE A DEAL?
ONE THAT'S MUTU-ALLY BENEFI-CIAL?
IF YOU TAKE ME TO THE PROPHECY BOOK...
...I'LL SHARE THE INTEL I'VE COLLECTED IN RETURN. HOW ABOUT IT?
...YOUR INTEL?
THE LOCATION OF...
...THE "KEY."
!

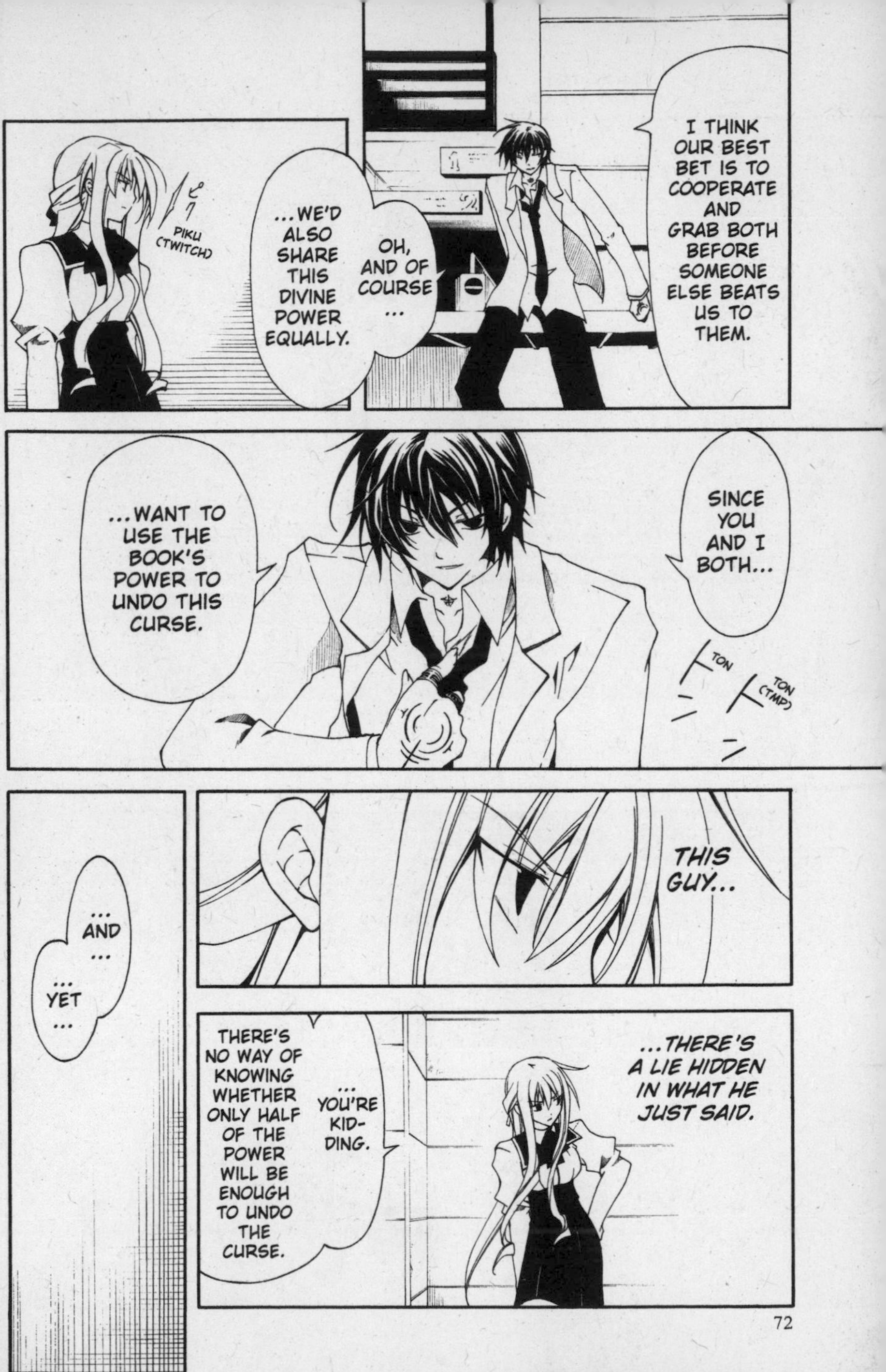
I THINK OUR BEST BET IS TO COOPERATE AND GRAB BOTH BEFORE SOMEONE ELSE BEATS US TO THEM.
OH, AND OF COURSE ...
...WE'D ALSO SHARE THIS DIVINE POWER EQUALLY.
ピク
PIKU (TWITCH)
SINCE YOU AND I BOTH...
...WANT TO USE THE BOOK'S POWER TO UNDO THIS CURSE.
TON
TON (TMP)
THIS GUY...
...THERE'S A LIE HIDDEN IN WHAT HE JUST SAID.
...YOU'RE KID-DING.
THERE'S NO WAY OF KNOWING WHETHER ONLY HALF OF THE POWER WILL BE ENOUGH TO UNDO THE CURSE.
...AND...
...YET...

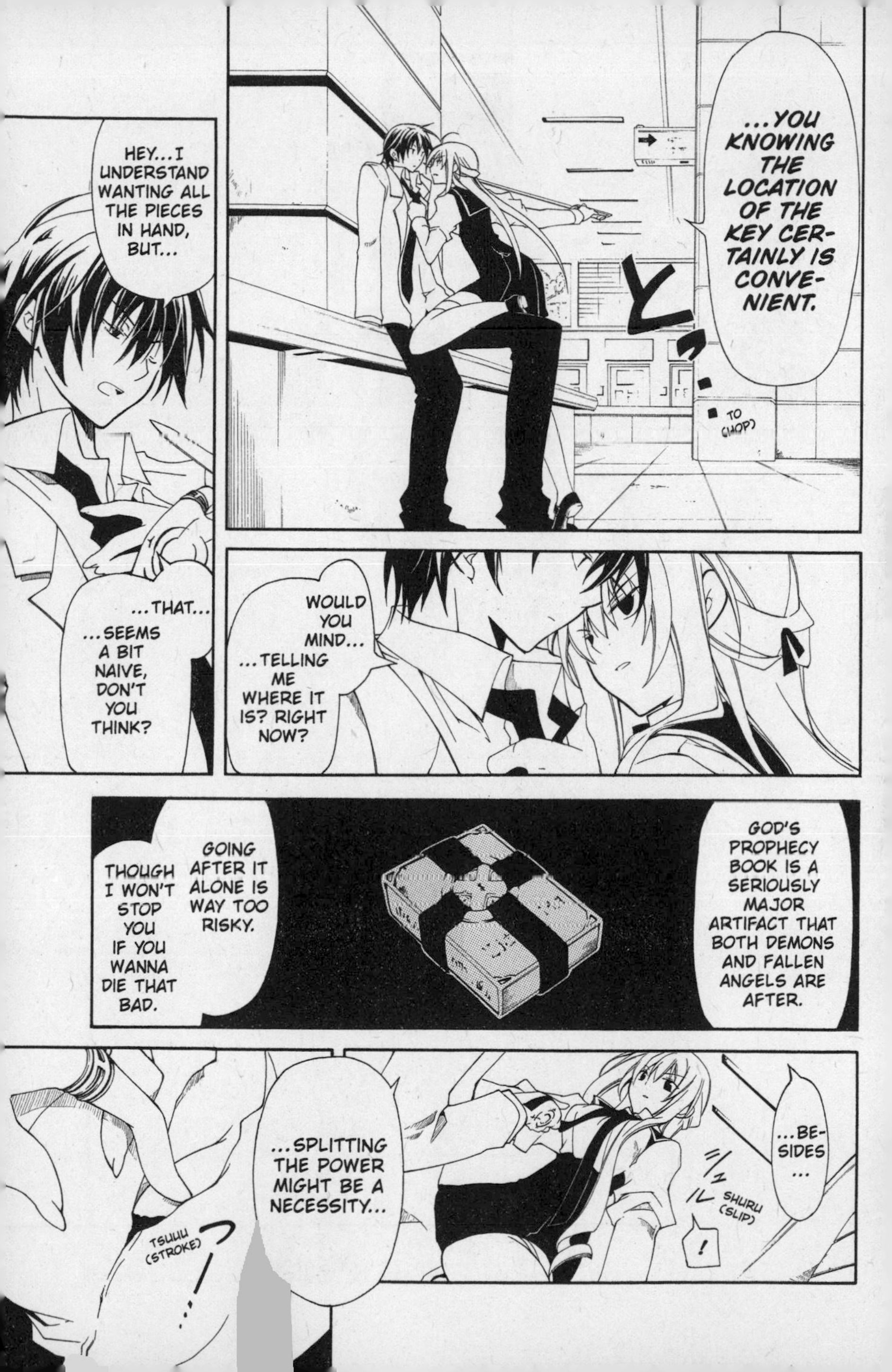

...YOU KNOWING THE LOCATION OF THE KEY CERTAINLY IS CONVENIENT.
TO (MOP)
WOULD YOU MIND...
...TELLING ME WHERE IT IS? RIGHT NOW?
HEY...I UNDERSTAND WANTING ALL THE PIECES IN HAND, BUT...
...THAT...
...SEEMS A BIT NAIVE, DON'T YOU THINK?
GOD'S PROPHECY BOOK IS A SERIOUSLY MAJOR ARTIFACT THAT BOTH DEMONS AND FALLEN ANGELS ARE AFTER.
GOING AFTER IT ALONE IS WAY TOO RISKY.
THOUGH I WON'T STOP YOU IF YOU WANNA DIE THAT BAD.
...BESIDES...
SHURU (SLIP)
!
...SPLITTING THE POWER MIGHT BE A NECESSITY...
TSUUU (STROKE)
...

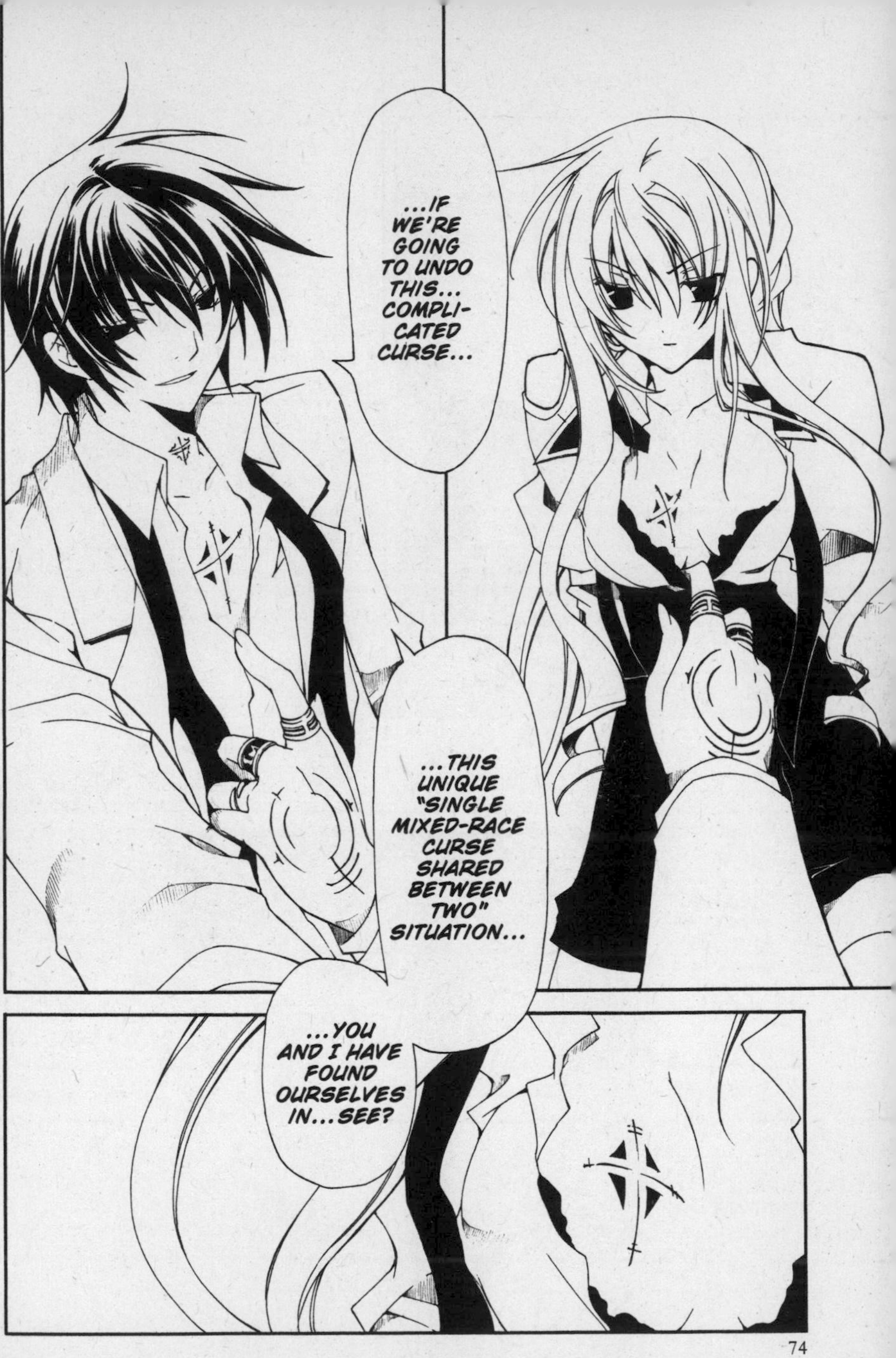
...IF WE'RE GOING TO UNDO THIS... COMPLICATED CURSE...
...THIS UNIQUE "SINGLE MIXED-RACE CURSE SHARED BETWEEN TWO" SITUATION...
...YOU AND I HAVE FOUND OURSELVES IN... SEE?

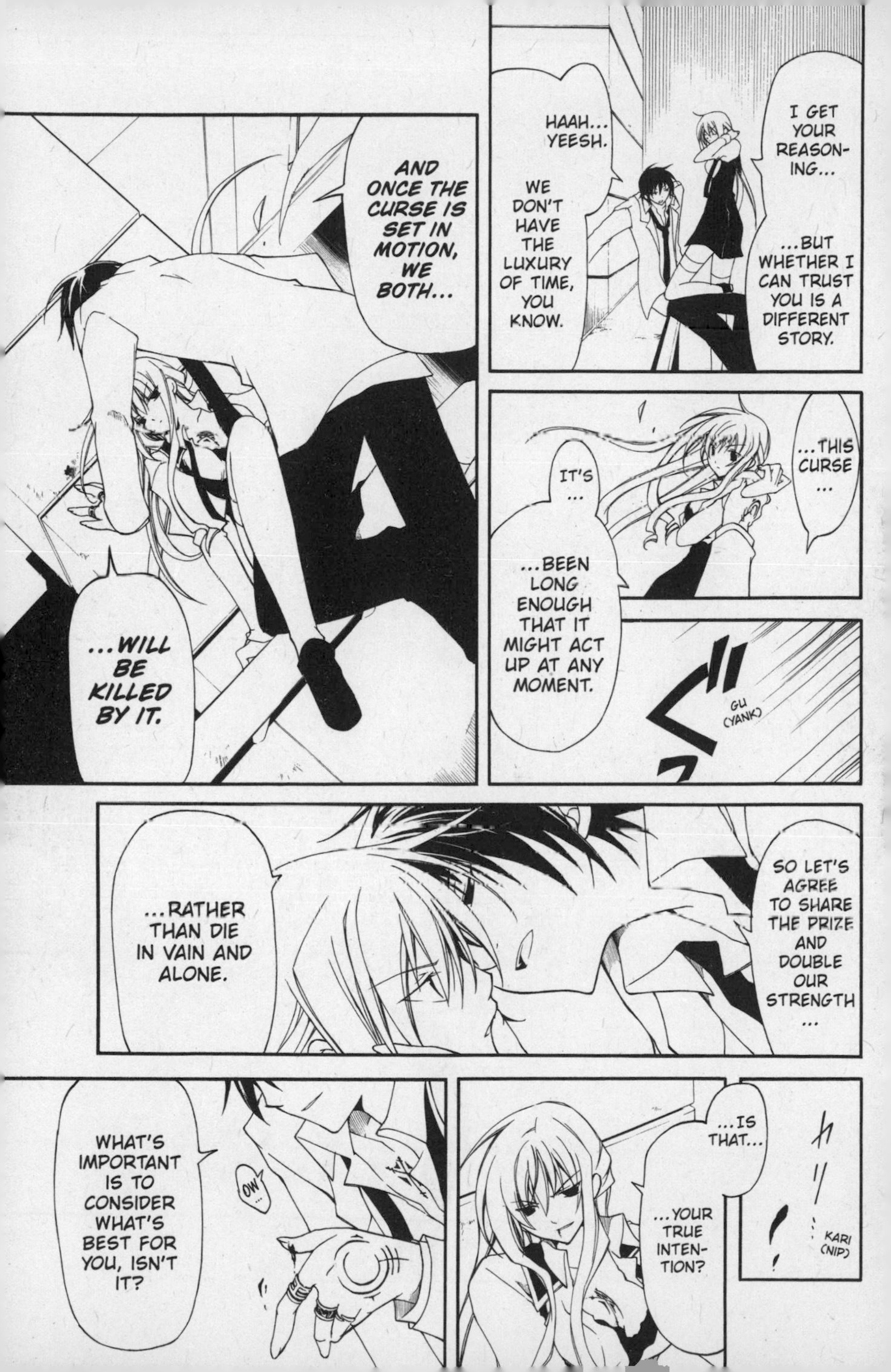
I GET YOUR REASONING...
...BUT WHETHER I CAN TRUST YOU IS A DIFFERENT STORY.
HAAH... YEESH.
WE DON'T HAVE THE LUXURY OF TIME, YOU KNOW.
...THIS CURSE...
IT'S...
...BEEN LONG ENOUGH THAT IT MIGHT ACT UP AT ANY MOMENT.
GU (YANK)
AND ONCE THE CURSE IS SET IN MOTION, WE BOTH...
...WILL BE KILLED BY IT.
SO LET'S AGREE TO SHARE THE PRIZE AND DOUBLE OUR STRENGTH...
...RATHER THAN DIE IN VAIN AND ALONE.
KARI (NIP)
...IS THAT...
...YOUR TRUE INTENTION?
OW...
WHAT'S IMPORTANT IS TO CONSIDER WHAT'S BEST FOR YOU, ISN'T IT?

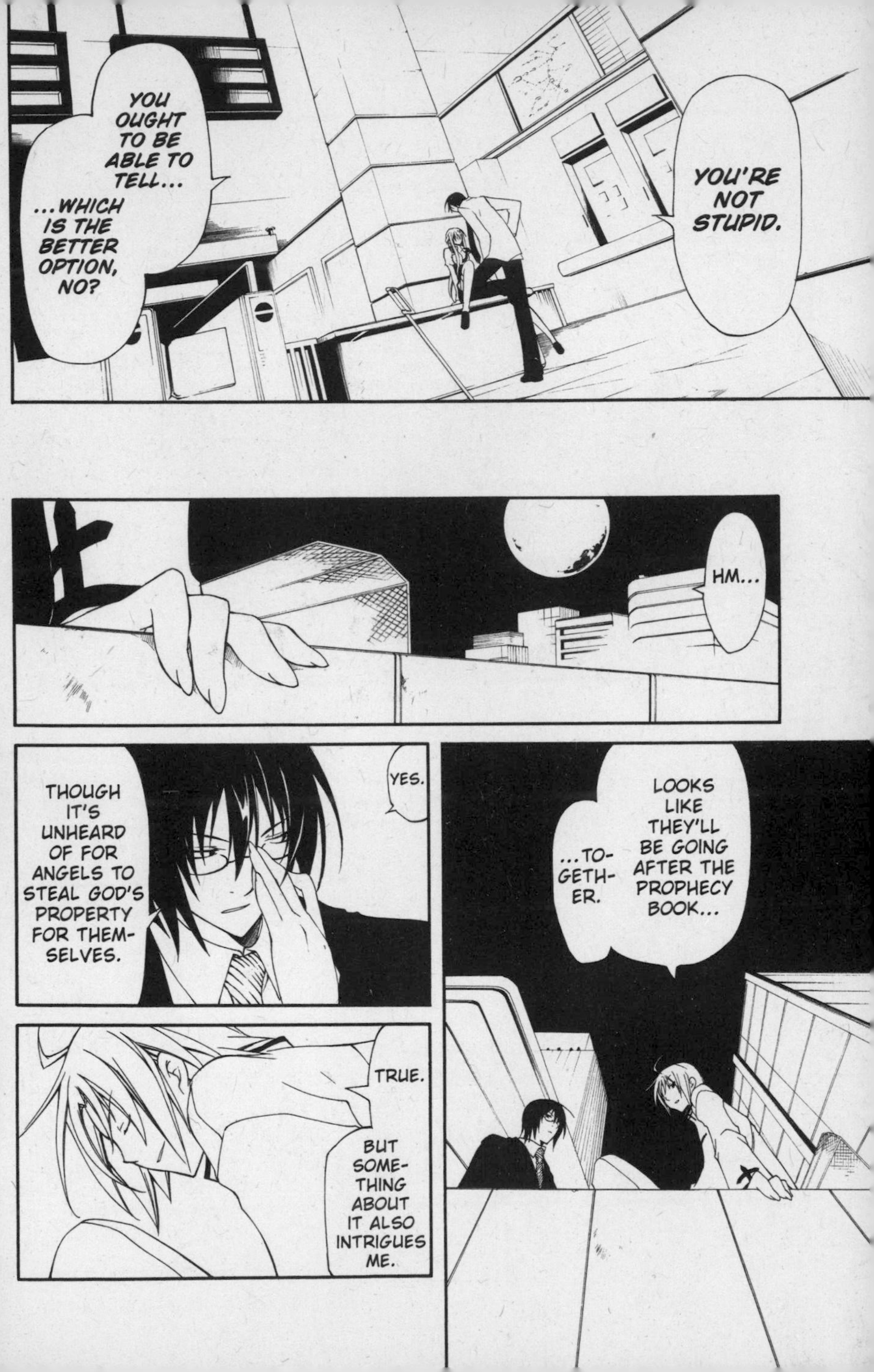
YOU'RE NOT STUPID.
YOU OUGHT TO BE ABLE TO TELL...
...WHICH IS THE BETTER OPTION, NO?
HM...
LOOKS LIKE THEY'LL BE GOING AFTER THE PROPHECY BOOK...
...TO-GETH-ER.
YES.
THOUGH IT'S UNHEARD OF FOR ANGELS TO STEAL GOD'S PROPERTY FOR THEM-SELVES.
TRUE.
BUT SOME-THING ABOUT IT ALSO INTRIGUES ME.

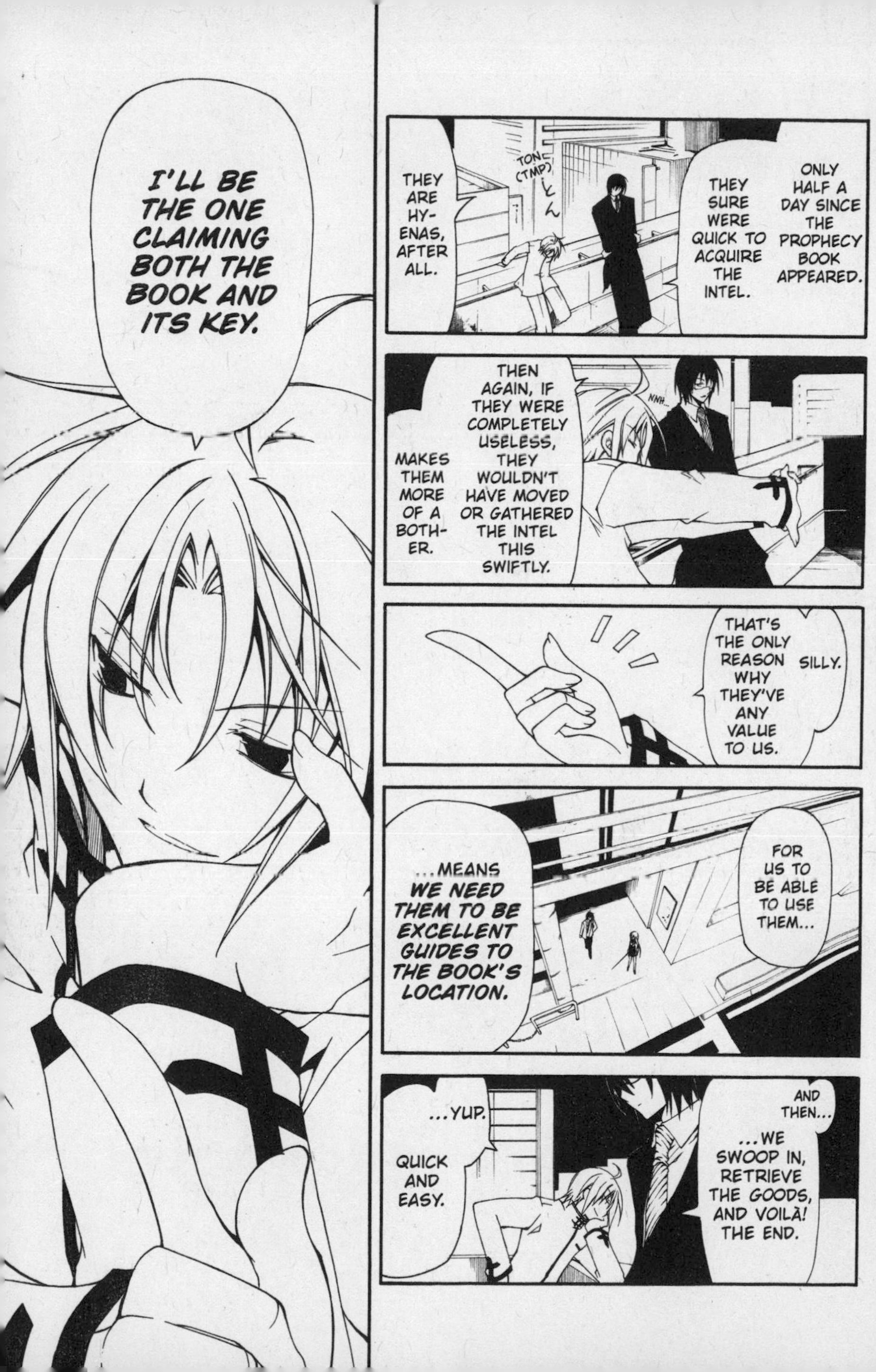
ONLY HALF A DAY SINCE THE PROPHECY BOOK APPEARED.
THEY SURE WERE QUICK TO ACQUIRE THE INTEL.
TON (TMP) とん
THEY ARE HY-ENAS, AFTER ALL.
NNH...
THEN AGAIN, IF THEY WERE COMPLETELY USELESS, THEY WOULDN'T HAVE MOVED OR GATHERED THE INTEL THIS SWIFTLY.
MAKES THEM MORE OF A BOTH-ER.
SILLY.
THAT'S THE ONLY REASON WHY THEY'VE ANY VALUE TO US.
FOR US TO BE ABLE TO USE THEM...
...MEANS WE NEED THEM TO BE EXCELLENT GUIDES TO THE BOOK'S LOCATION.
AND THEN...
...WE SWOOP IN, RETRIEVE THE GOODS, AND VOILÀ! THE END.
...YUP.
QUICK AND EASY.
I'LL BE THE ONE CLAIMING BOTH THE BOOK AND ITS KEY.

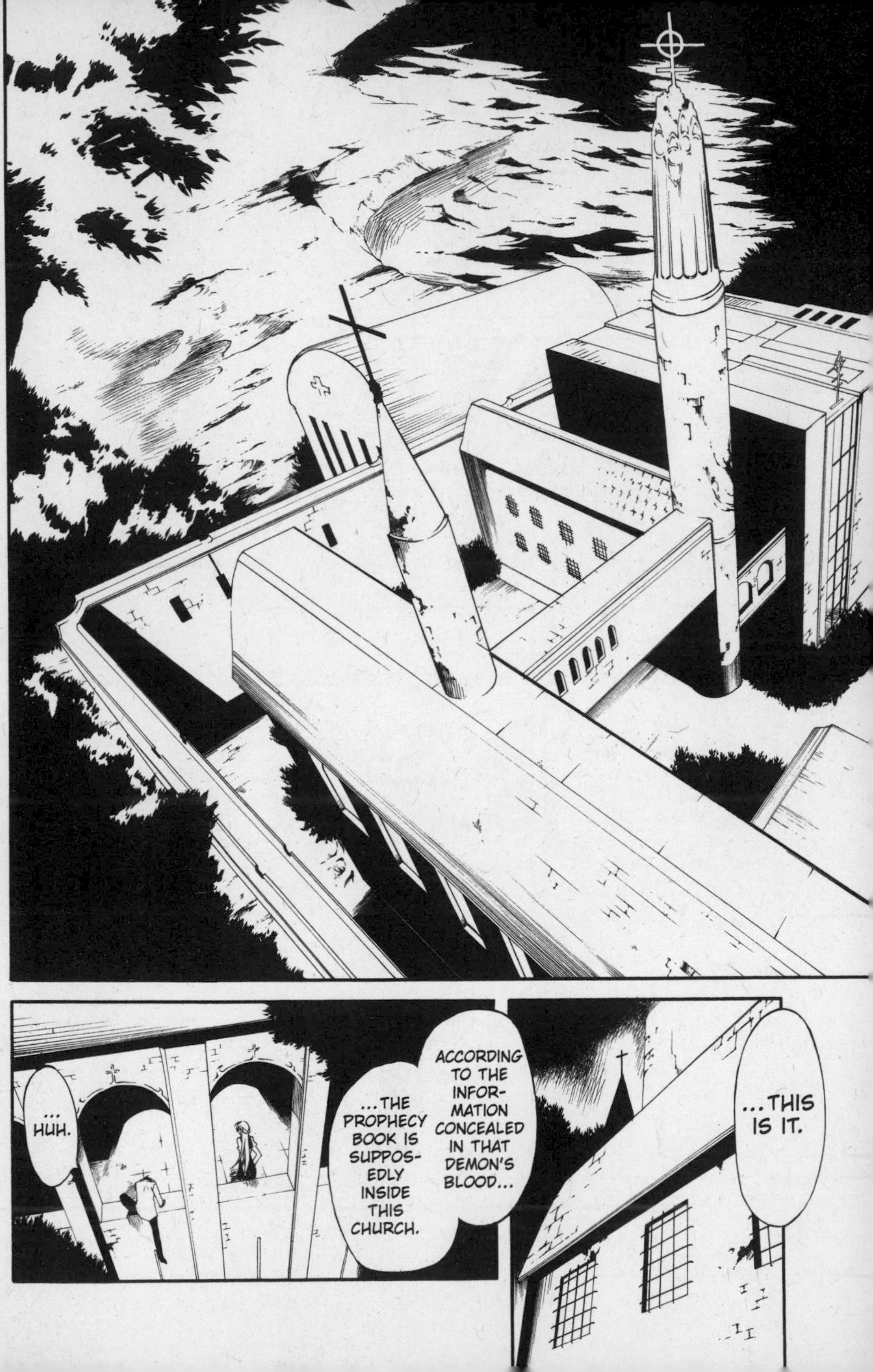
...THIS IS IT.
ACCORDING TO THE INFORMATION CONCEALED IN THAT DEMON'S BLOOD...
...THE PROPHECY BOOK IS SUPPOSEDLY INSIDE THIS CHURCH.
...HUH.

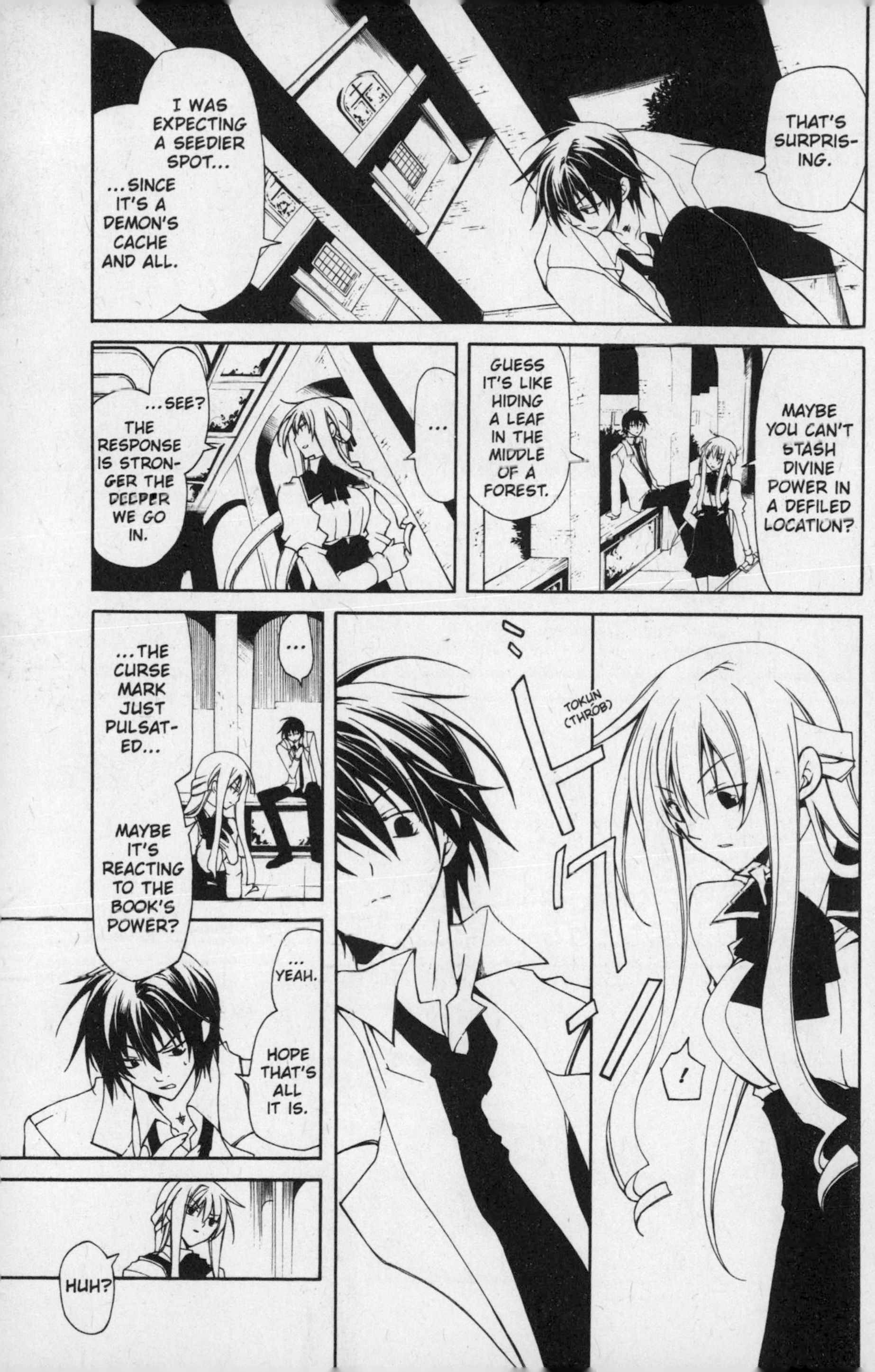
THAT'S SURPRISING.
I WAS EXPECTING A SEEDIER SPOT... ...SINCE IT'S A DEMON'S CACHE AND ALL.
MAYBE YOU CAN'T STASH DIVINE POWER IN A DEFILED LOCATION?
GUESS IT'S LIKE HIDING A LEAF IN THE MIDDLE OF A FOREST.
...
...SEE? THE RESPONSE IS STRONGER THE DEEPER WE GO IN.
TOKUN (THROB)
!
...
...THE CURSE MARK JUST PULSATED... MAYBE IT'S REACTING TO THE BOOK'S POWER?
...YEAH. HOPE THAT'S ALL IT IS.
HUH?

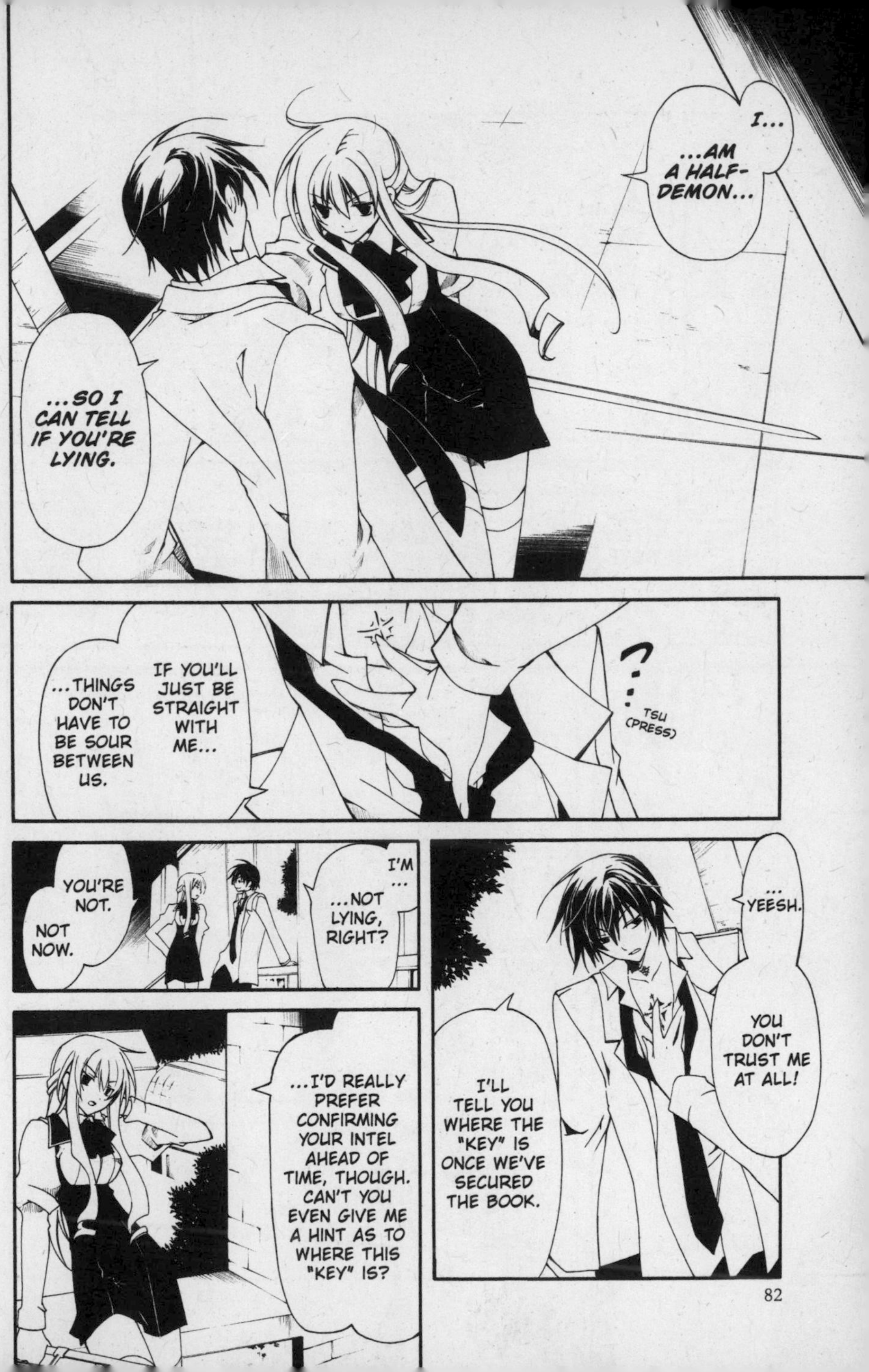
I...
...AM A HALF-DEMON...
...SO I CAN TELL IF YOU'RE LYING.
?
TSU (PRESS)
IF YOU'LL JUST BE STRAIGHT WITH ME...
...THINGS DON'T HAVE TO BE SOUR BETWEEN US.
...YEESH.
YOU DON'T TRUST ME AT ALL!
I'LL TELL YOU WHERE THE "KEY" IS ONCE WE'VE SECURED THE BOOK.
I'M...
...NOT LYING, RIGHT?
YOU'RE NOT.
NOT NOW.
...I'D REALLY PREFER CONFIRMING YOUR INTEL AHEAD OF TIME, THOUGH. CAN'T YOU EVEN GIVE ME A HINT AS TO WHERE THIS "KEY" IS?

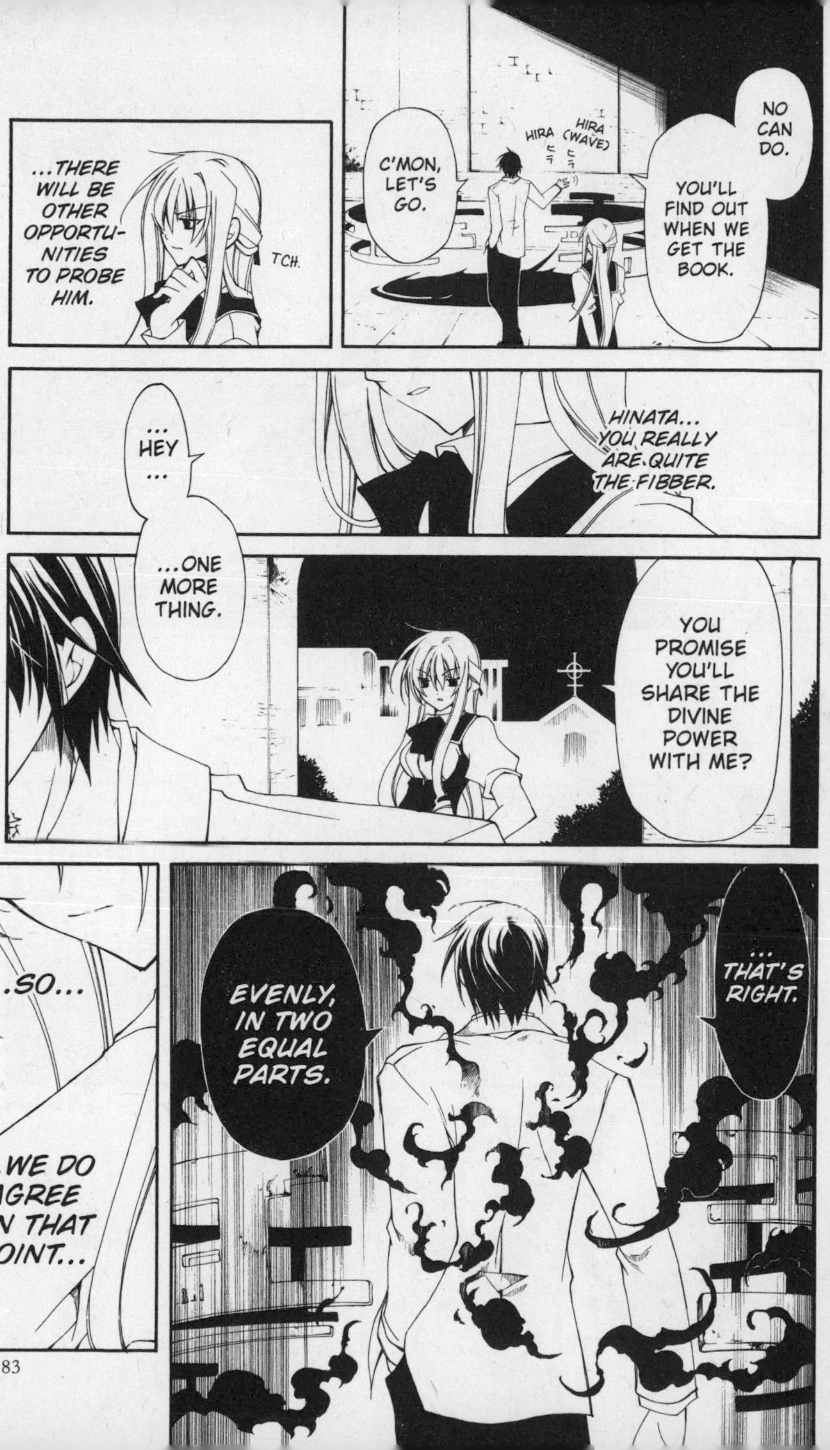
NO CAN DO.
YOU'LL FIND OUT WHEN WE GET THE BOOK.
HIRA HIRA (WAVE)
C'MON, LET'S GO.
...THERE WILL BE OTHER OPPORTU-NITIES TO PROBE HIM.
TCH.
HINATA... YOU REALLY ARE QUITE THE FIBBER.
...HEY...
...ONE MORE THING.
YOU PROMISE YOU'LL SHARE THE DIVINE POWER WITH ME?
...THAT'S RIGHT.
EVENLY, IN TWO EQUAL PARTS.
...SO...
...WE DO AGREE ON THAT POINT...

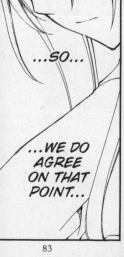

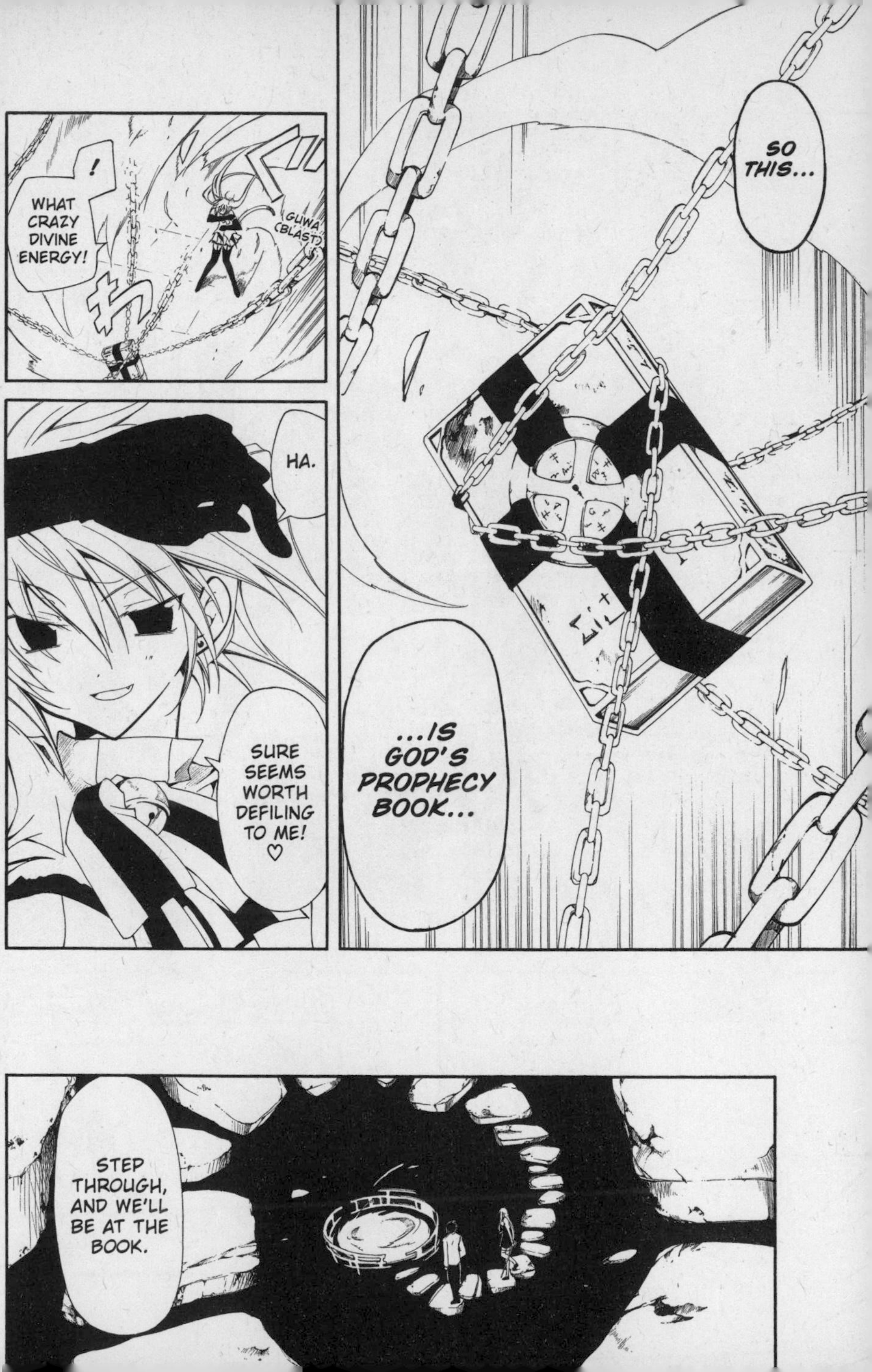
SO THIS...
...IS GOD'S PROPHECY BOOK...
GUWA (BLAST)
! WHAT CRAZY DIVINE ENERGY!
HA.
SURE SEEMS WORTH DEFILING TO ME! ♡
STEP THROUGH, AND WE'LL BE AT THE BOOK.

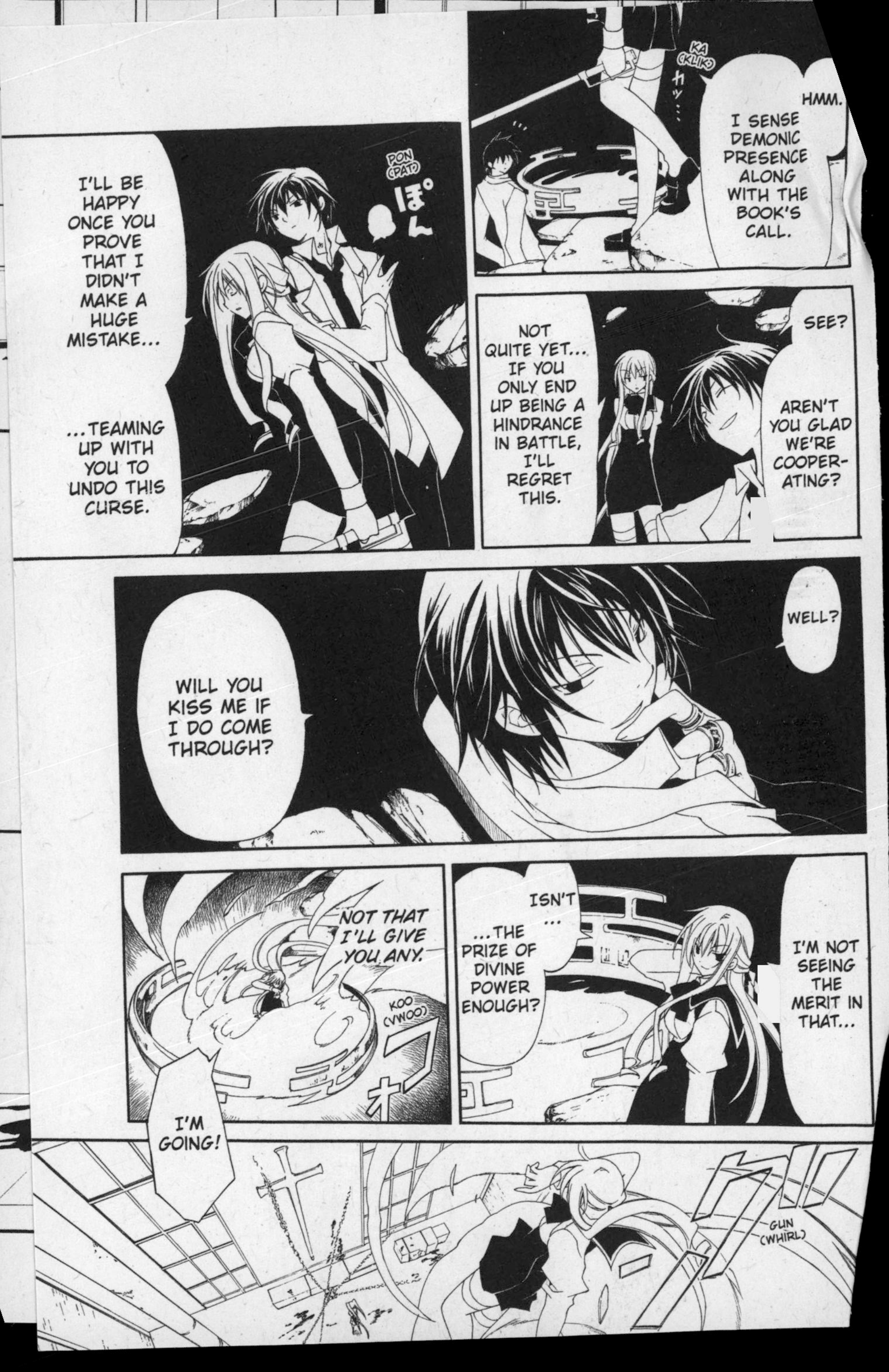
KA (KLIK)
カッ…
HMM.
I SENSE DEMONIC PRESENCE ALONG WITH THE BOOK'S CALL.
SEE?
AREN'T YOU GLAD WE'RE COOPER-ATING?
NOT QUITE YET… IF YOU ONLY END UP BEING A HINDRANCE IN BATTLE, I'LL REGRET THIS.
PON (PAT)
ぽん
I'LL BE HAPPY ONCE YOU PROVE THAT I DIDN'T MAKE A HUGE MISTAKE…
…TEAMING UP WITH YOU TO UNDO THIS CURSE.
WELL?
WILL YOU KISS ME IF I DO COME THROUGH?
I'M NOT SEEING THE MERIT IN THAT…
ISN'T …
…THE PRIZE OF DIVINE POWER ENOUGH?
NOT THAT I'LL GIVE YOU ANY.
KOO (VWOO)
GUN (WHIRL)
I'M GOING!

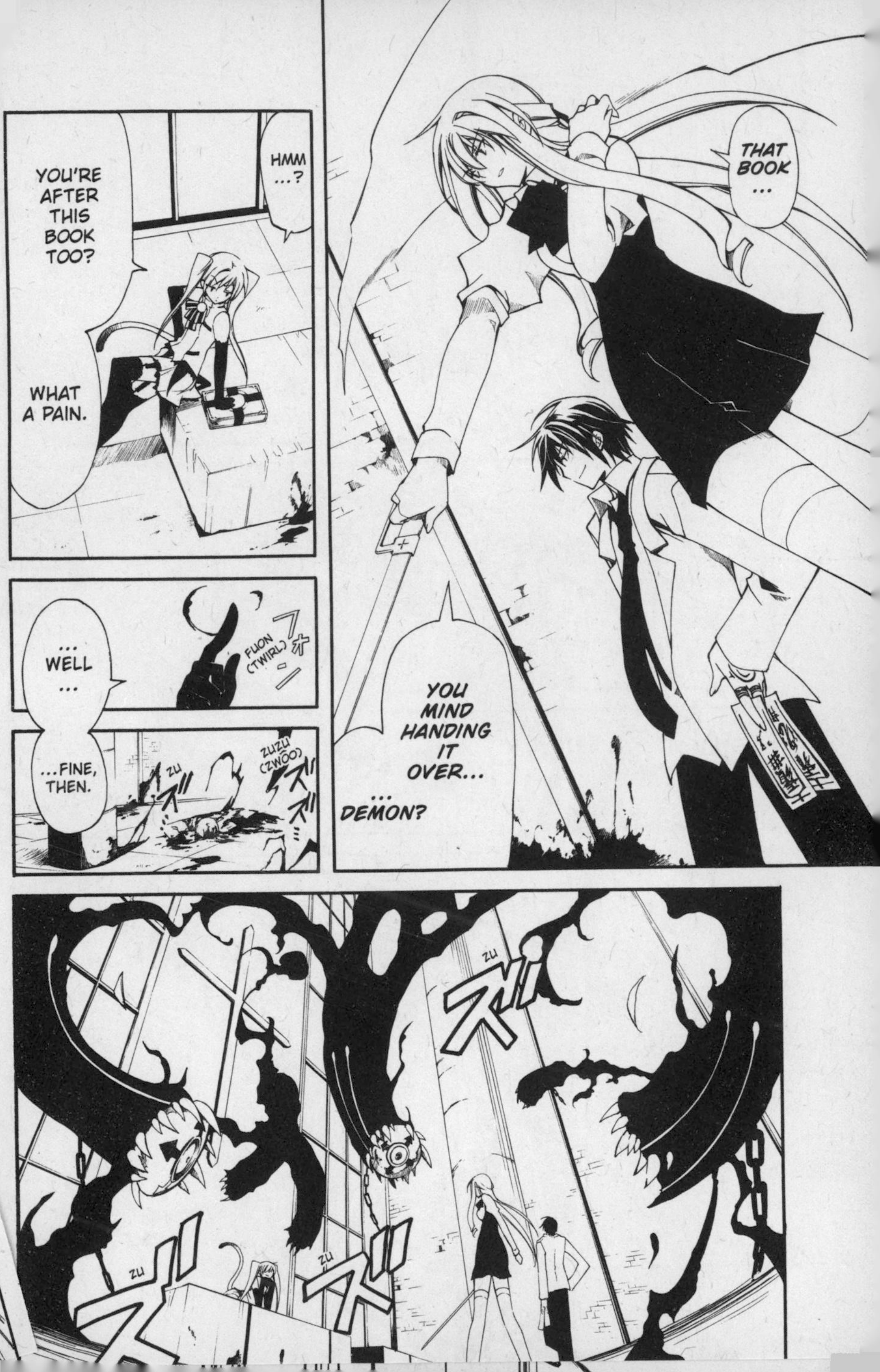
THAT BOOK ...
YOU MIND HANDING IT OVER...
... DEMON?
HMM ...?
YOU'RE AFTER THIS BOOK TOO?
WHAT A PAIN.
FUON (TWIRL)
... WELL ...
ZUZU (ZWOO)
ZU
...FINE, THEN.
ZU
ZU
ZU

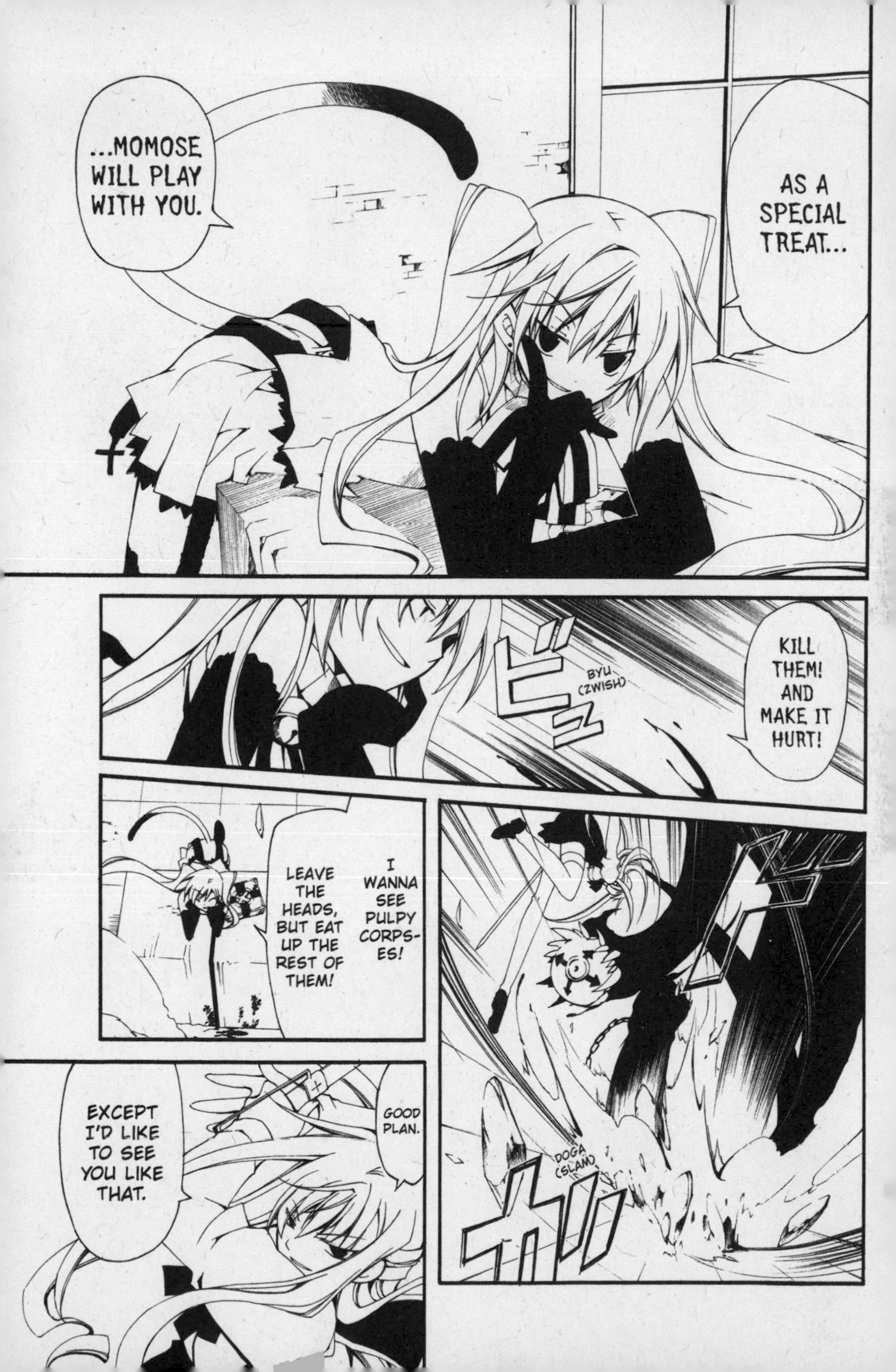
AS A SPECIAL TREAT...
...MOMOSE WILL PLAY WITH YOU.
KILL THEM! AND MAKE IT HURT!
BYU (ZWISH)
DOGA (SLAM)
I WANNA SEE PULPY CORPSES!
LEAVE THE HEADS, BUT EAT UP THE REST OF THEM!
GOOD PLAN.
EXCEPT I'D LIKE TO SEE YOU LIKE THAT.

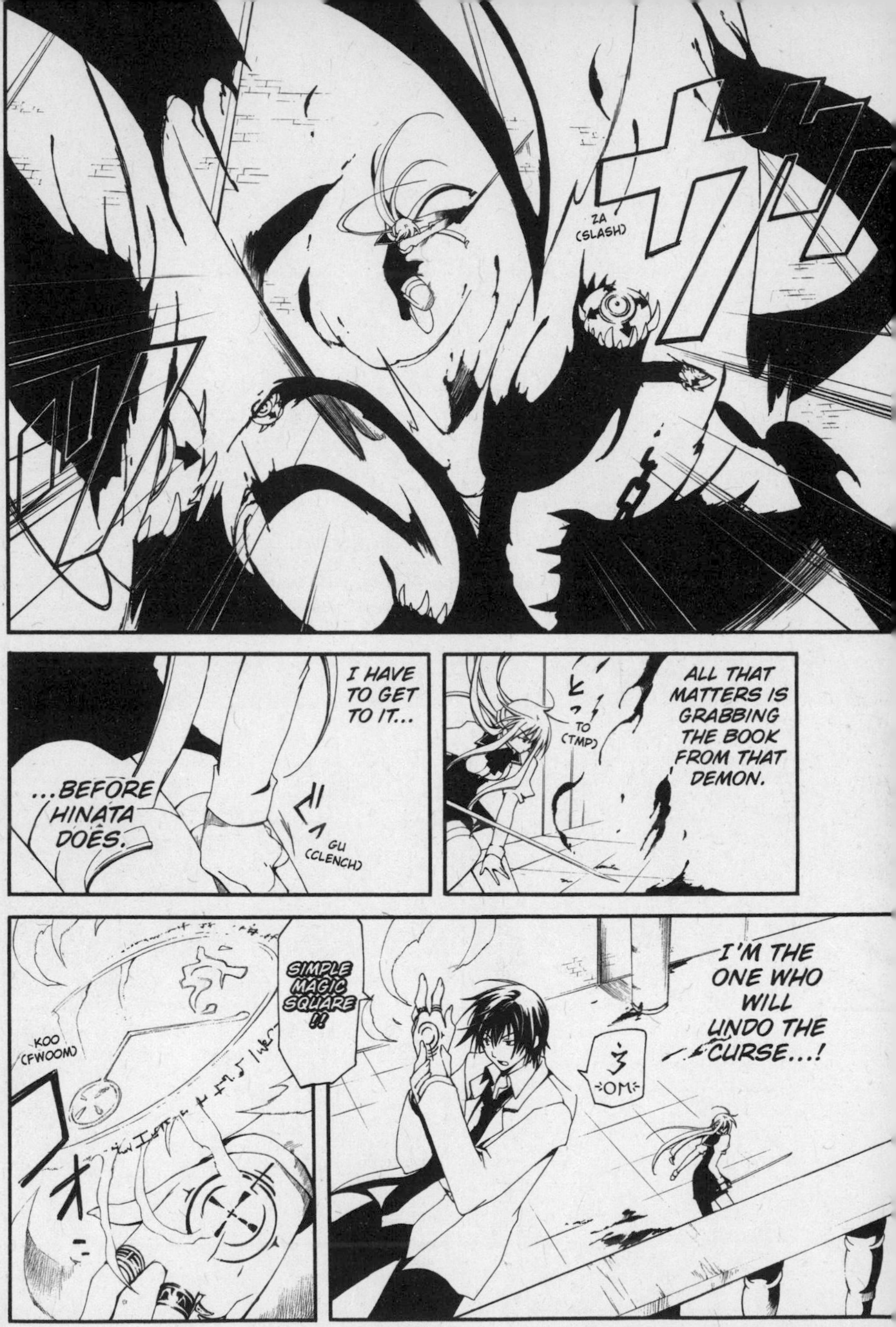

ZA (SLASH)
ALL THAT MATTERS IS GRABBING THE BOOK FROM THAT DEMON.
TO (TMP)
I HAVE TO GET TO IT...
...BEFORE HINATA DOES.
GU (CLENCH)
I'M THE ONE WHO WILL UNDO THE CURSE...!
SIMPLE MAGIC SQUARE!!
OM
KOO (FWOOM)

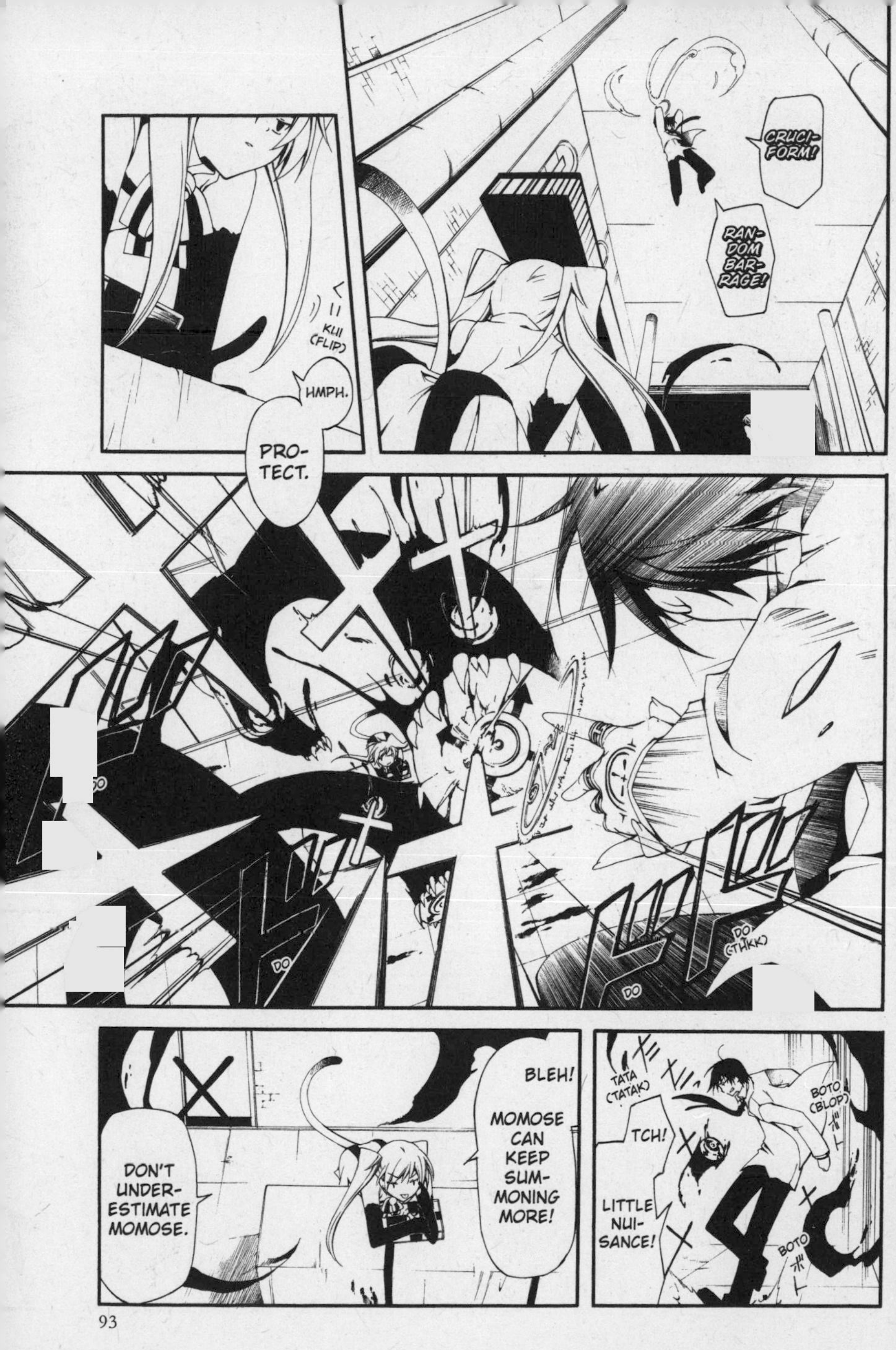
CRUCI-FORM!
RAN-DOM BAR-RAGE!
KUI (FLIP)
HMPH.
PRO-TECT.
DO
DO (THKK)
DO
DO
TATA (TATAK)
BOTO (BLOP)
TCH!
LITTLE NUI-SANCE!
BOTO
BLEH!
MOMOSE CAN KEEP SUM-MONING MORE!
DON'T UNDER-ESTIMATE MOMOSE.

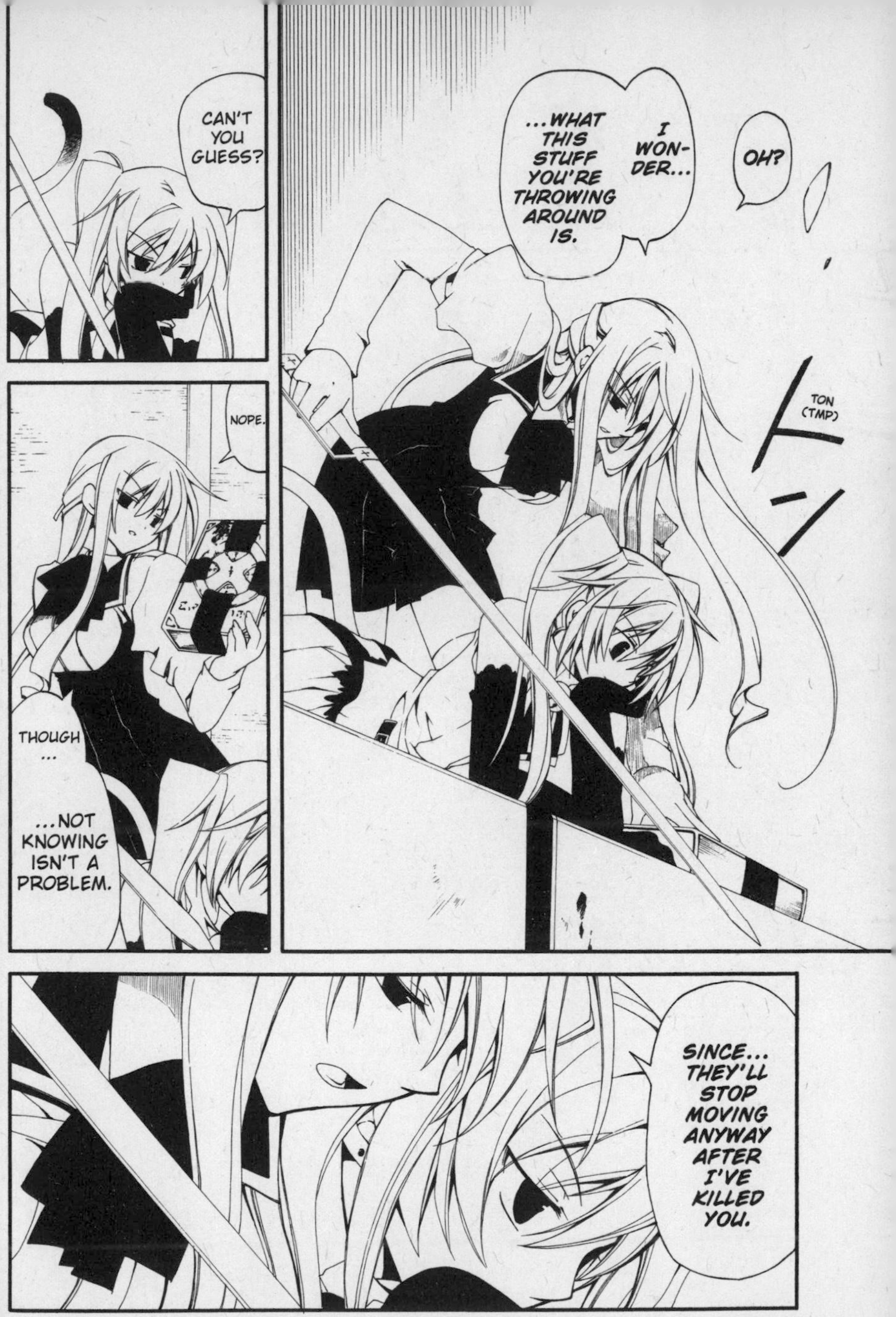
OH?
I WONDER...
...WHAT THIS STUFF YOU'RE THROWING AROUND IS.
TON (TMP)
CAN'T YOU GUESS?
NOPE.
THOUGH...
...NOT KNOWING ISN'T A PROBLEM.
SINCE... THEY'LL STOP MOVING ANYWAY AFTER I'VE KILLED YOU.

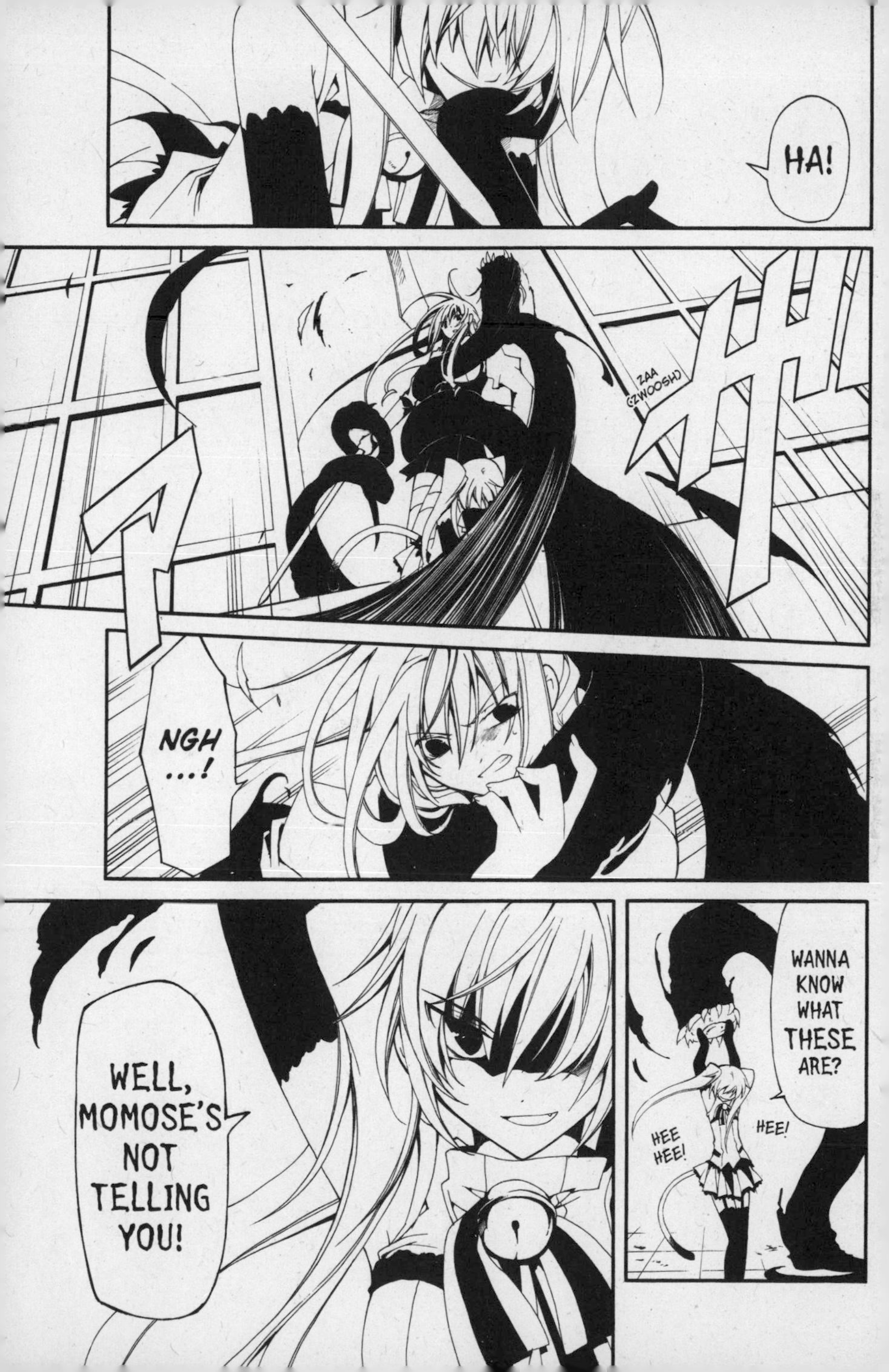
HA!
ZAA (ZWOOSH)
NGH ...!
WANNA KNOW WHAT THESE ARE?
HEE!
HEE HEE!
WELL, MOMOSE'S NOT TELLING YOU!

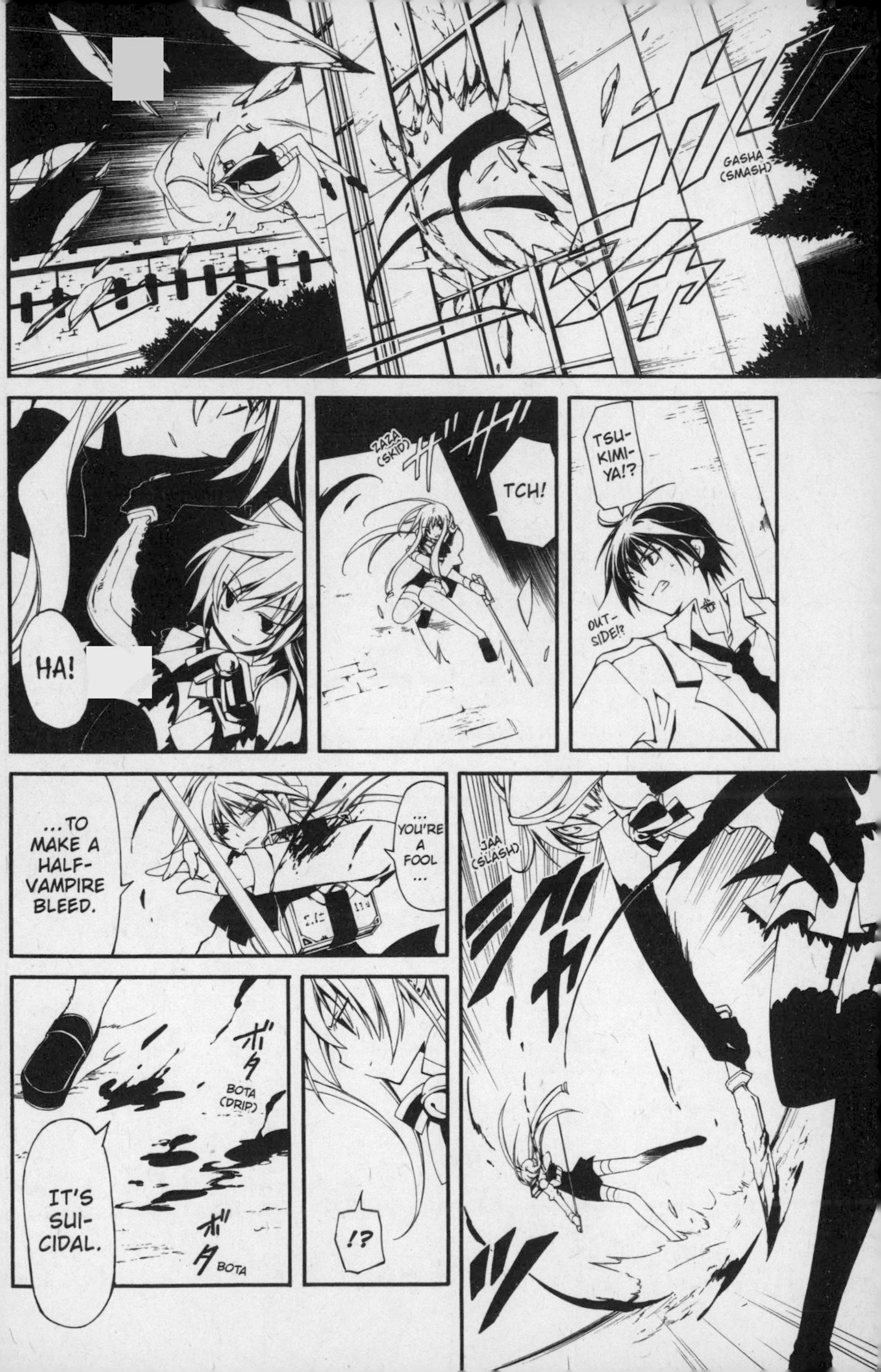
GASHA (SMASH)
TSU-KIMI-YA!?
OUT-SIDE!?
ZAZA (SKID)
TCH!
HA!
JAA (SLASH)
... YOU'RE A FOOL ...
... TO MAKE A HALF-VAMPIRE BLEED.
!?
BOTA (DRIP)
IT'S SUI-CIDAL.
BOTA

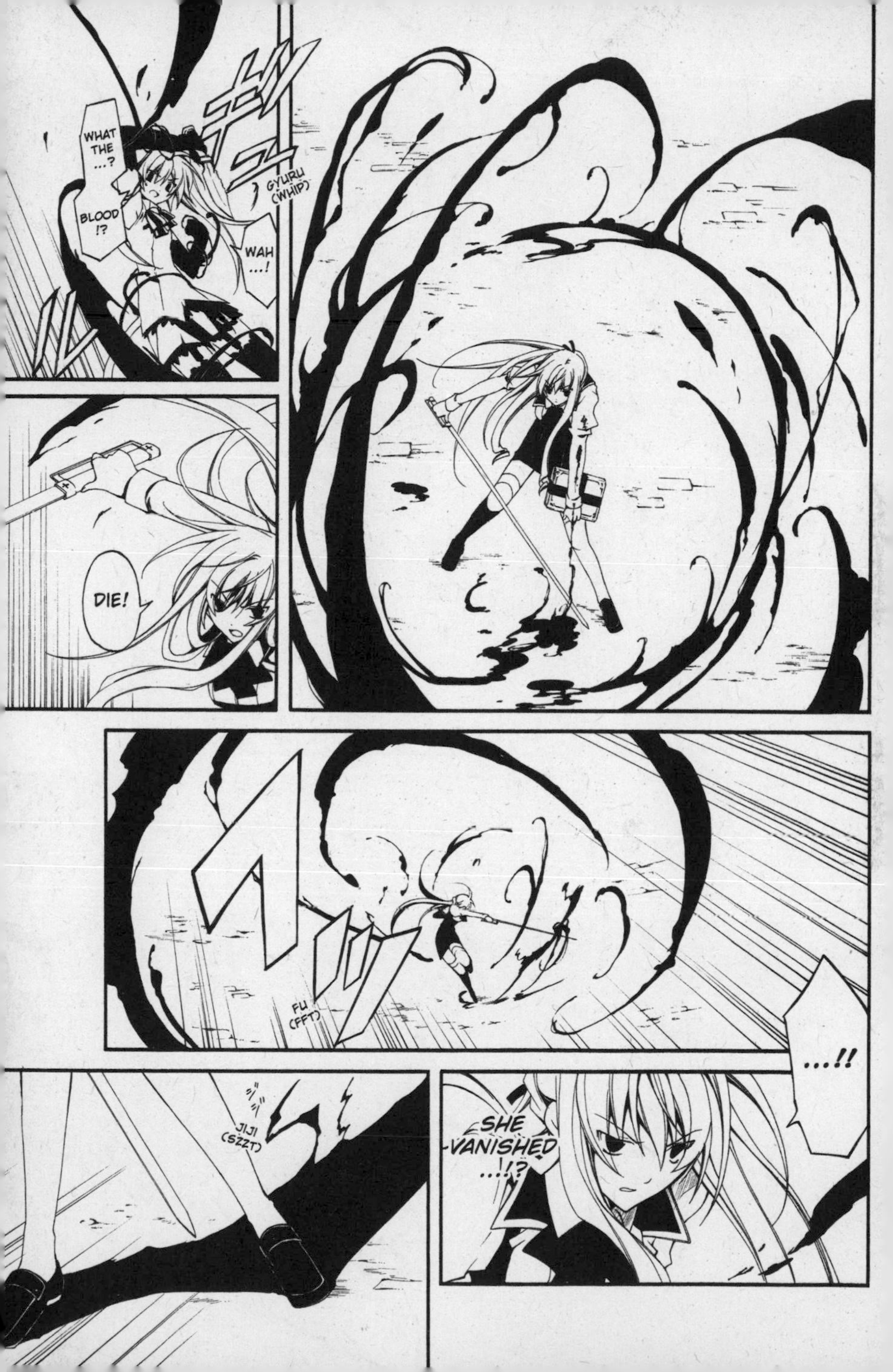
GYURU (WHIP)
WAH ...!
WHAT THE ...?
BLOOD !?
DIE!
FU (FFT)
...!!
SHE VANISHED ...!?
JIJI (SZZT)

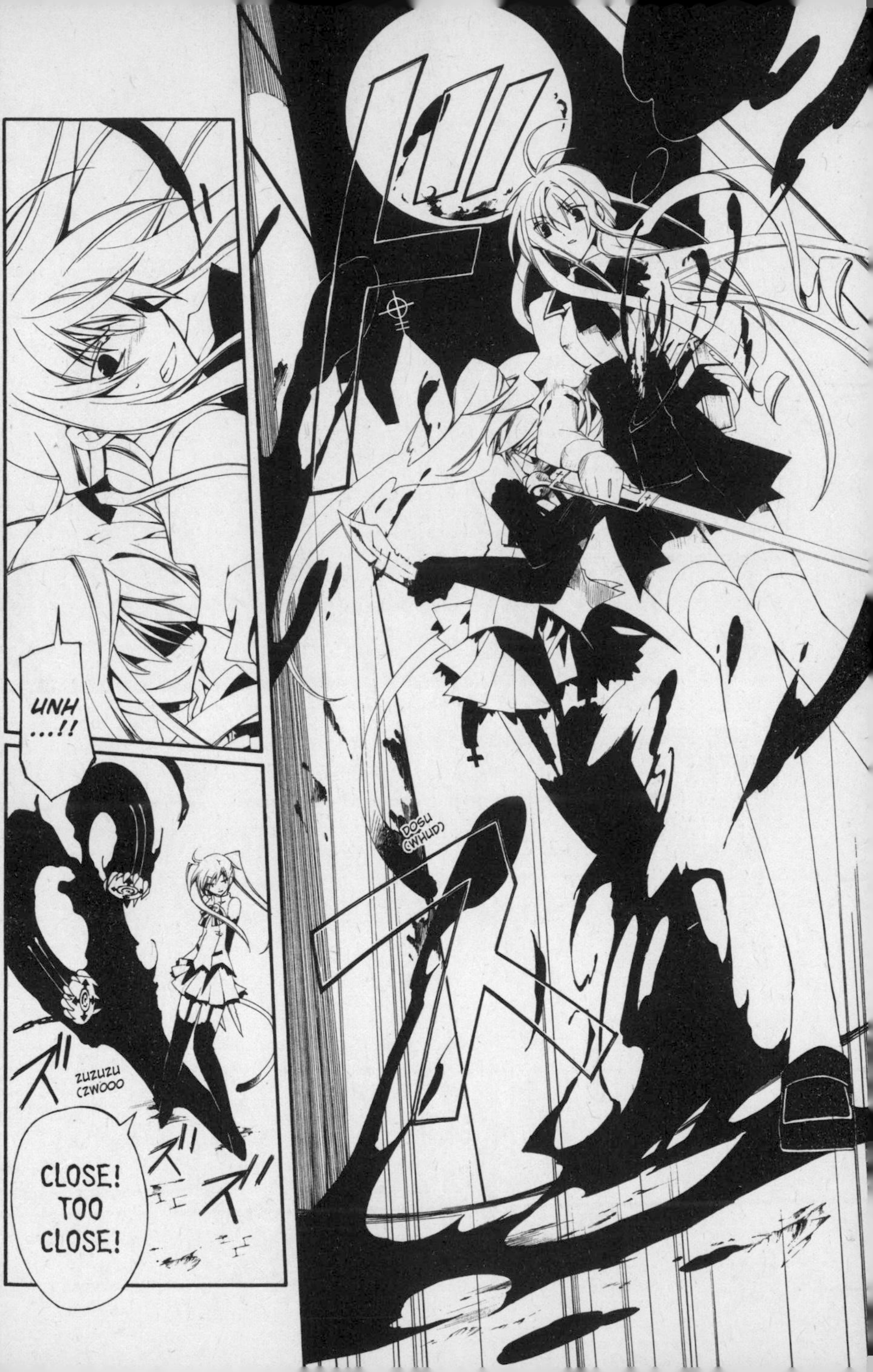
DOSU (WHUD)
UNH ...!!
ZUZUZU (ZWOOO)
CLOSE! TOO CLOSE!

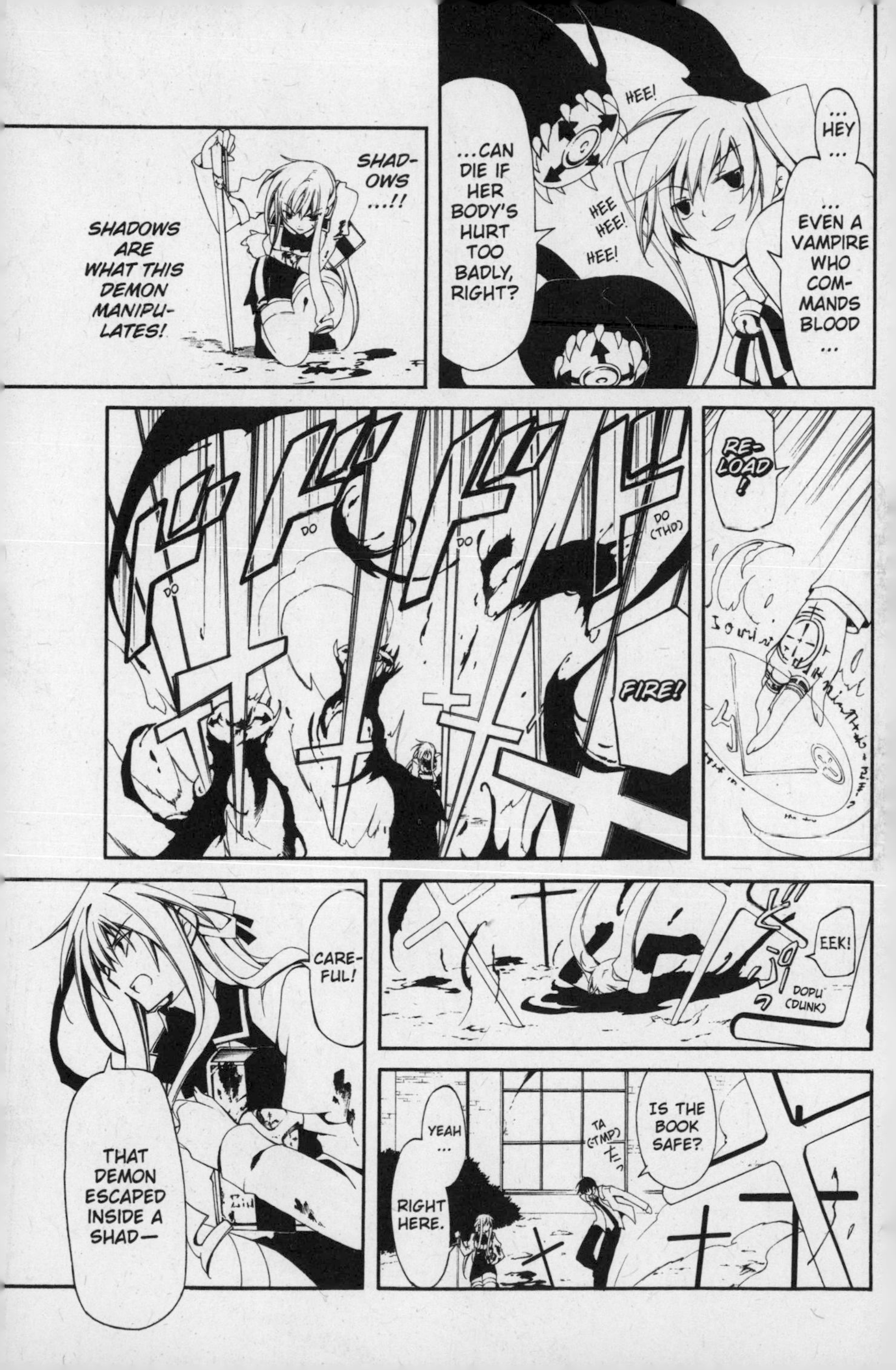
... HEY ...
... EVEN A VAMPIRE WHO COMMANDS BLOOD ...
HEE!
HEE HEE!
HEE!
...CAN DIE IF HER BODY'S HURT TOO BADLY, RIGHT?
SHADOWS ...!!
SHADOWS ARE WHAT THIS DEMON MANIPULATES!
RELOAD!
FIRE!
DO (THD)
DO
DO
DO
EEK!
DOPU (DUNK)
CAREFUL!
THAT DEMON ESCAPED INSIDE A SHAD—
IS THE BOOK SAFE?
TA (-TMP)
YEAH ...
RIGHT HERE.

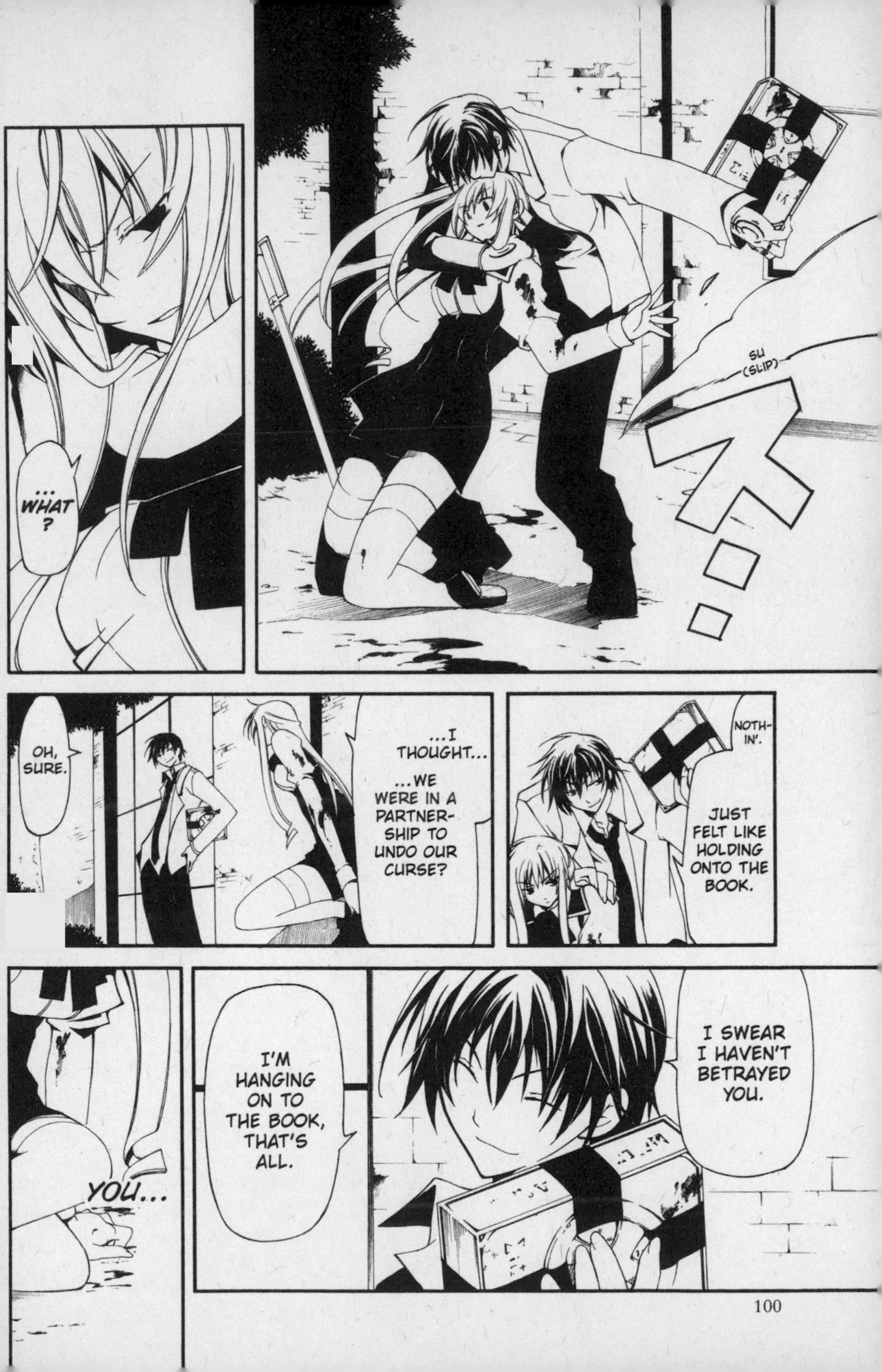
SU (SLIP)
...WHAT?
NOTHIN'.
JUST FELT LIKE HOLDING ONTO THE BOOK.
...I THOUGHT...
...WE WERE IN A PARTNERSHIP TO UNDO OUR CURSE?
OH, SURE.
I SWEAR I HAVEN'T BETRAYED YOU.
I'M HANGING ON TO THE BOOK, THAT'S ALL.
YOU...

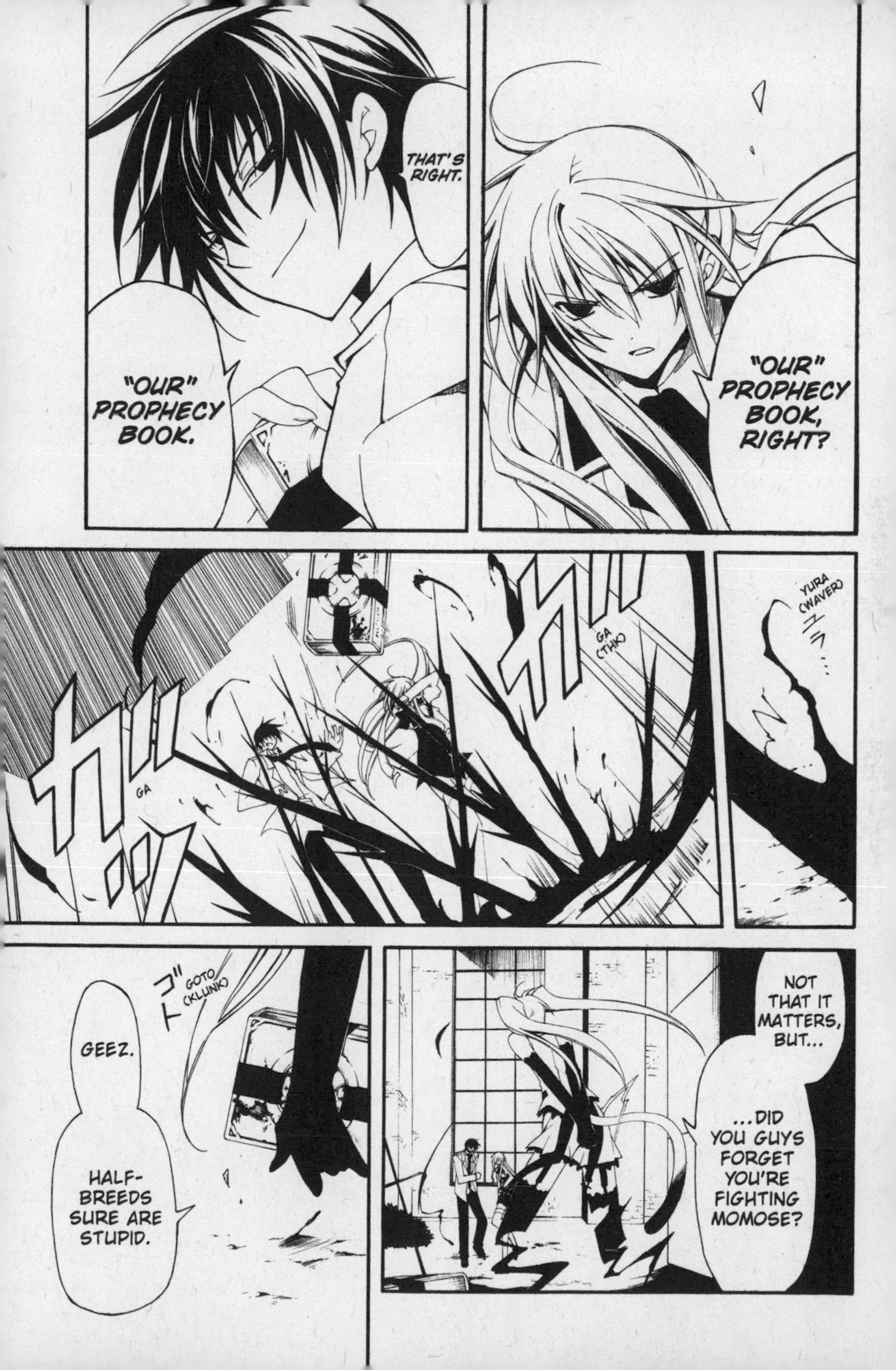
"OUR" PROPHECY BOOK, RIGHT?
THAT'S RIGHT.
"OUR" PROPHECY BOOK.
YURA (WAVER)
GA (THK)
GA
NOT THAT IT MATTERS, BUT...
...DID YOU GUYS FORGET YOU'RE FIGHTING MOMOSE?
GOTO (KLUNK)
GEEZ.
HALF-BREEDS SURE ARE STUPID.

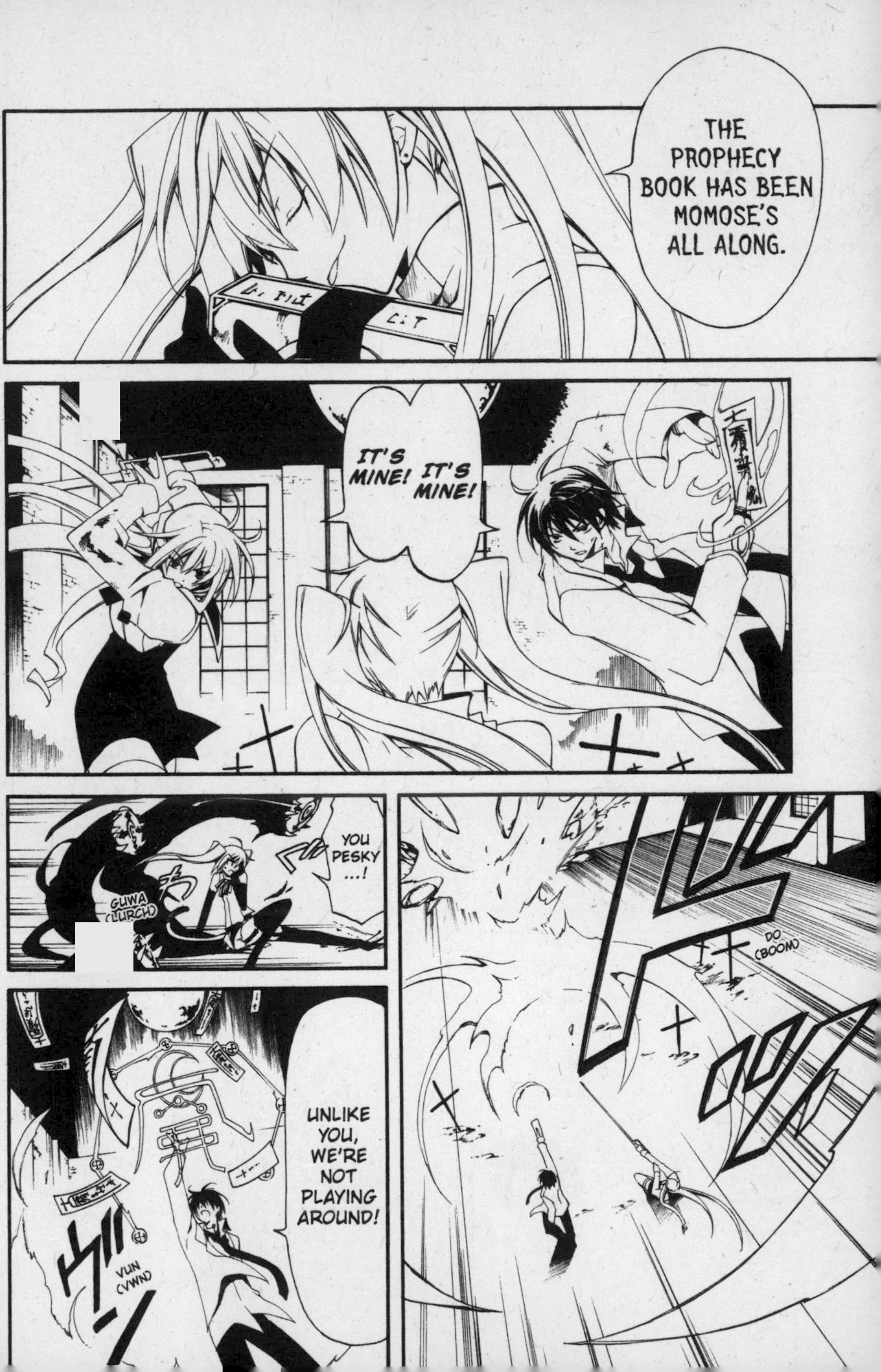
THE PROPHECY BOOK HAS BEEN MOMOSE'S ALL ALONG.
IT'S MINE! IT'S MINE!
DO (BOOM)
YOU PESKY ...!
GUWA (LURCH)
UNLIKE YOU, WE'RE NOT PLAYING AROUND!
VUN (VWN)

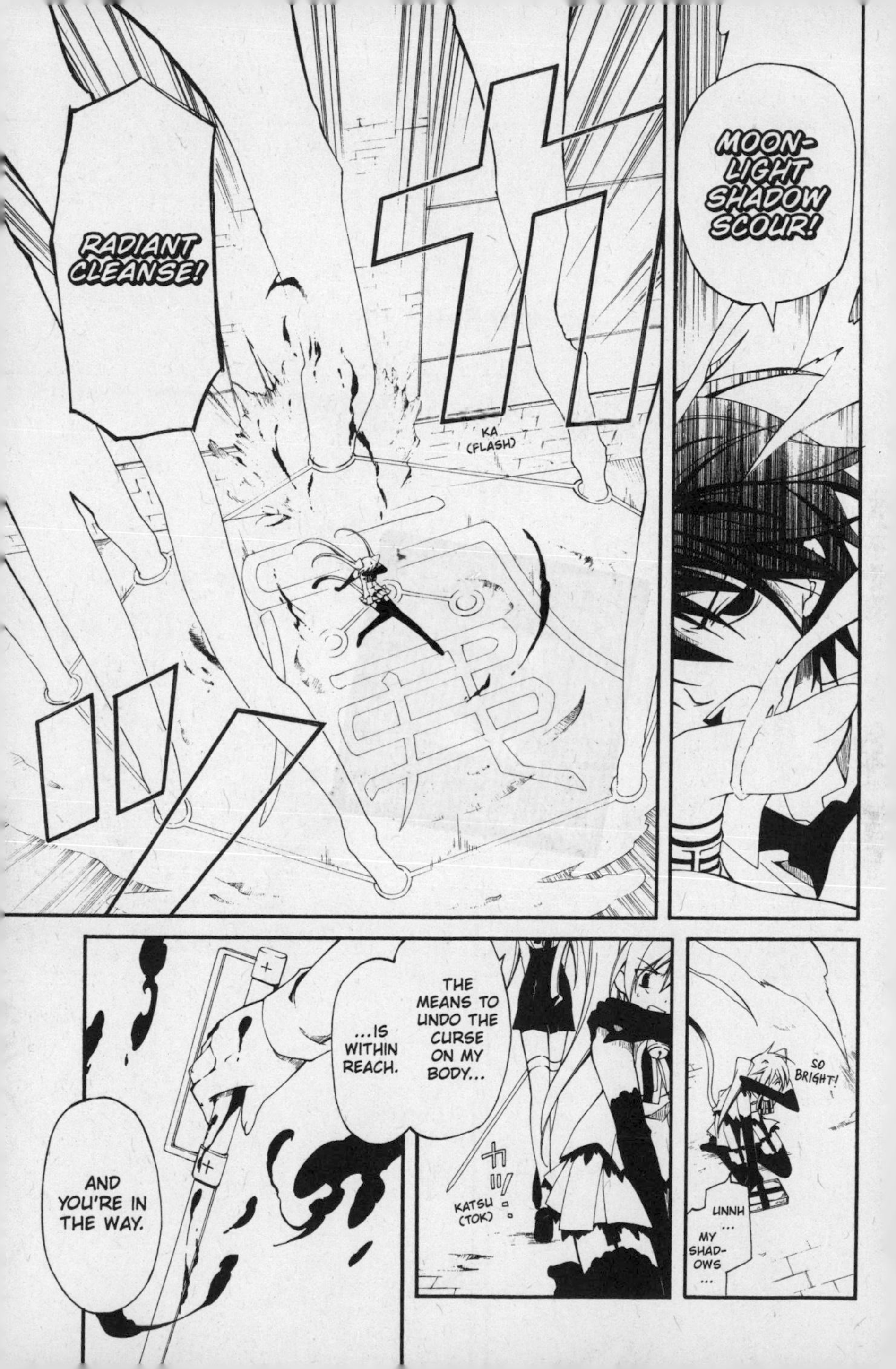
MOON-LIGHT SHADOW SCOUR!
RADIANT CLEANSE!
KA (FLASH)
SO BRIGHT!
UNNH ... MY SHAD-OWS ...
THE MEANS TO UNDO THE CURSE ON MY BODY...
...IS WITHIN REACH.
KATSU (TOK)
AND YOU'RE IN THE WAY.

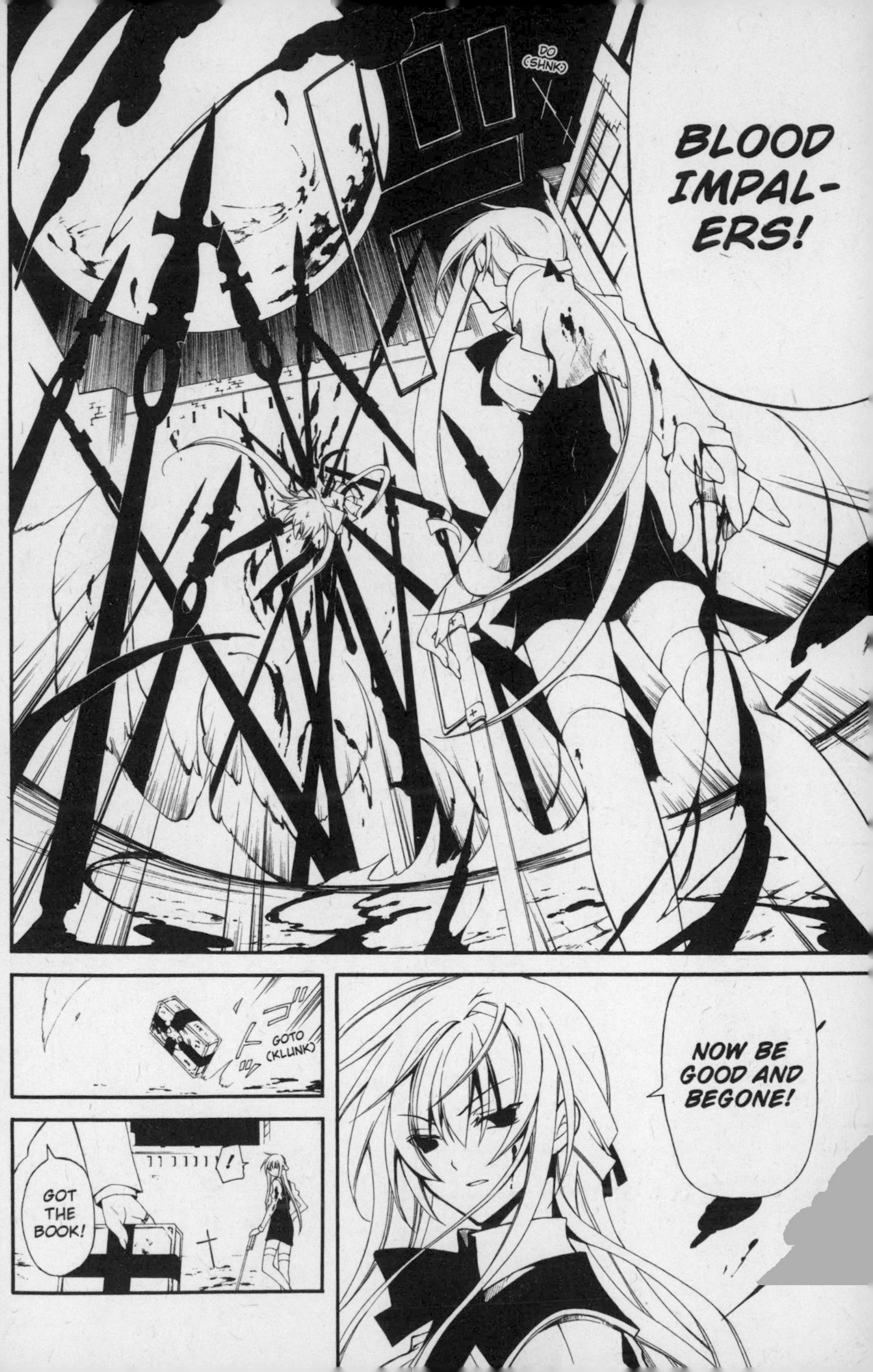
BLOOD IMPAL-ERS!
DO (SHNK)
NOW BE GOOD AND BEGONE!
GOTO (KLUNK)
!
GOT THE BOOK!

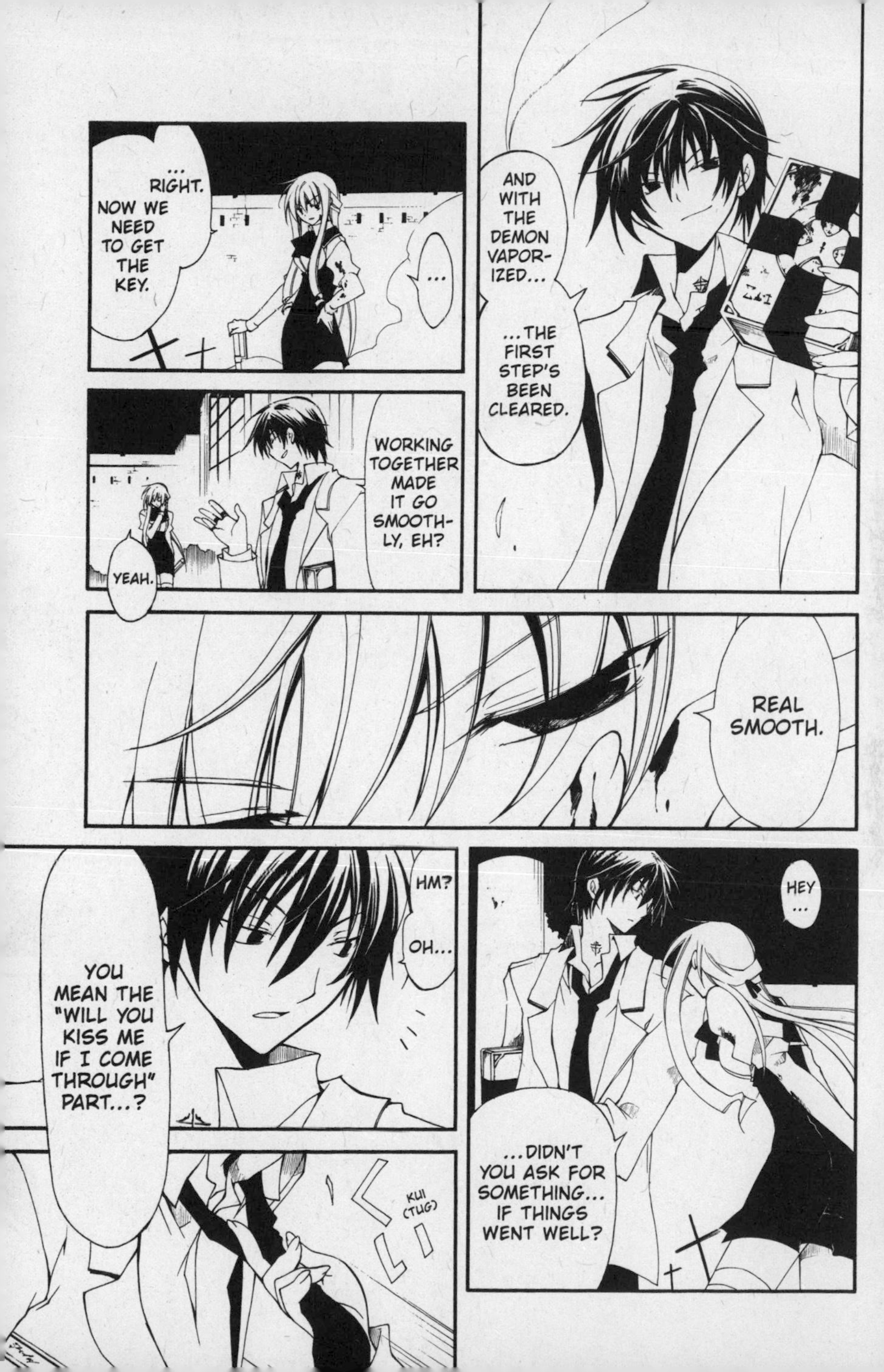
AND WITH THE DEMON VAPORIZED...
...THE FIRST STEP'S BEEN CLEARED.
...
...RIGHT. NOW WE NEED TO GET THE KEY.
WORKING TOGETHER MADE IT GO SMOOTHLY, EH?
YEAH.
REAL SMOOTH.
HEY...
...DIDN'T YOU ASK FOR SOMETHING... IF THINGS WENT WELL?
HM?
OH...
YOU MEAN THE "WILL YOU KISS ME IF I COME THROUGH" PART...?
KUI (TUG)

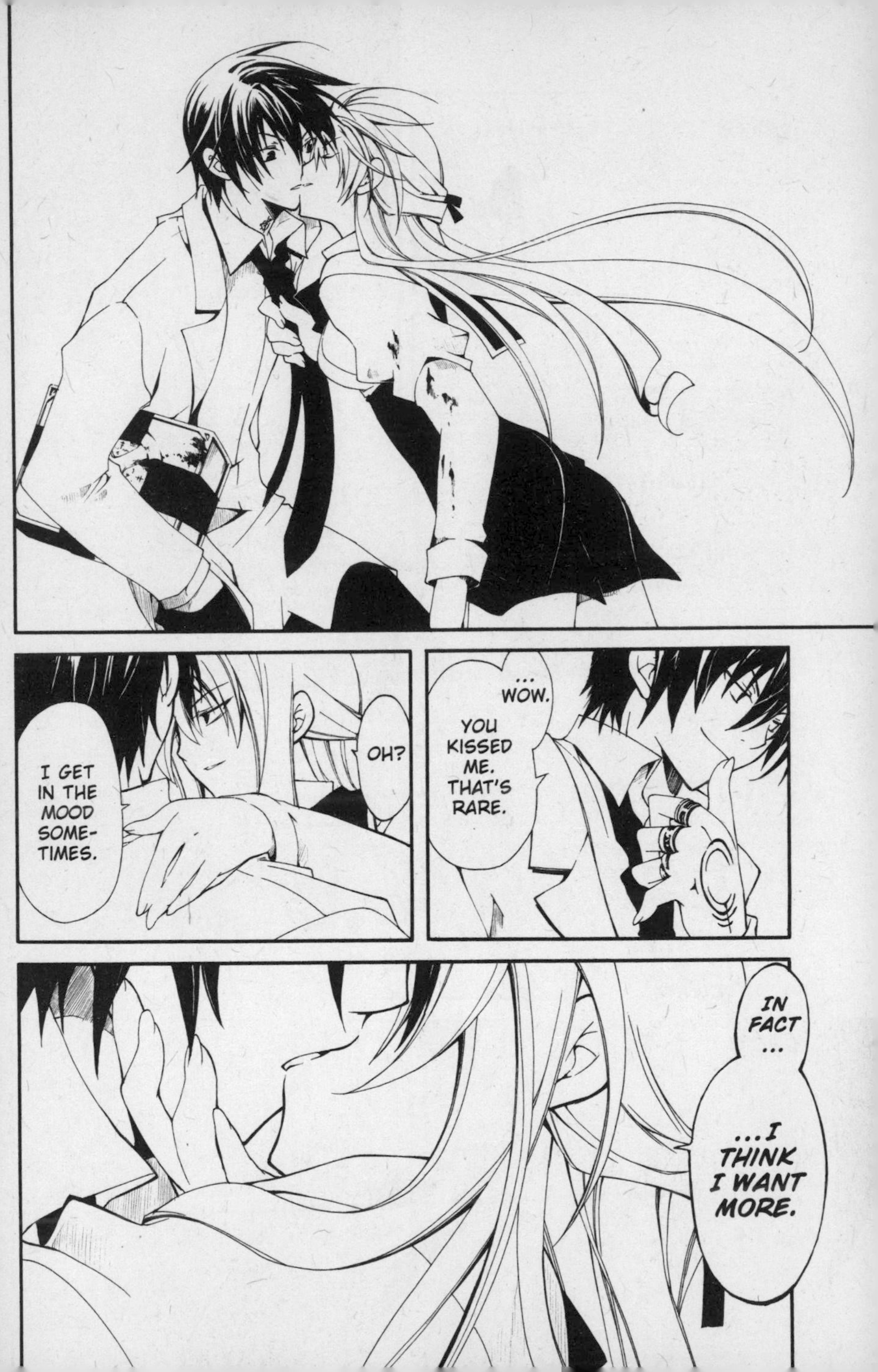
...WOW.
YOU KISSED ME. THAT'S RARE.
OH?
I GET IN THE MOOD SOMETIMES.
IN FACT...
...I THINK I WANT MORE.

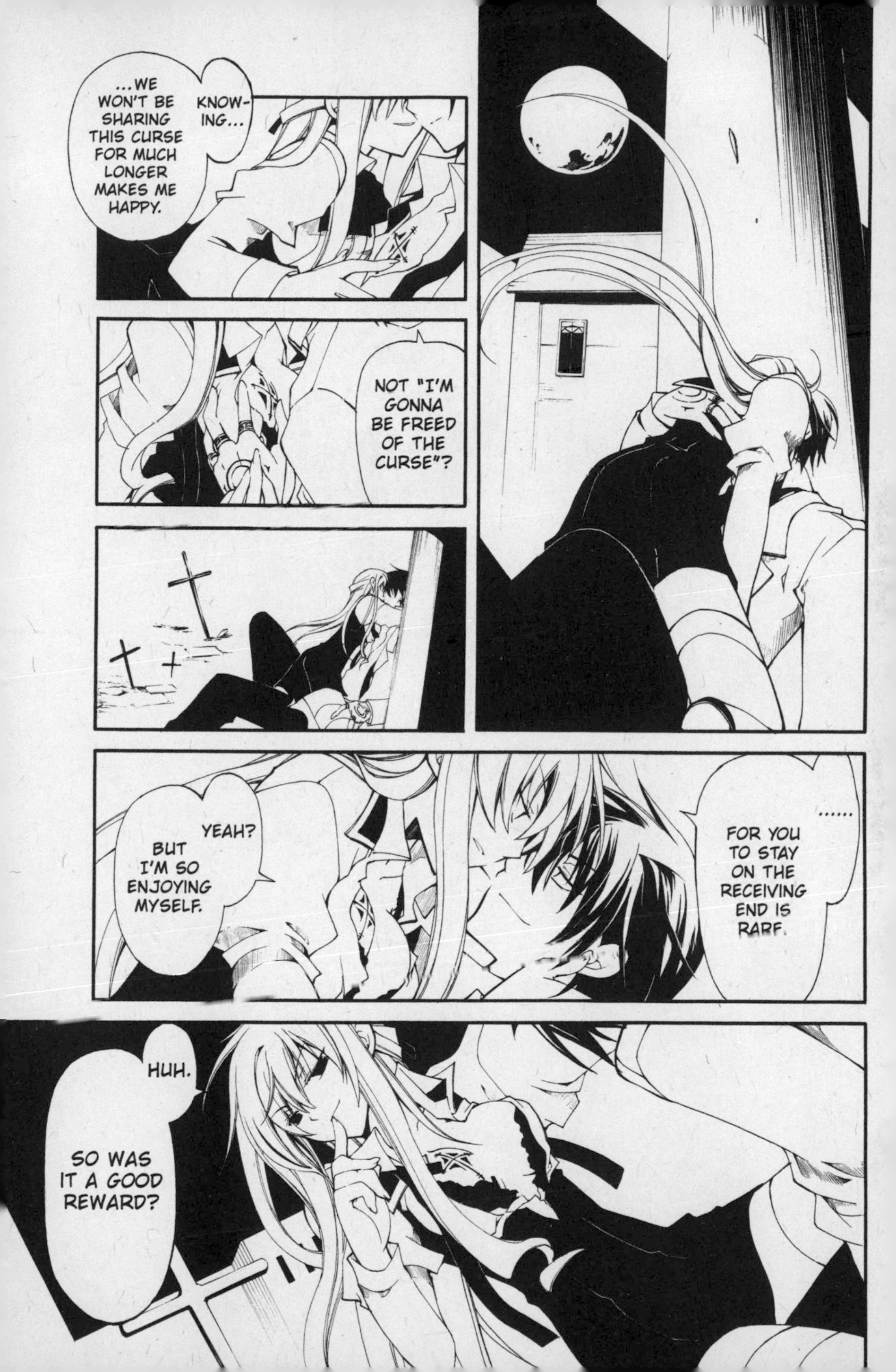
KNOW-ING...
...WE WON'T BE SHARING THIS CURSE FOR MUCH LONGER MAKES ME HAPPY.
NOT "I'M GONNA BE FREED OF THE CURSE"?
......
FOR YOU TO STAY ON THE RECEIVING END IS RARF.
YEAH? BUT I'M SO ENJOYING MYSELF.
HUH.
SO WAS IT A GOOD REWARD?

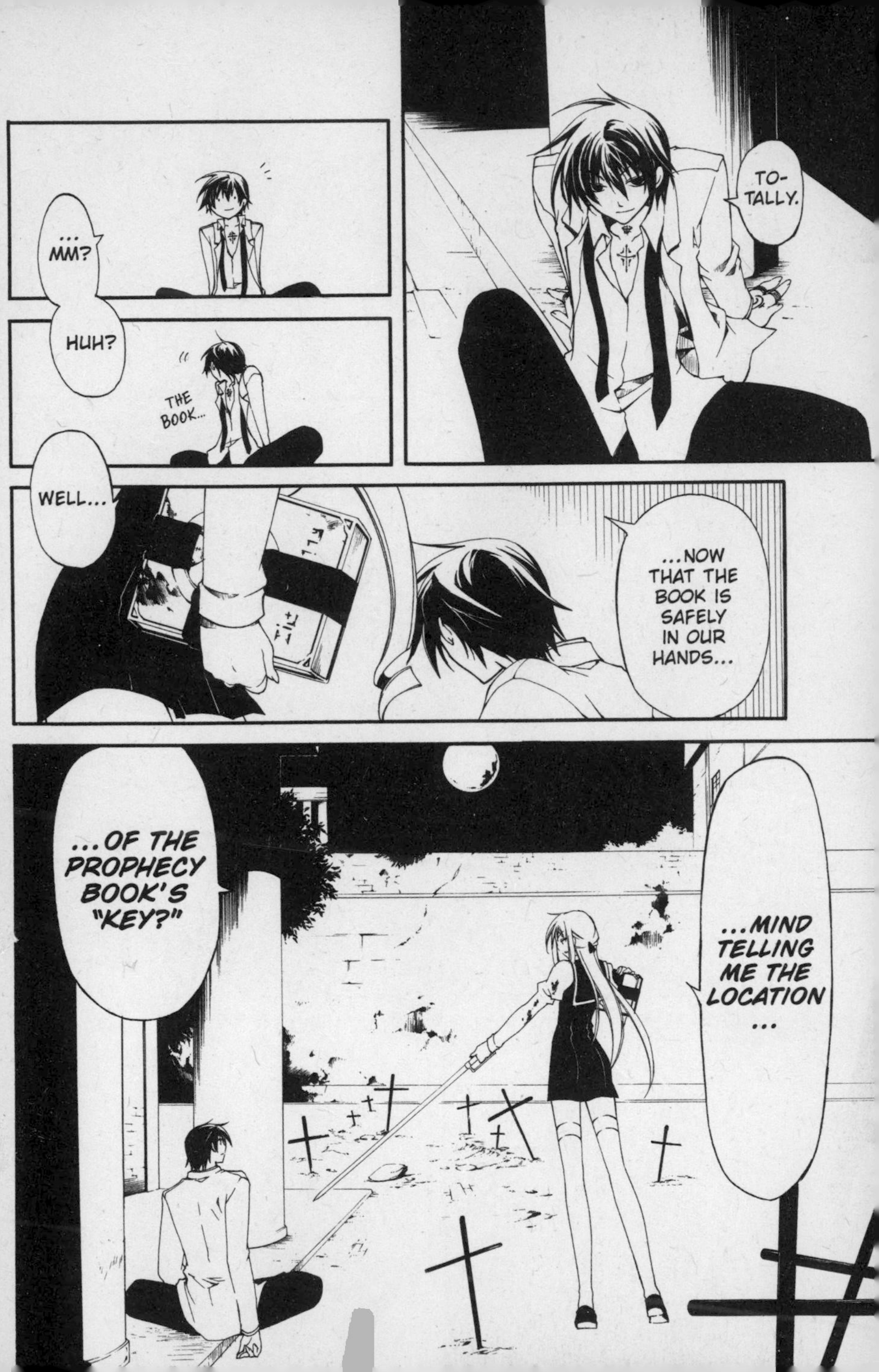
TO-TALLY.
...MM?
HUH?
THE BOOK...
WELL...
...NOW THAT THE BOOK IS SAFELY IN OUR HANDS...
...MIND TELLING ME THE LOCATION...
...OF THE PROPHECY BOOK'S "KEY?"

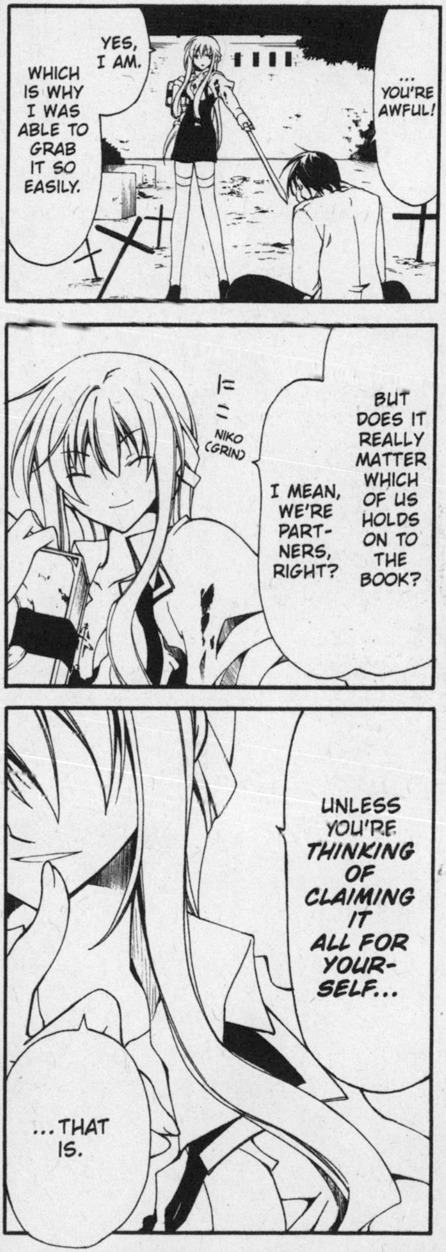
...YOU'RE AWFUL!
YES, I AM.
WHICH IS WHY I WAS ABLE TO GRAB IT SO EASILY.
BUT DOES IT REALLY MATTER WHICH OF US HOLDS ON TO THE BOOK?
I MEAN, WE'RE PART-NERS, RIGHT?
ニコ
NIKO (GRIN)
UNLESS YOU'RE THINKING OF CLAIMING IT ALL FOR YOUR-SELF...
...THAT IS.
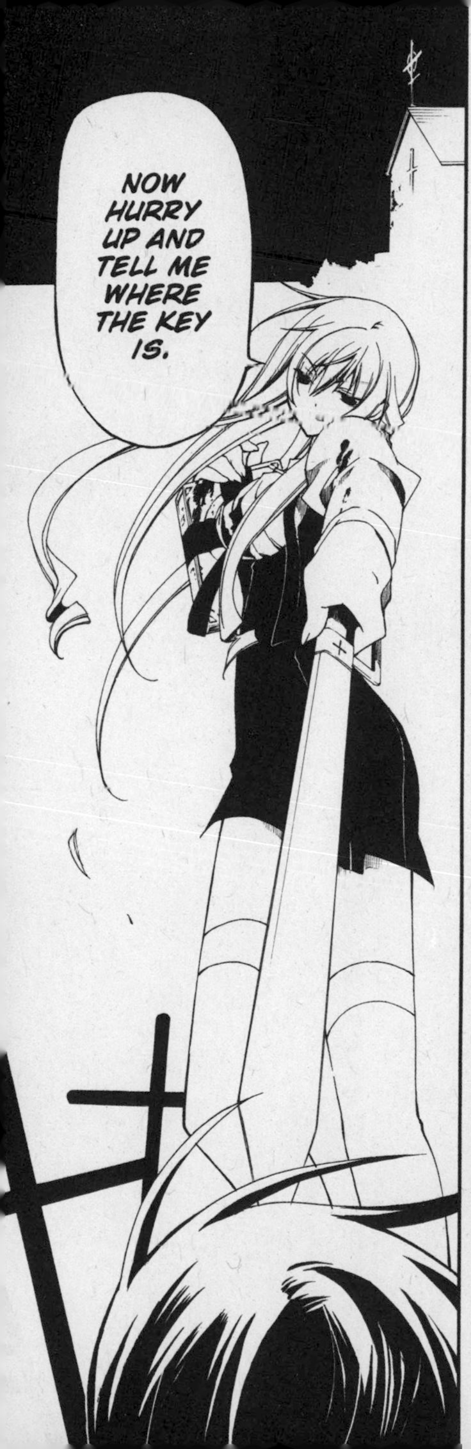
NOW HURRY UP AND TELL ME WHERE THE KEY IS.

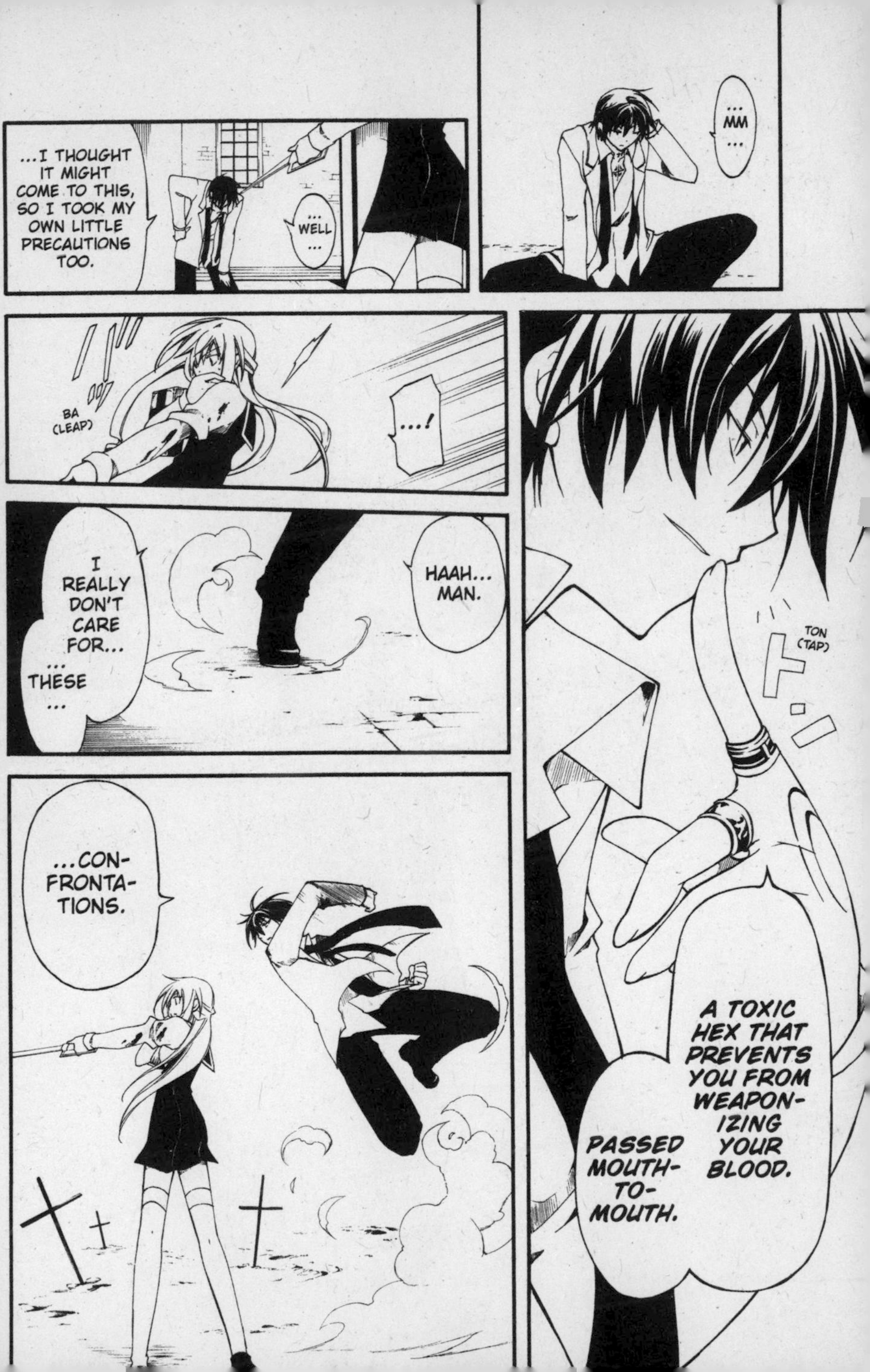
...MM...
...I THOUGHT IT MIGHT COME TO THIS, SO I TOOK MY OWN LITTLE PRECAUTIONS TOO.
...WELL...
TON (TAP)
A TOXIC HEX THAT PREVENTS YOU FROM WEAPON-IZING YOUR BLOOD.
PASSED MOUTH-TO-MOUTH.
BA (LEAP)
...!
HAAH... MAN.
I REALLY DON'T CARE FOR... ...THESE...
...CON-FRONTA-TIONS.

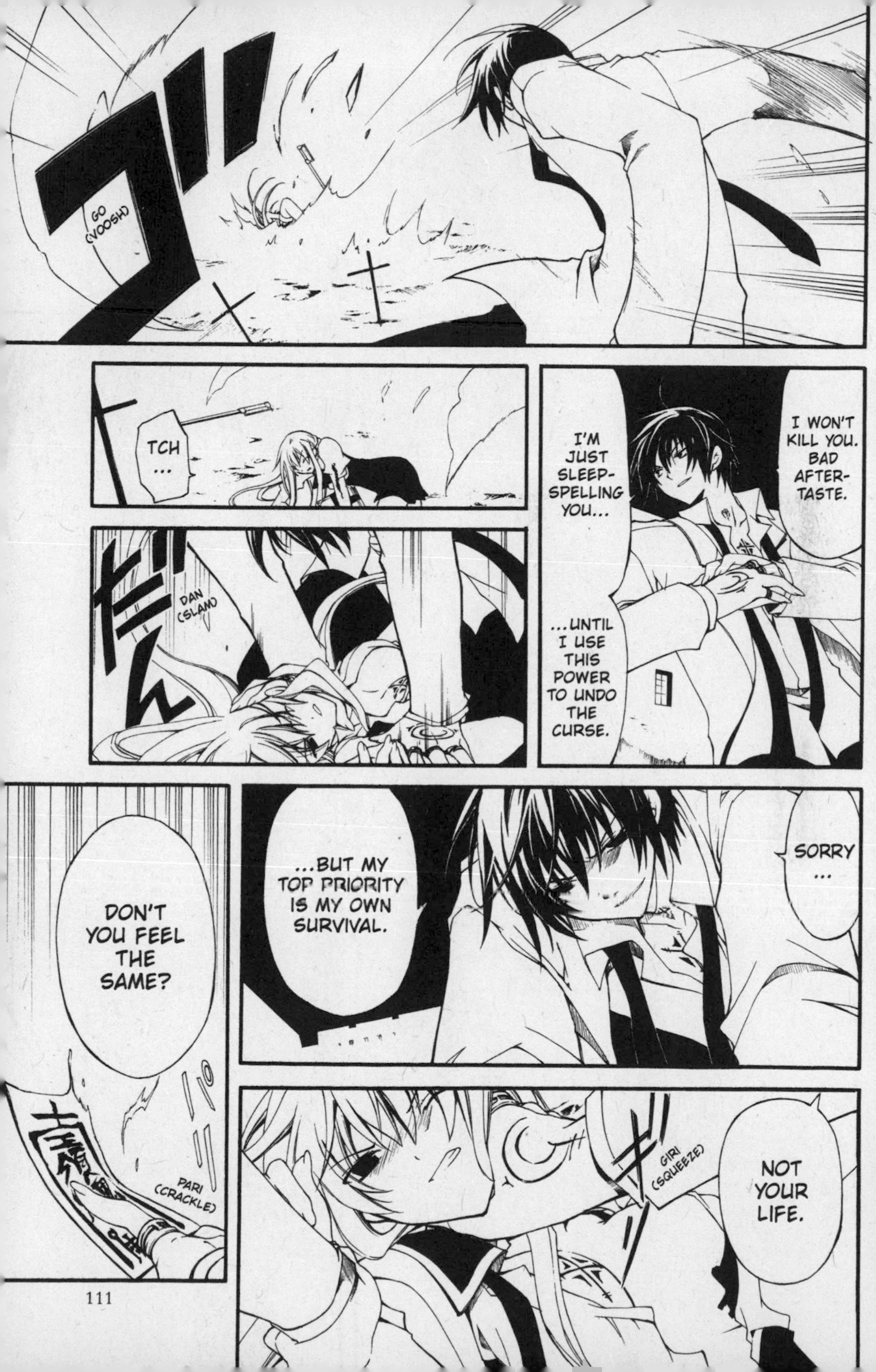
GO (VOOSH)
I WON'T KILL YOU. BAD AFTER-TASTE.
I'M JUST SLEEP-SPELLING YOU...
...UNTIL I USE THIS POWER TO UNDO THE CURSE.
TCH ...
DAN (SLAM)
SORRY ...
...BUT MY TOP PRIORITY IS MY OWN SURVIVAL.
GIRI (SQUEEZE)
NOT YOUR LIFE.
DON'T YOU FEEL THE SAME?
PARI (CRACKLE)

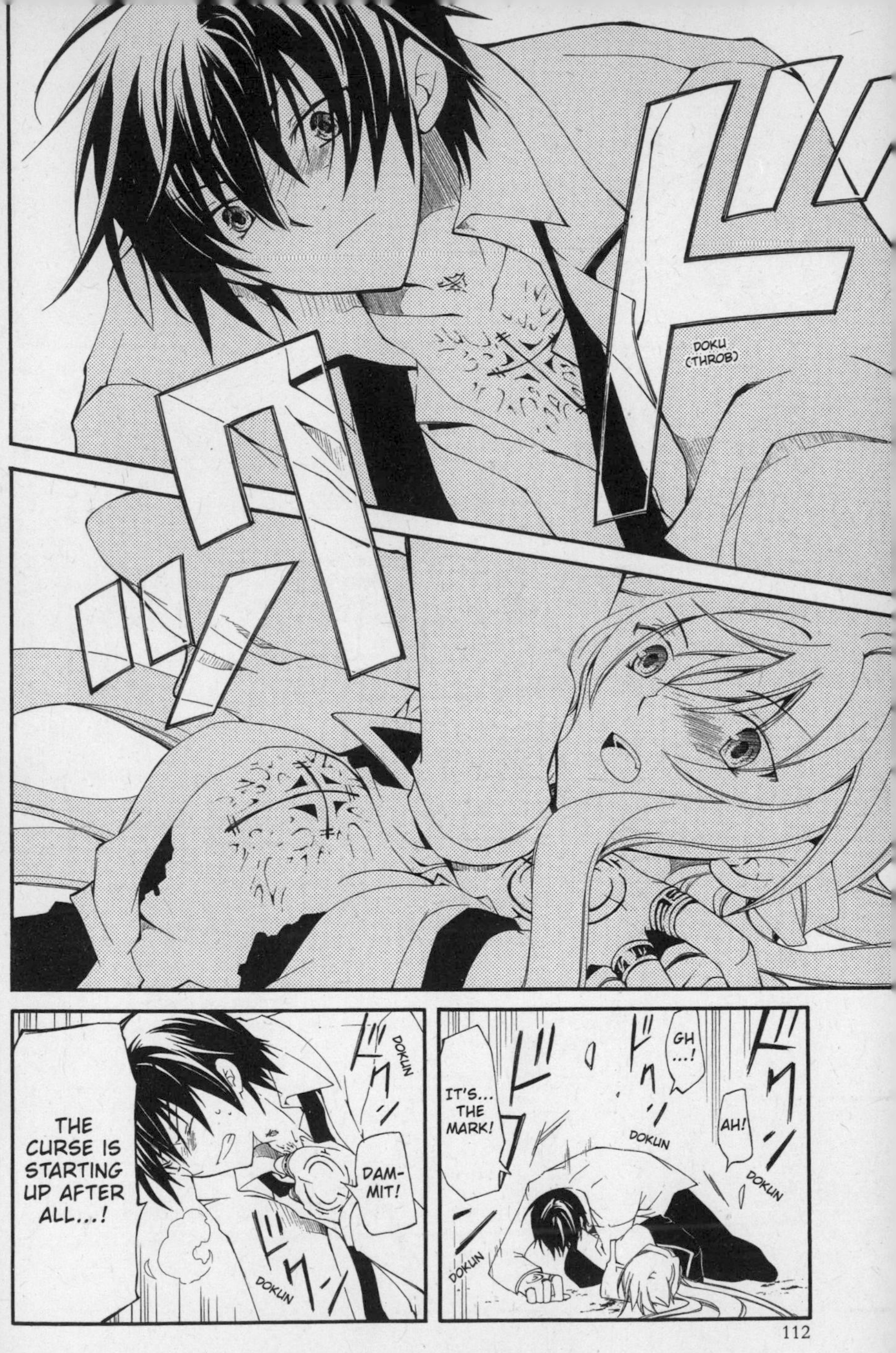
DOKU (THROB)
GH ...!
AH!
IT'S... THE MARK!
DOKUN
DOKUN
DOKUN
DOKUN
DAM-MIT!
THE CURSE IS STARTING UP AFTER ALL...!
DOKUN

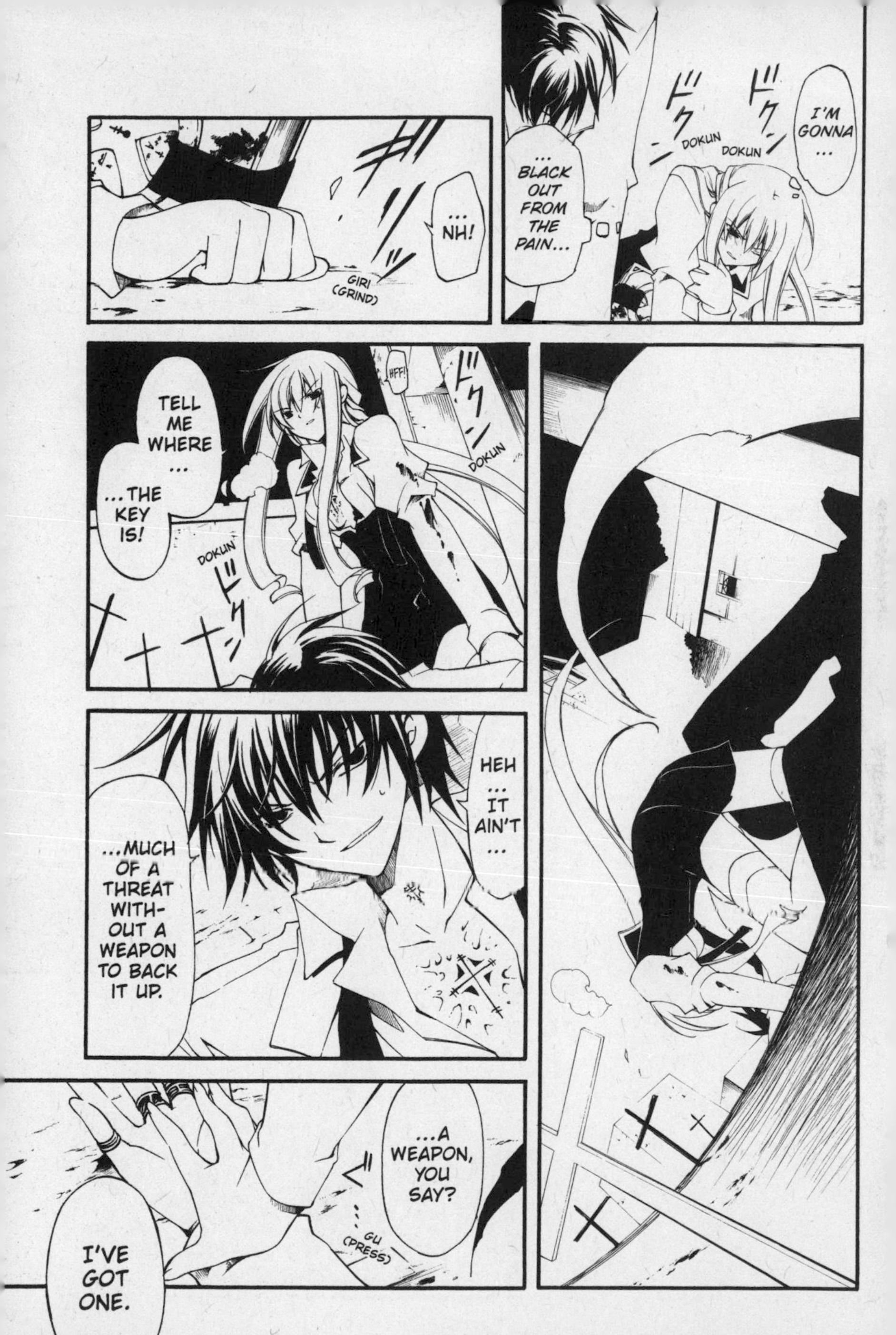
I'M GONNA ...
DOKUN
DOKUN
... BLACK OUT FROM THE PAIN...
... NH!
GIRI (GRIND)
TELL ME WHERE ...
...THE KEY IS!
HFF!
DOKUN
DOKUN
HEH ... IT AIN'T ...
...MUCH OF A THREAT WITH-OUT A WEAPON TO BACK IT UP.
...A WEAPON, YOU SAY?
GU (PRESS)
I'VE GOT ONE.

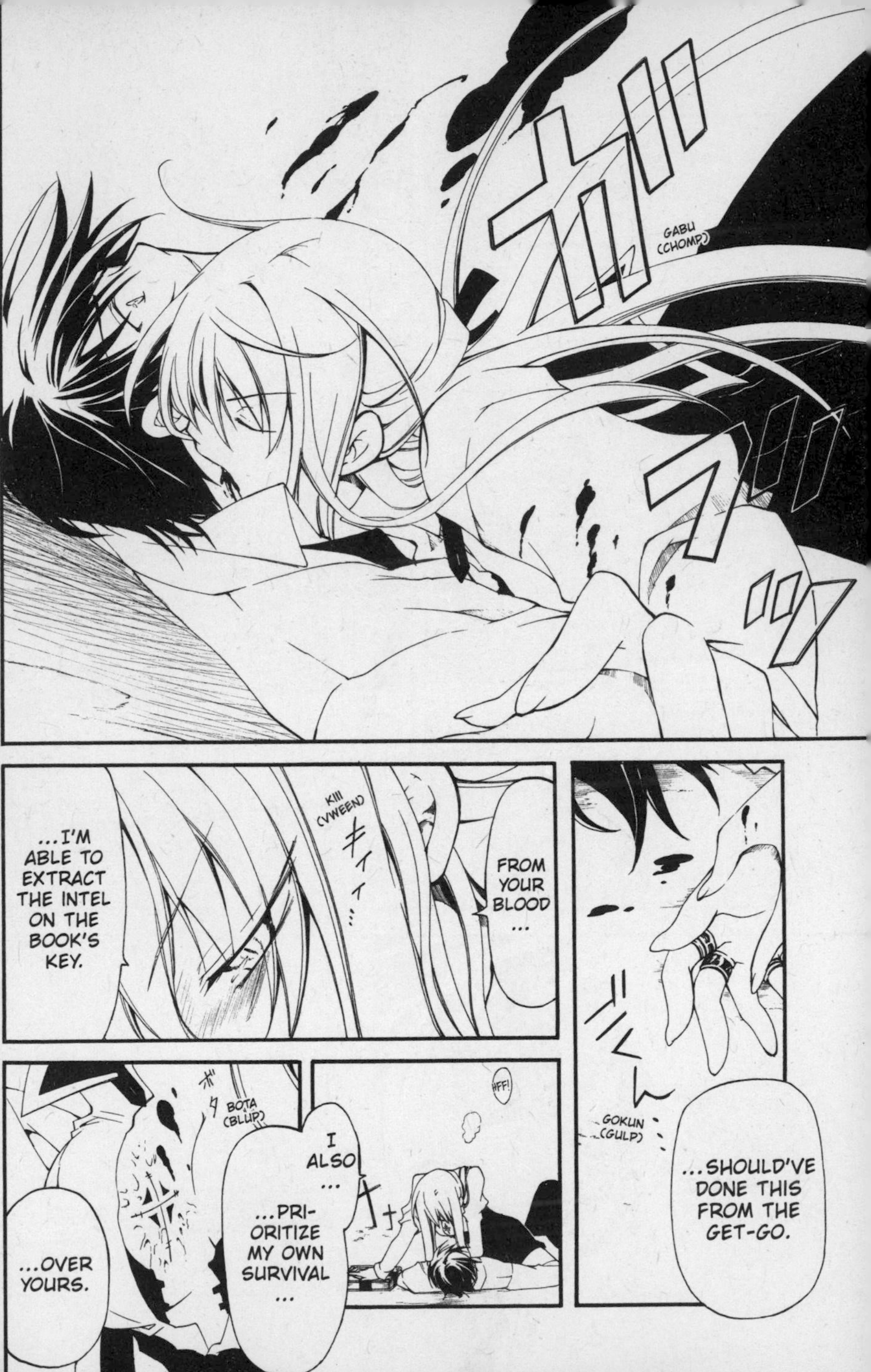
GABU (CHOMP)
GOKUN (GULP)
...SHOULD'VE DONE THIS FROM THE GET-GO.
FROM YOUR BLOOD...
KIII (VWEEND)
...I'M ABLE TO EXTRACT THE INTEL ON THE BOOK'S KEY.
HFF!
I ALSO...
...PRI-ORITIZE MY OWN SURVIVAL...
BOTA (BLUP)
...OVER YOURS.

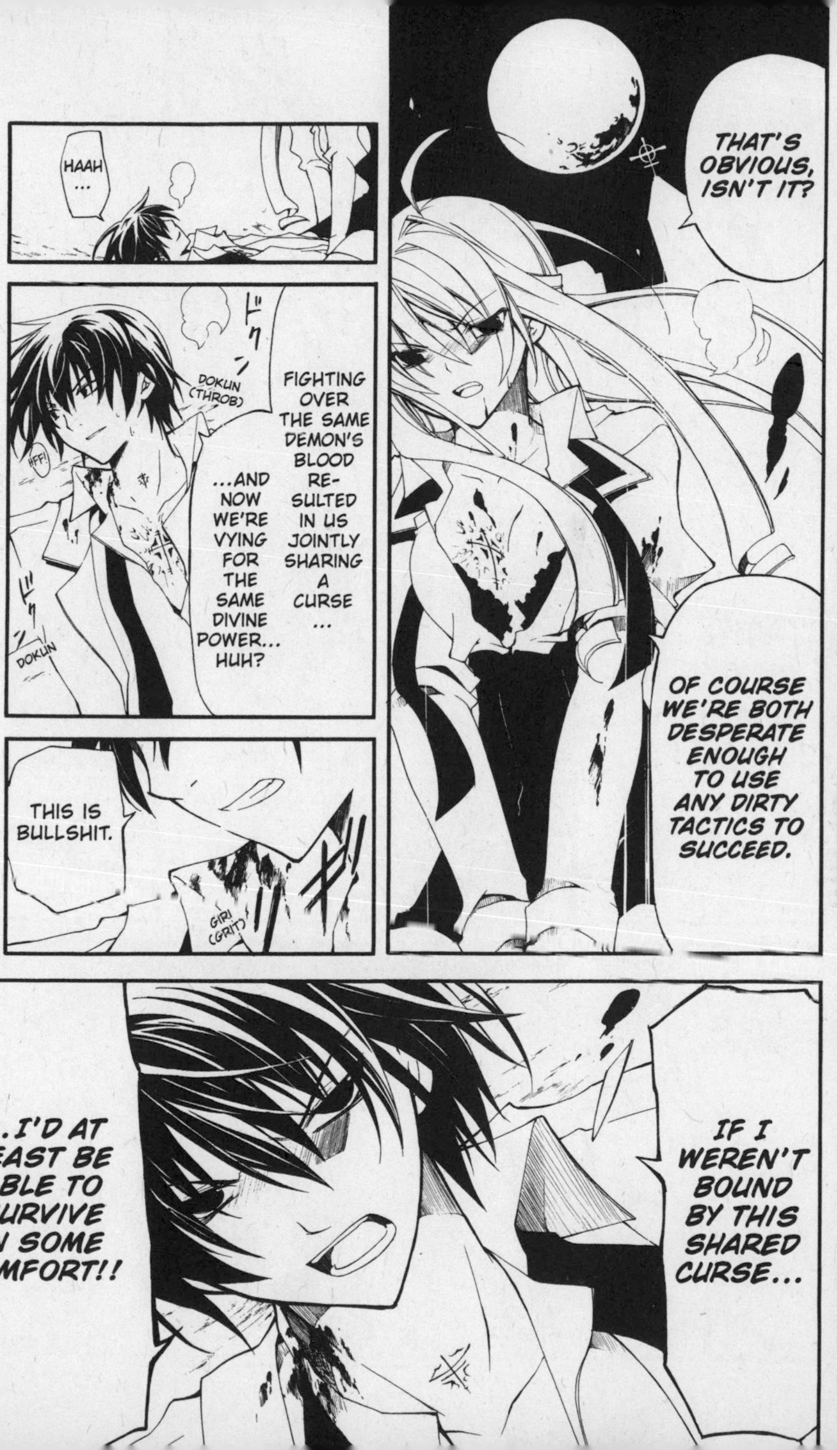
THAT'S OBVIOUS, ISN'T IT?
OF COURSE WE'RE BOTH DESPERATE ENOUGH TO USE ANY DIRTY TACTICS TO SUCCEED.
HAAH ...
ドクン
DOKUN (THROB)
FIGHTING OVER THE SAME DEMON'S BLOOD RE-SULTED IN US JOINTLY SHARING A CURSE ...
...AND NOW WE'RE VYING FOR THE SAME DIVINE POWER... HUH?
HFF!
ドクン
DOKUN
THIS IS BULLSHIT.
GIRI (GRIT)
IF I WEREN'T BOUND BY THIS SHARED CURSE...
...I'D AT LEAST BE ABLE TO SURVIVE IN SOME COMFORT!!

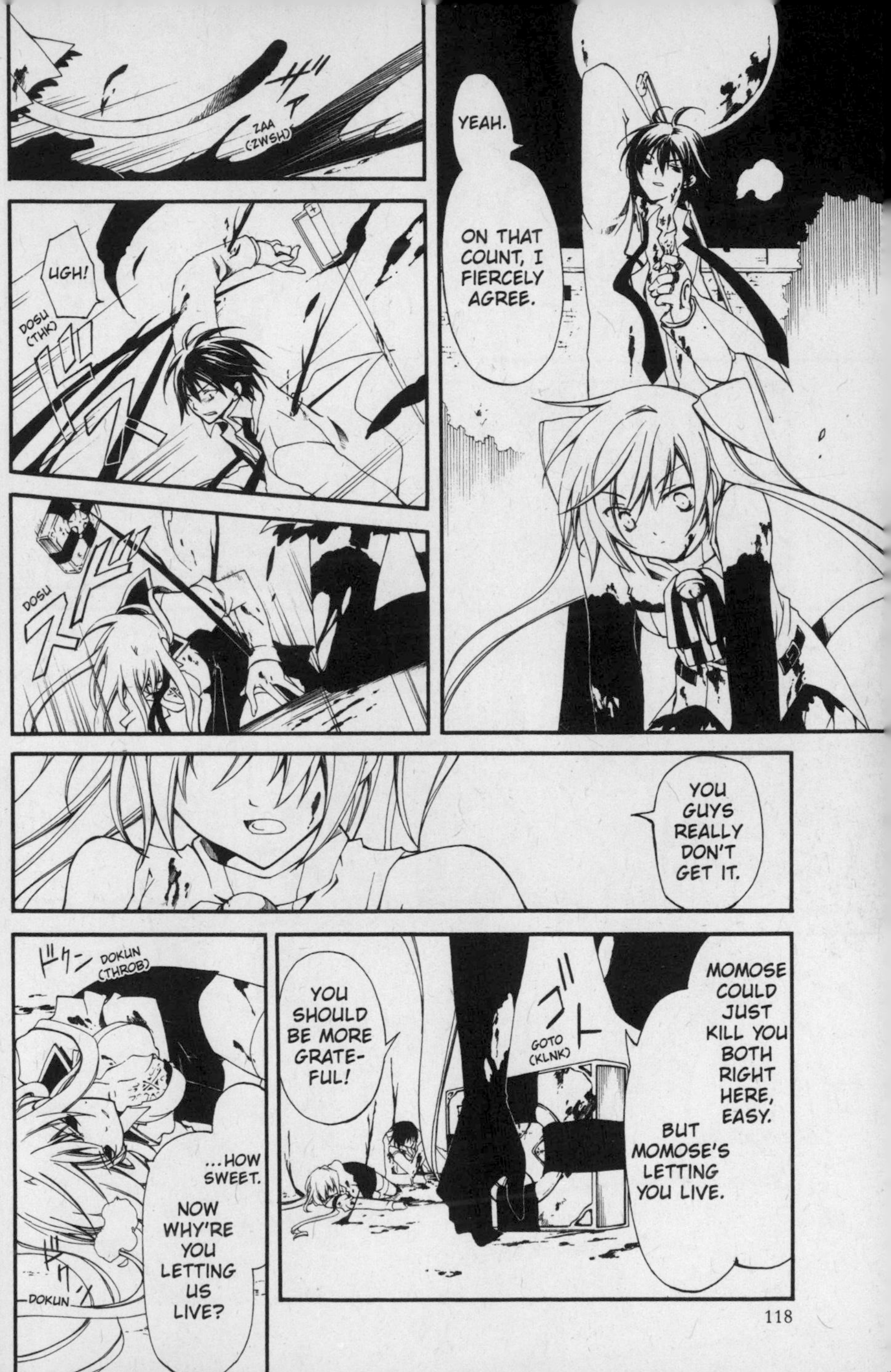
YEAH.
ON THAT COUNT, I FIERCELY AGREE.
ZAA (ZWSH)
UGH!
DOSU (THK)
DOSU
YOU GUYS REALLY DON'T GET IT.
MOMOSE COULD JUST KILL YOU BOTH RIGHT HERE, EASY.
BUT MOMOSE'S LETTING YOU LIVE.
GOTO (KLNK)
YOU SHOULD BE MORE GRATE-FUL!
DOKUN (THROB)
...HOW SWEET.
NOW WHY'RE YOU LETTING US LIVE?
DOKUN

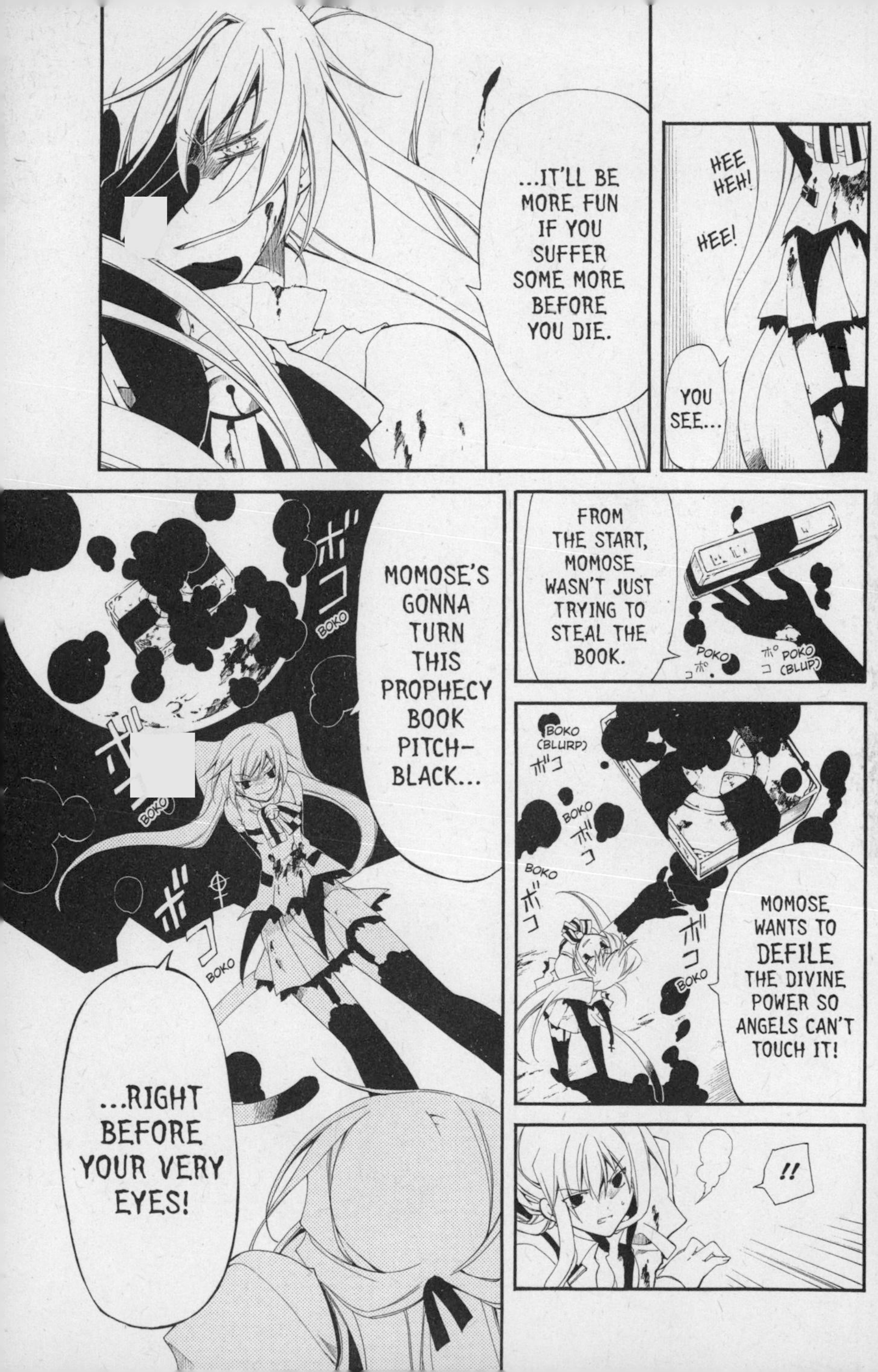
HEE HEH!
HEE!
YOU SEE...
...IT'LL BE MORE FUN IF YOU SUFFER SOME MORE BEFORE YOU DIE.
FROM THE START, MOMOSE WASN'T JUST TRYING TO STEAL THE BOOK.
ポコ POKO
ポコ POKO (BLUP)
ボコ BOKO (BLURP)
ボコ BOKO
ボコ BOKO
ボコ BOKO
MOMOSE WANTS TO DEFILE THE DIVINE POWER SO ANGELS CAN'T TOUCH IT!
!!
ボコ BOKO
MOMOSE'S GONNA TURN THIS PROPHECY BOOK PITCH-BLACK...
ボコ BOKO
ボコ BOKO
...RIGHT BEFORE YOUR VERY EYES!

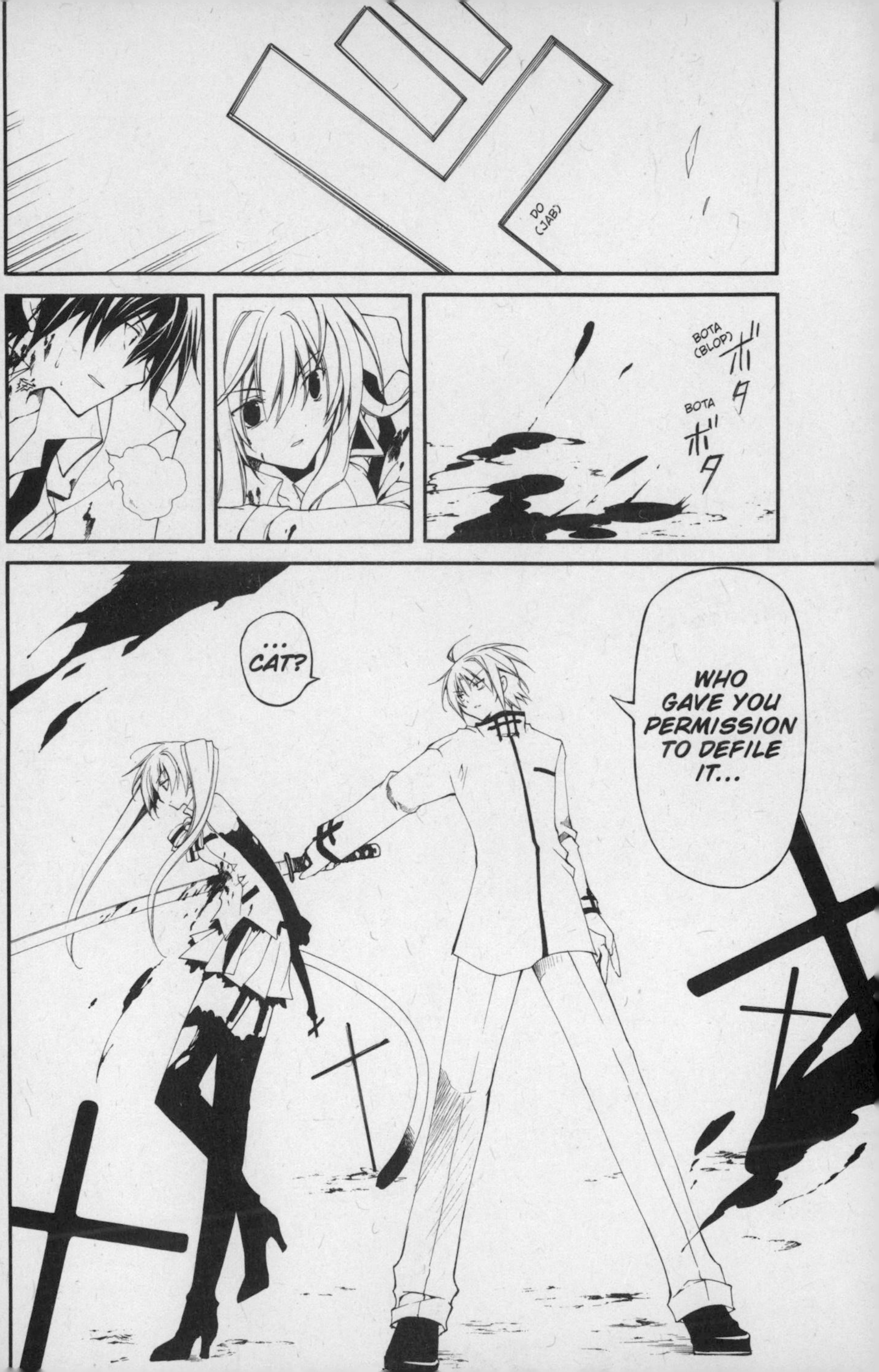
DO (JAB)
BOTA (BLOP)
ボタ
BOTA
ボタ
WHO GAVE YOU PERMISSION TO DEFILE IT...
...CAT?

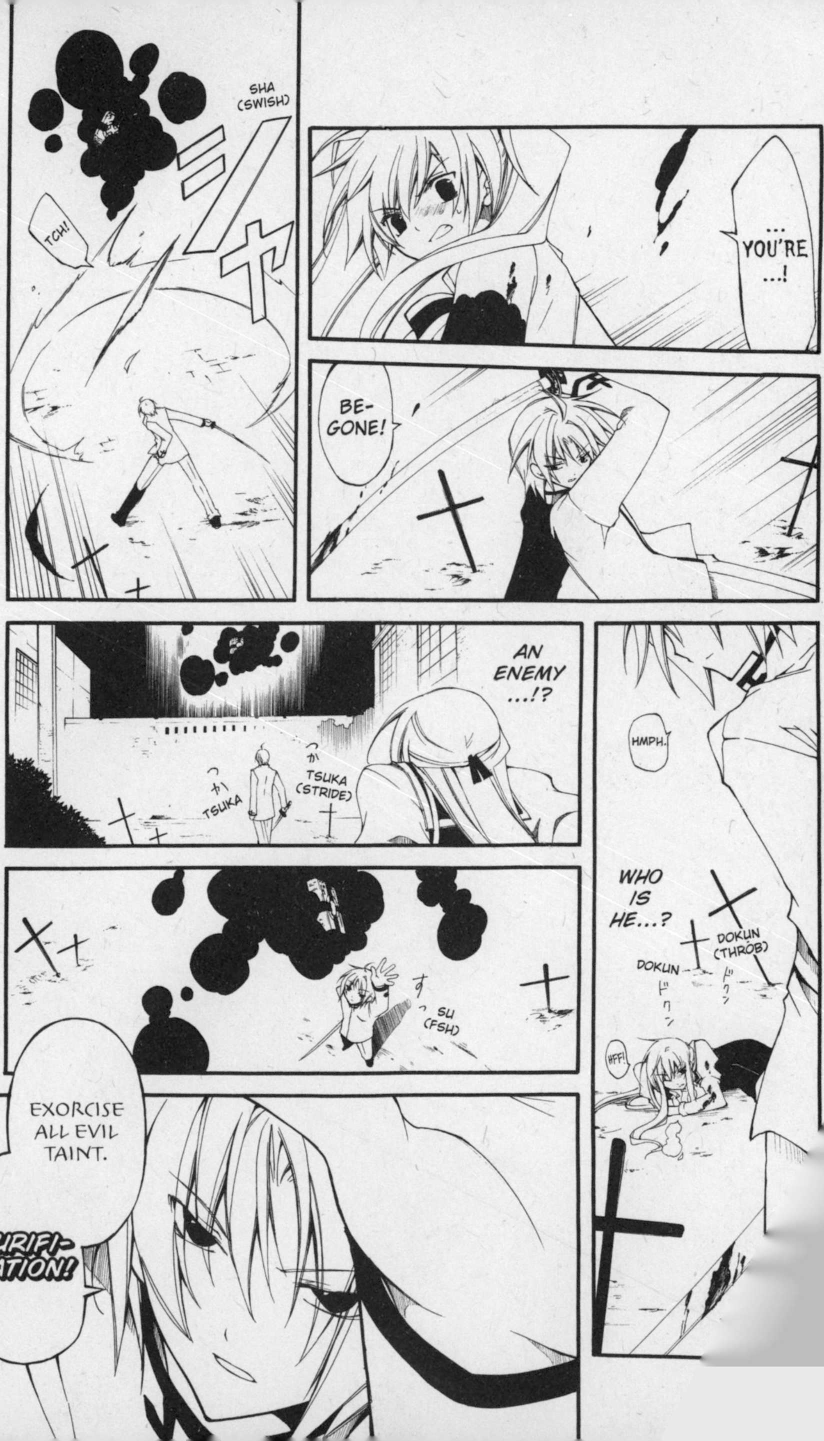
... YOU'RE ...!
BE-GONE!
SHA (SWISH)
TCH!
HMPH.
WHO IS HE...?
DOKUN (THROB)
DOKUN
HFF!
AN ENEMY ...!?
TSUKA (STRIDE)
TSUKA
SU (FSH)
EXORCISE ALL EVIL TAINT.
PURIFI-CATION!

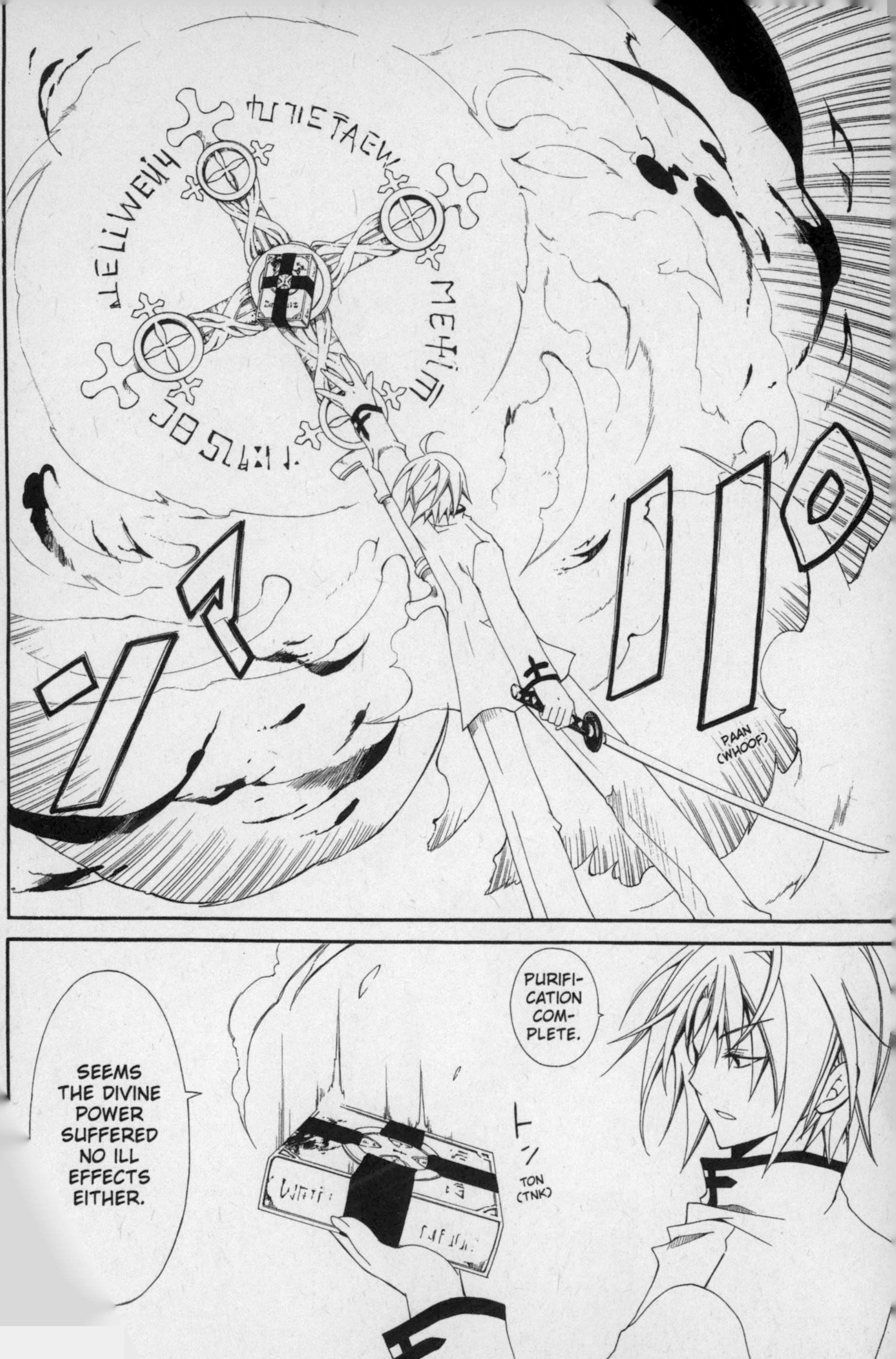
PAAN (WHOOF)
PURIFICATION COMPLETE.
TON (TNK)
SEEMS THE DIVINE POWER SUFFERED NO ILL EFFECTS EITHER.

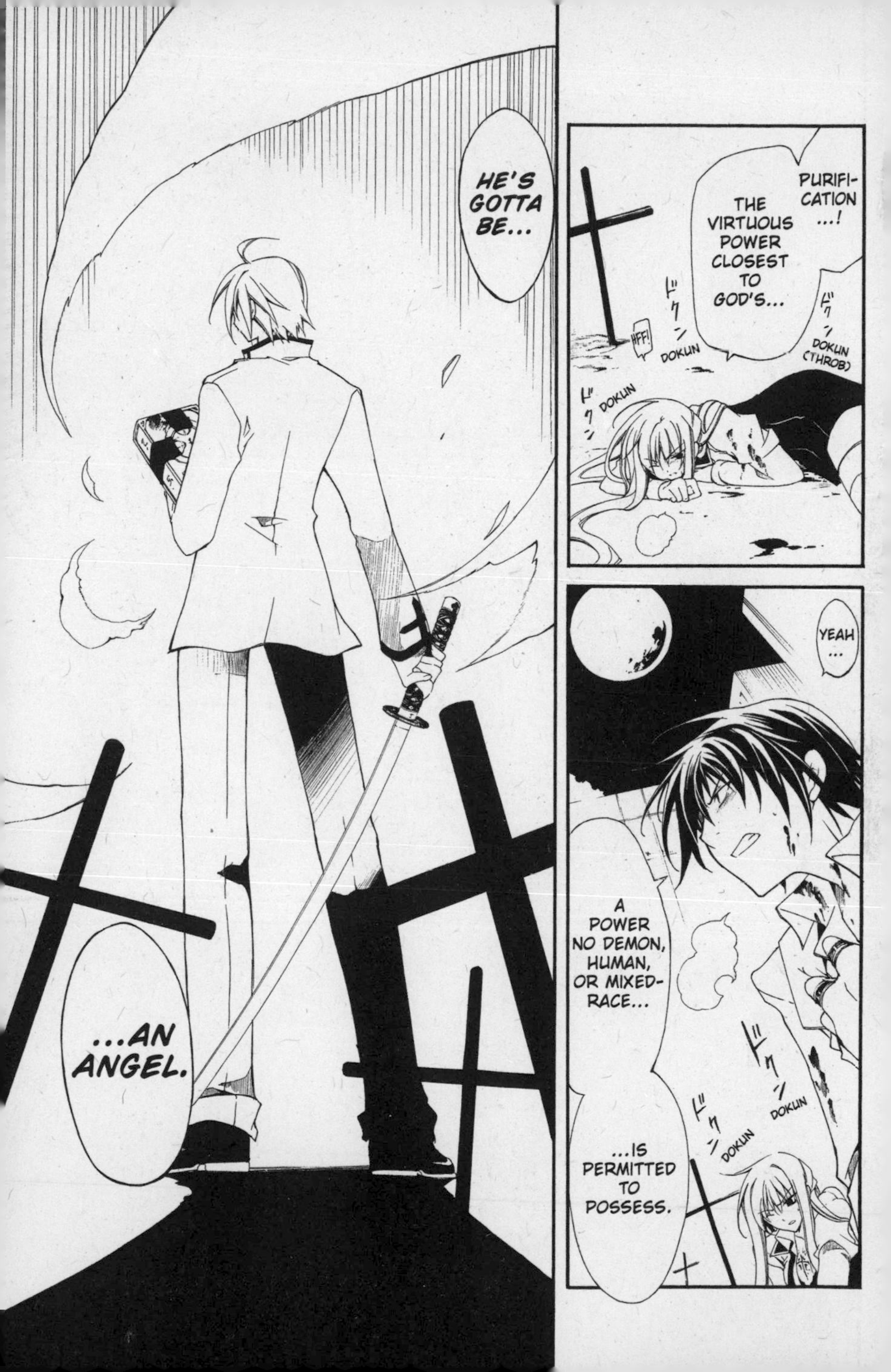
PURIFI-CATION ...!
THE VIRTUOUS POWER CLOSEST TO GOD'S...
ドクン DOKUN (THROB)
HFF!
ドクン DOKUN
ドクン DOKUN
YEAH ...
A POWER NO DEMON, HUMAN, OR MIXED-RACE...
...IS PERMITTED TO POSSESS.
ドクン DOKUN
ドクン DOKUN
HE'S GOTTA BE...
...AN ANGEL.

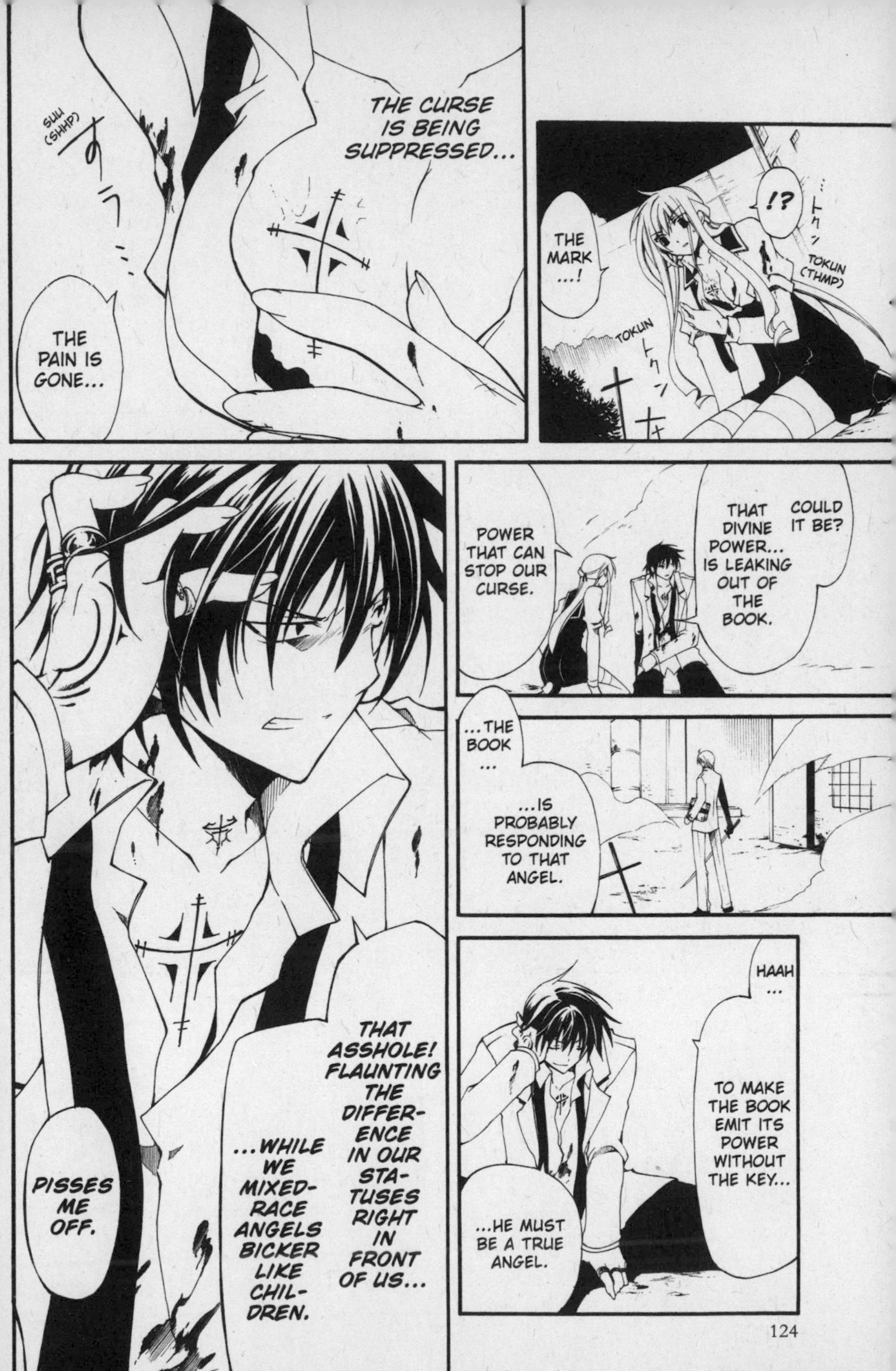

!?
TOKUN (THMP)
THE MARK ...!
TOKUN
THE CURSE IS BEING SUPPRESSED...
SUU (SHHP)
THE PAIN IS GONE...
COULD IT BE?
THAT DIVINE POWER... IS LEAKING OUT OF THE BOOK.
POWER THAT CAN STOP OUR CURSE.
...THE BOOK ...
...IS PROBABLY RESPONDING TO THAT ANGEL.
HAAH ...
TO MAKE THE BOOK EMIT ITS POWER WITHOUT THE KEY...
...HE MUST BE A TRUE ANGEL.
THAT ASSHOLE! FLAUNTING THE DIFFER-ENCE IN OUR STA-TUSES RIGHT IN FRONT OF US...
...WHILE WE MIXED-RACE ANGELS BICKER LIKE CHIL-DREN.
PISSES ME OFF.

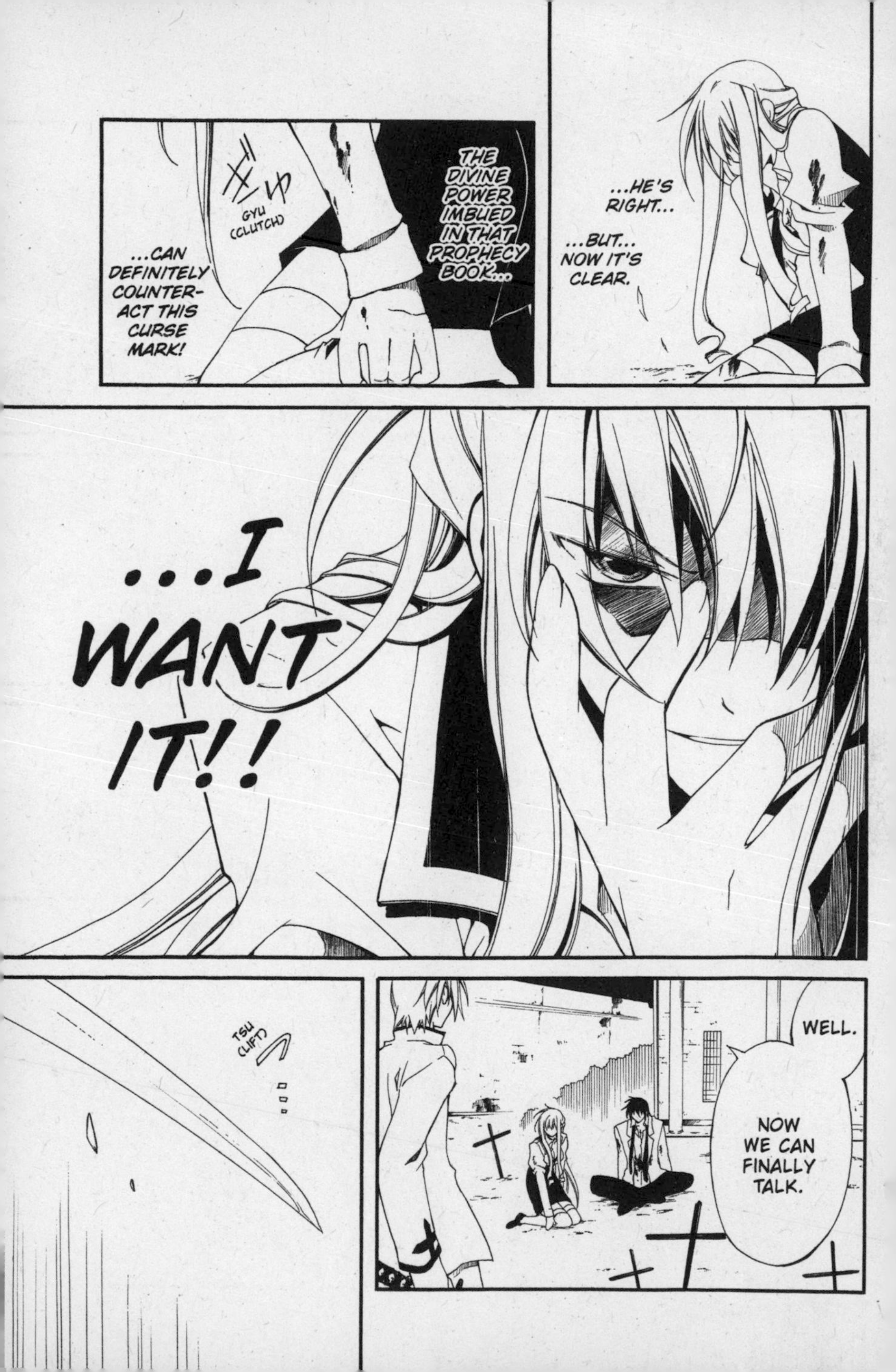
...HE'S RIGHT...
...BUT... NOW IT'S CLEAR.
THE DIVINE POWER IMBUED IN THAT PROPHECY BOOK...
GYU (CLUTCH)
...CAN DEFINITELY COUNTER-ACT THIS CURSE MARK!
...I WANT IT!!
WELL.
NOW WE CAN FINALLY TALK.
TSU (LIFT)

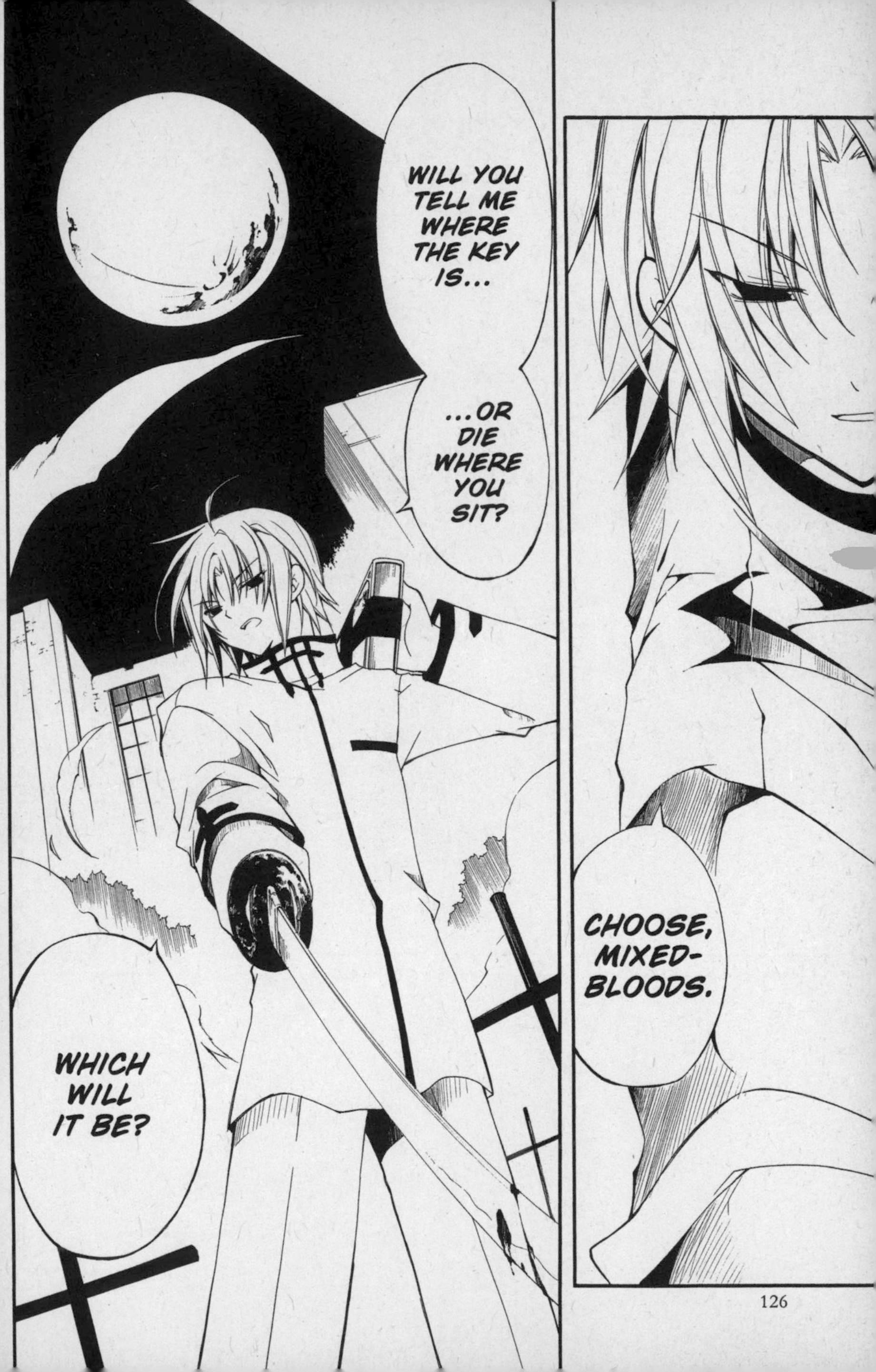
CHOOSE, MIXED-BLOODS.
WILL YOU TELL ME WHERE THE KEY IS...
...OR DIE WHERE YOU SIT?
WHICH WILL IT BE?

BLOODY CROSS

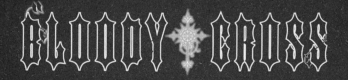

BLOODY CROSS

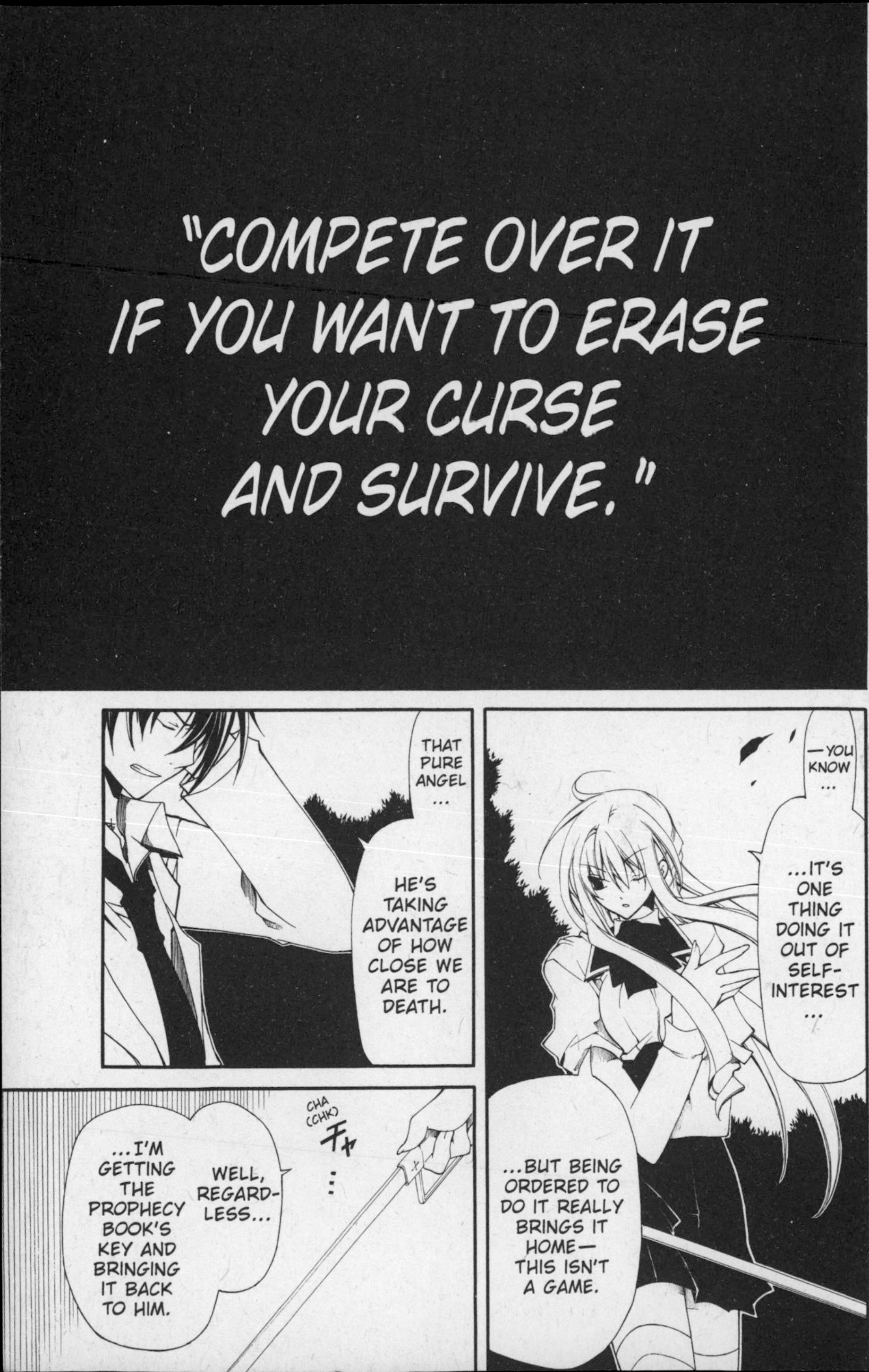
"COMPETE OVER IT IF YOU WANT TO ERASE YOUR CURSE AND SURVIVE."
—YOU KNOW ...
...IT'S ONE THING DOING IT OUT OF SELF-INTEREST ...
...BUT BEING ORDERED TO DO IT REALLY BRINGS IT HOME— THIS ISN'T A GAME.
THAT PURE ANGEL ...
HE'S TAKING ADVANTAGE OF HOW CLOSE WE ARE TO DEATH.
CHA (CHK)
チャ
...
WELL, REGARDLESS...
...I'M GETTING THE PROPHECY BOOK'S KEY AND BRINGING IT BACK TO HIM.

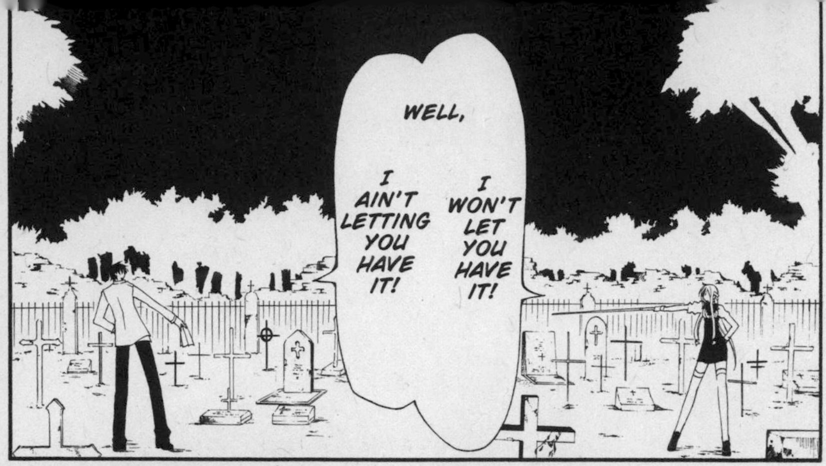
WELL,
I WON'T LET YOU HAVE IT!
I AIN'T LETTING YOU HAVE IT!

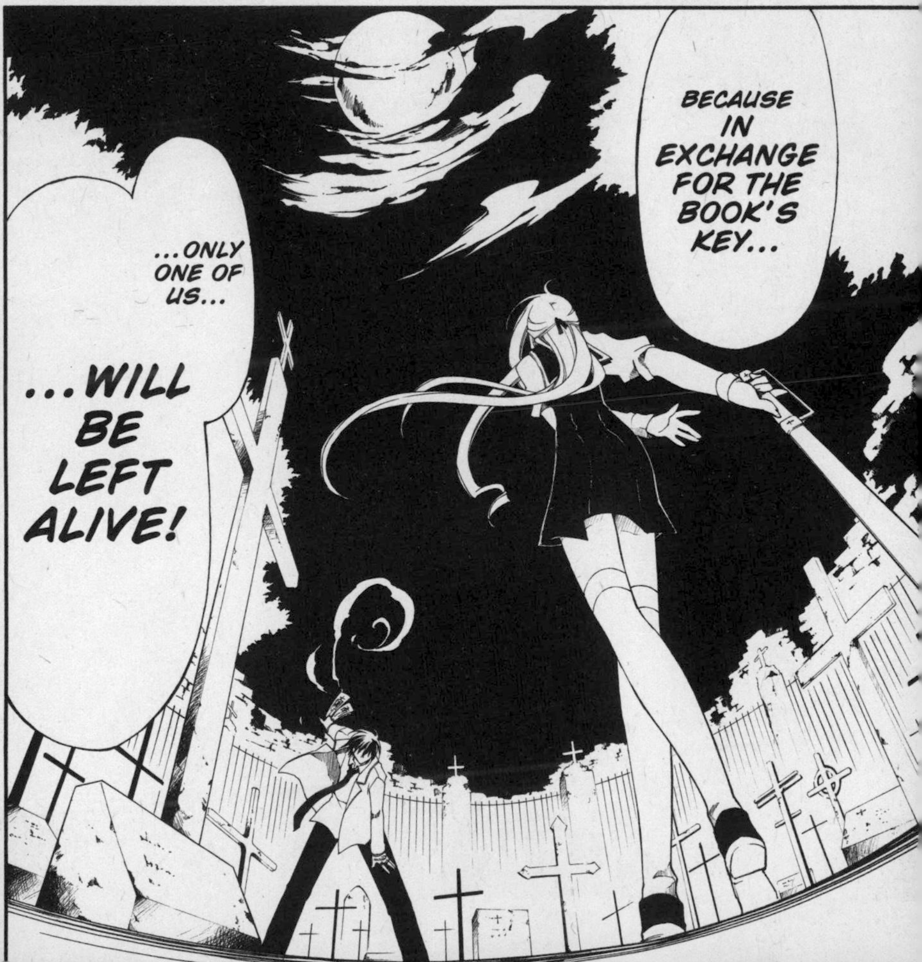
BECAUSE IN EXCHANGE FOR THE BOOK'S KEY...
...ONLY ONE OF US...
...WILL BE LEFT ALIVE!

Chapter 2
The Prophecy Book's Key

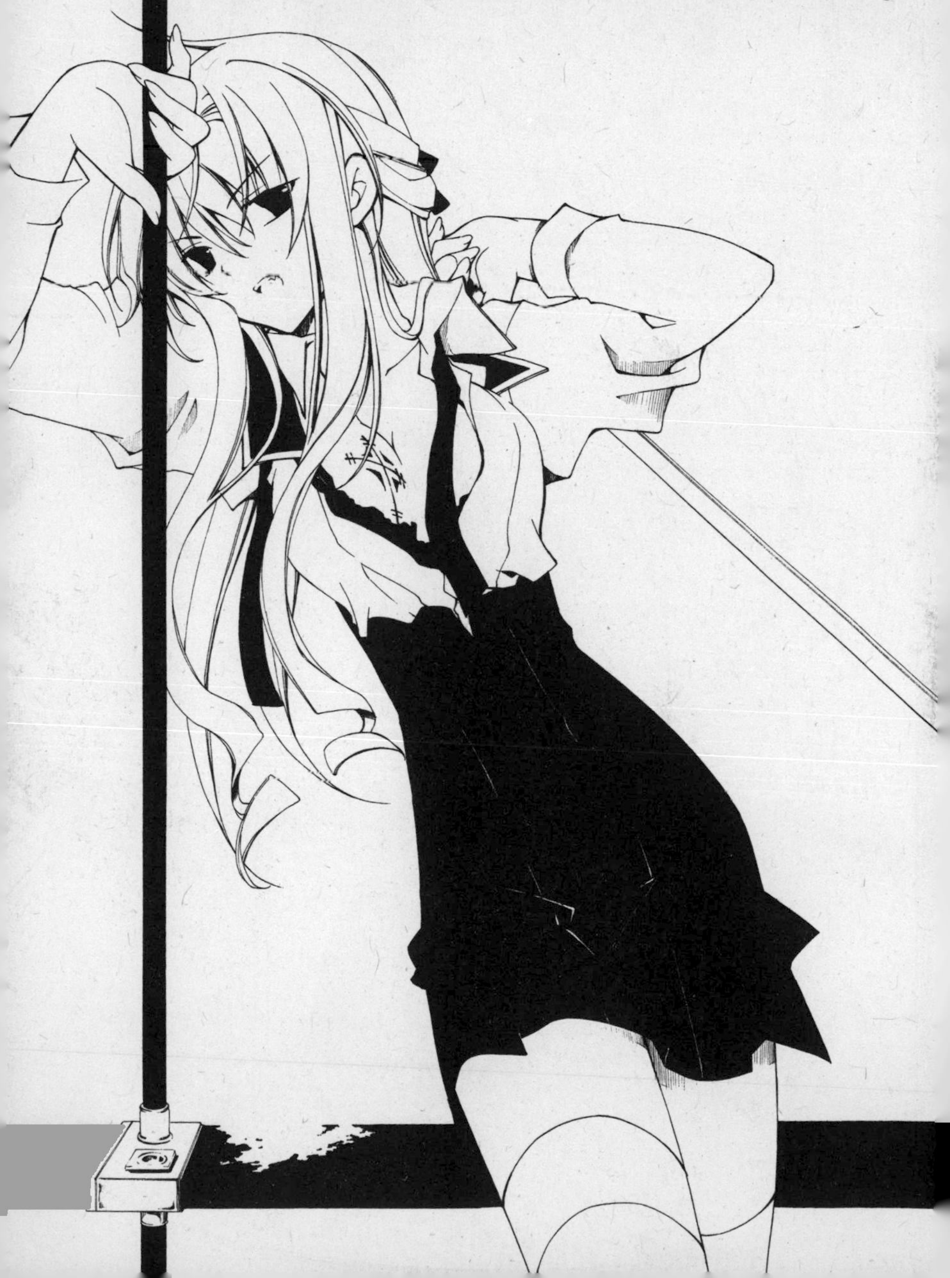

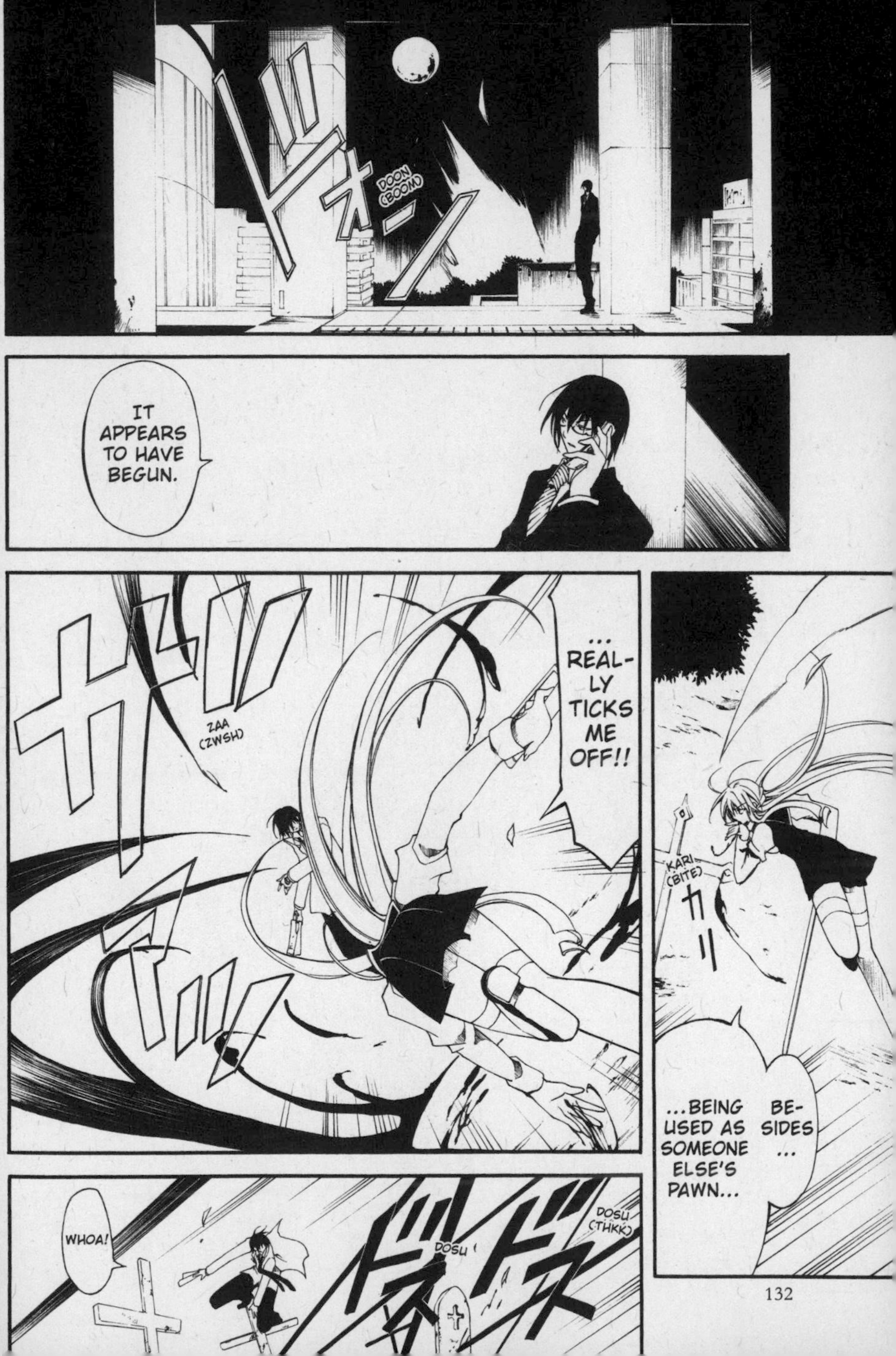
DOON (BOOM)
IT APPEARS TO HAVE BEGUN.
KARI (BITE)
BESIDES...
...BEING USED AS SOMEONE ELSE'S PAWN...
...REALLY TICKS ME OFF!!
ZAA (ZWSH)
DOSU (THKK)
DOSU
WHOA!

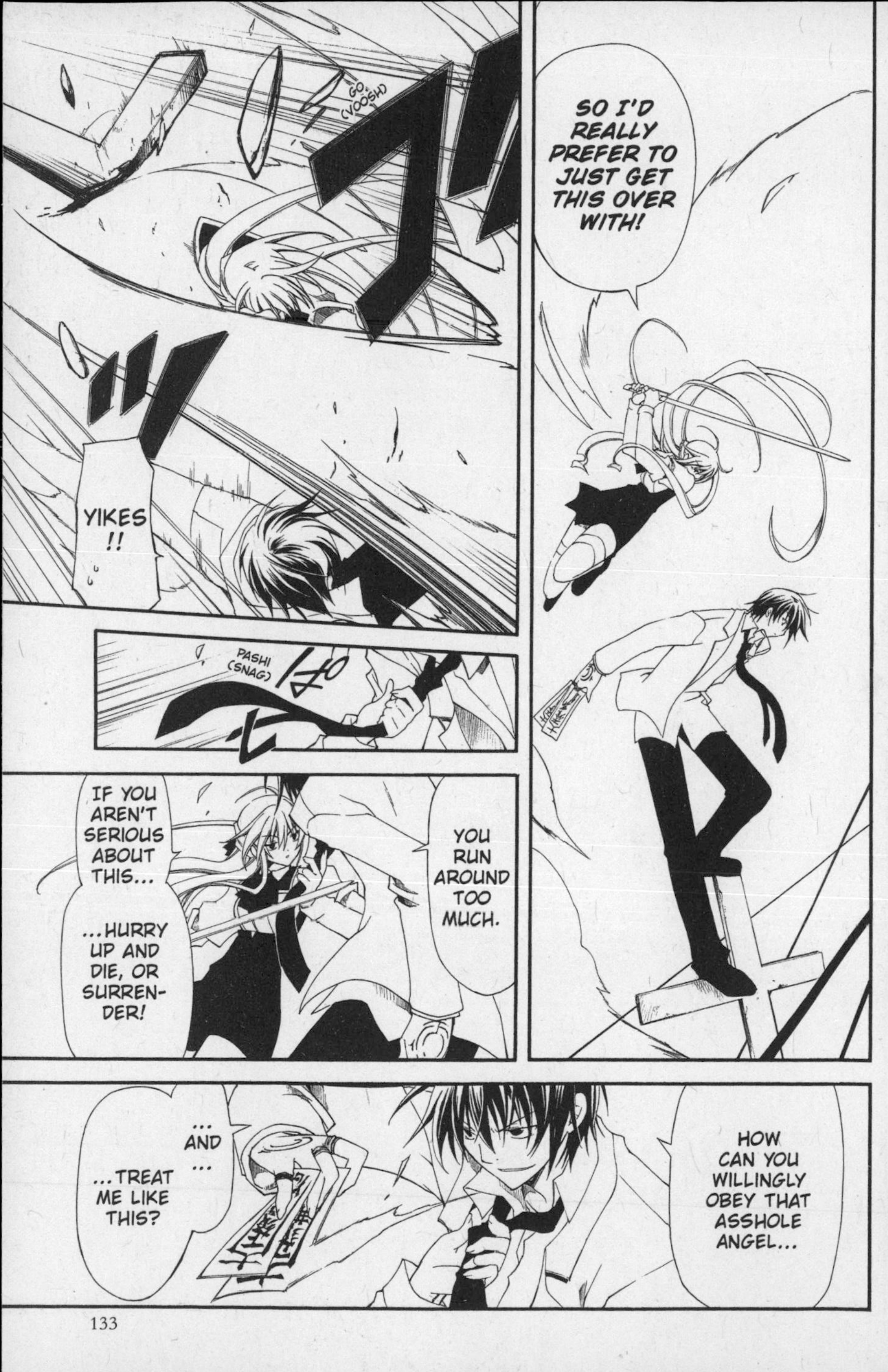
SO I'D REALLY PREFER TO JUST GET THIS OVER WITH!
GO (VOOSH)
YIKES !!
PASHI (SNAG)
YOU RUN AROUND TOO MUCH.
IF YOU AREN'T SERIOUS ABOUT THIS...
...HURRY UP AND DIE, OR SURRENDER!
HOW CAN YOU WILLINGLY OBEY THAT ASSHOLE ANGEL...
... AND ...
...TREAT ME LIKE THIS?

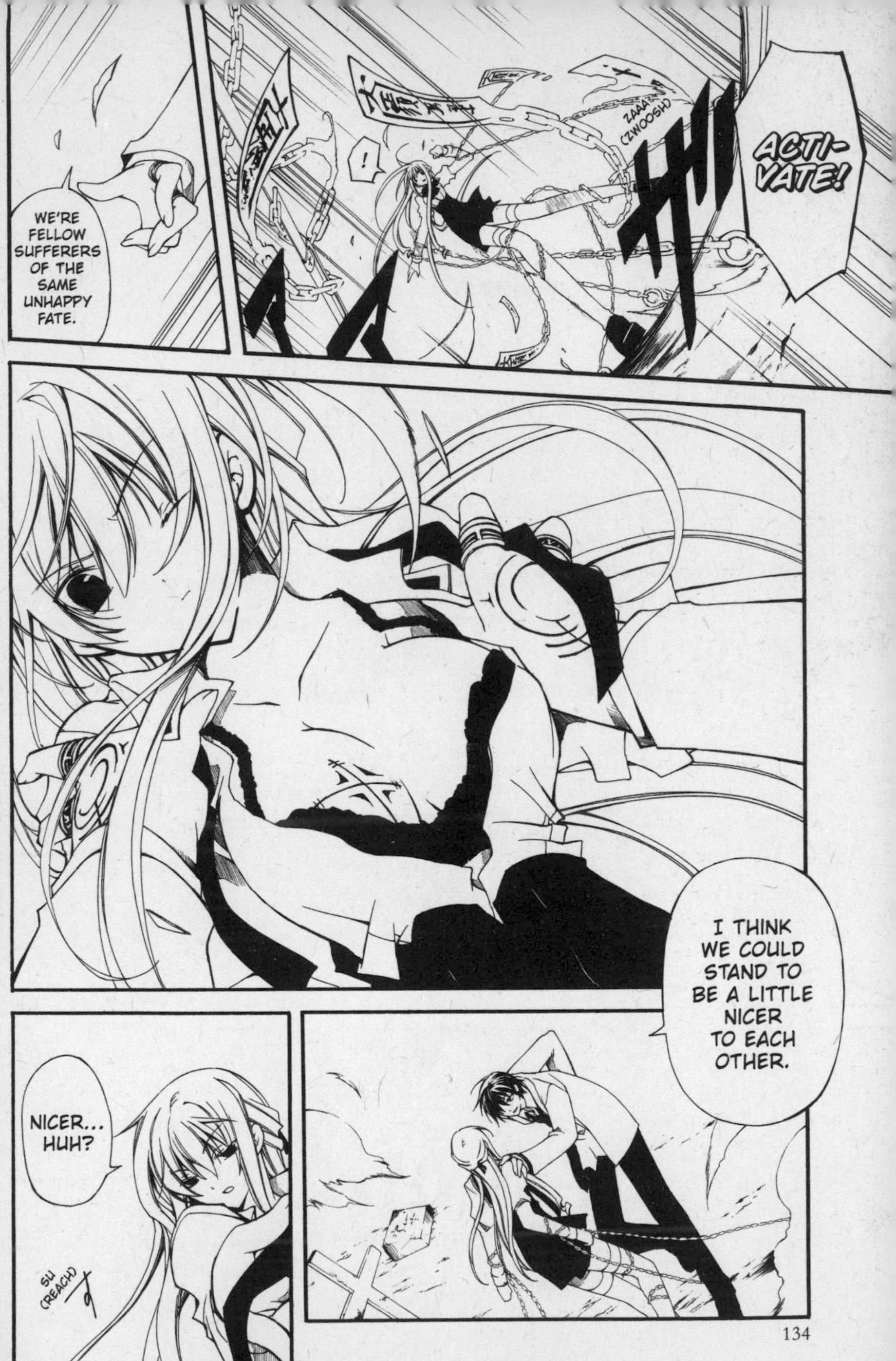
ACTI-VATE!
ZAAAA (ZWOOSH)
!
WE'RE FELLOW SUFFERERS OF THE SAME UNHAPPY FATE.
I THINK WE COULD STAND TO BE A LITTLE NICER TO EACH OTHER.
NICER... HUH?
SU (REACH)

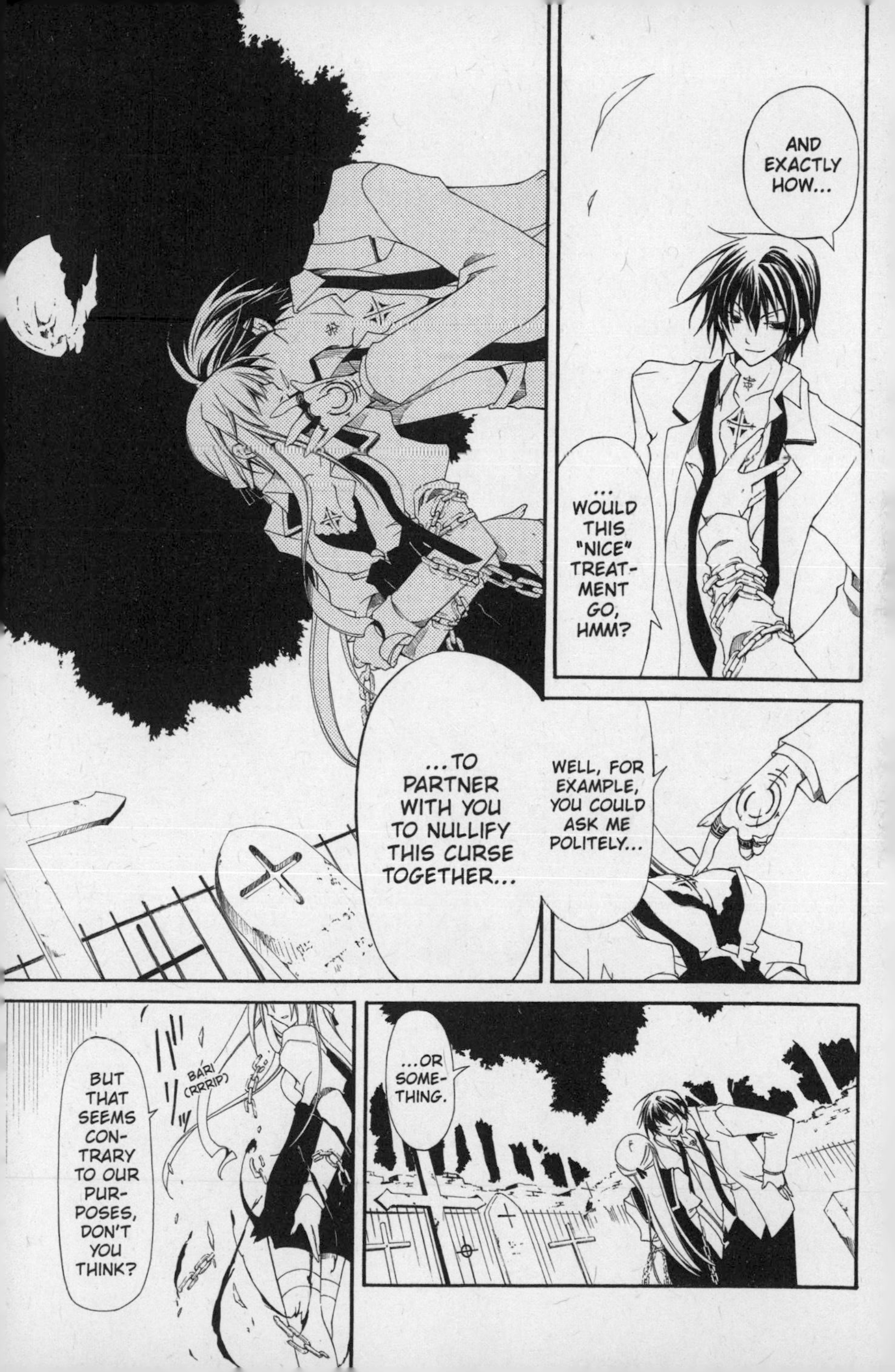
AND EXACTLY HOW...
...WOULD THIS "NICE" TREATMENT GO, HMM?
WELL, FOR EXAMPLE, YOU COULD ASK ME POLITELY...
...TO PARTNER WITH YOU TO NULLIFY THIS CURSE TOGETHER...
...OR SOMETHING.
BARI (RRRIP)
BUT THAT SEEMS CONTRARY TO OUR PURPOSES, DON'T YOU THINK?

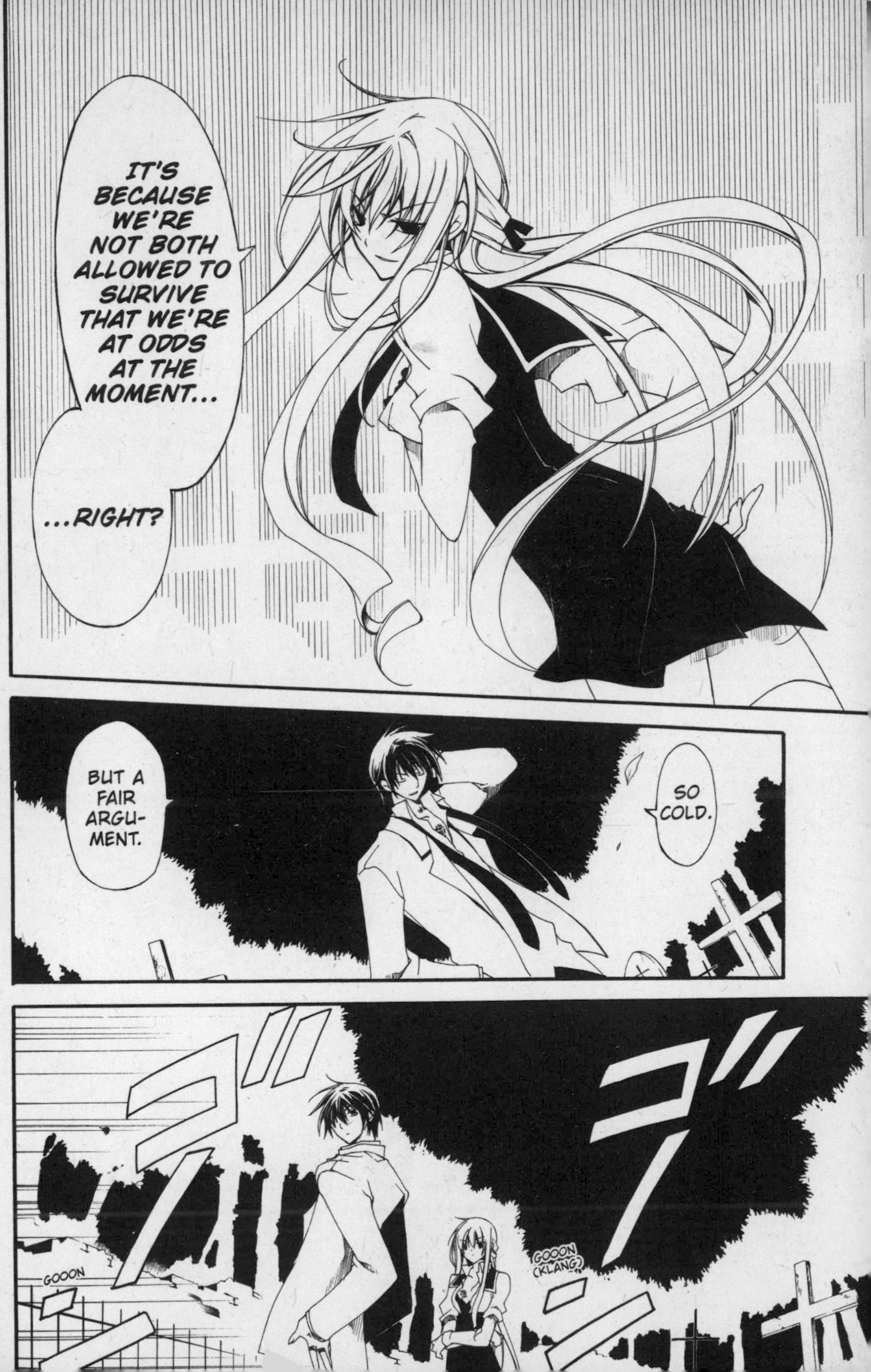
IT'S BECAUSE WE'RE NOT BOTH ALLOWED TO SURVIVE THAT WE'RE AT ODDS AT THE MOMENT...
...RIGHT?
SO COLD.
BUT A FAIR ARGU-MENT.
GOOON (KLANG)
GOOON

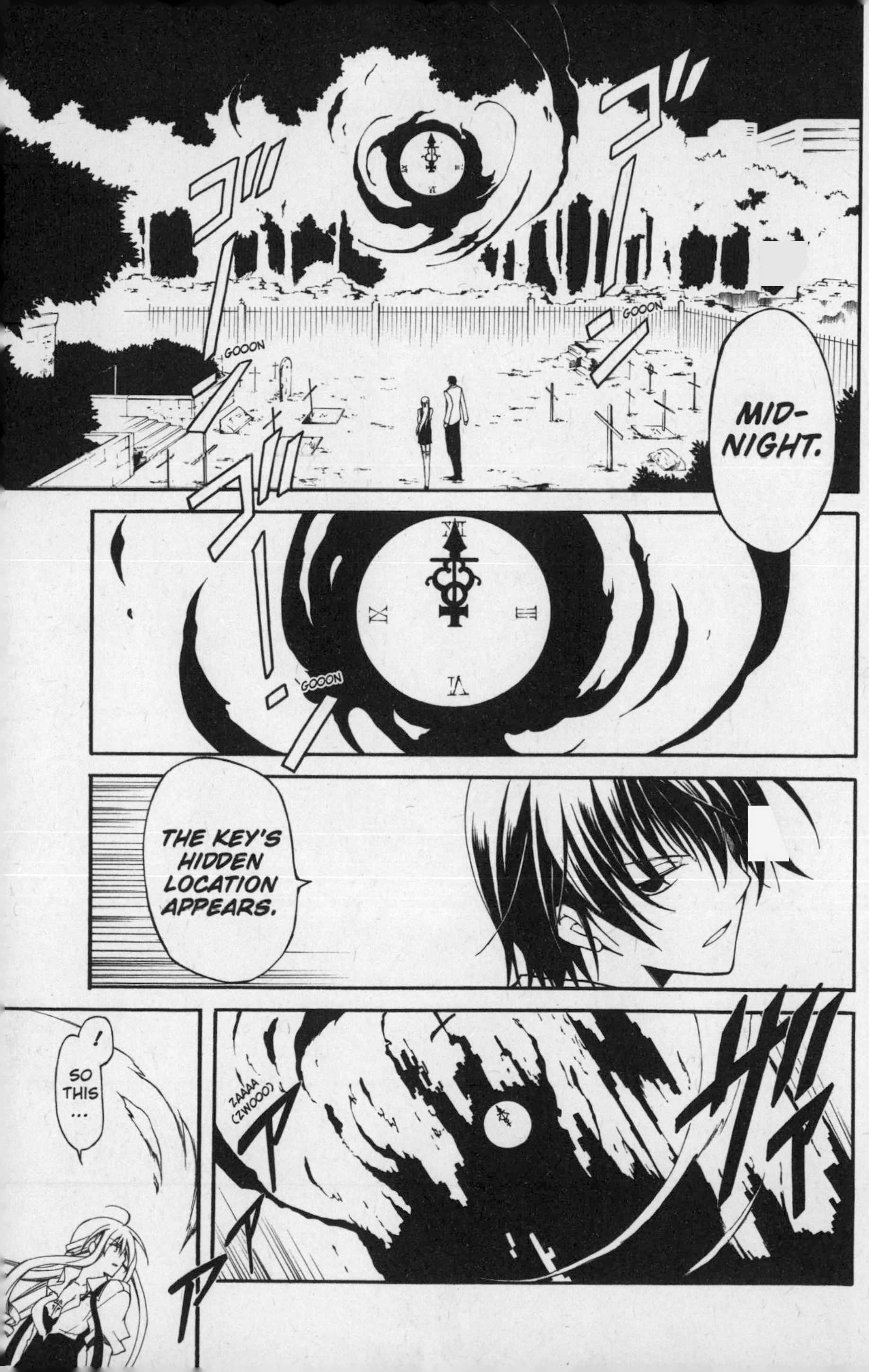
GOOON
GOOON
MID-NIGHT.
GOOON
THE KEY'S HIDDEN LOCATION APPEARS.
ZAAAA (ZWOOO)
!
SO THIS ...

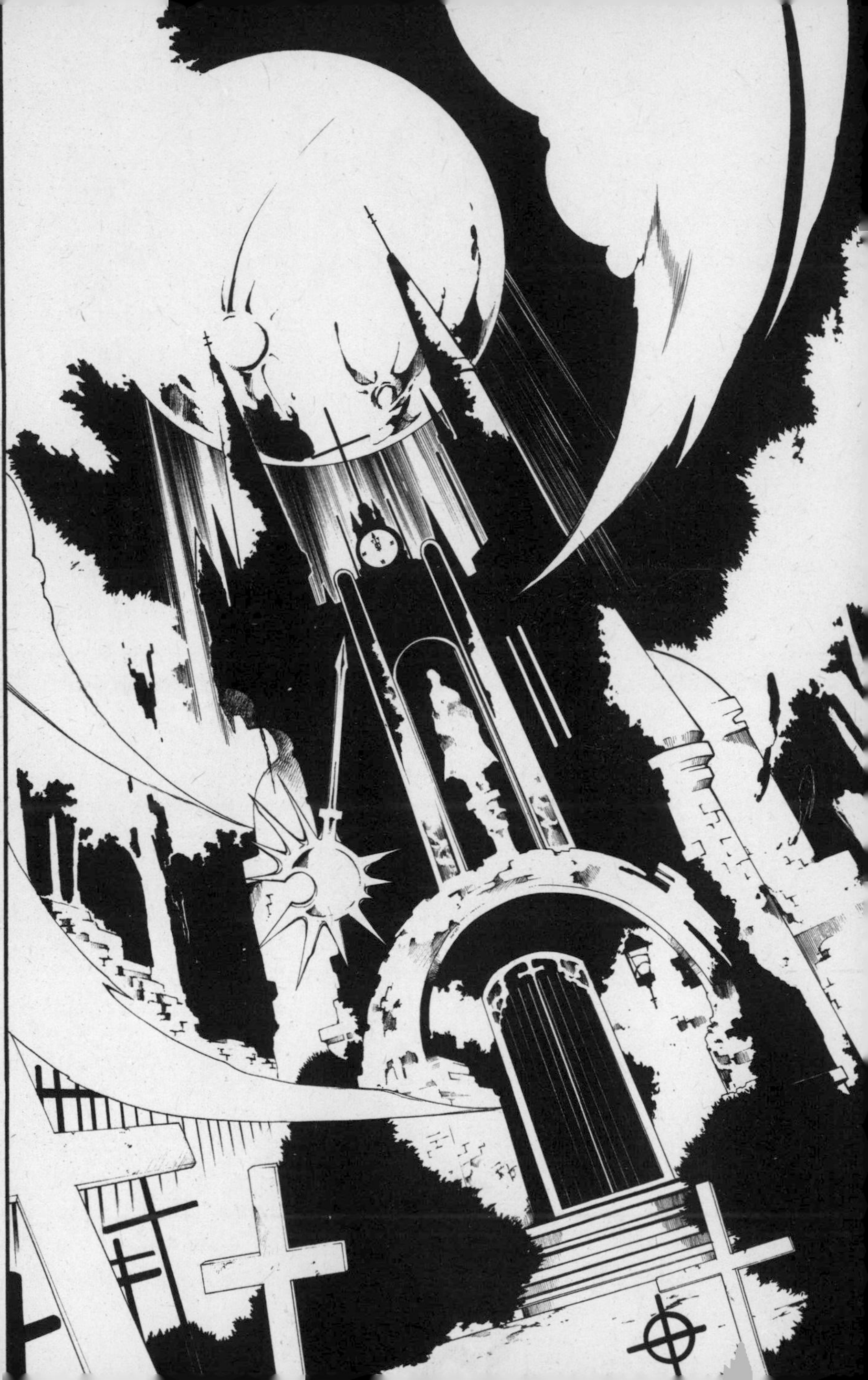

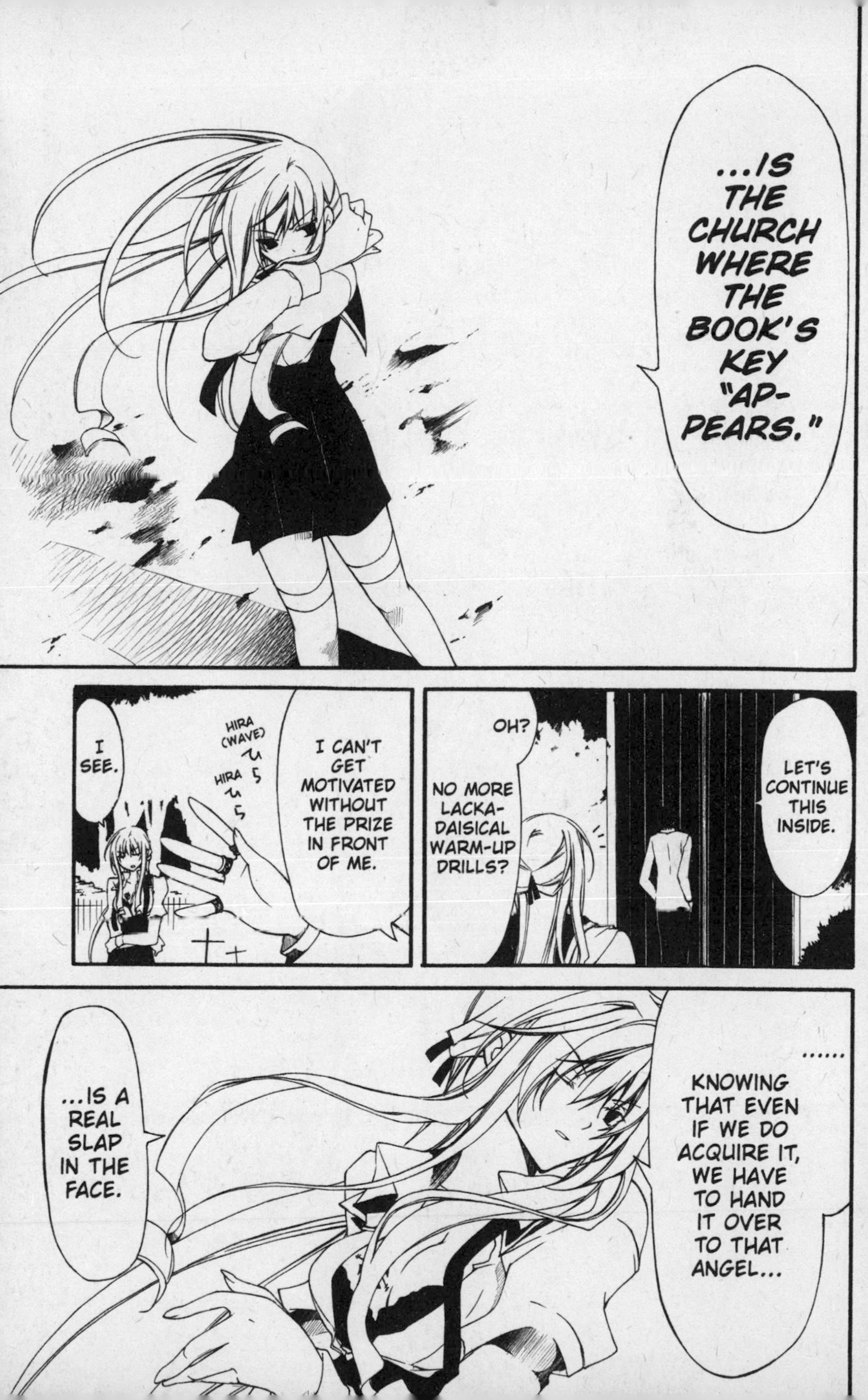
...IS THE CHURCH WHERE THE BOOK'S KEY "AP-PEARS."
LET'S CONTINUE THIS INSIDE.
OH?
NO MORE LACKA-DAISICAL WARM-UP DRILLS?
I CAN'T GET MOTIVATED WITHOUT THE PRIZE IN FRONT OF ME.
HIRA (WAVE)
HIRA
I SEE.
......
KNOWING THAT EVEN IF WE DO ACQUIRE IT, WE HAVE TO HAND IT OVER TO THAT ANGEL...
...IS A REAL SLAP IN THE FACE.

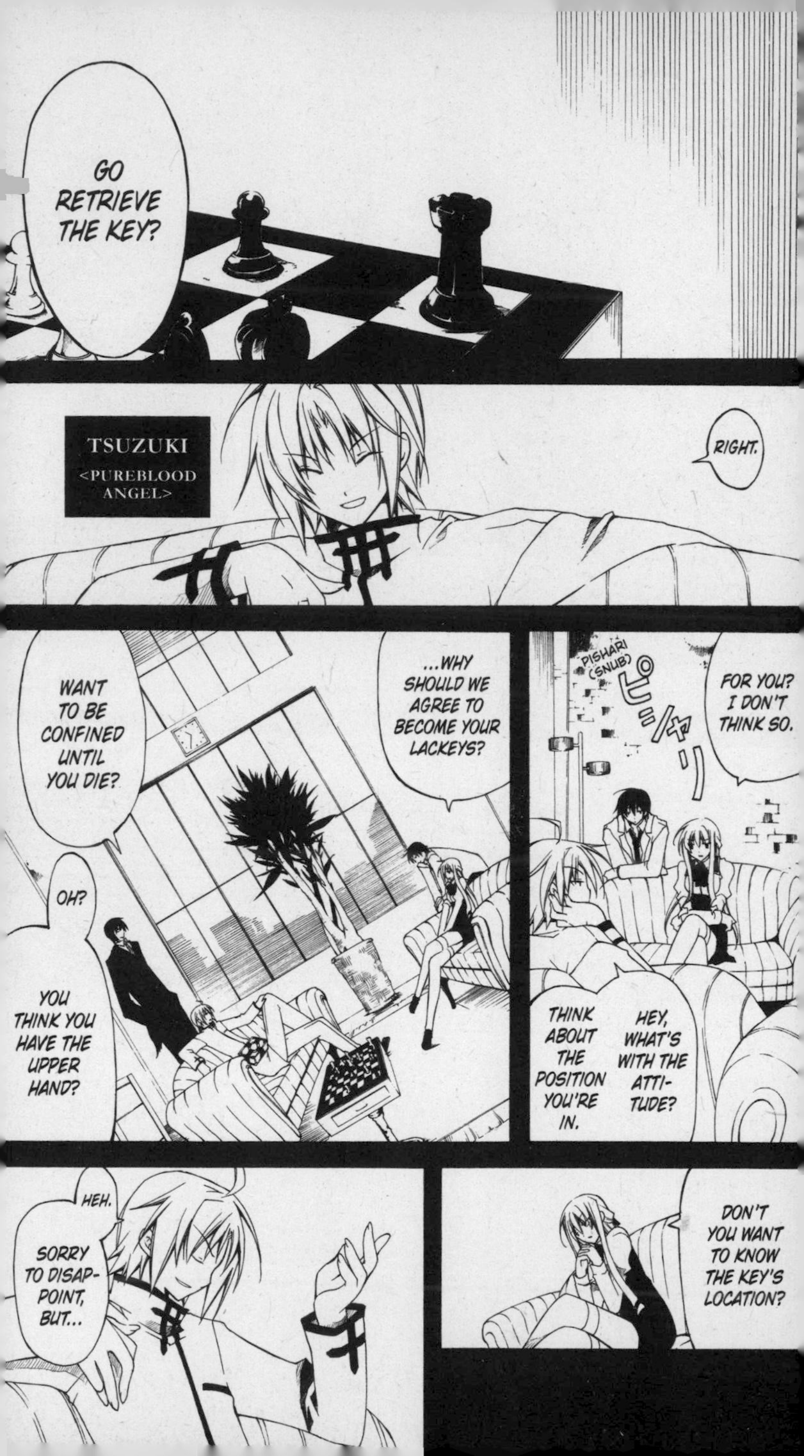
GO RETRIEVE THE KEY?
RIGHT.
TSUZUKI
<PUREBLOOD ANGEL>
FOR YOU? I DON'T THINK SO.
PISHARI (SNUB)
ピシャリ
HEY, WHAT'S WITH THE ATTI-TUDE?
THINK ABOUT THE POSITION YOU'RE IN.
...WHY SHOULD WE AGREE TO BECOME YOUR LACKEYS?
WANT TO BE CONFINED UNTIL YOU DIE?
OH?
YOU THINK YOU HAVE THE UPPER HAND?
DON'T YOU WANT TO KNOW THE KEY'S LOCATION?
HEH.
SORRY TO DISAP-POINT, BUT...

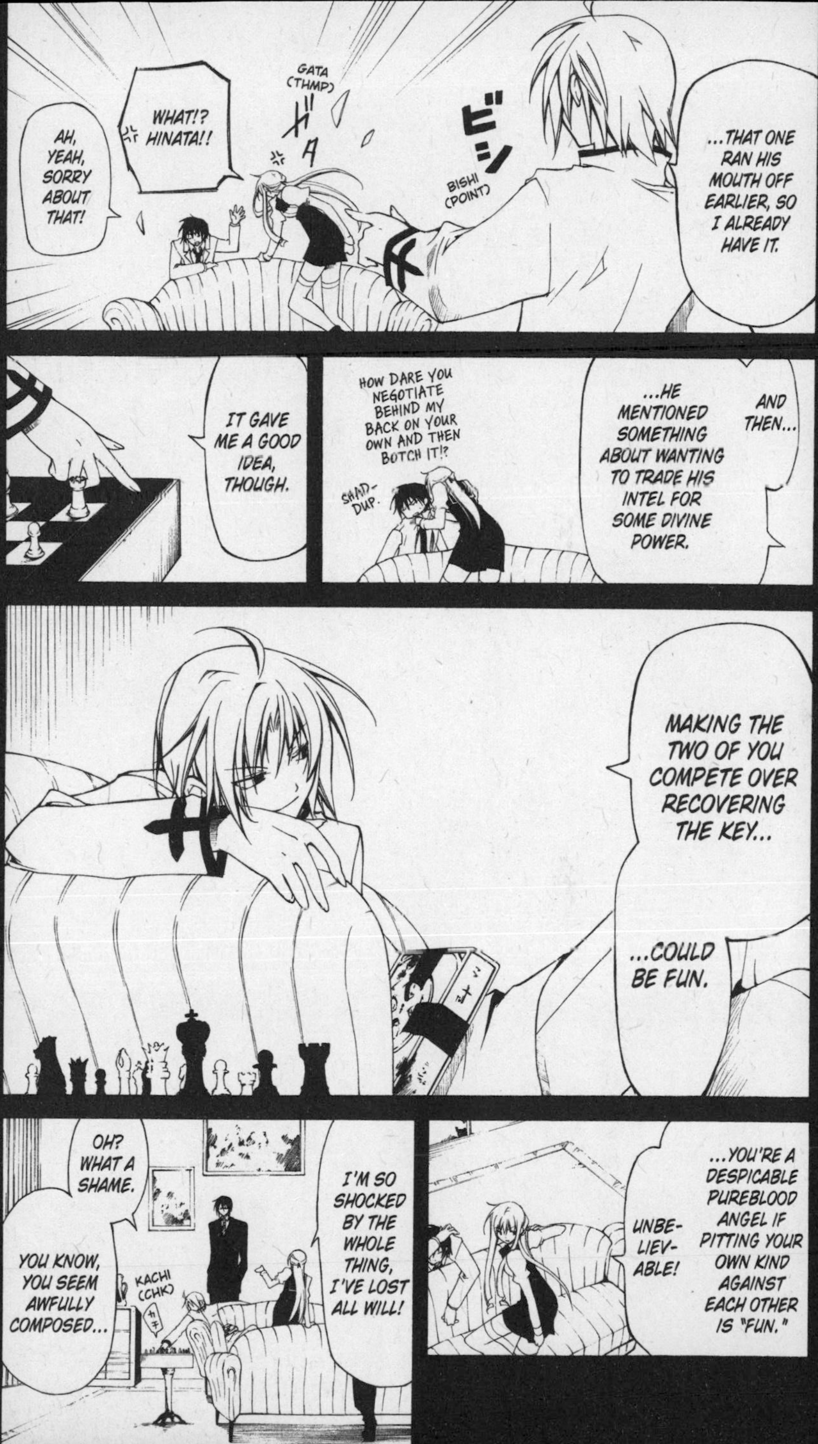
...THAT ONE RAN HIS MOUTH OFF EARLIER, SO I ALREADY HAVE IT.
ビシ
BISHI (POINT)
ガタ
GATA (THMP)
WHAT!? HINATA!!
AH, YEAH, SORRY ABOUT THAT!
AND THEN...
...HE MENTIONED SOMETHING ABOUT WANTING TO TRADE HIS INTEL FOR SOME DIVINE POWER.
HOW DARE YOU NEGOTIATE BEHIND MY BACK ON YOUR OWN AND THEN BOTCH IT!?
SHAD-DUP.
IT GAVE ME A GOOD IDEA, THOUGH.
MAKING THE TWO OF YOU COMPETE OVER RECOVERING THE KEY...
...COULD BE FUN.
...YOU'RE A DESPICABLE PUREBLOOD ANGEL IF PITTING YOUR OWN KIND AGAINST EACH OTHER IS "FUN."
UNBE-LIEV-ABLE!
I'M SO SHOCKED BY THE WHOLE THING, I'VE LOST ALL WILL!
OH? WHAT A SHAME.
カチ
KACHI (CHK)
YOU KNOW, YOU SEEM AWFULLY COMPOSED...

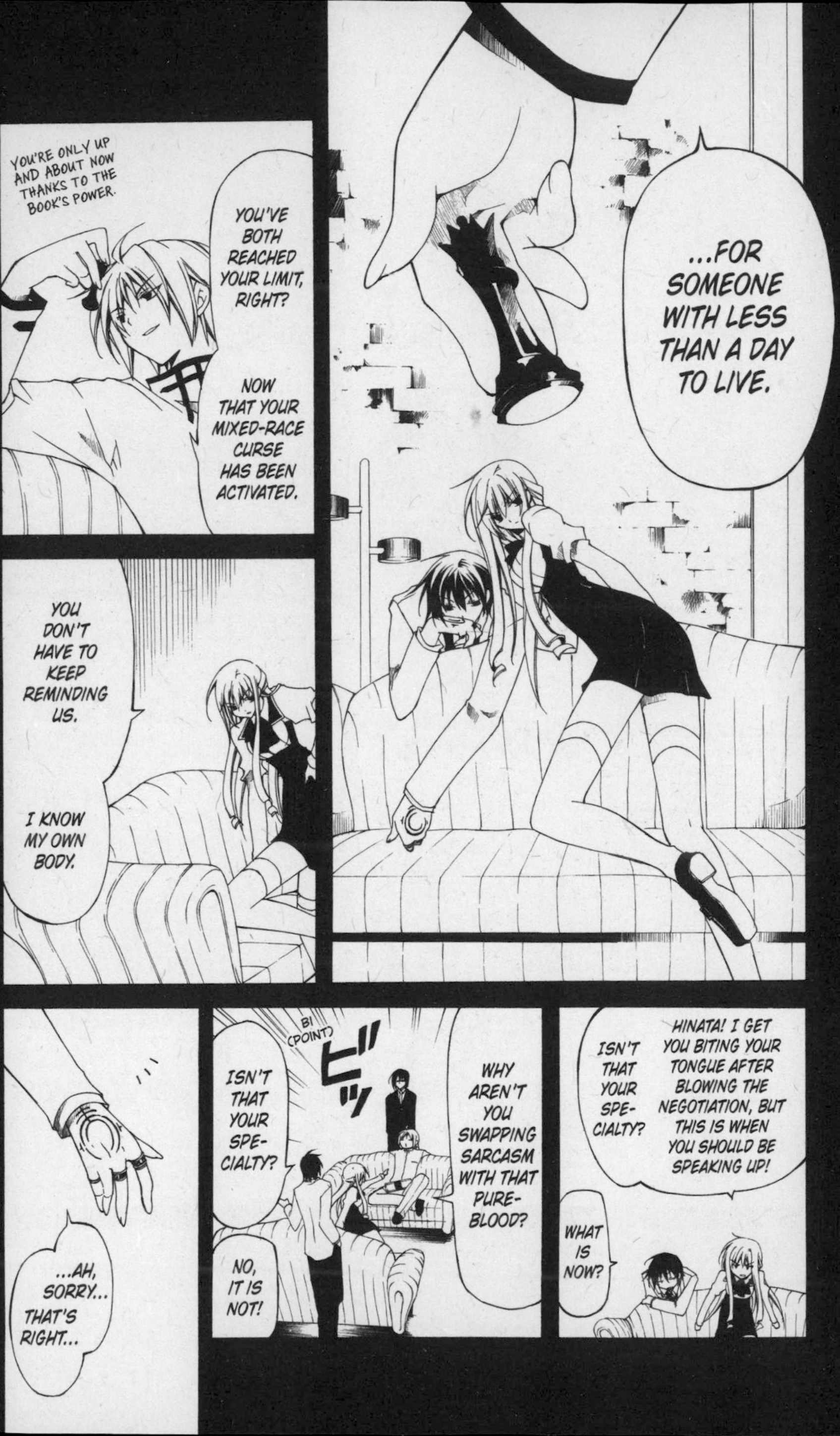
...FOR SOMEONE WITH LESS THAN A DAY TO LIVE.
YOU'VE BOTH REACHED YOUR LIMIT, RIGHT?
YOU'RE ONLY UP AND ABOUT NOW THANKS TO THE BOOK'S POWER.
NOW THAT YOUR MIXED-RACE CURSE HAS BEEN ACTIVATED.
YOU DON'T HAVE TO KEEP REMINDING US.
I KNOW MY OWN BODY.
HINATA! I GET YOU BITING YOUR TONGUE AFTER BLOWING THE NEGOTIATION, BUT THIS IS WHEN YOU SHOULD BE SPEAKING UP!
ISN'T THAT YOUR SPE-CIALTY?
WHAT IS NOW?
WHY AREN'T YOU SWAPPING SARCASM WITH THAT PURE-BLOOD?
BI (POINT)
ISN'T THAT YOUR SPE-CIALTY?
NO, IT IS NOT!
...AH, SORRY... THAT'S RIGHT...

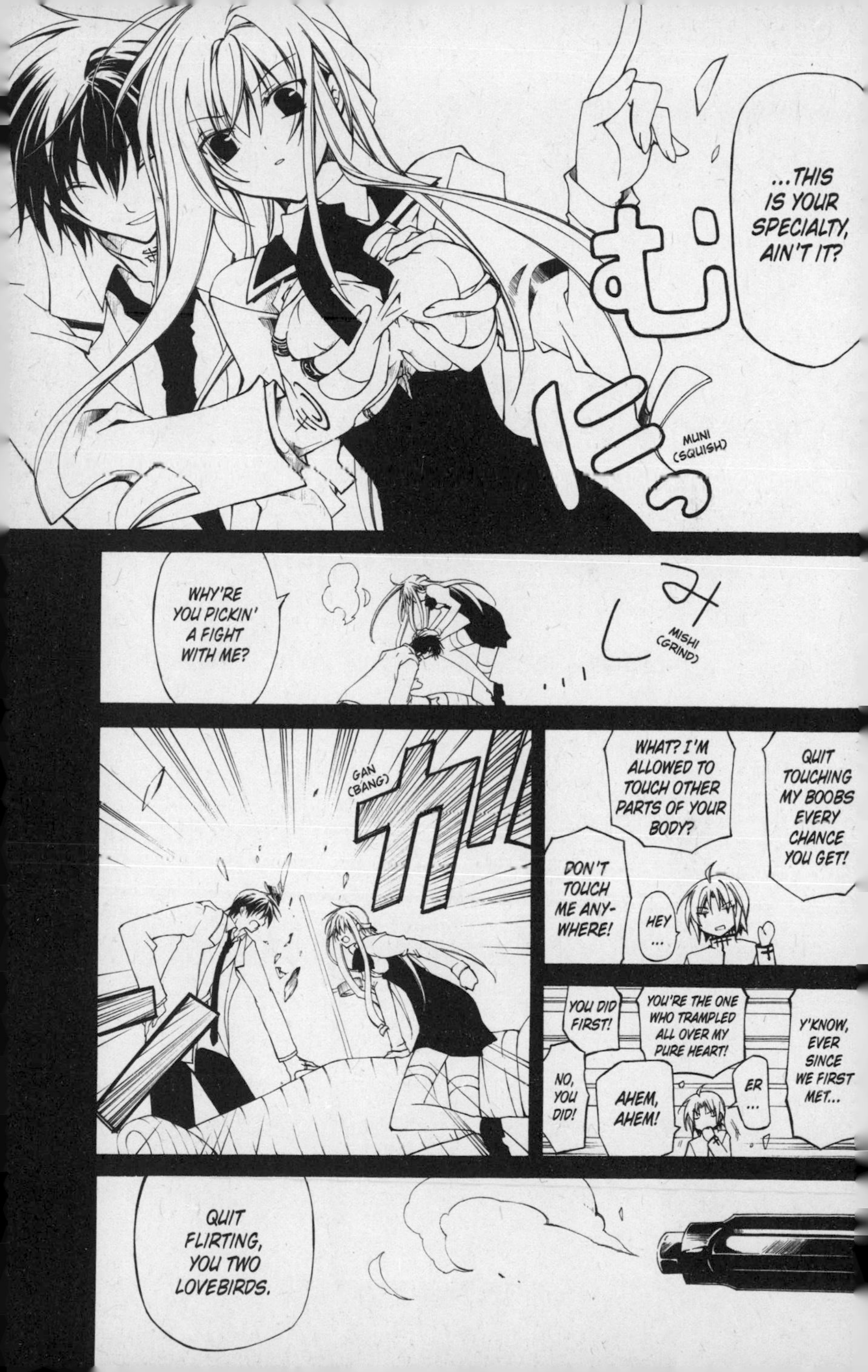
...THIS IS YOUR SPECIALTY, AIN'T IT?
むにっ
MUNI (SQUISH)
みし
MISHI (GRIND)
WHY'RE YOU PICKIN' A FIGHT WITH ME?
QUIT TOUCHING MY BOOBS EVERY CHANCE YOU GET!
WHAT? I'M ALLOWED TO TOUCH OTHER PARTS OF YOUR BODY?
HEY ...
DON'T TOUCH ME ANY-WHERE!
Y'KNOW, EVER SINCE WE FIRST MET...
ER ...
YOU'RE THE ONE WHO TRAMPLED ALL OVER MY PURE HEART!
YOU DID FIRST!
AHEM, AHEM!
NO, YOU DID!
GAN (BANG)
QUIT FLIRTING, YOU TWO LOVEBIRDS.

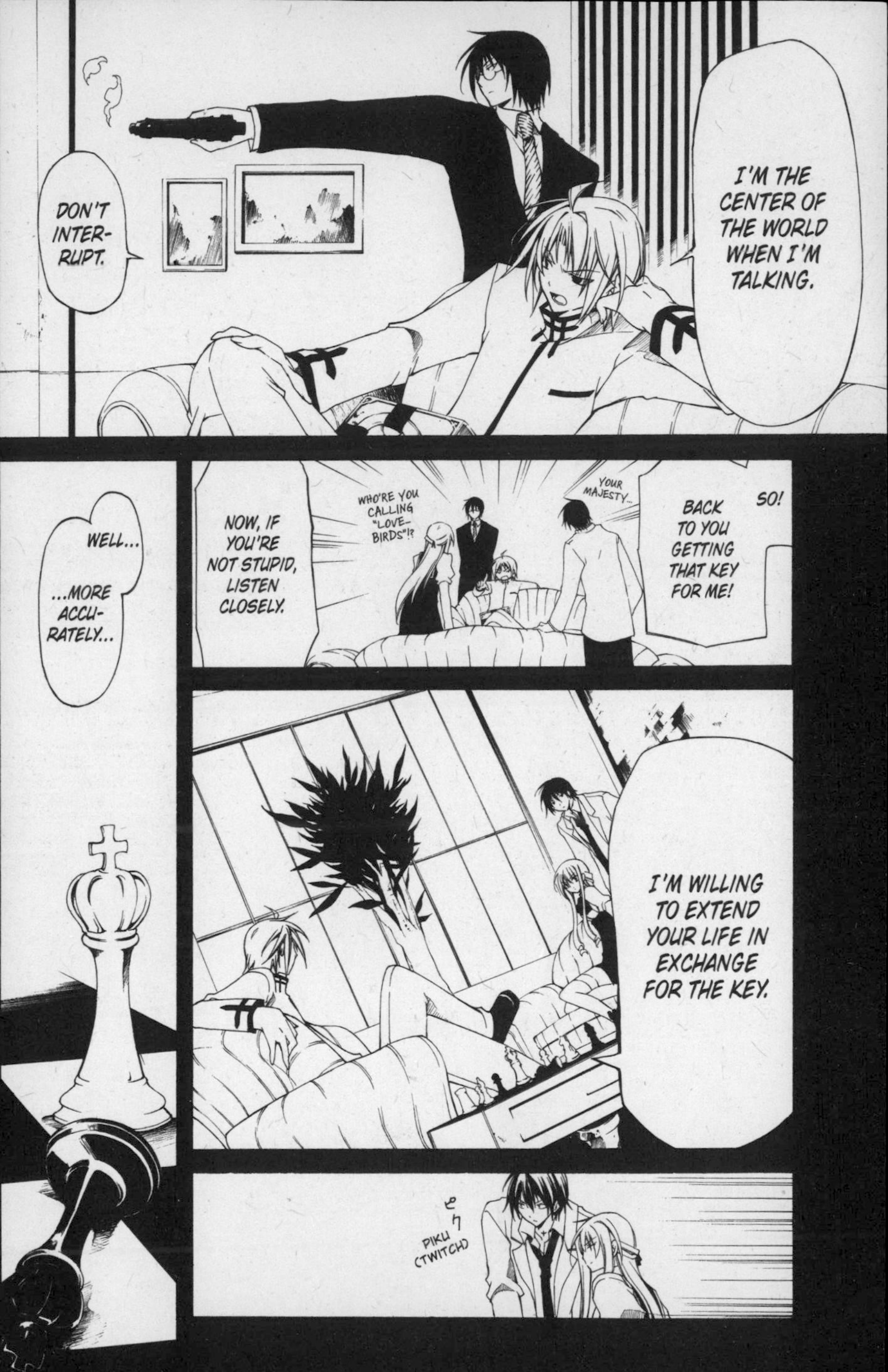
I'M THE CENTER OF THE WORLD WHEN I'M TALKING.
DON'T INTER-RUPT.
SO!
BACK TO YOU GETTING THAT KEY FOR ME!
YOUR MAJESTY...
WHO'RE YOU CALLING "LOVE-BIRDS"!?
NOW, IF YOU'RE NOT STUPID, LISTEN CLOSELY.
I'M WILLING TO EXTEND YOUR LIFE IN EXCHANGE FOR THE KEY.
ピク
PIKU (TWITCH)
WELL...
...MORE ACCURATELY...

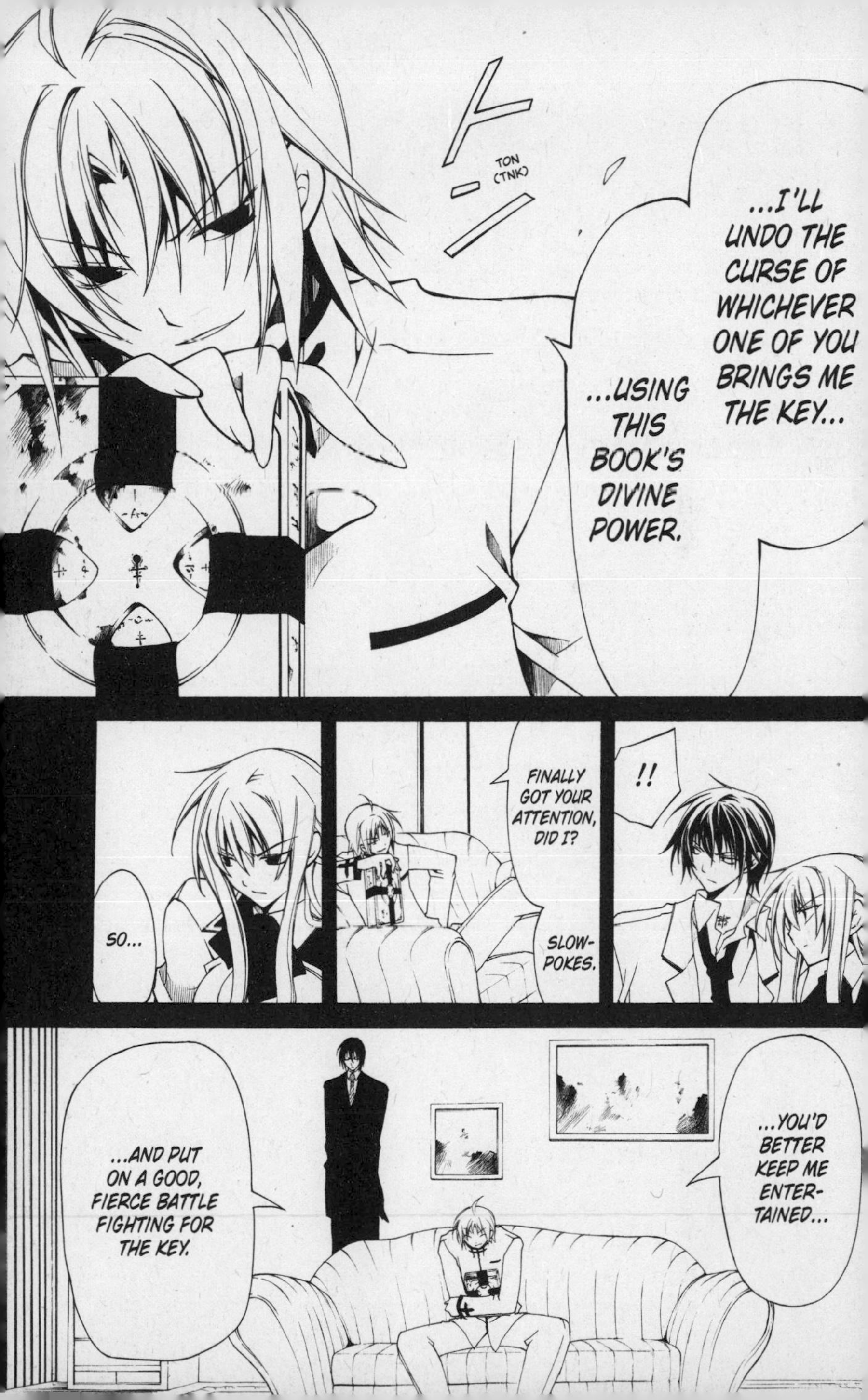
...I'LL UNDO THE CURSE OF WHICHEVER ONE OF YOU BRINGS ME THE KEY...
TON (TNK)
...USING THIS BOOK'S DIVINE POWER.
!!
FINALLY GOT YOUR ATTENTION, DID I?
SLOW-POKES.
SO...
...YOU'D BETTER KEEP ME ENTER-TAINED...
...AND PUT ON A GOOD, FIERCE BATTLE FIGHTING FOR THE KEY.

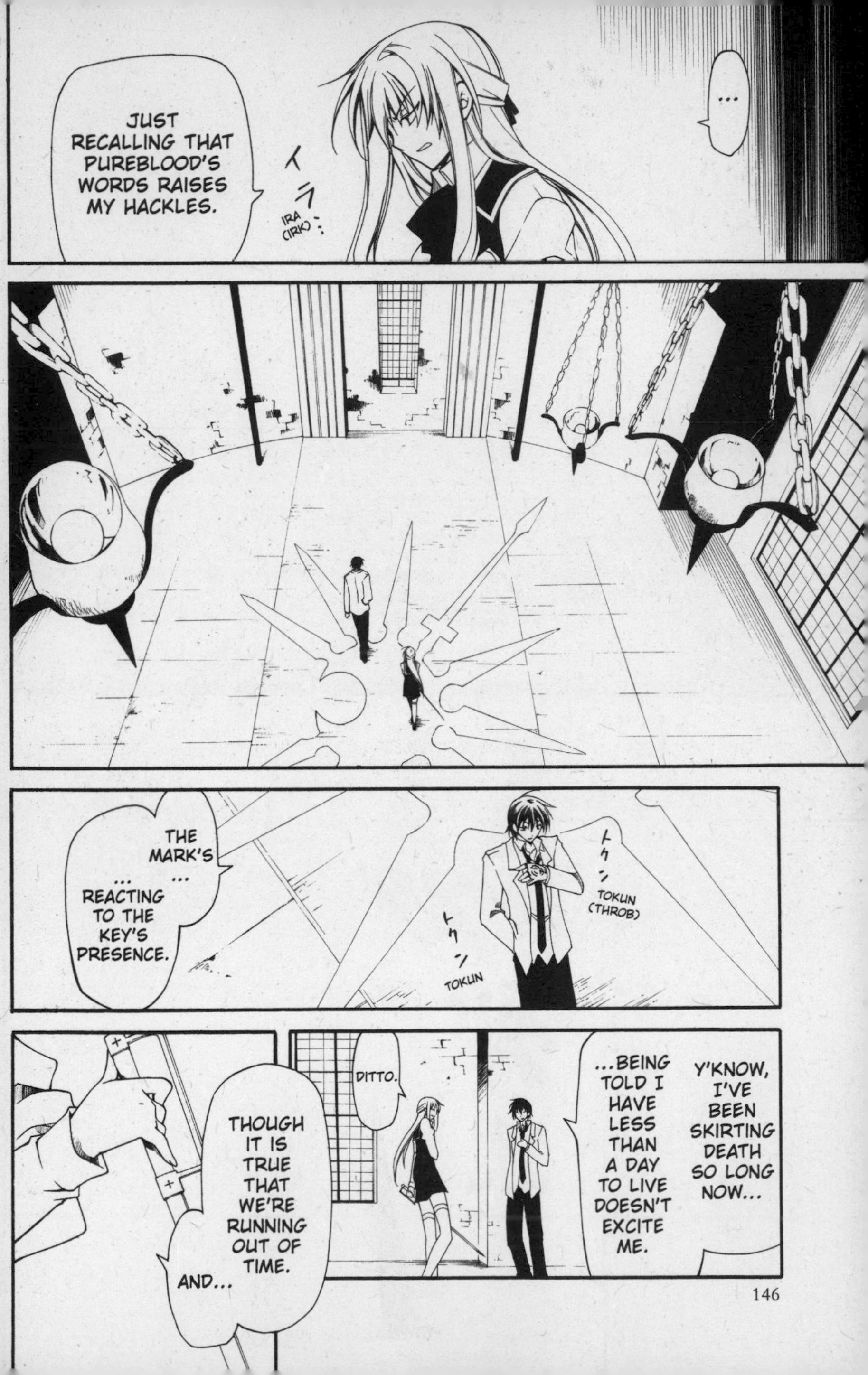
...
JUST RECALLING THAT PUREBLOOD'S WORDS RAISES MY HACKLES.
IRA (IRK)
TOKUN (THROB)
TOKUN
THE MARK'S ... REACTING TO THE KEY'S PRESENCE.
Y'KNOW, I'VE BEEN SKIRTING DEATH SO LONG NOW...
...BEING TOLD I HAVE LESS THAN A DAY TO LIVE DOESN'T EXCITE ME.
DITTO.
THOUGH IT IS TRUE THAT WE'RE RUNNING OUT OF TIME.
AND...

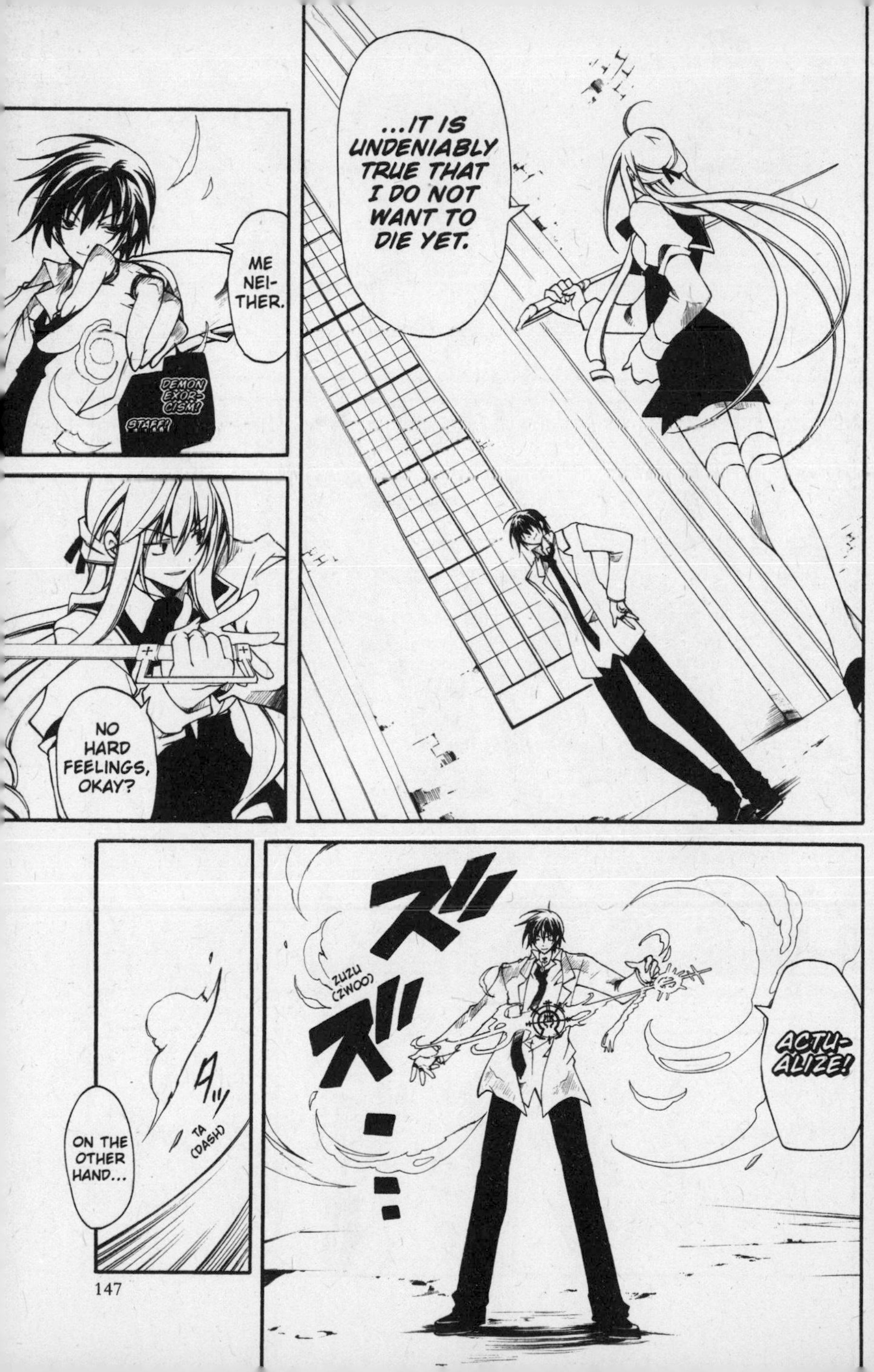
...IT IS UNDENIABLY TRUE THAT I DO NOT WANT TO DIE YET.
ME NEI-THER.
DEMON EXOR-CISM!
STAFF!
NO HARD FEELINGS, OKAY?
ACTU-ALIZE!
ズズッ
ZUZU (ZWOO)
タッ
TA (DASH)
ON THE OTHER HAND...

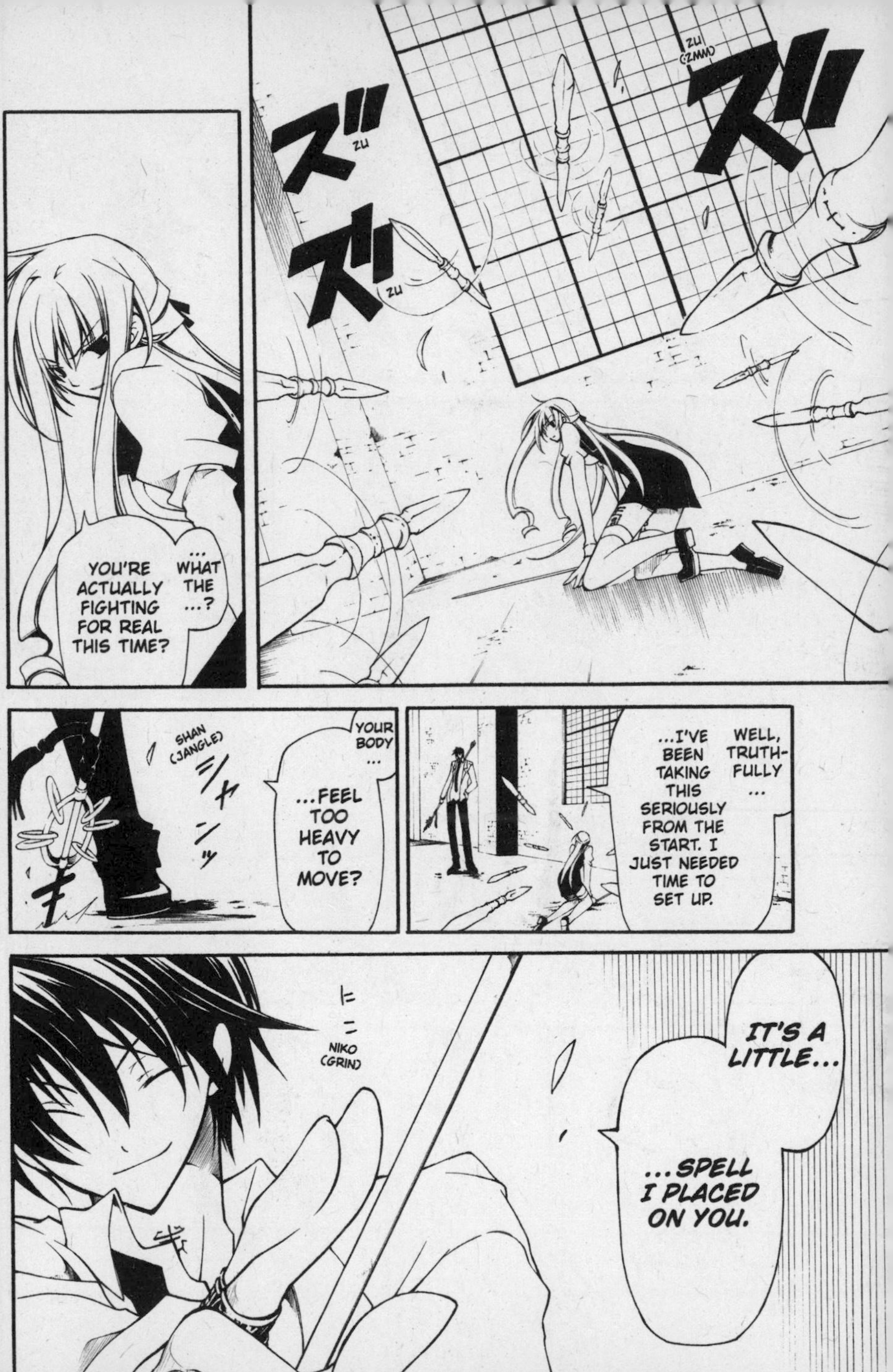
ズ
ZU (ZMM)
ズ
ZU
ズ
ZU
...WHAT THE...?
YOU'RE ACTUALLY FIGHTING FOR REAL THIS TIME?
WELL, TRUTHFULLY...
...I'VE BEEN TAKING THIS SERIOUSLY FROM THE START. I JUST NEEDED TIME TO SET UP.
YOUR BODY...
...FEEL TOO HEAVY TO MOVE?
シャンッ
SHAN (JANGLE)
IT'S A LITTLE...
...SPELL I PLACED ON YOU.
にこ
NIKO (GRIN)

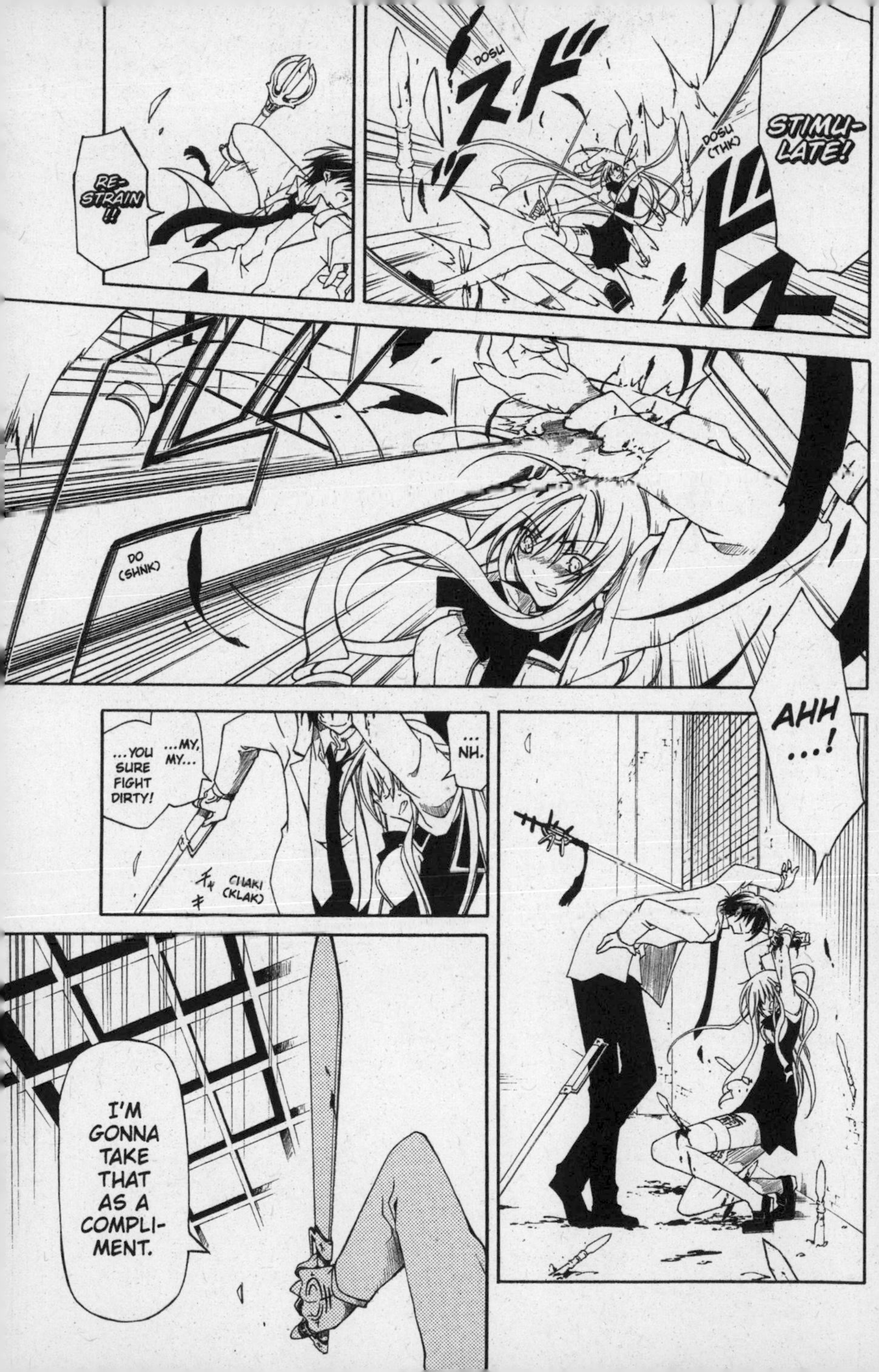
ドス
DOSU
DOSU (THK)
ドス
STIMU-LATE!
RE-STRAIN!!
DO (SHNK)
AHH...!
...NH.
...MY, MY...
...YOU SURE FIGHT DIRTY!
CHAKI (KLAK)
I'M GONNA TAKE THAT AS A COMPLIMENT.

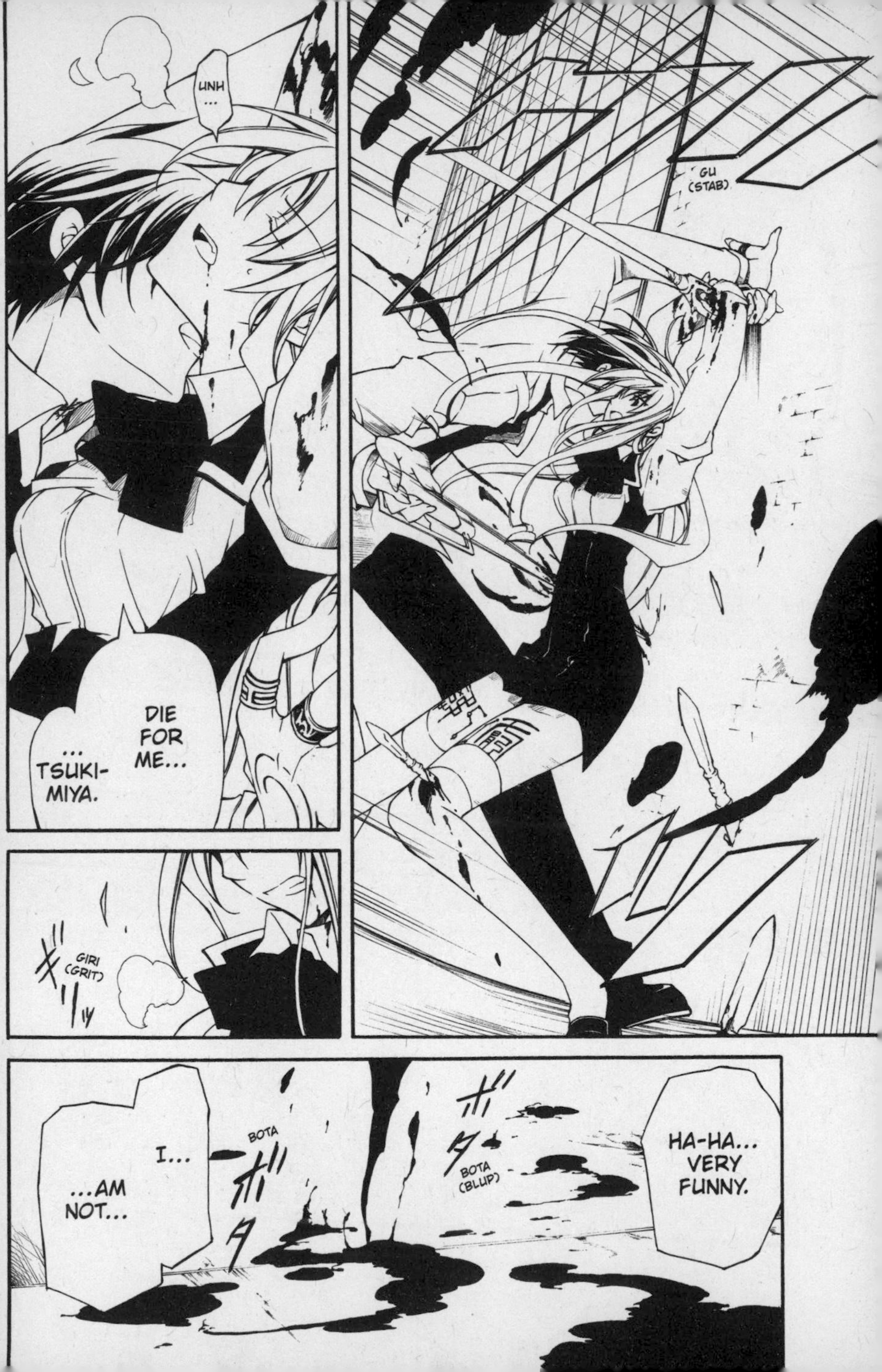
GU (STAB)
UNH ...
DIE FOR ME...
...TSUKIMIYA.
GIRI (GRIT)
HA-HA... VERY FUNNY.
BOTA (BLUP)
BOTA
I...
...AM NOT...

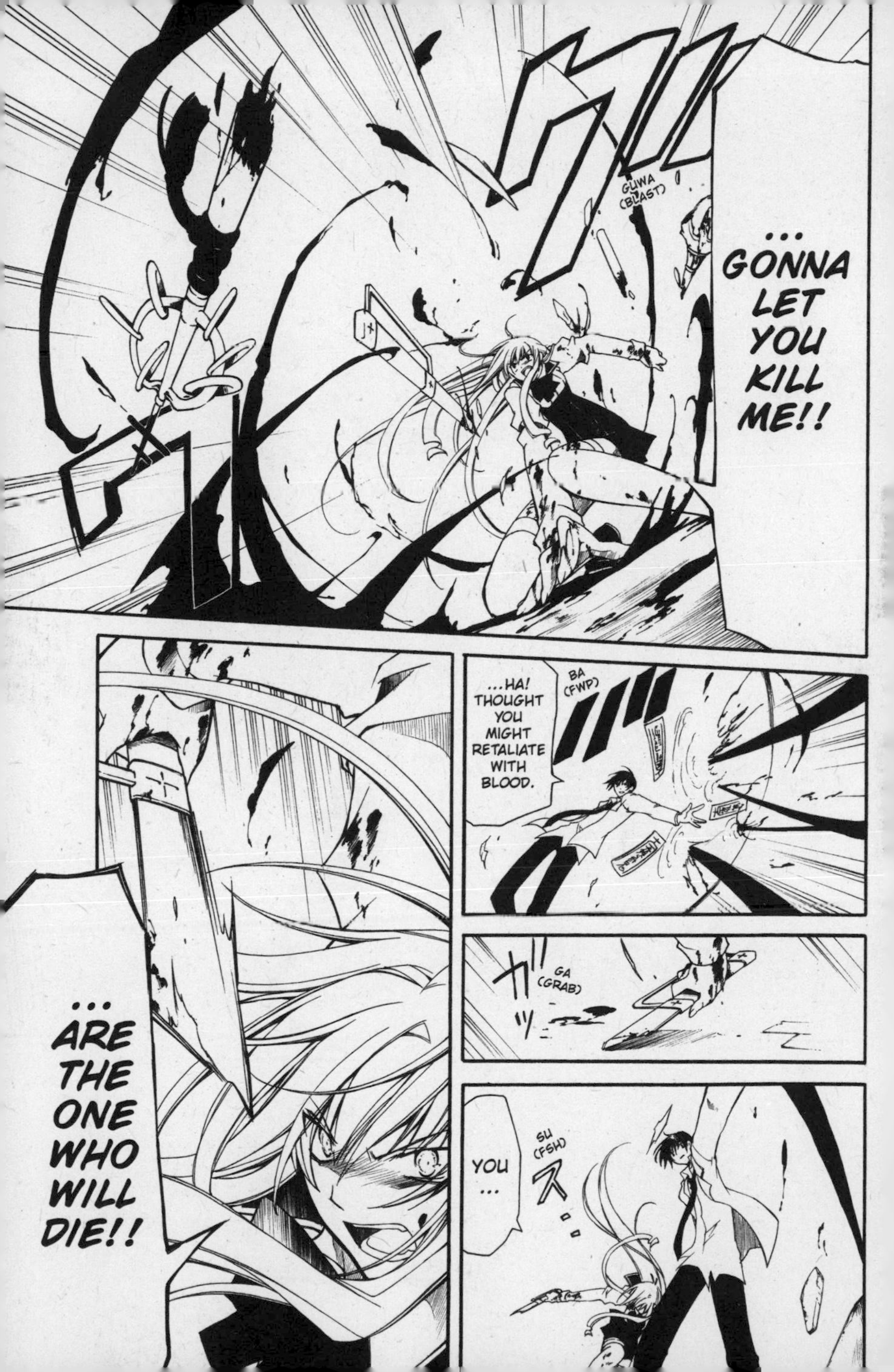

...GONNA LET YOU KILL ME!!
GUWA (BLAST)
BA (FWP)
...HA! THOUGHT YOU MIGHT RETALIATE WITH BLOOD.
GA (GRAB)
SU (FSH)
YOU ...
...ARE THE ONE WHO WILL DIE!!

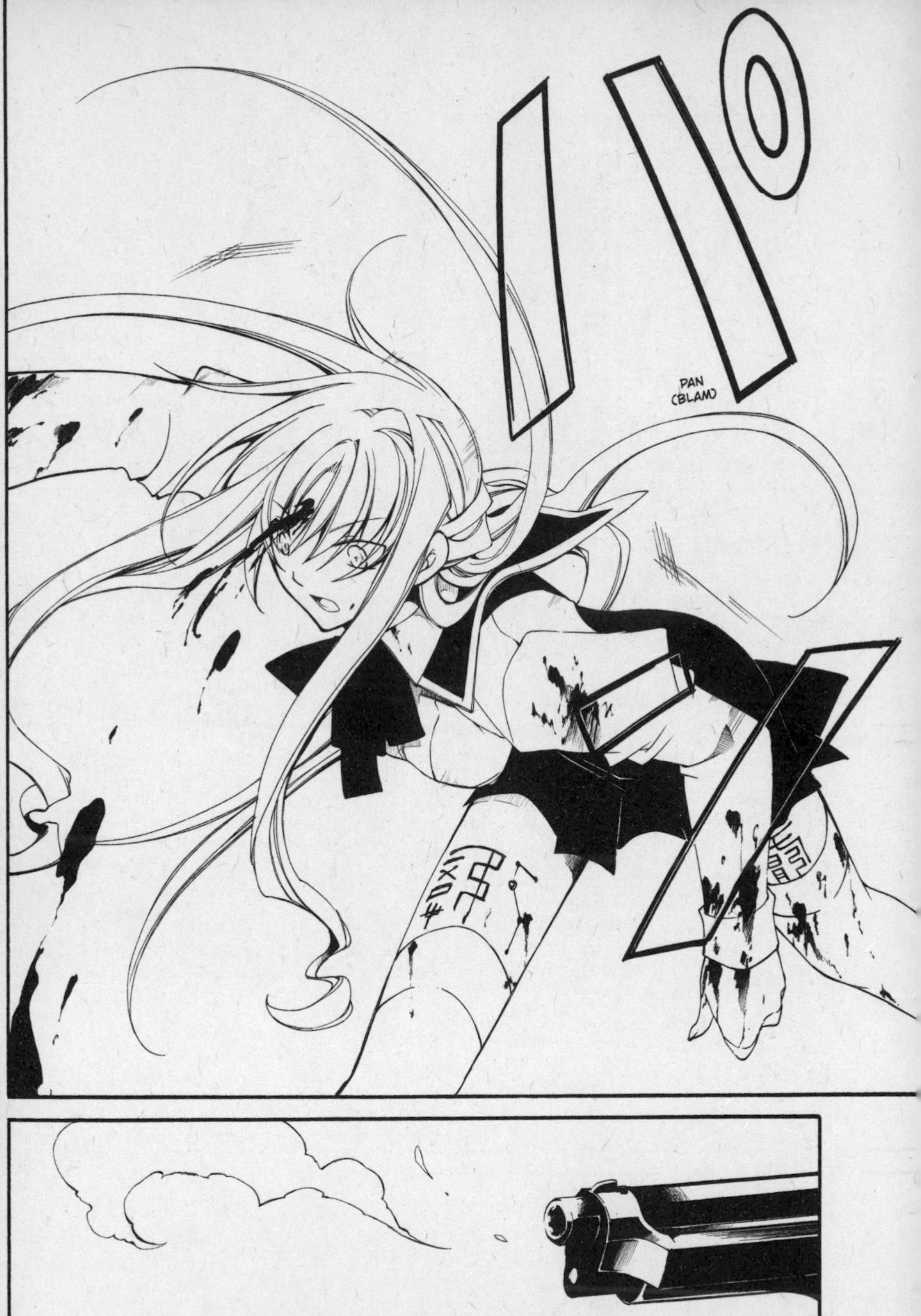
PAN
(BLAM)

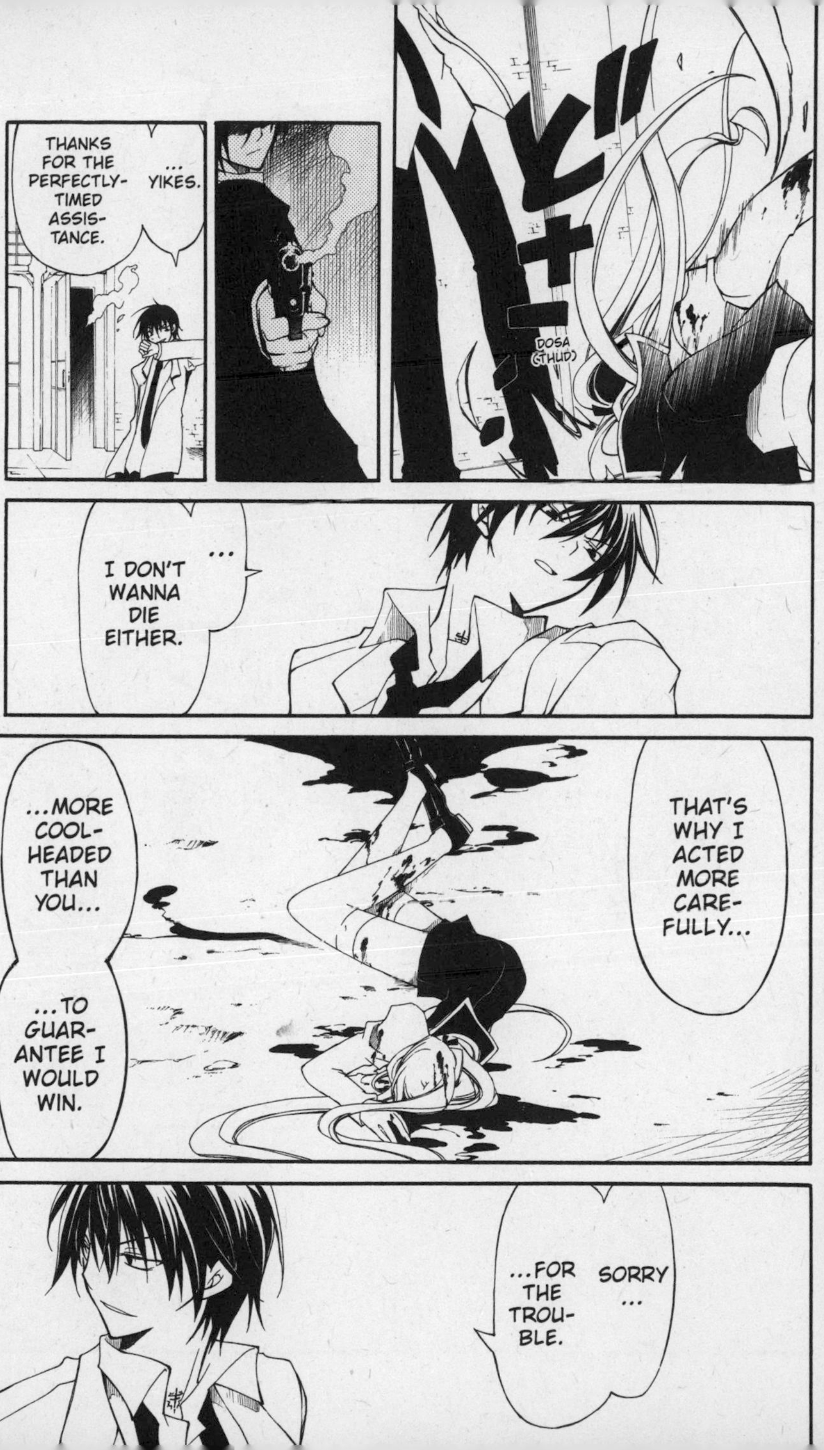
DOSA (THUD)
... YIKES.
THANKS FOR THE PERFECTLY-TIMED ASSISTANCE.
... I DON'T WANNA DIE EITHER.
THAT'S WHY I ACTED MORE CAREFULLY...
...MORE COOL-HEADED THAN YOU...
...TO GUARANTEE I WOULD WIN.
SORRY...
...FOR THE TROUBLE.

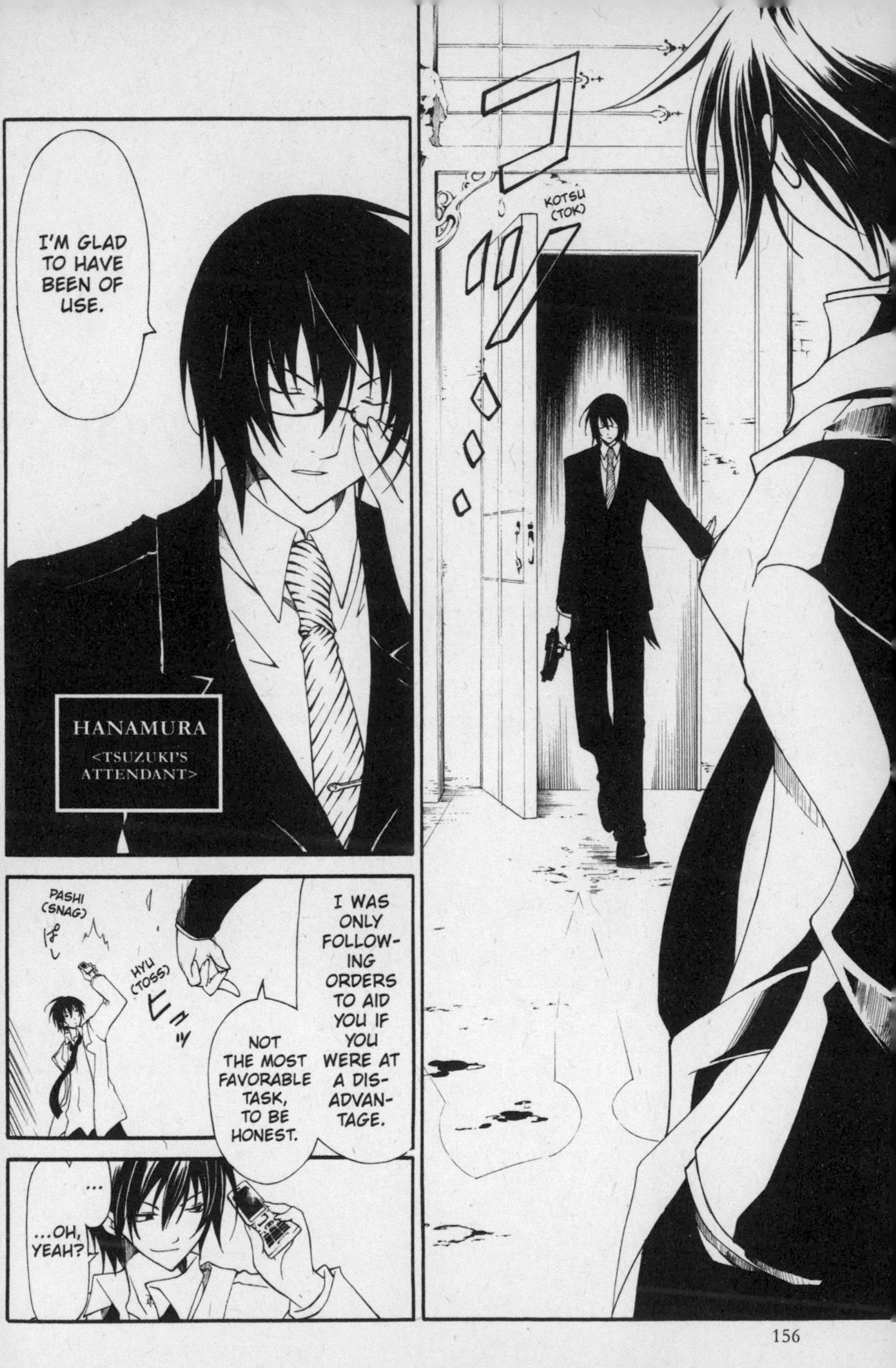
KOTSU (TOK)
I'M GLAD TO HAVE BEEN OF USE.
HANAMURA
<TSUZUKI'S ATTENDANT>
I WAS ONLY FOLLOWING ORDERS TO AID YOU IF YOU WERE AT A DISADVANTAGE.
NOT THE MOST FAVORABLE TASK, TO BE HONEST.
HYU (TOSS)
PASHI (SNAG)
...
...OH, YEAH?

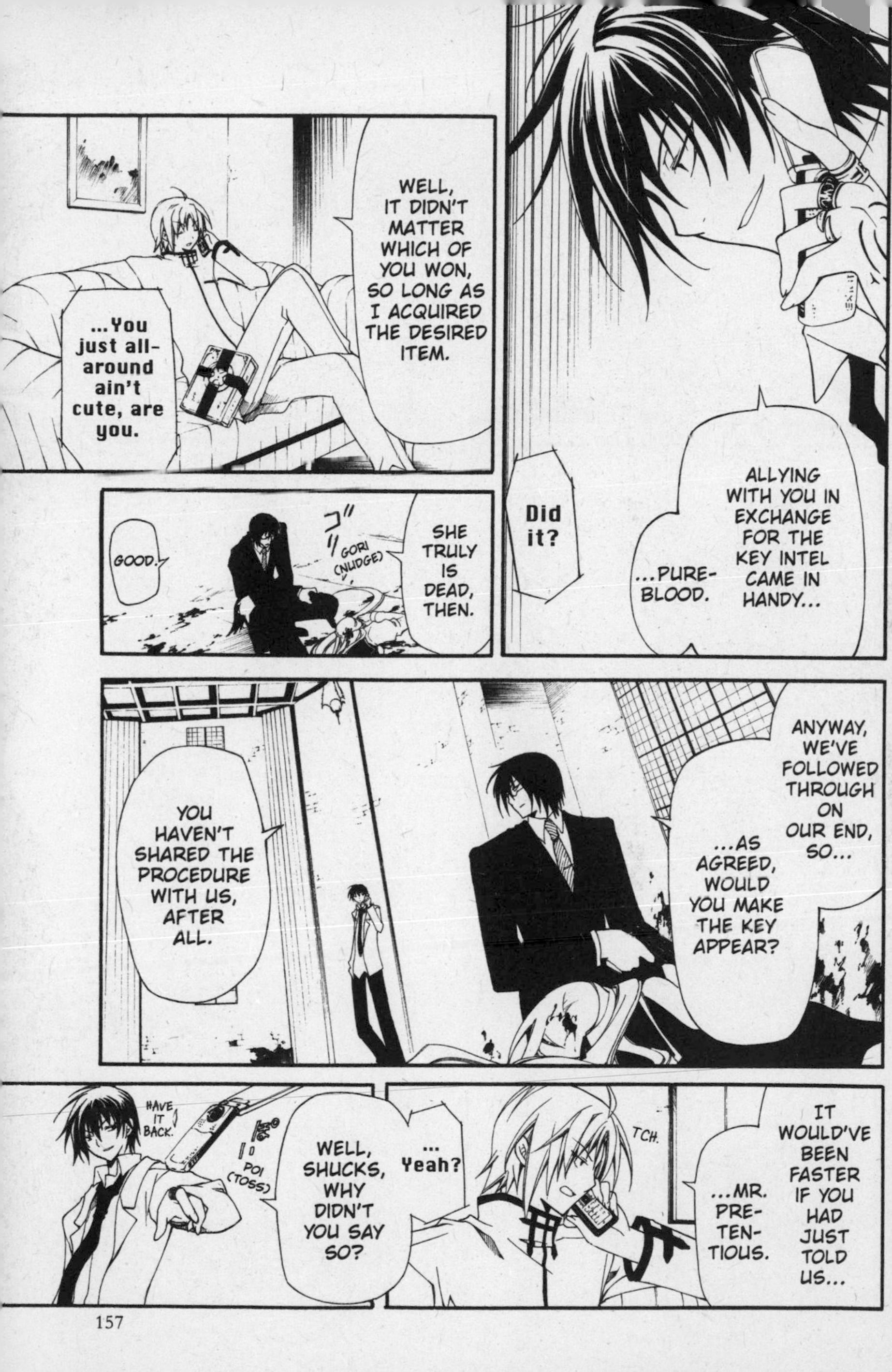
ALLYING WITH YOU IN EXCHANGE FOR THE KEY INTEL CAME IN HANDY...
...PURE-BLOOD.
Did it?
WELL, IT DIDN'T MATTER WHICH OF YOU WON, SO LONG AS I ACQUIRED THE DESIRED ITEM.
...You just all-around ain't cute, are you.
SHE TRULY IS DEAD, THEN.
GORI (NUDGE)
GOOD.
ANYWAY, WE'VE FOLLOWED THROUGH ON OUR END, SO...
...AS AGREED, WOULD YOU MAKE THE KEY APPEAR?
YOU HAVEN'T SHARED THE PROCEDURE WITH US, AFTER ALL.
IT WOULD'VE BEEN FASTER IF YOU HAD JUST TOLD US...
...MR. PRETENTIOUS.
TCH.
... Yeah?
WELL, SHUCKS, WHY DIDN'T YOU SAY SO?
POI (TOSS)
HAVE IT BACK.

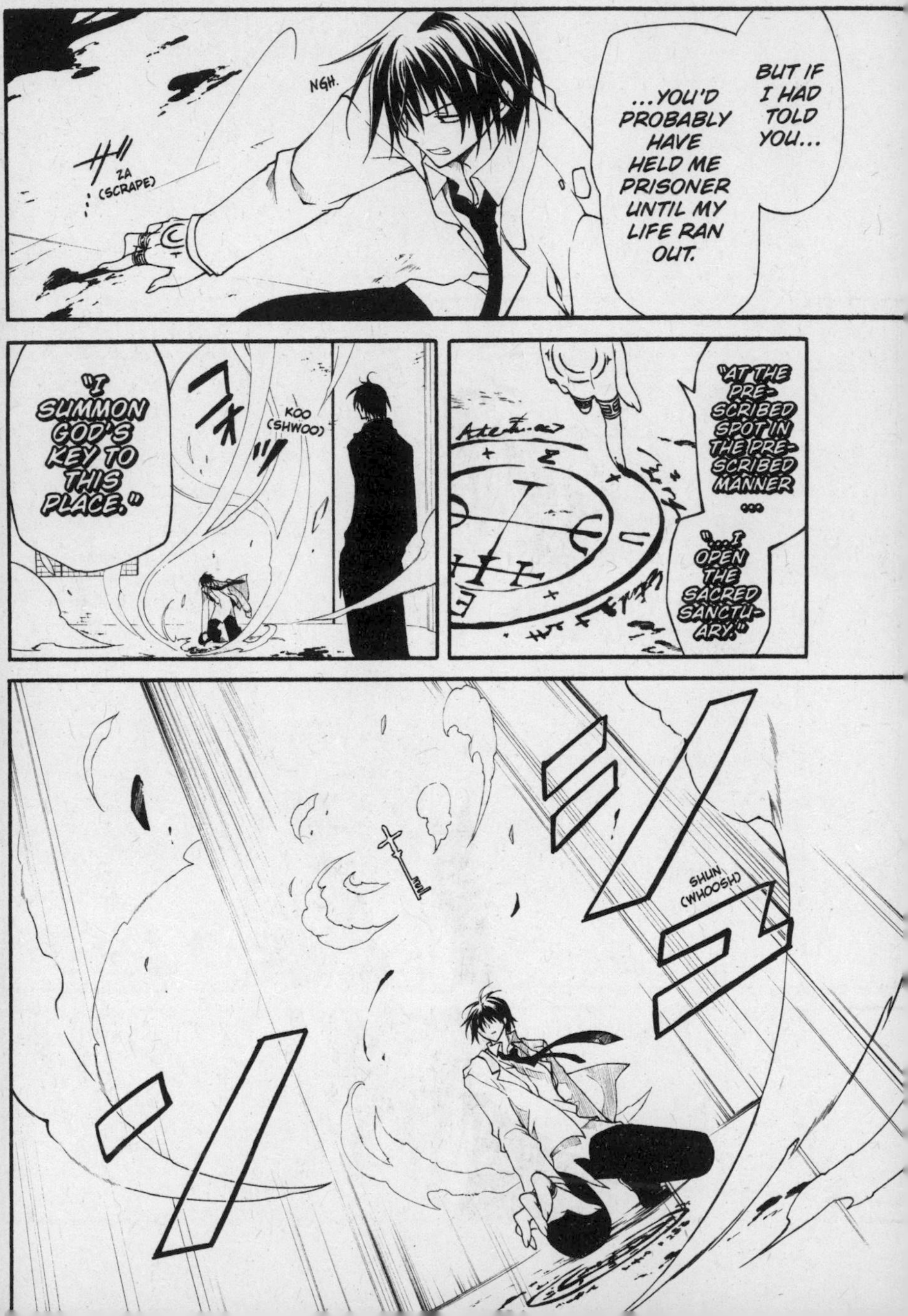
BUT IF I HAD TOLD YOU...
...YOU'D PROBABLY HAVE HELD ME PRISONER UNTIL MY LIFE RAN OUT.
NGH.
ZA (SCRAPE)
"AT THE PRE-SCRIBED SPOT IN THE PRE-SCRIBED MANNER...
"...I OPEN THE SACRED SANCTU-ARY."
"I SUMMON GOD'S KEY TO THIS PLACE."
KOO (SHWOO)
SHUN (WHOOSH)

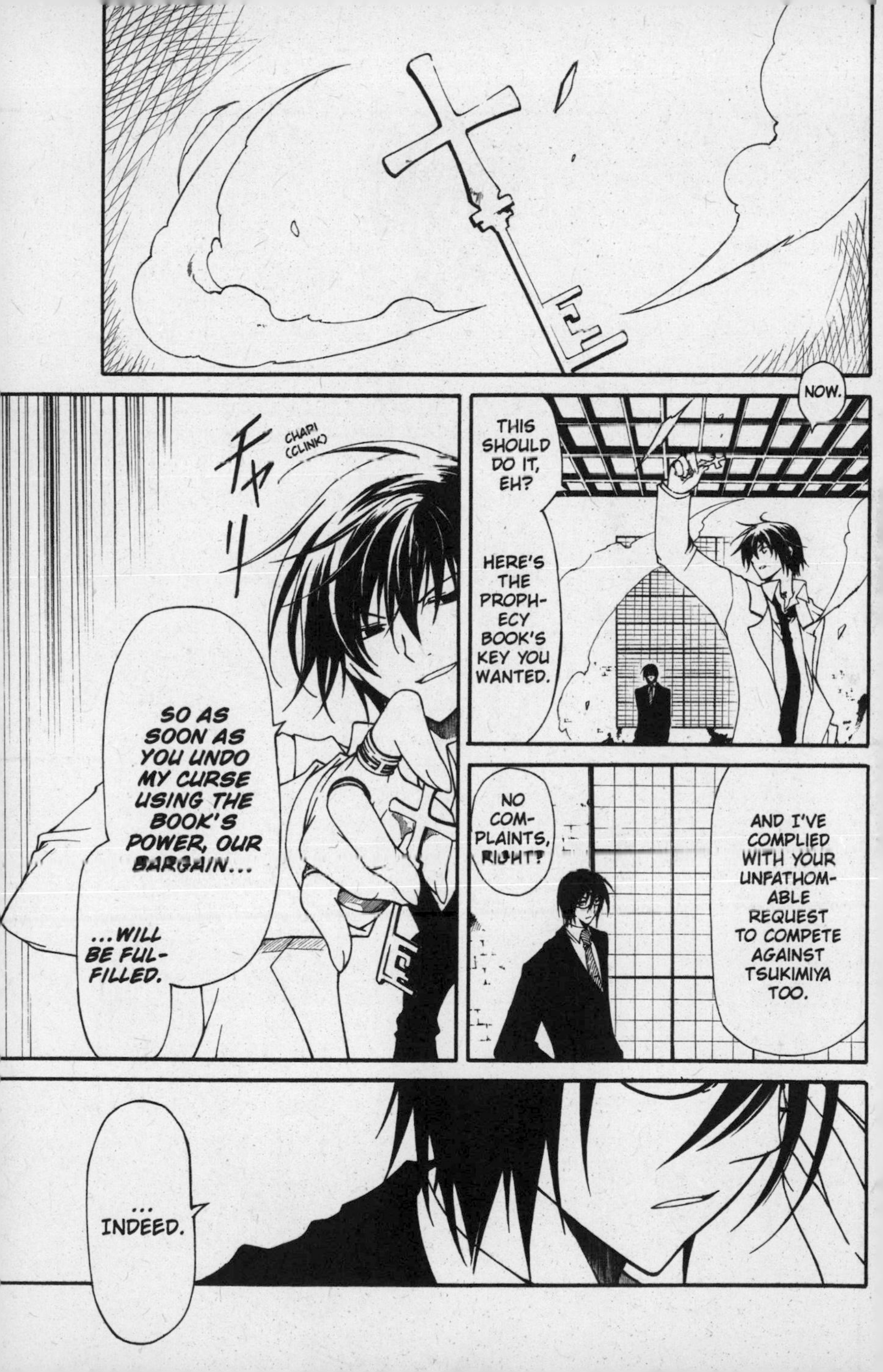

NOW.
THIS SHOULD DO IT, EH?
HERE'S THE PROPHECY BOOK'S KEY YOU WANTED.
AND I'VE COMPLIED WITH YOUR UNFATHOMABLE REQUEST TO COMPETE AGAINST TSUKIMIYA TOO.
NO COMPLAINTS, RIGHT?
チャリ
CHARI (CLINK)
SO AS SOON AS YOU UNDO MY CURSE USING THE BOOK'S POWER, OUR BARGAIN...
...WILL BE FULFILLED.
... INDEED.

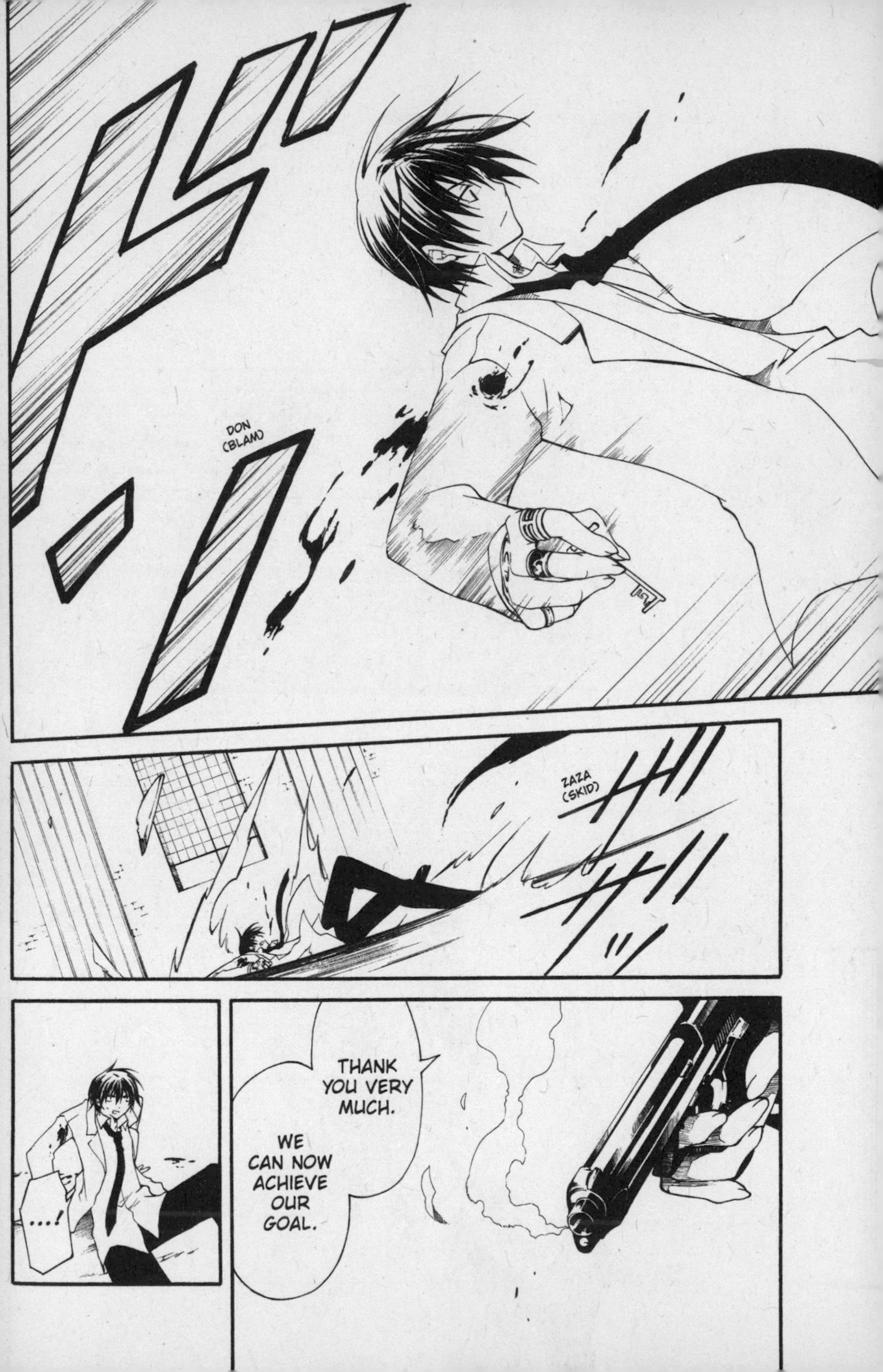
DON (BLAM)
ZAZA (SKID)
THANK YOU VERY MUCH.
WE CAN NOW ACHIEVE OUR GOAL.
....!

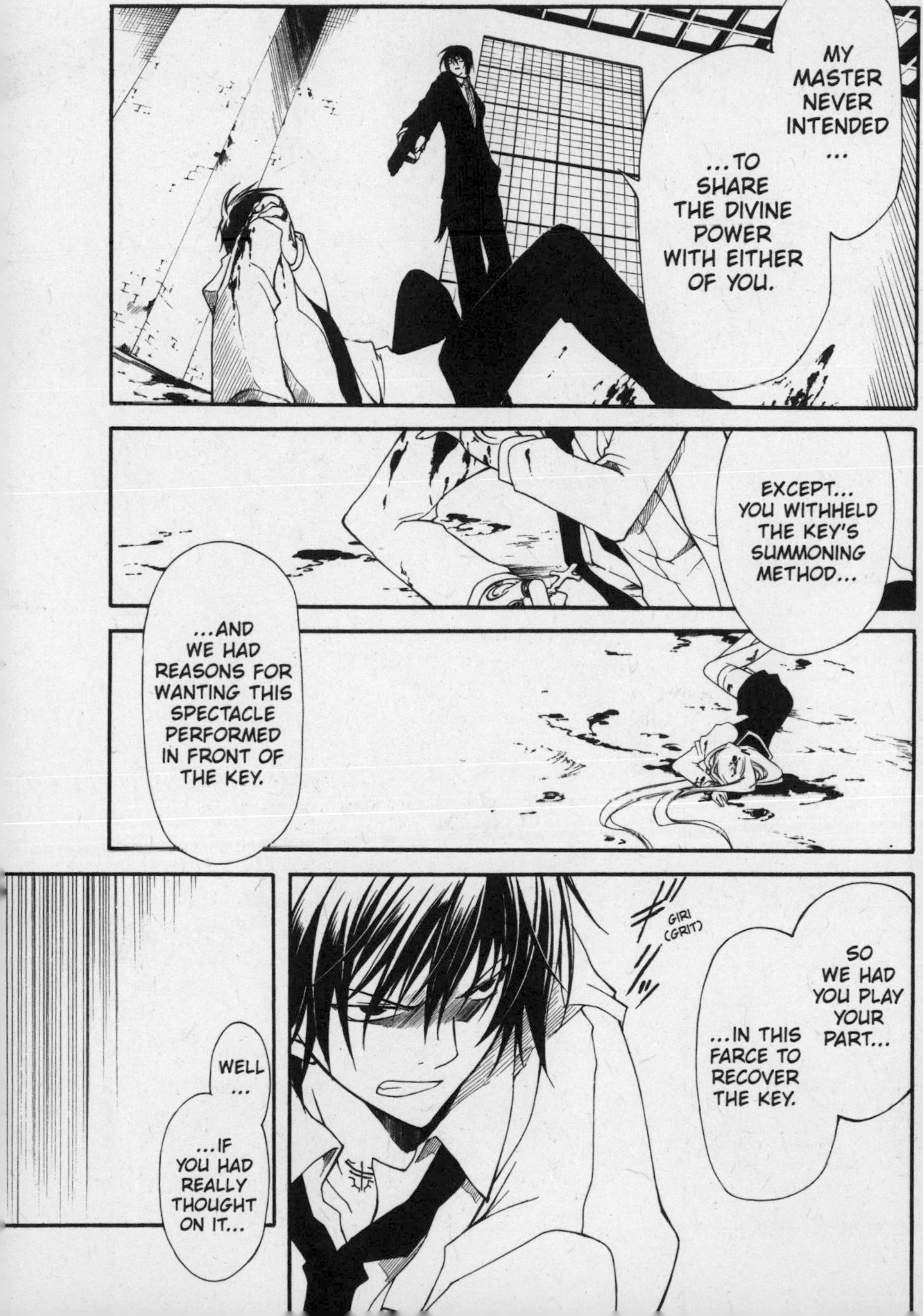
MY MASTER NEVER INTENDED ...
...TO SHARE THE DIVINE POWER WITH EITHER OF YOU.
EXCEPT... YOU WITHHELD THE KEY'S SUMMONING METHOD...
...AND WE HAD REASONS FOR WANTING THIS SPECTACLE PERFORMED IN FRONT OF THE KEY.
GIRI (GRIT)
SO WE HAD YOU PLAY YOUR PART...
...IN THIS FARCE TO RECOVER THE KEY.
WELL ...
...IF YOU HAD REALLY THOUGHT ON IT...

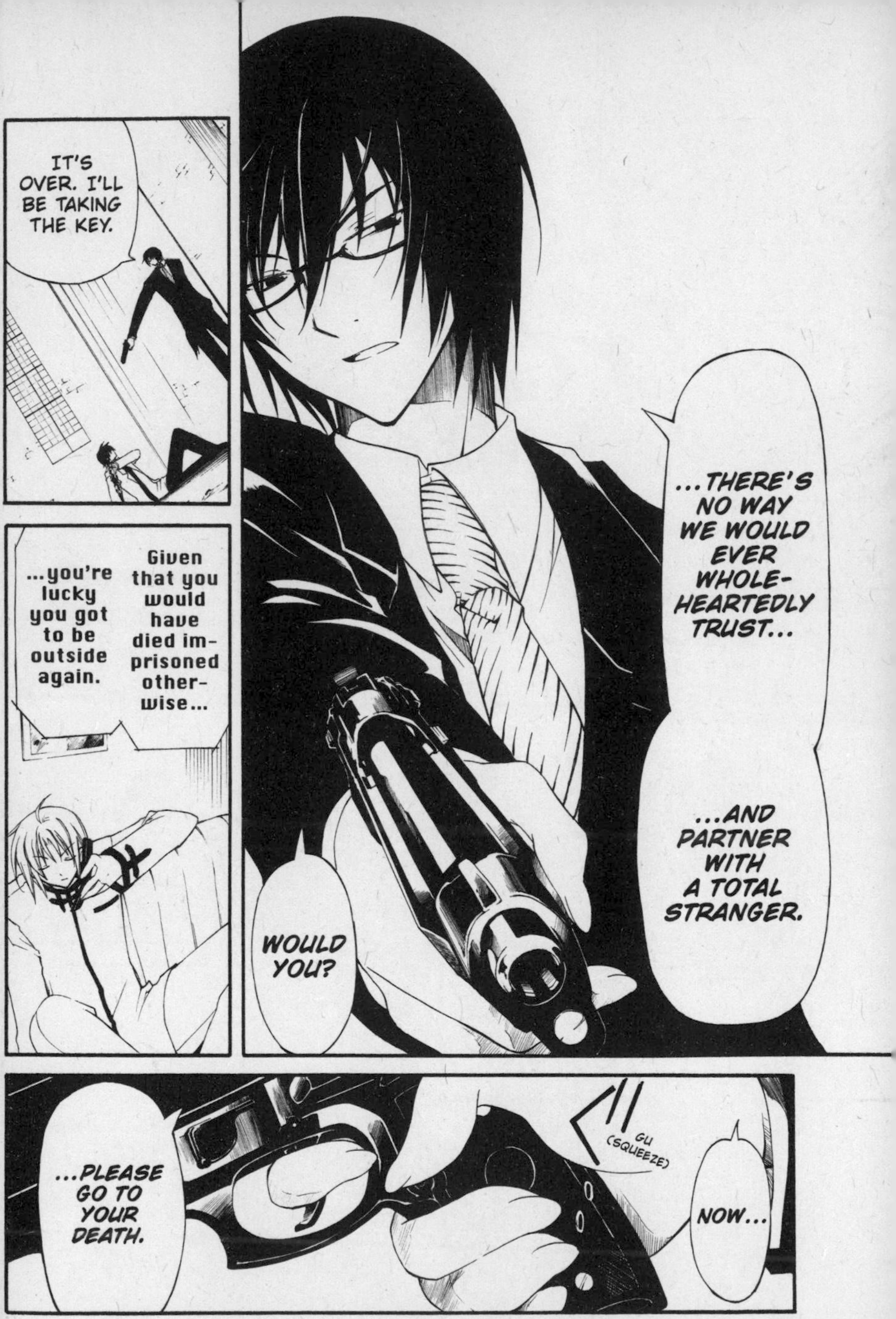
...THERE'S NO WAY WE WOULD EVER WHOLE-HEARTEDLY TRUST...
...AND PARTNER WITH A TOTAL STRANGER.
WOULD YOU?
IT'S OVER. I'LL BE TAKING THE KEY.
Given that you would have died im-prisoned other-wise...
...you're lucky you got to be outside again.
NOW...
GU (SQUEEZE)
...PLEASE GO TO YOUR DEATH.

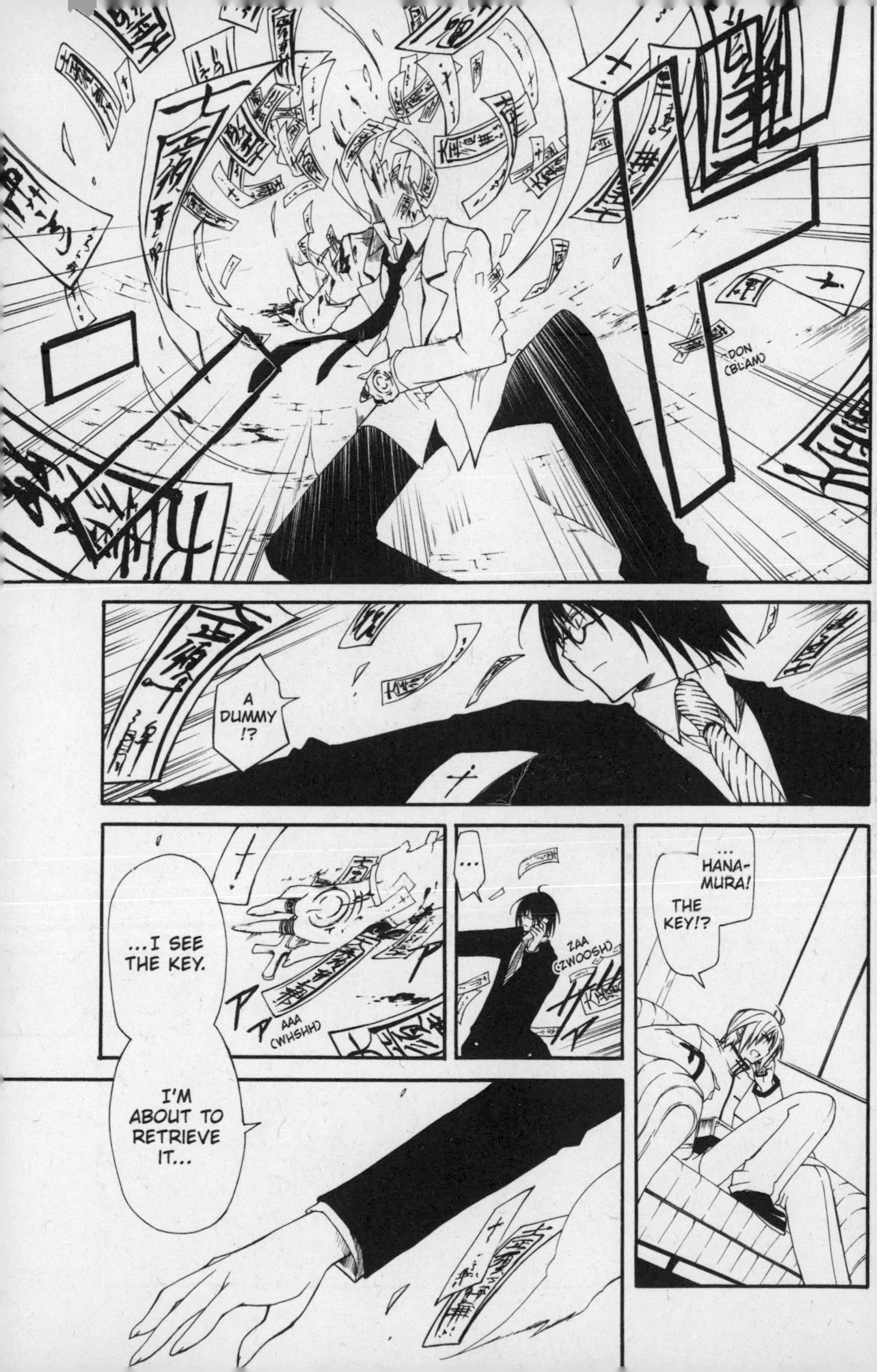
DON (BLAM)
A DUMMY!?
...HANA-MURA!
THE KEY!?
...
ZAA (ZWOOSH)
...I SEE THE KEY.
AAA (WHSHH)
I'M ABOUT TO RETRIEVE IT...

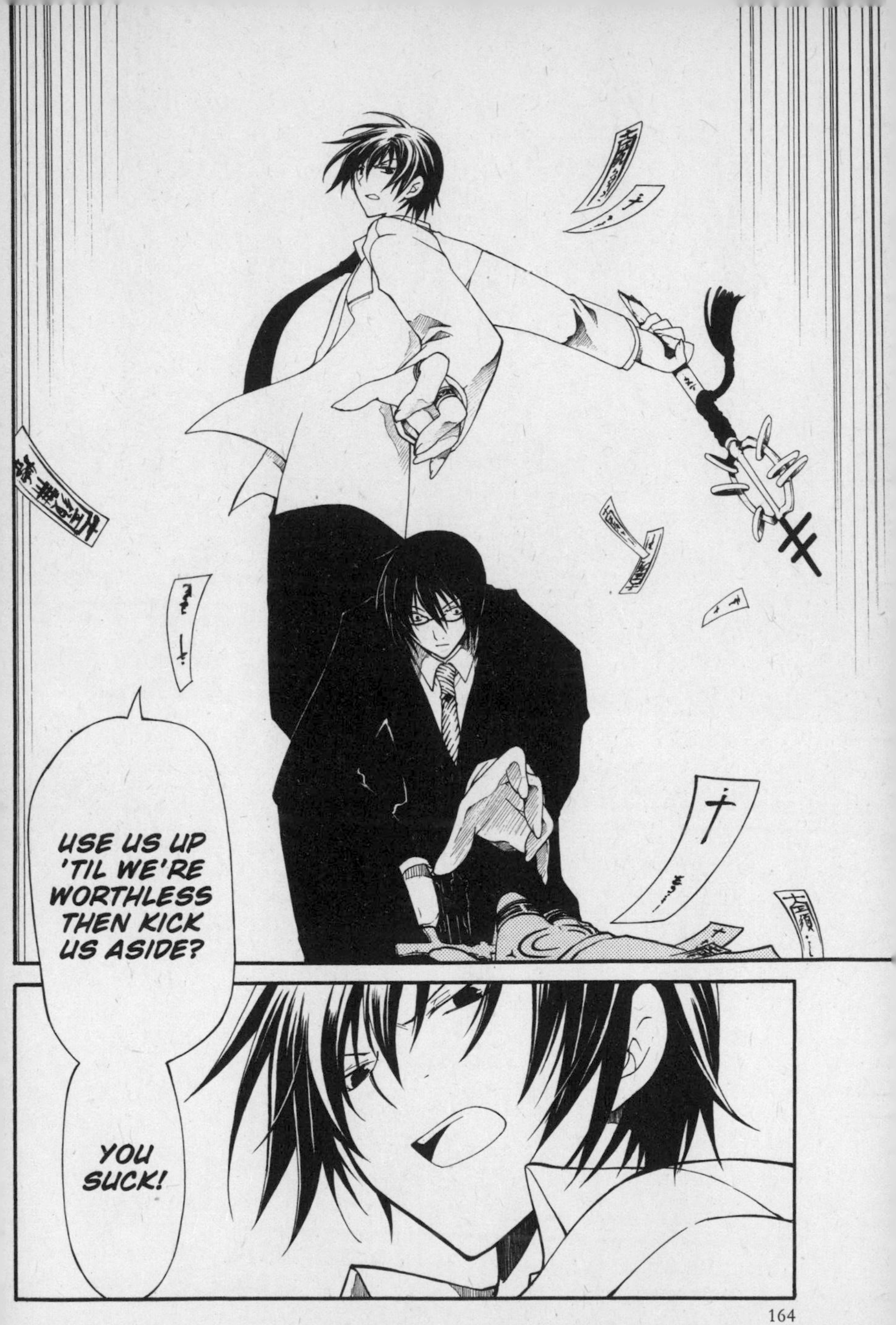
USE US UP 'TIL WE'RE WORTHLESS THEN KICK US ASIDE?
YOU SUCK!

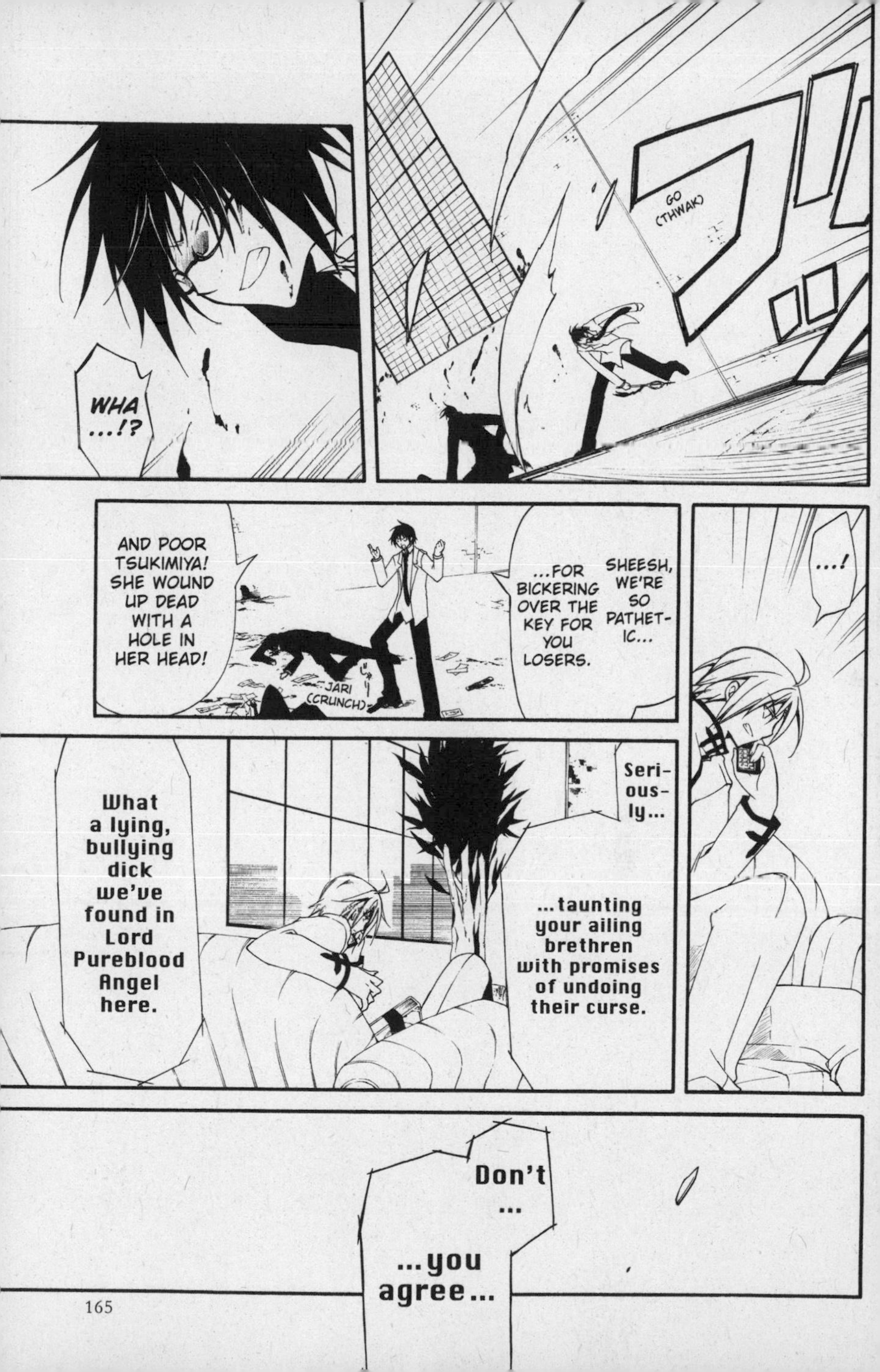
GO (THWAK)
WHA ...!?
...!
SHEESH, WE'RE SO PATHETIC...
...FOR BICKERING OVER THE KEY FOR YOU LOSERS.
JARI (CRUNCH)
AND POOR TSUKIMIYA! SHE WOUND UP DEAD WITH A HOLE IN HER HEAD!
Seriously...
...taunting your ailing brethren with promises of undoing their curse.
What a lying, bullying dick we've found in Lord Pureblood Angel here.
Don't ...
...you agree...

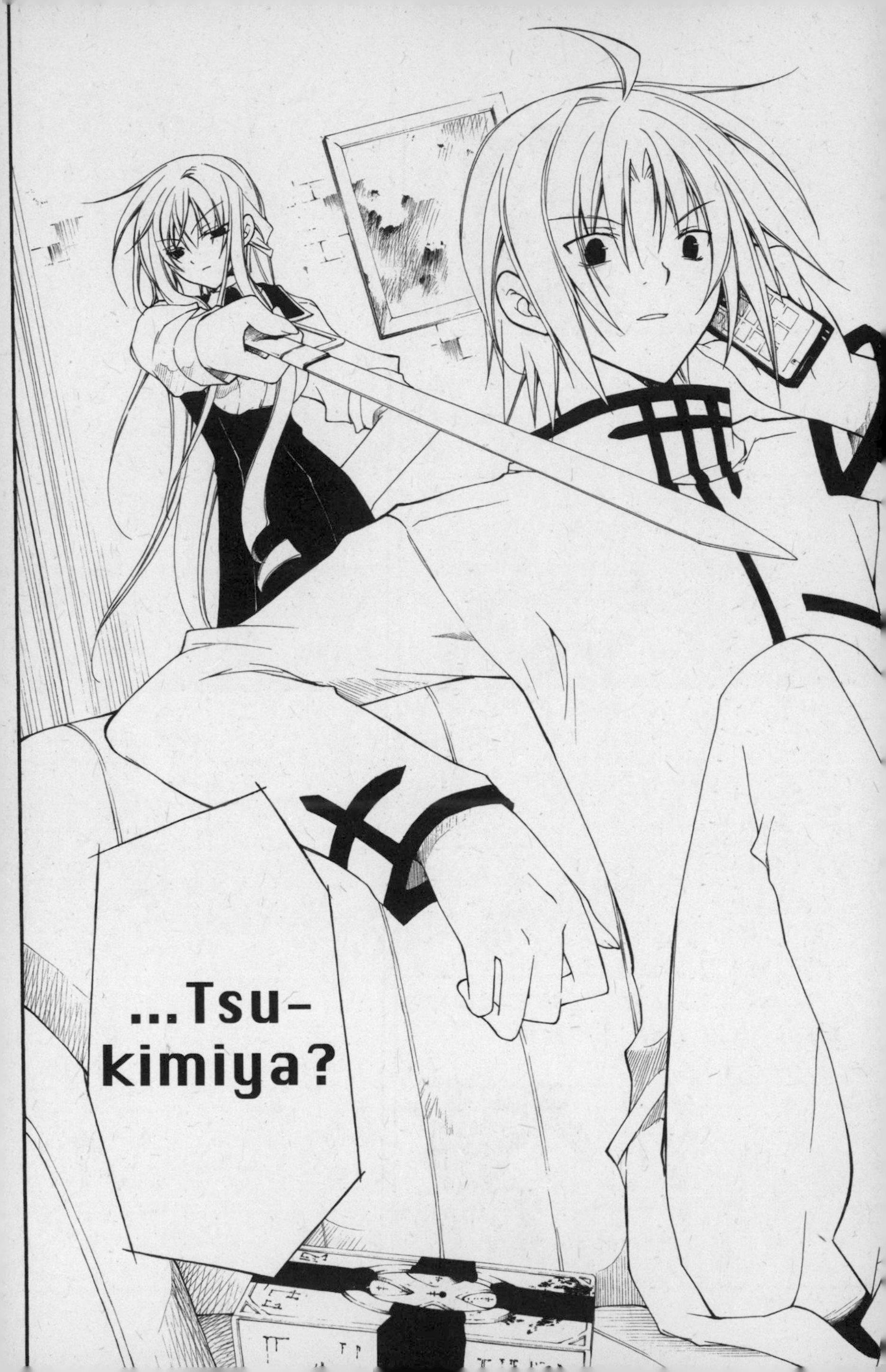
...Tsu-kimiya?

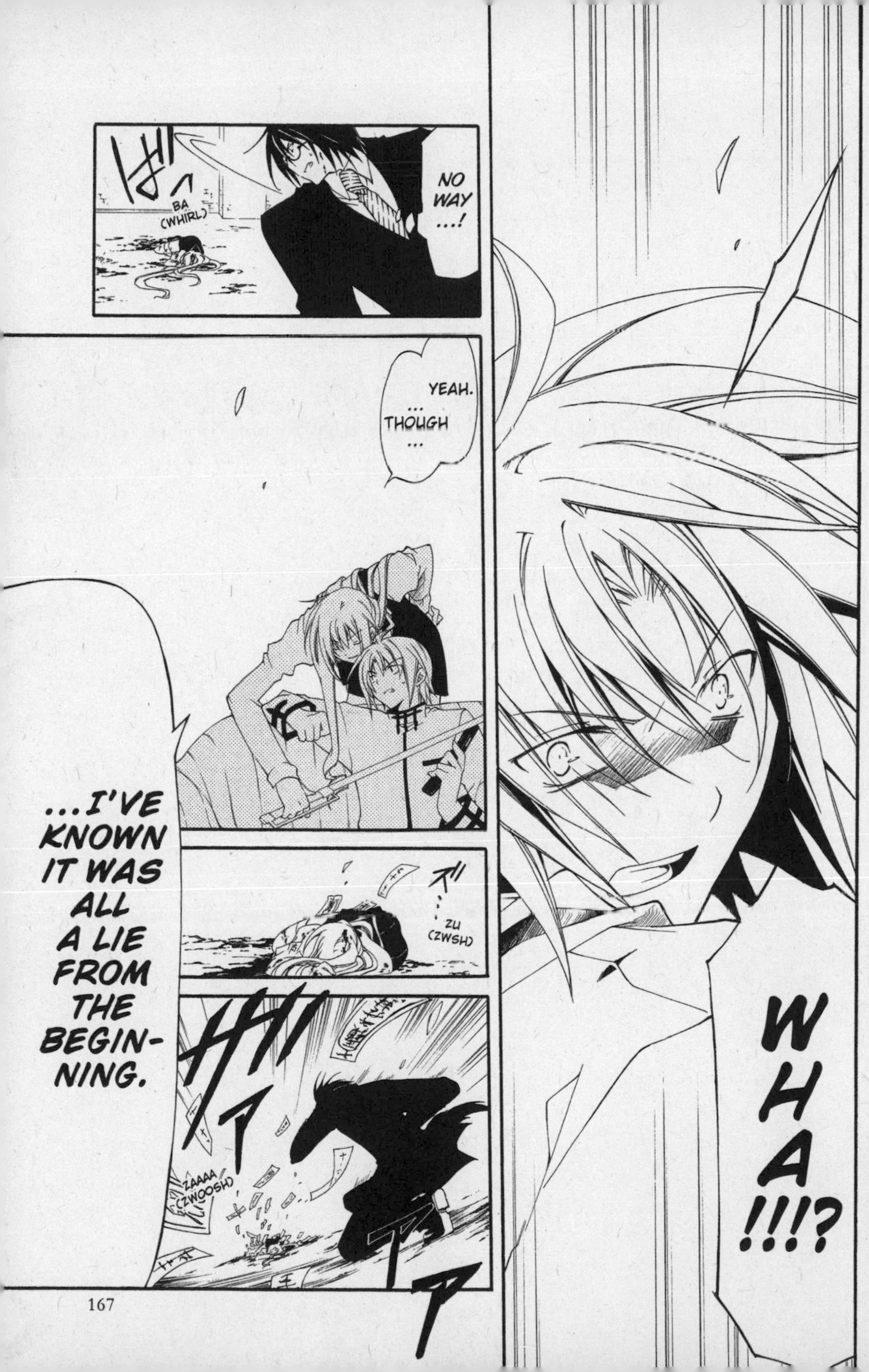

WHA!!!?
BA (WHIRL)
NO WAY...!
YEAH. ...THOUGH...
...I'VE KNOWN IT WAS ALL A LIE FROM THE BEGINNING.
ZU (ZWSH)
ZAAAA (ZWOOSH)

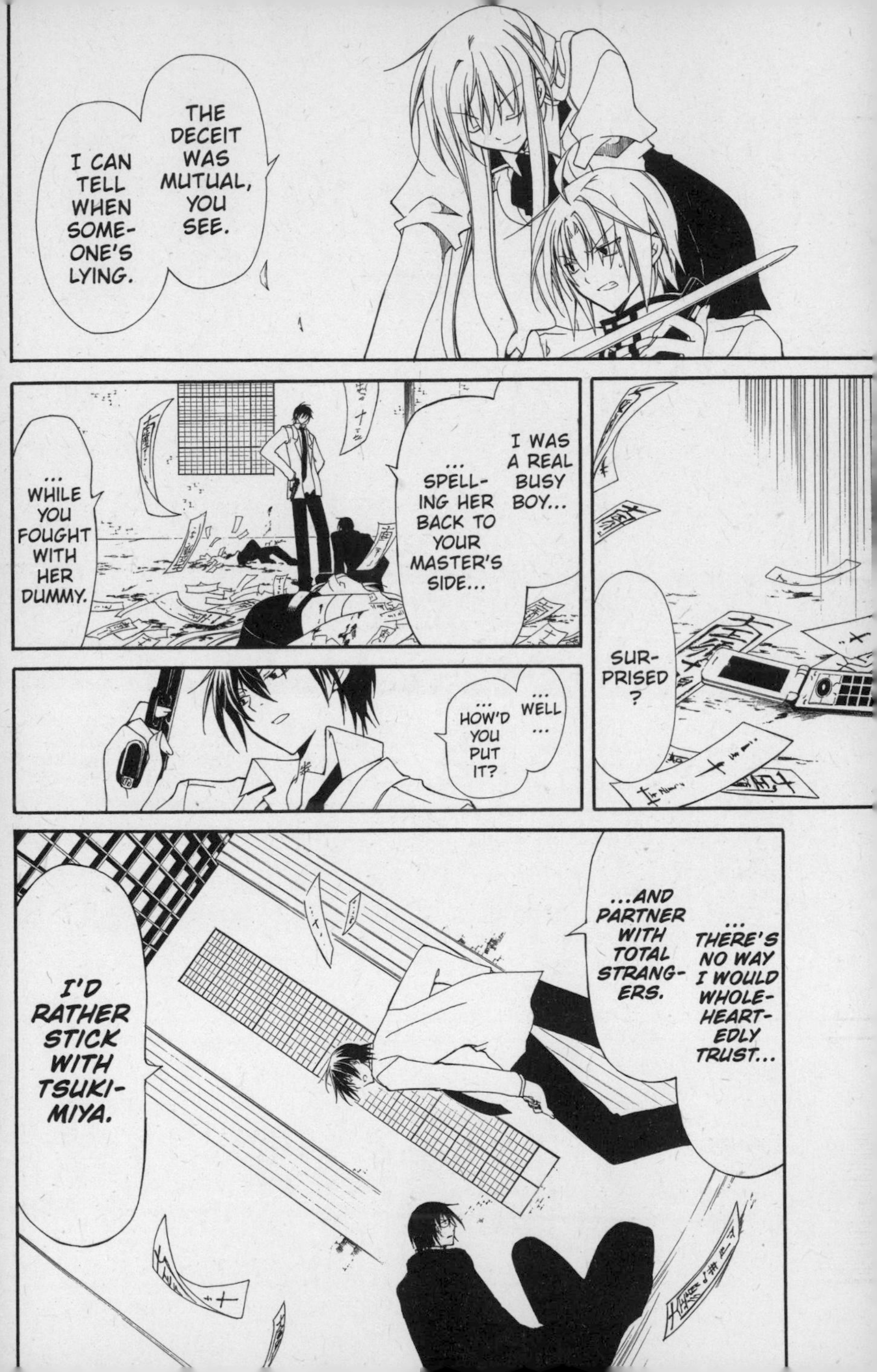
THE DECEIT WAS MUTUAL, YOU SEE.
I CAN TELL WHEN SOMEONE'S LYING.
SURPRISED?
I WAS A REAL BUSY BOY...
...SPELLING HER BACK TO YOUR MASTER'S SIDE...
...WHILE YOU FOUGHT WITH HER DUMMY.
...WELL...
...HOW'D YOU PUT IT?
...THERE'S NO WAY I WOULD WHOLEHEARTEDLY TRUST...
...AND PARTNER WITH TOTAL STRANGERS.
I'D RATHER STICK WITH TSUKIMIYA.

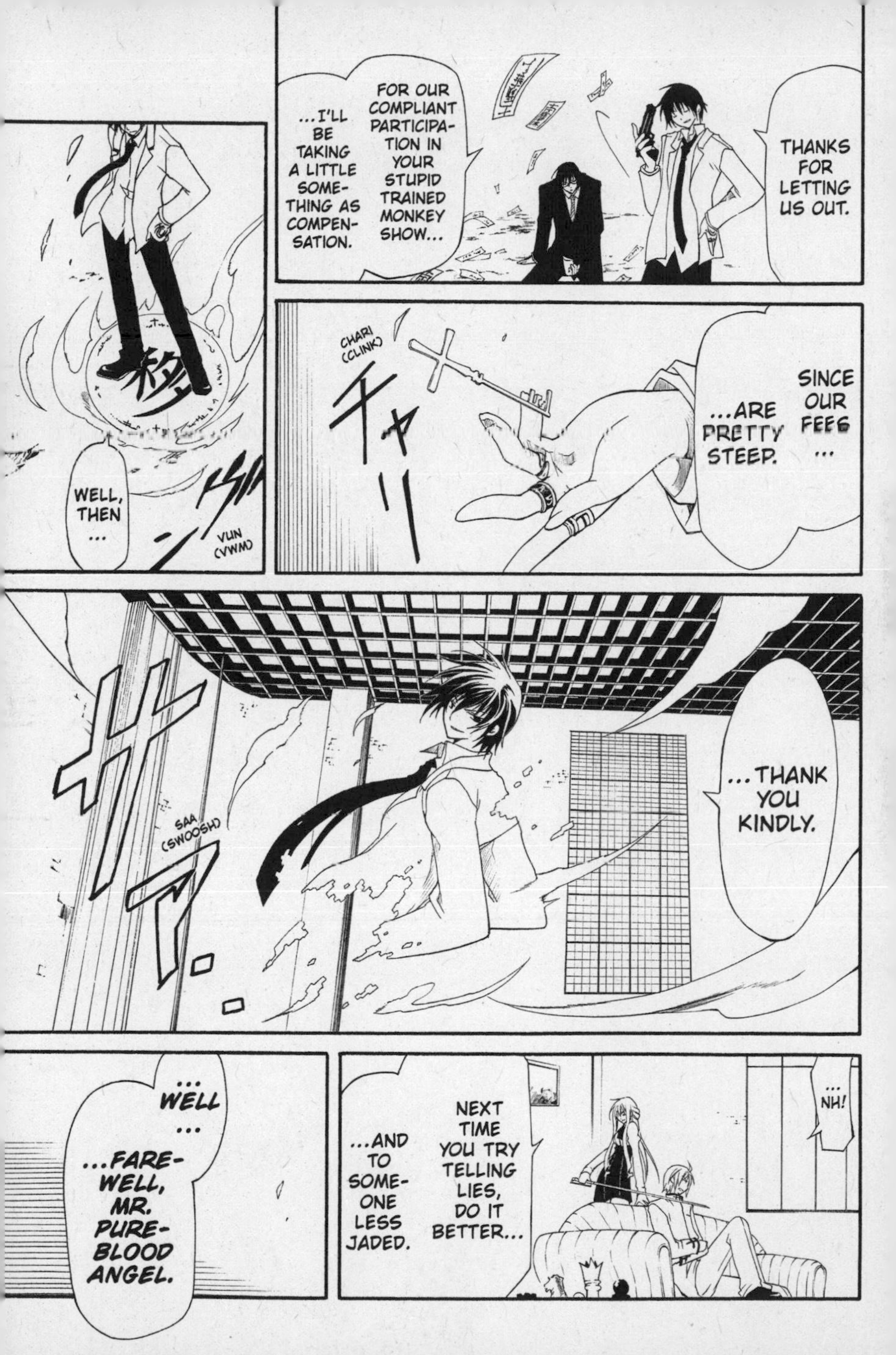
THANKS FOR LETTING US OUT.
FOR OUR COMPLIANT PARTICIPATION IN YOUR STUPID TRAINED MONKEY SHOW...
...I'LL BE TAKING A LITTLE SOMETHING AS COMPENSATION.
SINCE OUR FEES...
...ARE PRETTY STEEP.
CHARI (CLINK)
WELL, THEN...
VUN (VWM)
...THANK YOU KINDLY.
SAA (SWOOSH)
...NH!
NEXT TIME YOU TRY TELLING LIES, DO IT BETTER...
...AND TO SOMEONE LESS JADED.
...WELL...
...FAREWELL, MR. PURE-BLOOD ANGEL.

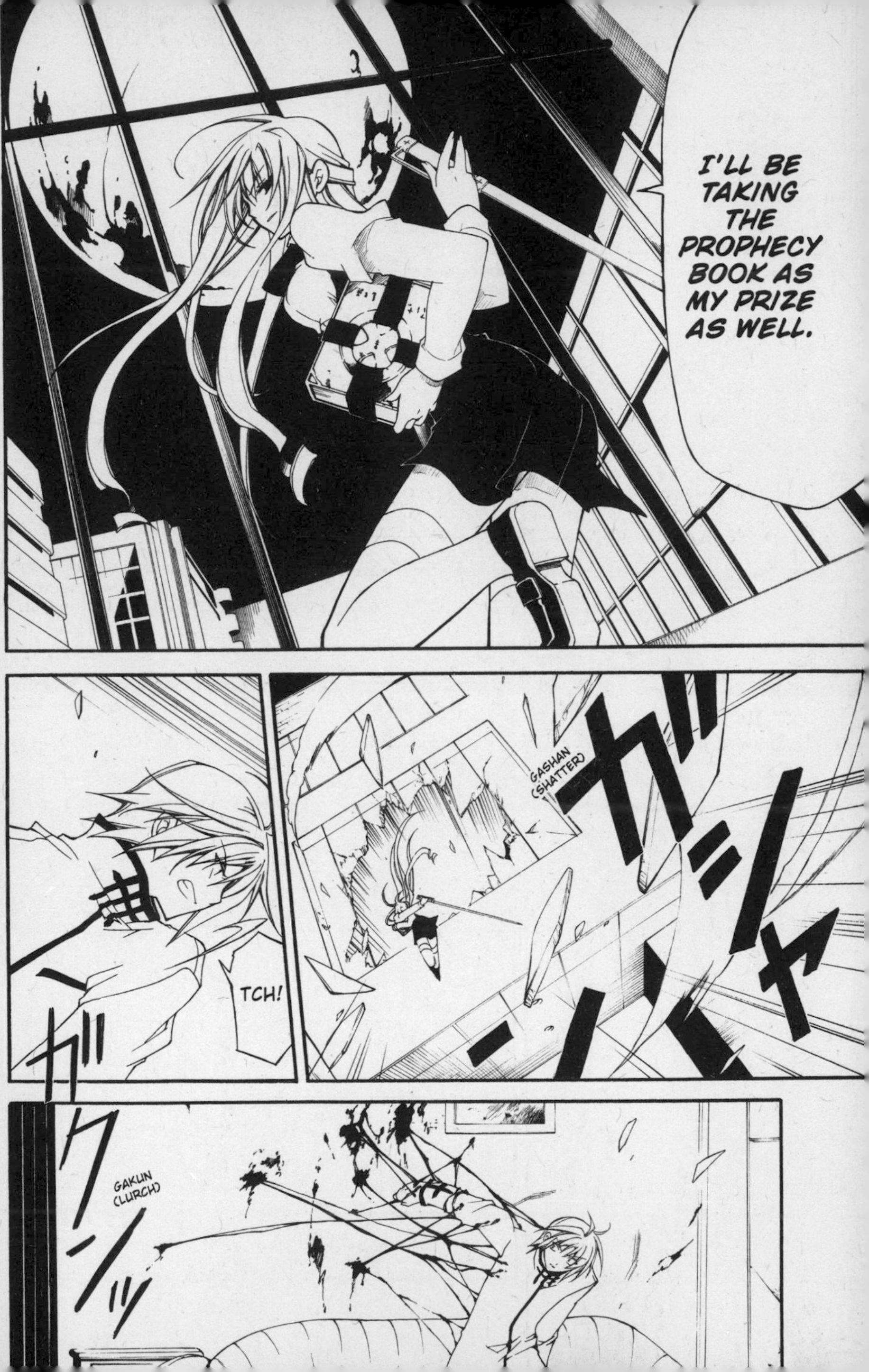
I'LL BE TAKING THE PROPHECY BOOK AS MY PRIZE AS WELL.
GASHAN (SHATTER)
TCH!
GAKUN (LURCH)

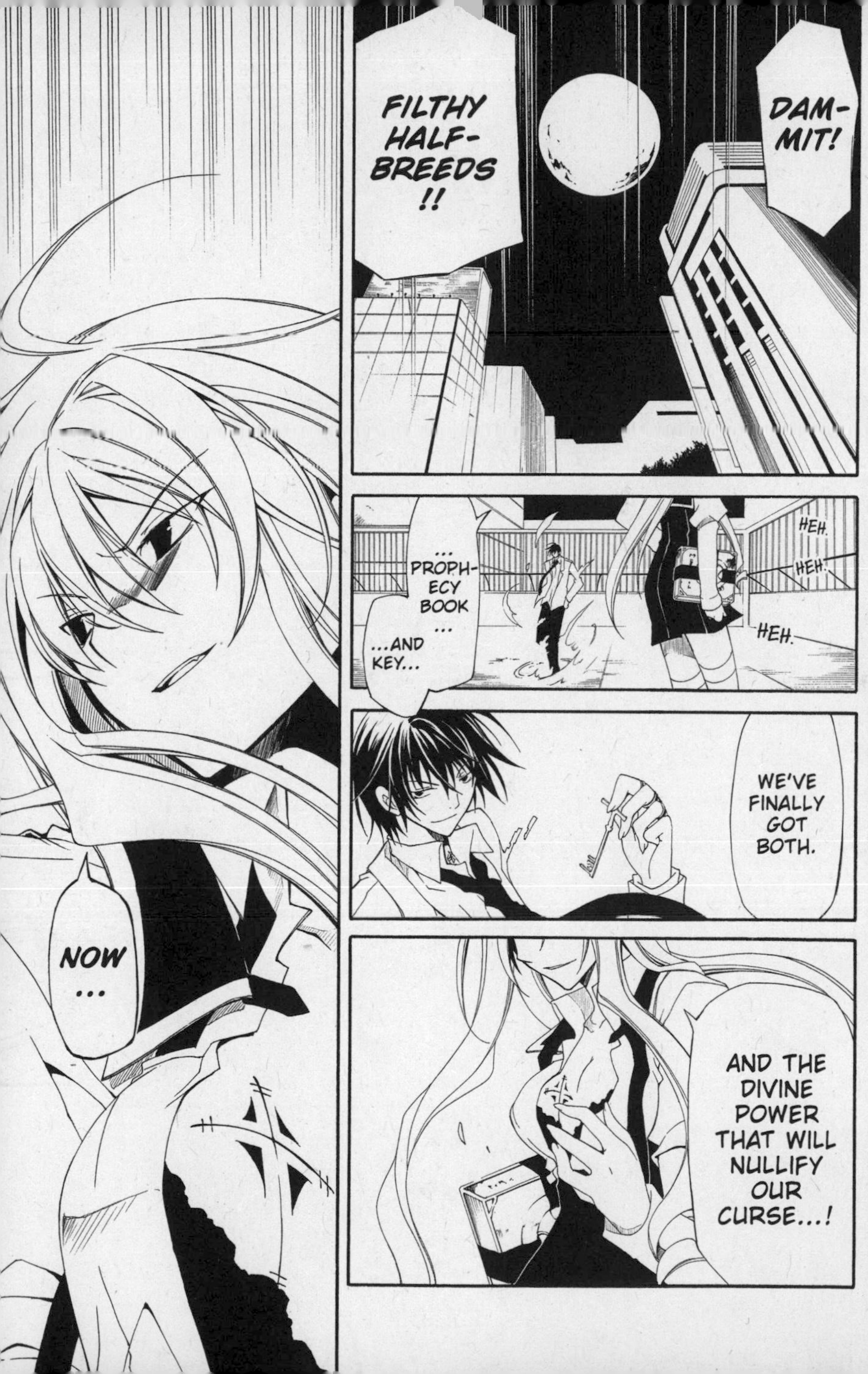
DAM-MIT!
FILTHY HALF-BREEDS!!
HEH.
HEH.
HEH.
...PROPHECY BOOK...
...AND KEY...
WE'VE FINALLY GOT BOTH.
AND THE DIVINE POWER THAT WILL NULLIFY OUR CURSE...!
NOW...

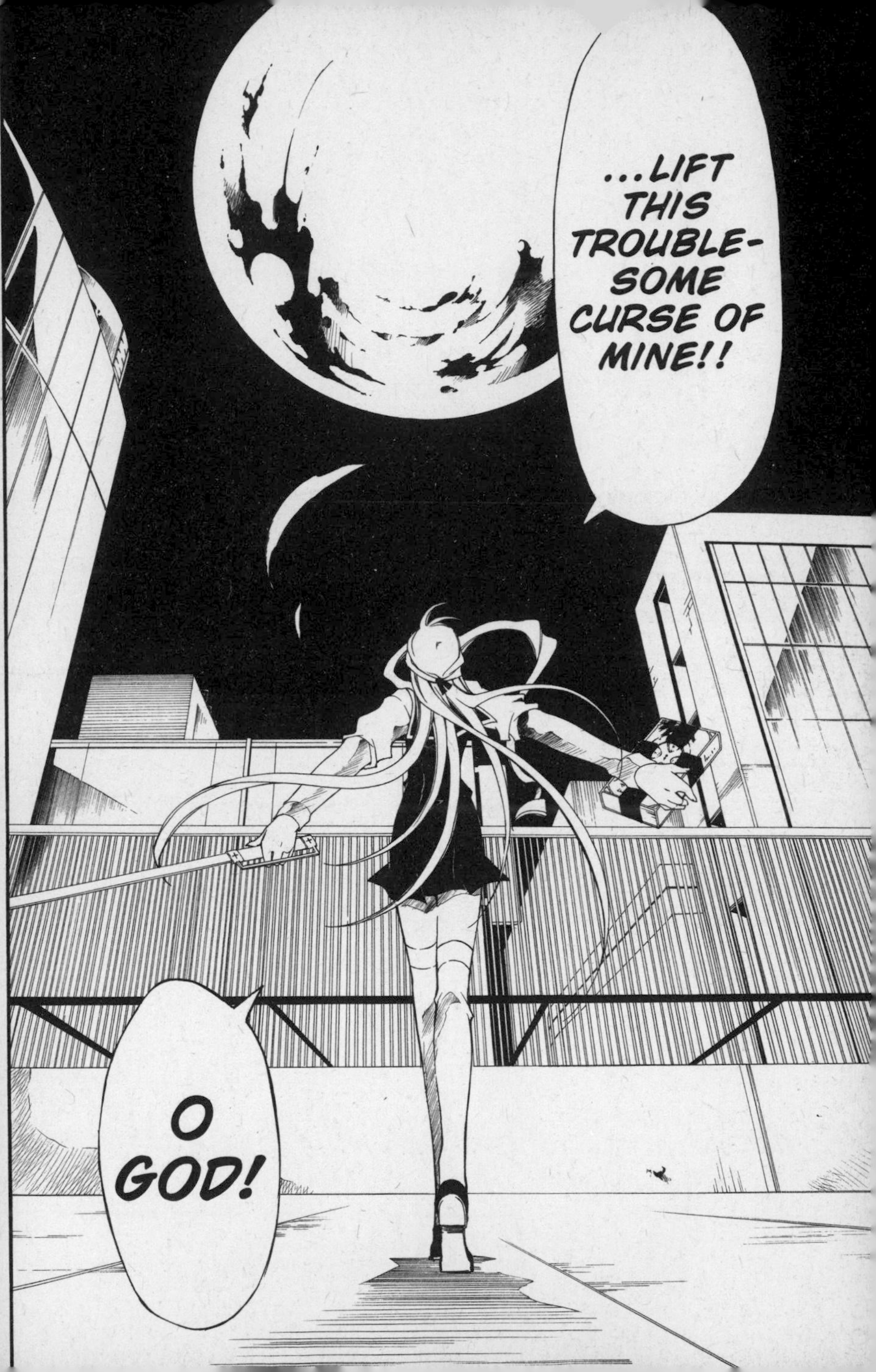
...LIFT THIS TROUBLE-SOME CURSE OF MINE!!
O GOD!

BLOODY CROSS

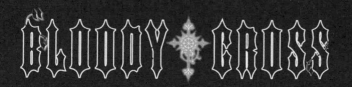

BLOODY CROSS

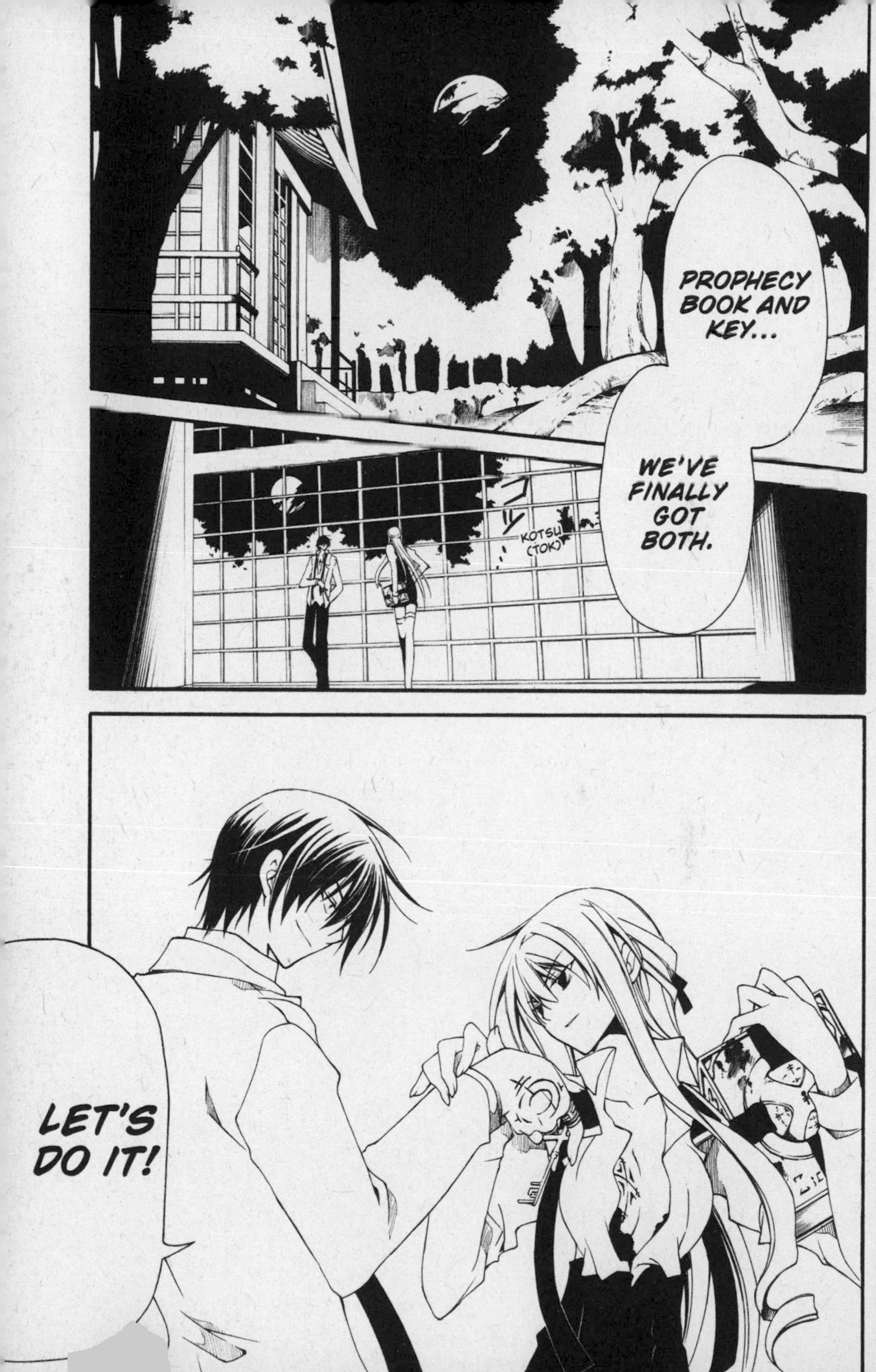
PROPHECY BOOK AND KEY...
WE'VE FINALLY GOT BOTH.
KOTSU (TOK)
LET'S DO IT!

LET'S UN-LOCK...
KACHI (CLICK)
...THE DIVINE POWER THAT WILL UNDO OUR CURSE ...!

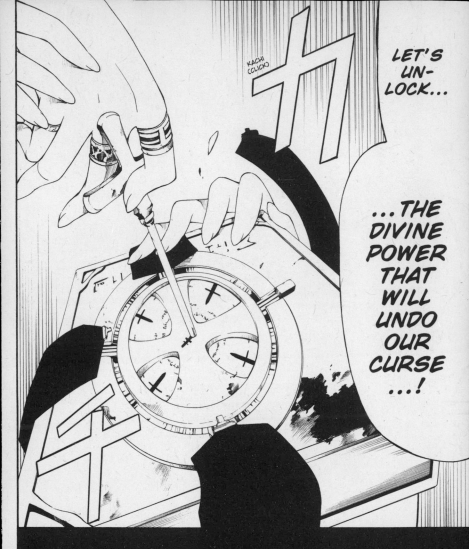

Chapter 3
The Divine Power

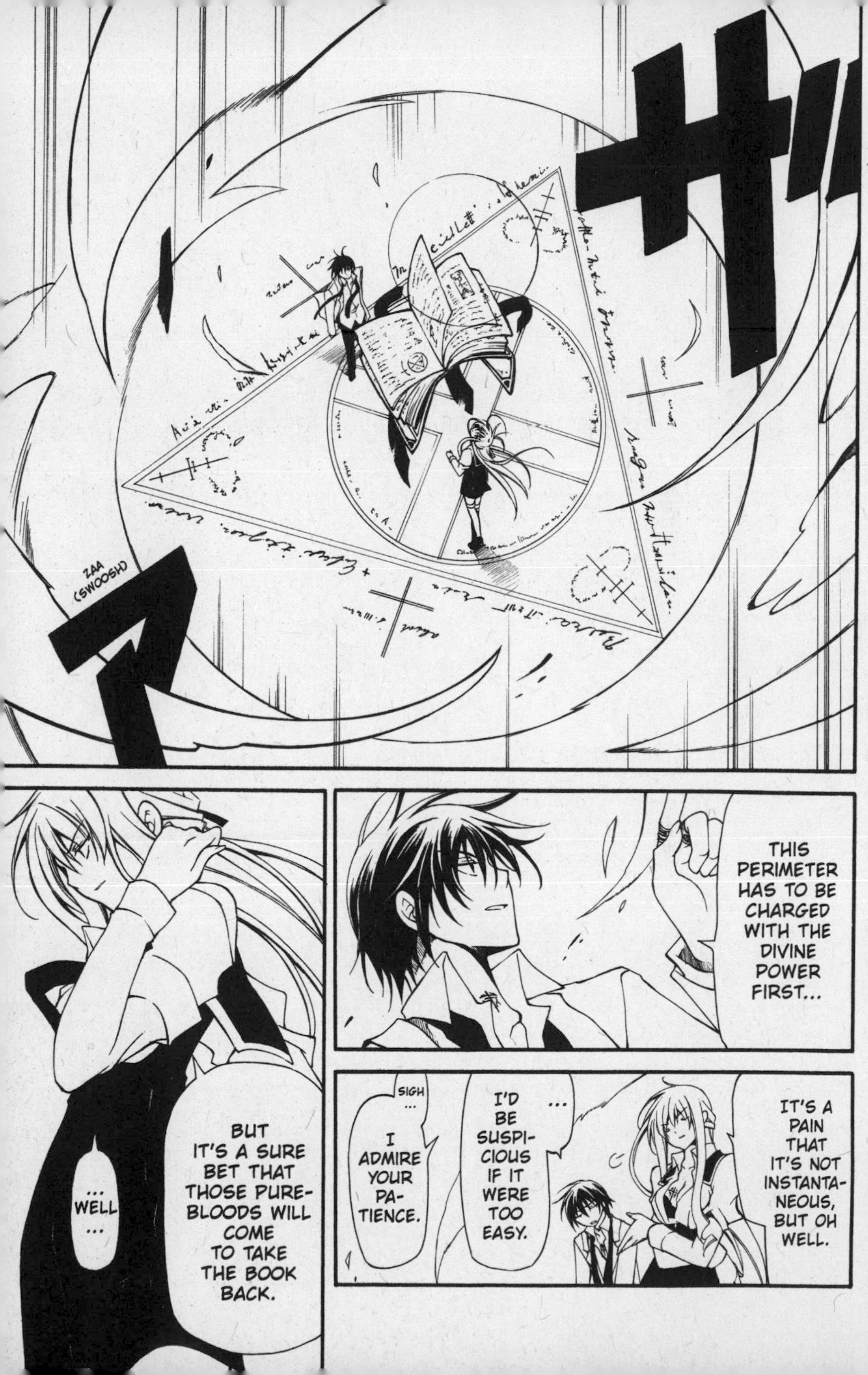
ZAA (SWOOSH)
THIS PERIMETER HAS TO BE CHARGED WITH THE DIVINE POWER FIRST...
IT'S A PAIN THAT IT'S NOT INSTANTANEOUS, BUT OH WELL.
I'D BE SUSPICIOUS IF IT WERE TOO EASY.
...
SIGH ...
I ADMIRE YOUR PATIENCE.
... WELL ...
BUT IT'S A SURE BET THAT THOSE PURE-BLOODS WILL COME TO TAKE THE BOOK BACK.

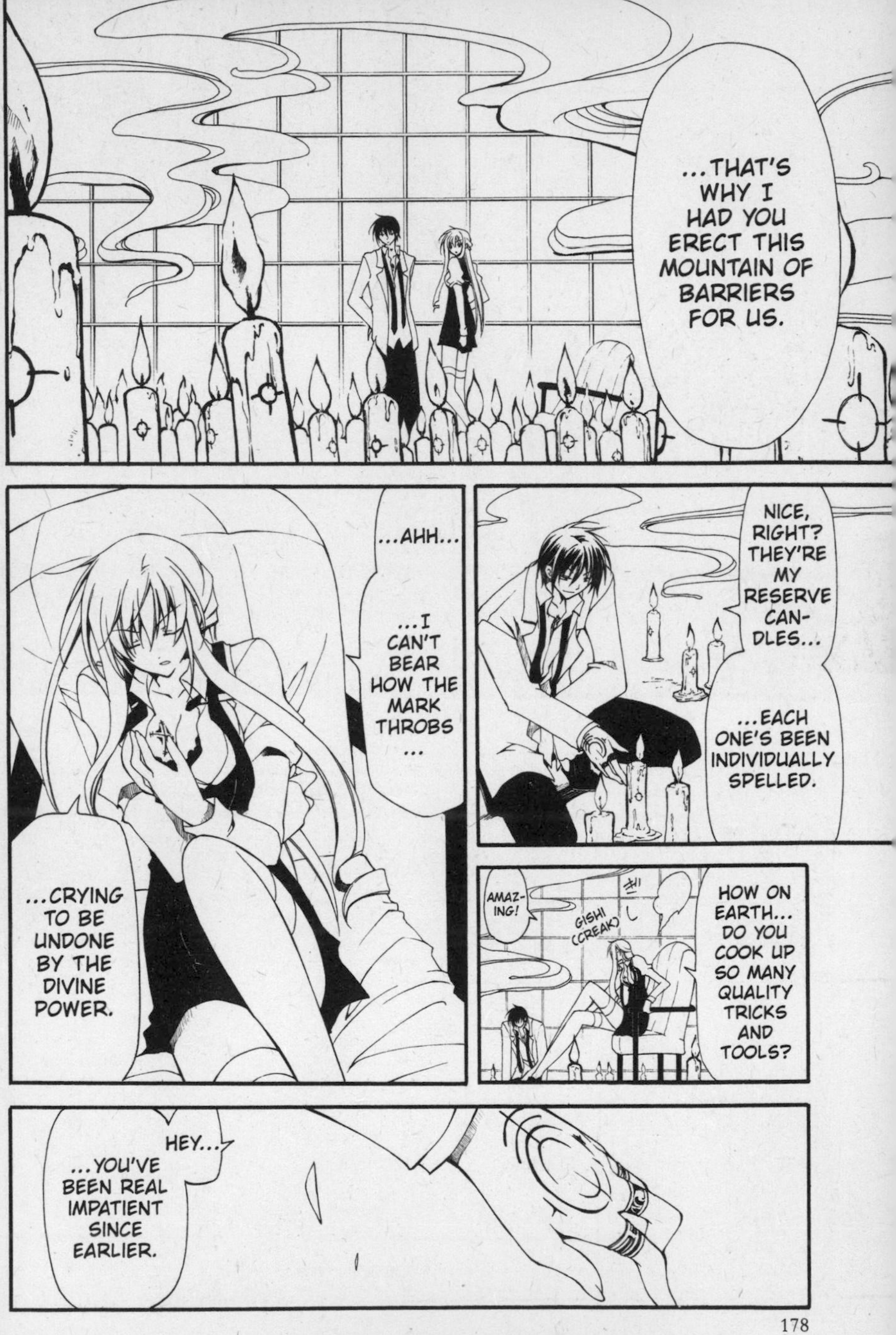
...THAT'S WHY I HAD YOU ERECT THIS MOUNTAIN OF BARRIERS FOR US.
NICE, RIGHT? THEY'RE MY RESERVE CAN-DLES...
...EACH ONE'S BEEN INDIVIDUALLY SPELLED.
HOW ON EARTH... DO YOU COOK UP SO MANY QUALITY TRICKS AND TOOLS?
ぎし
GISHI (CREAK)
AMAZ-ING!
...AHH...
...I CAN'T BEAR HOW THE MARK THROBS ...
...CRYING TO BE UNDONE BY THE DIVINE POWER.
HEY...
...YOU'VE BEEN REAL IMPATIENT SINCE EARLIER.

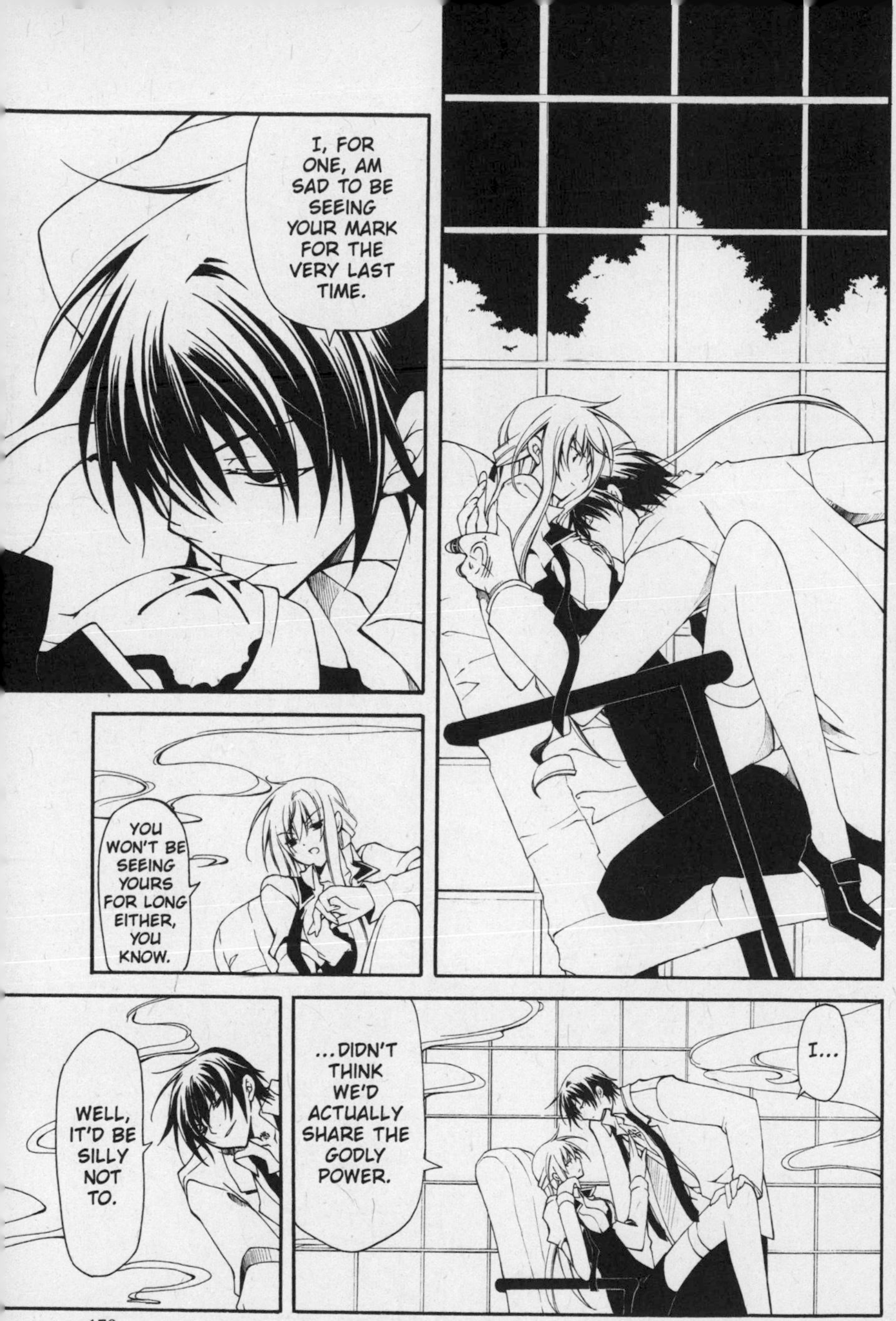
I, FOR ONE, AM SAD TO BE SEEING YOUR MARK FOR THE VERY LAST TIME.
YOU WON'T BE SEEING YOURS FOR LONG EITHER, YOU KNOW.
I...
...DIDN'T THINK WE'D ACTUALLY SHARE THE GODLY POWER.
WELL, IT'D BE SILLY NOT TO.

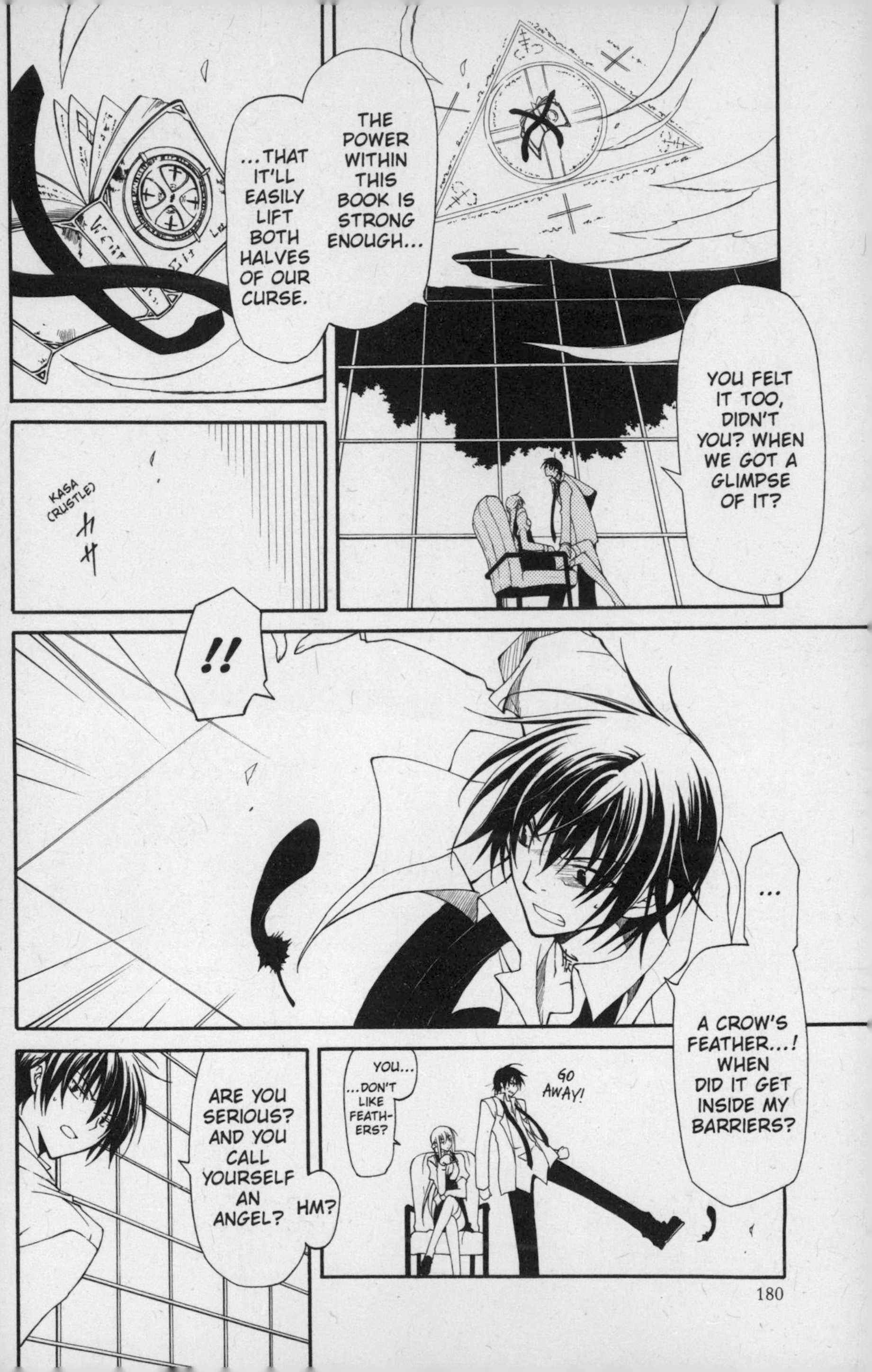
THE POWER WITHIN THIS BOOK IS STRONG ENOUGH...
...THAT IT'LL EASILY LIFT BOTH HALVES OF OUR CURSE.
YOU FELT IT TOO, DIDN'T YOU? WHEN WE GOT A GLIMPSE OF IT?
KASA (RUSTLE)
!!
...
A CROW'S FEATHER...! WHEN DID IT GET INSIDE MY BARRIERS?
GO AWAY!
YOU...
...DON'T LIKE FEATHERS?
HM?
ARE YOU SERIOUS? AND YOU CALL YOURSELF AN ANGEL?

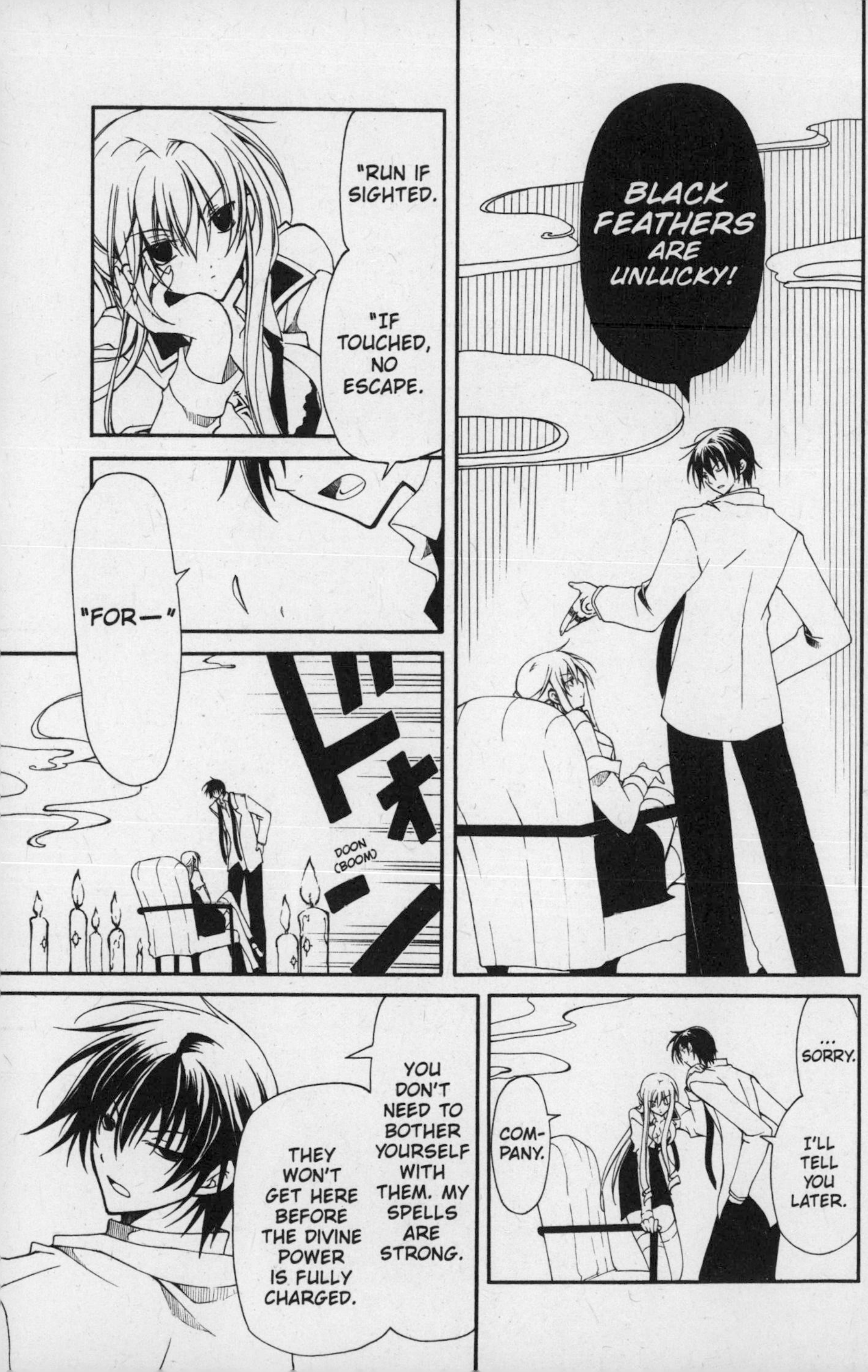
BLACK FEATHERS ARE UNLUCKY!
"RUN IF SIGHTED.
"IF TOUCHED, NO ESCAPE.
"FOR—"
ドォン
DOON (BOOM)
... SORRY.
I'LL TELL YOU LATER.
COM-PANY.
YOU DON'T NEED TO BOTHER YOURSELF WITH THEM. MY SPELLS ARE STRONG.
THEY WON'T GET HERE BEFORE THE DIVINE POWER IS FULLY CHARGED.

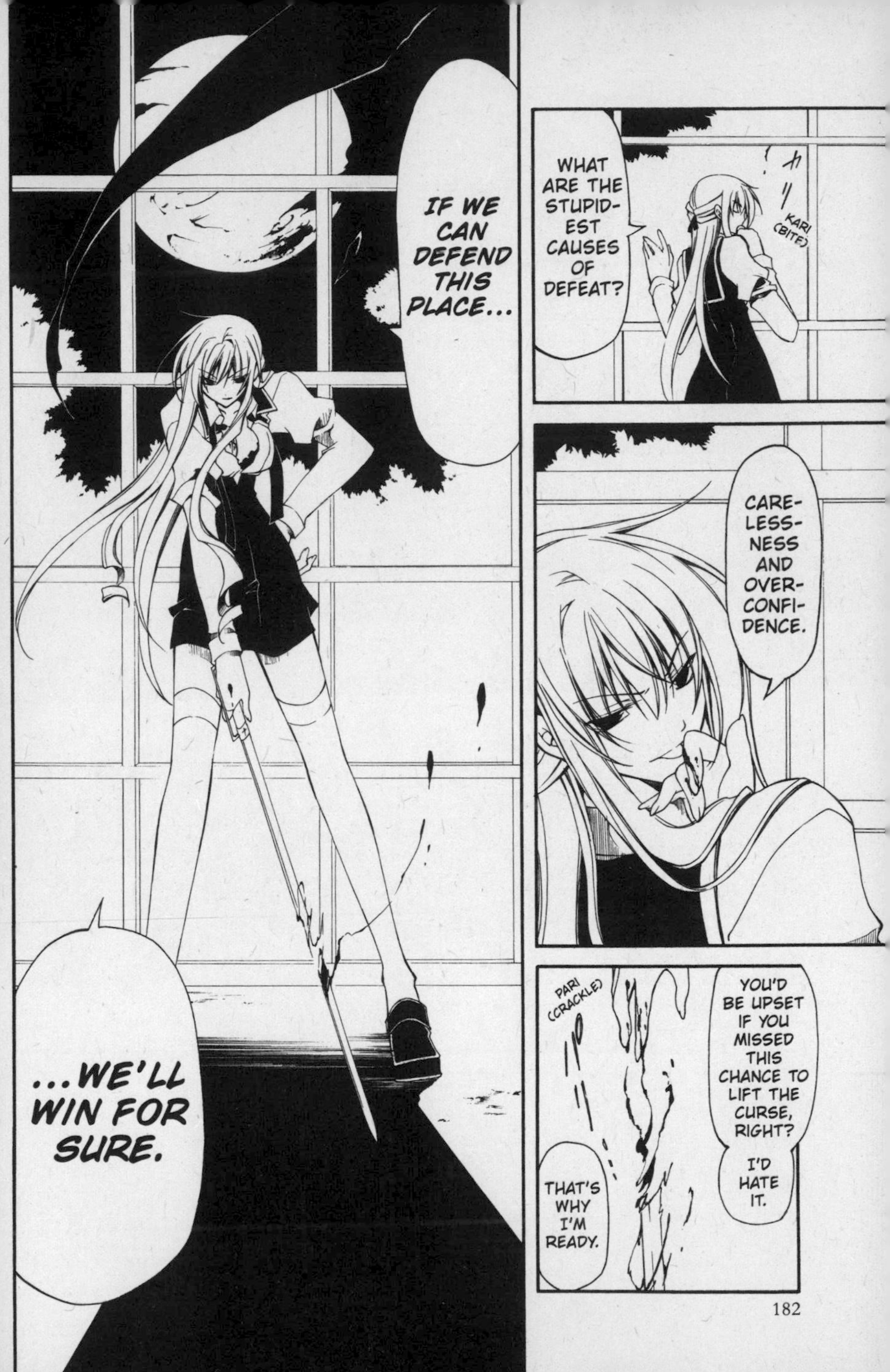
WHAT ARE THE STUPID-EST CAUSES OF DEFEAT?
KARI (BITE)
CARE-LESS-NESS AND OVER-CONFI-DENCE.
YOU'D BE UPSET IF YOU MISSED THIS CHANCE TO LIFT THE CURSE, RIGHT?
I'D HATE IT.
PARI (CRACKLE)
THAT'S WHY I'M READY.
IF WE CAN DEFEND THIS PLACE...
...WE'LL WIN FOR SURE.

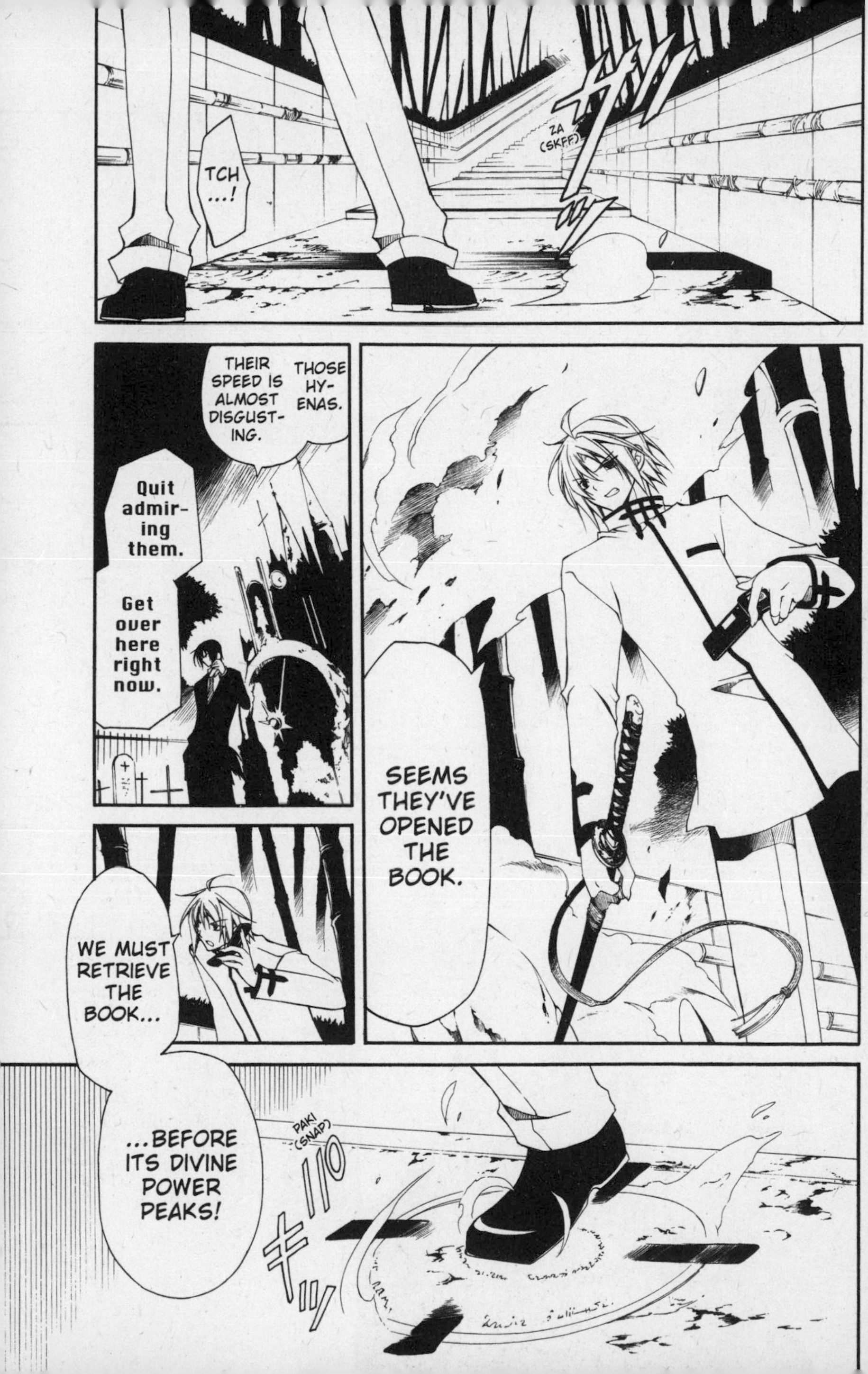
ZA (SKFF)
TCH ...!
SEEMS THEY'VE OPENED THE BOOK.
THOSE HY-ENAS.
THEIR SPEED IS ALMOST DISGUST-ING.
Quit admir-ing them.
Get over here right now.
WE MUST RETRIEVE THE BOOK...
...BEFORE ITS DIVINE POWER PEAKS!
PAKI (SNAP)

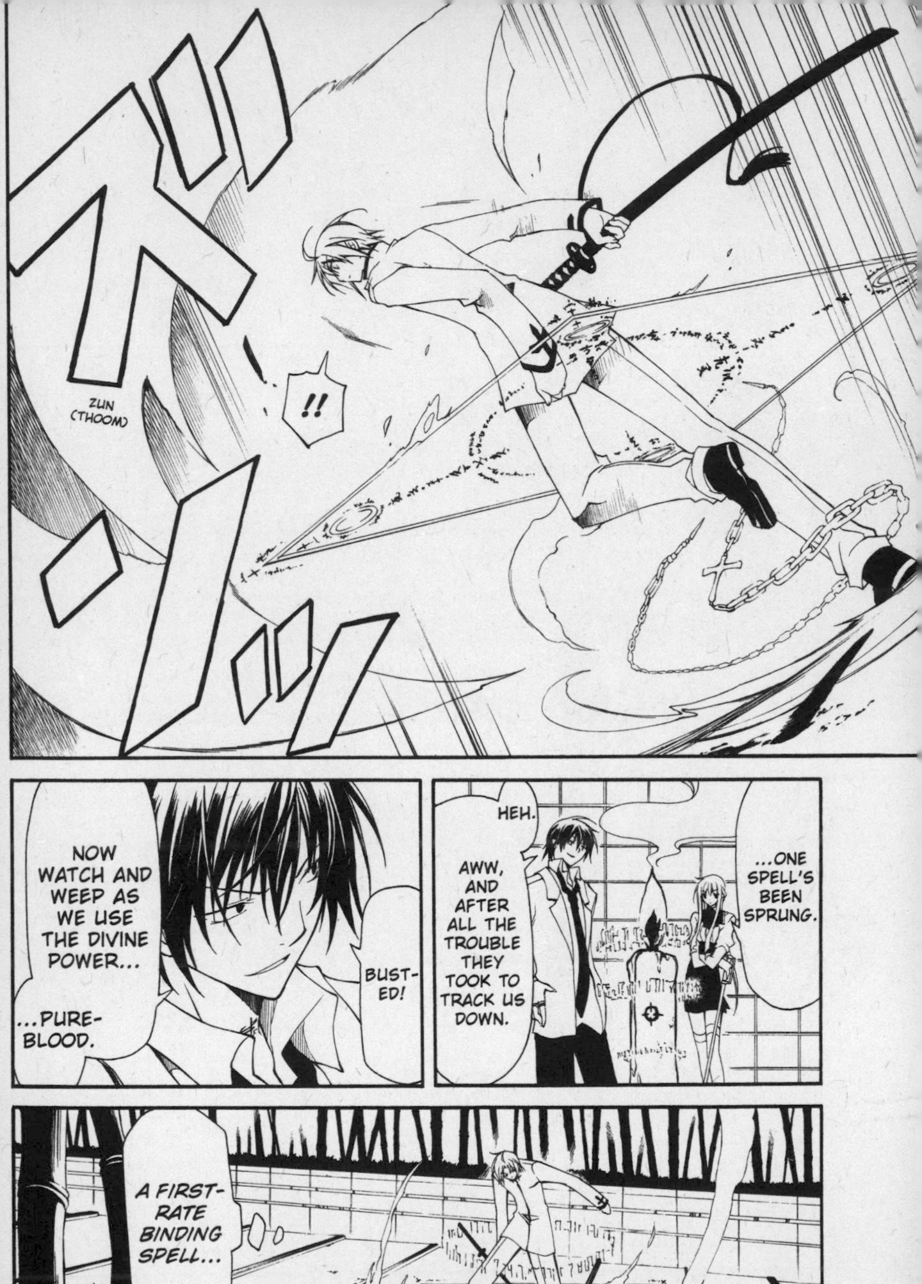
ZUN (THOOM)
!!
...ONE SPELL'S BEEN SPRUNG.
HEH.
AWW, AND AFTER ALL THE TROUBLE THEY TOOK TO TRACK US DOWN.
BUST-ED!
NOW WATCH AND WEEP AS WE USE THE DIVINE POWER...
...PURE-BLOOD.
A FIRST-RATE BINDING SPELL...

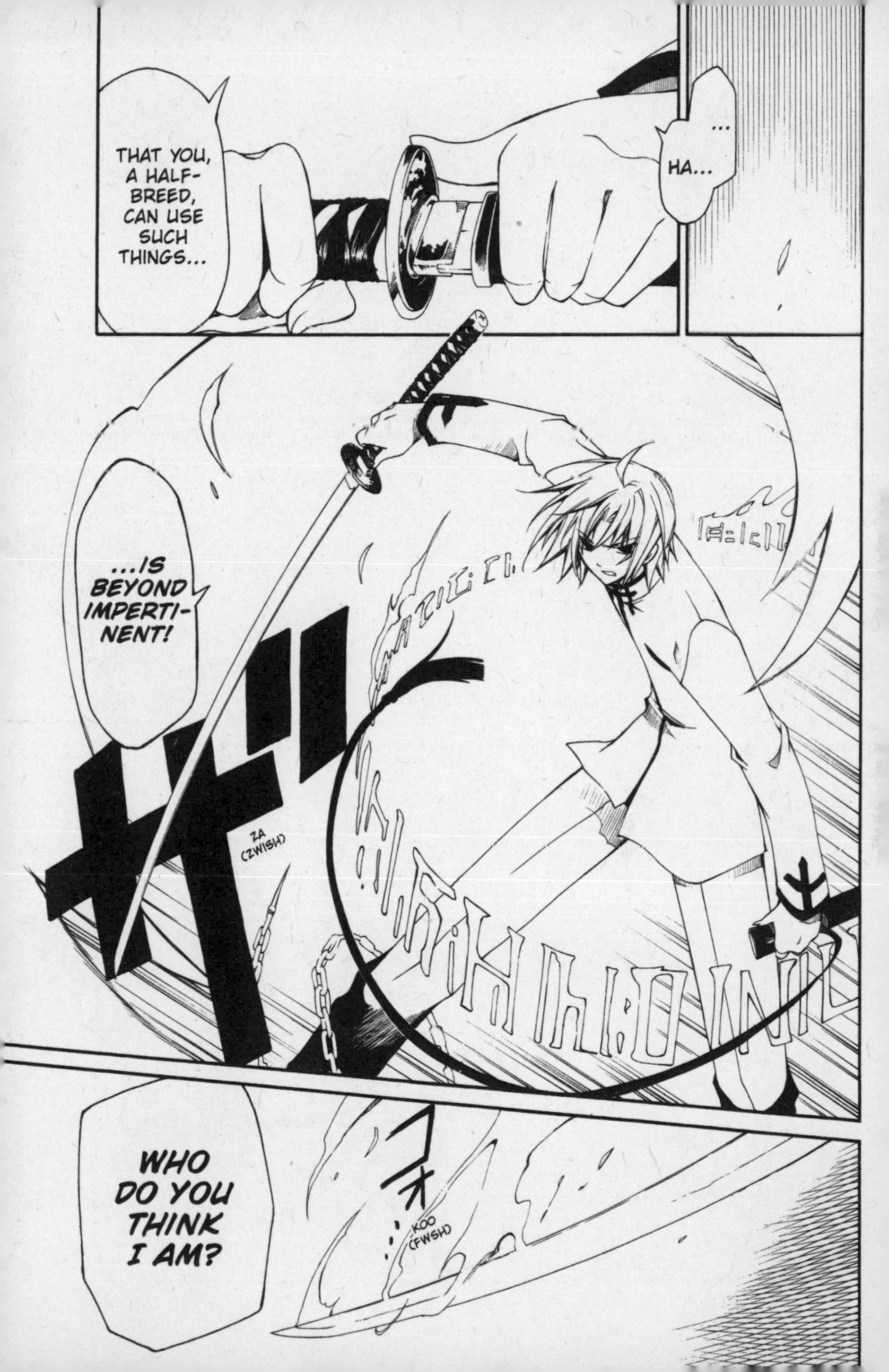
... HA...
THAT YOU, A HALF-BREED, CAN USE SUCH THINGS...
...IS BEYOND IMPERTINENT!
ZA (ZWISH)
KOO (FWSH)
WHO DO YOU THINK I AM?

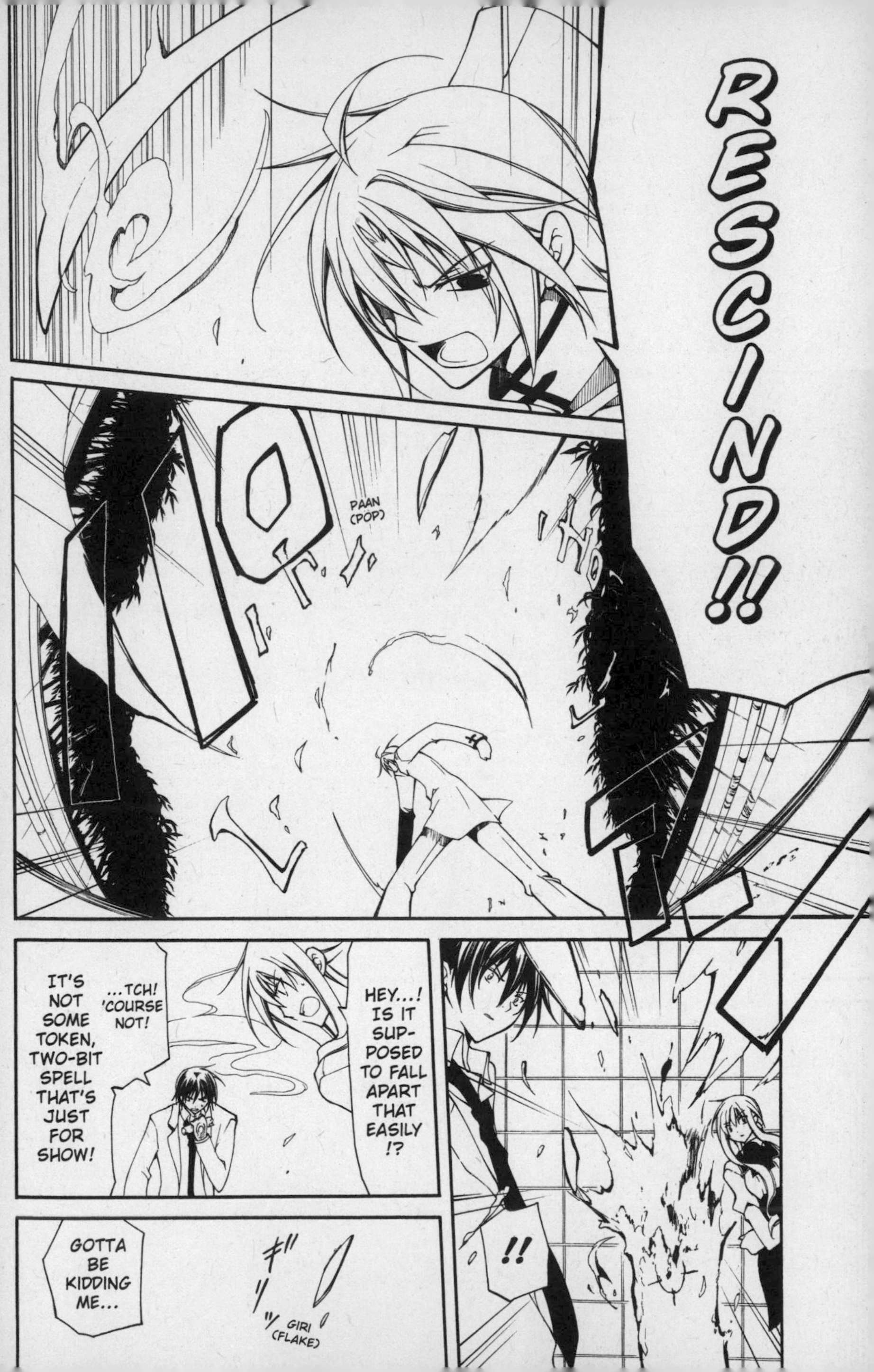
RESCIND!!
PAAN (POP)
HEY...! IS IT SUP-POSED TO FALL APART THAT EASILY !?
!!
...TCH! 'COURSE NOT!
IT'S NOT SOME TOKEN, TWO-BIT SPELL THAT'S JUST FOR SHOW!
GOTTA BE KIDDING ME...
GIRI (FLAKE)

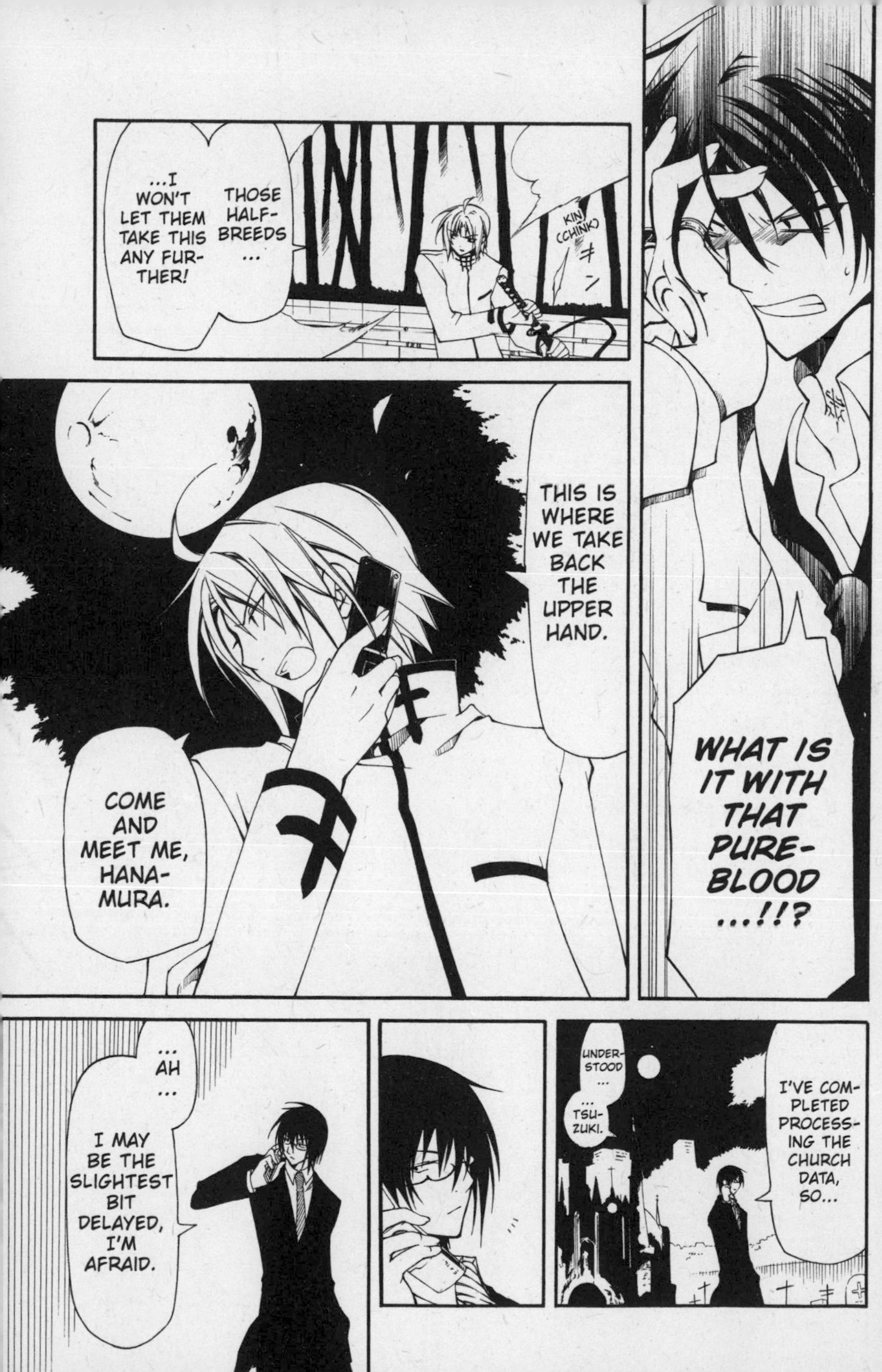
WHAT IS IT WITH THAT PURE-BLOOD ...!!?
KIN (CHINK)
キン
THOSE HALF-BREEDS ...
...I WON'T LET THEM TAKE THIS ANY FURTHER!
THIS IS WHERE WE TAKE BACK THE UPPER HAND.
COME AND MEET ME, HANAMURA.
I'VE COMPLETED PROCESSING THE CHURCH DATA, SO...
UNDERSTOOD ...
... TSUZUKI.
... AH ...
I MAY BE THE SLIGHTEST BIT DELAYED, I'M AFRAID.

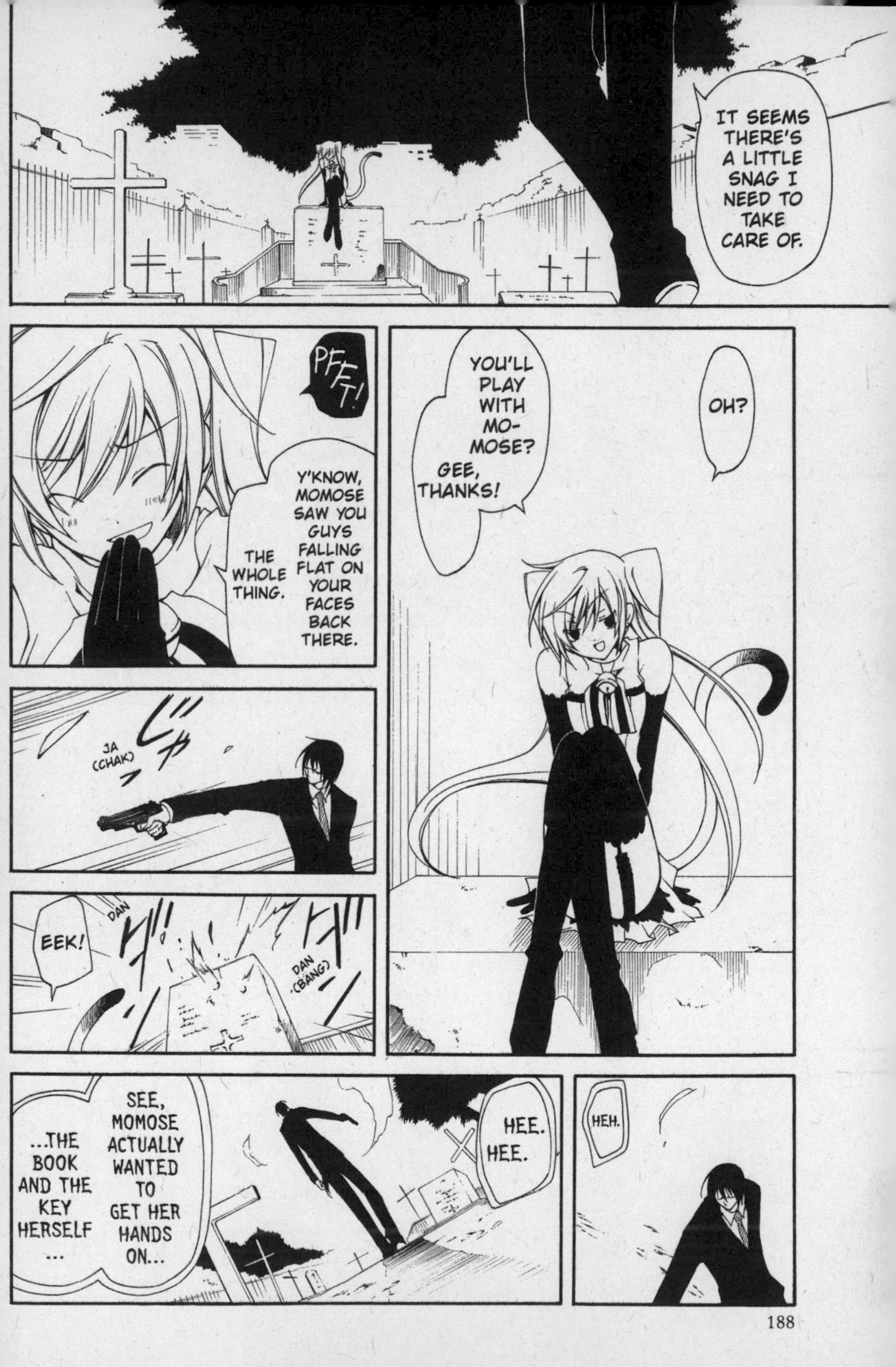
IT SEEMS THERE'S A LITTLE SNAG I NEED TO TAKE CARE OF.
OH?
YOU'LL PLAY WITH MO-MOSE? GEE, THANKS!
PFFT!
Y'KNOW, MOMOSE SAW YOU GUYS FALLING FLAT ON YOUR FACES BACK THERE.
THE WHOLE THING.
JA (CHAK)
DAN
EEK!
DAN (BANG)
HEH.
HEE. HEE.
SEE, MOMOSE ACTUALLY WANTED TO GET HER HANDS ON...
...THE BOOK AND THE KEY HERSELF...

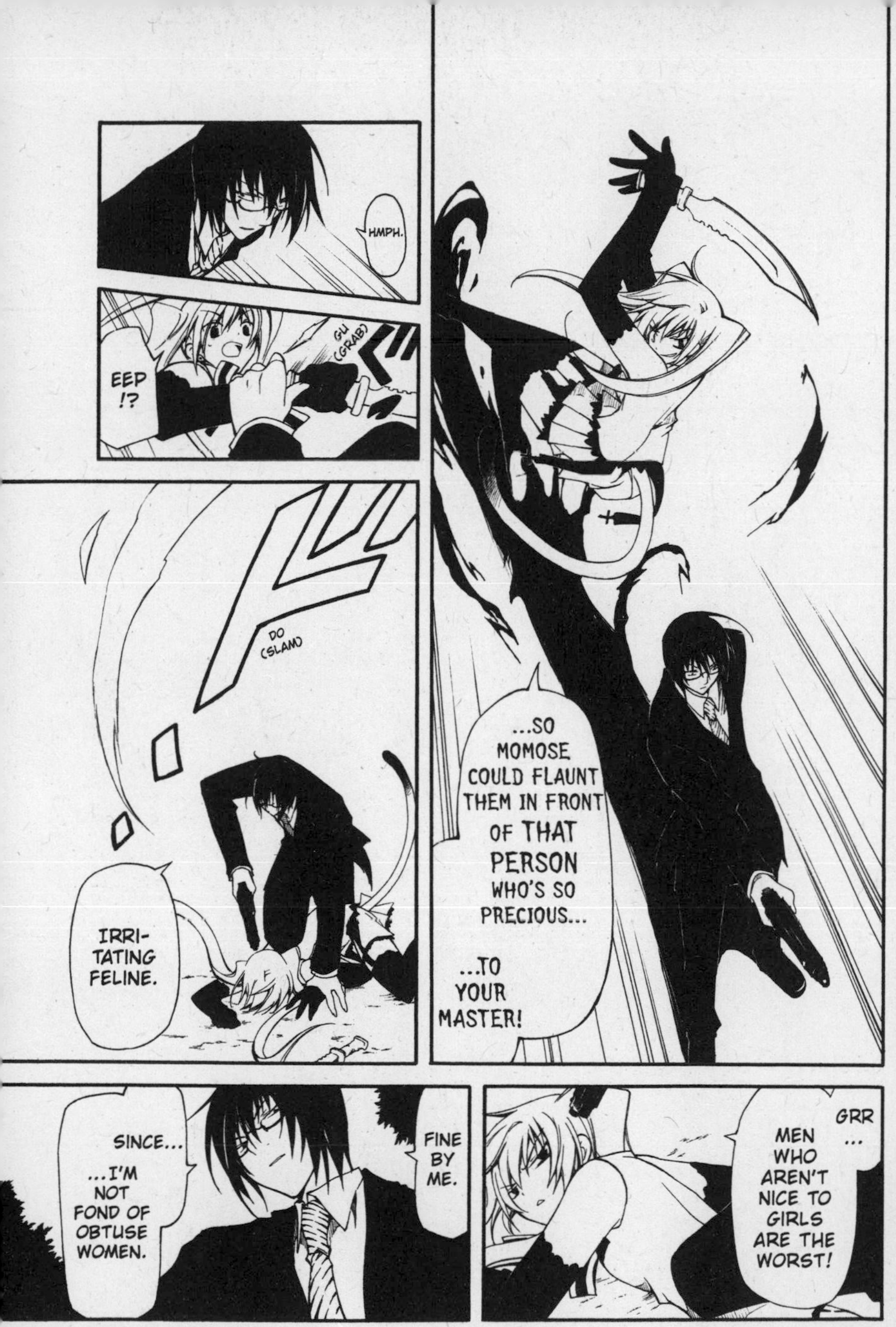
...SO MOMOSE COULD FLAUNT THEM IN FRONT OF THAT PERSON WHO'S SO PRECIOUS...
...TO YOUR MASTER!
HMPH.
GU (GRAB)
EEP !?
DO (SLAM)
IRRI- TATING FELINE.
GRR ...
MEN WHO AREN'T NICE TO GIRLS ARE THE WORST!
FINE BY ME.
SINCE...
...I'M NOT FOND OF OBTUSE WOMEN.

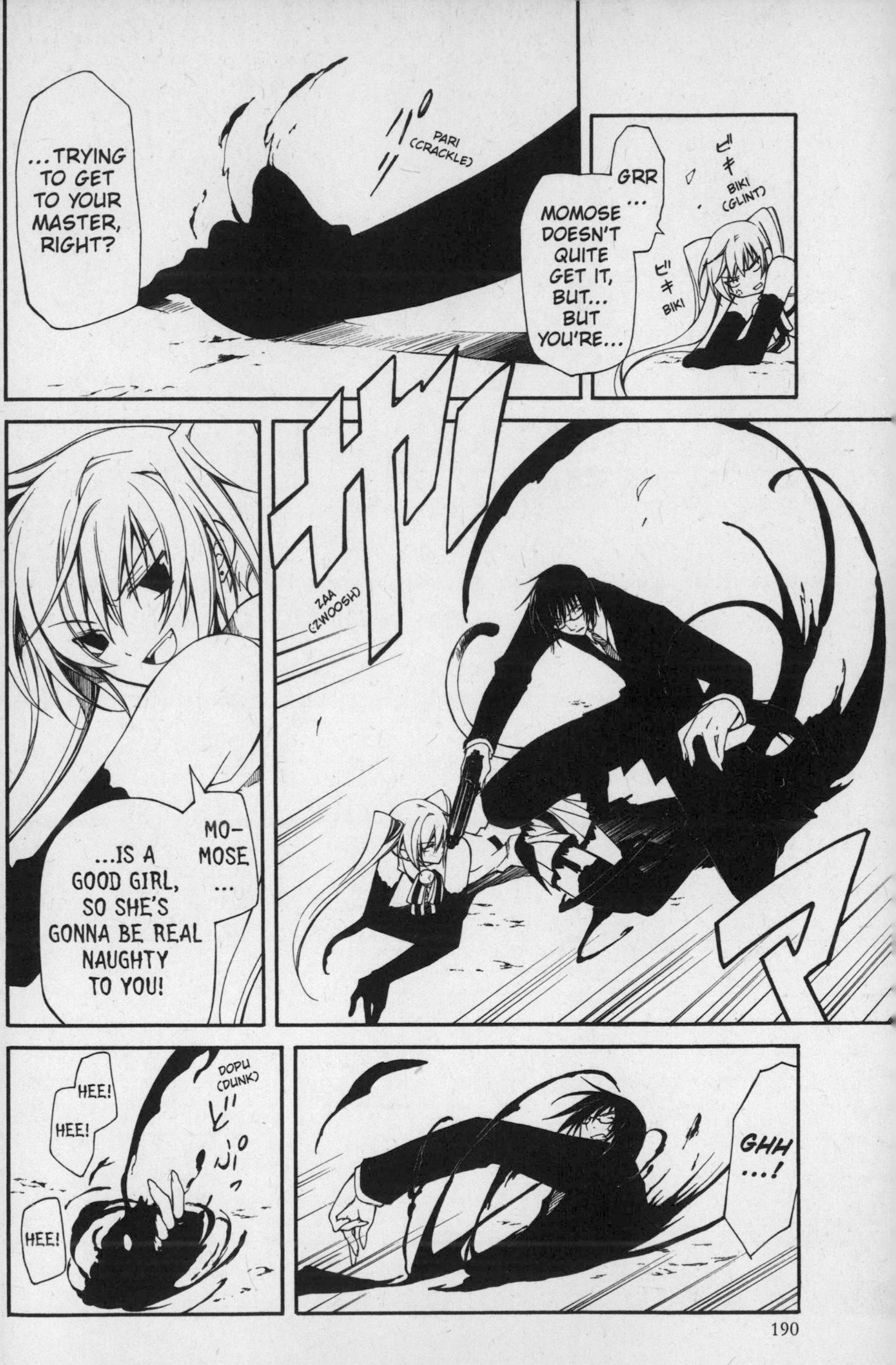
GRR ...
MOMOSE DOESN'T QUITE GET IT, BUT... BUT YOU'RE...
ビキ
BIKI (GLINT)
ビキ
BIKI
PARI (CRACKLE)
...TRYING TO GET TO YOUR MASTER, RIGHT?
ZAA (ZWOOSH)
MO-MOSE ...
...IS A GOOD GIRL, SO SHE'S GONNA BE REAL NAUGHTY TO YOU!
GHH ...!
DOPU (DUNK)
HEE!
HEE!
HEE!

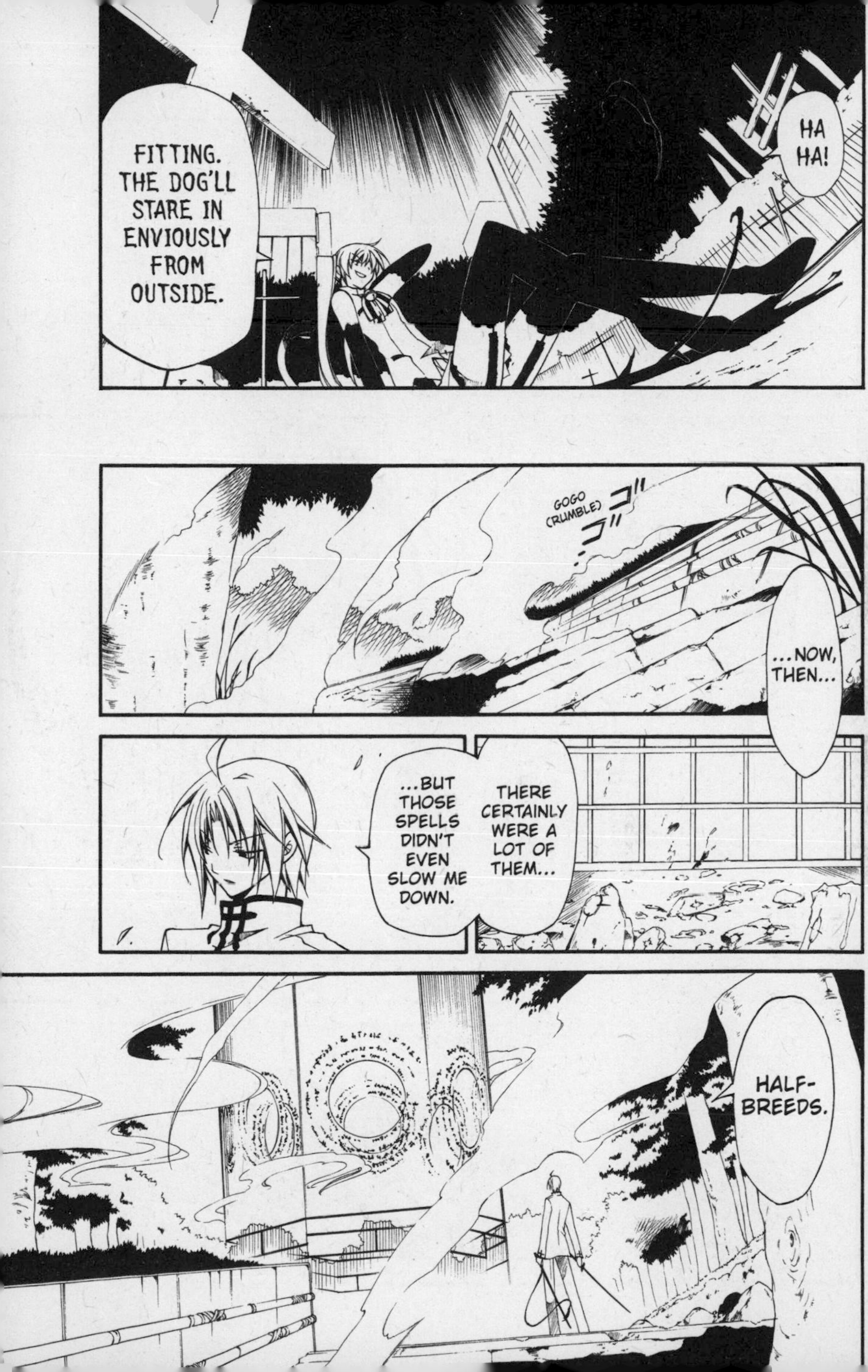
HA HA!
FITTING. THE DOG'LL STARE IN ENVIOUSLY FROM OUTSIDE.
GOGO (RUMBLE) ゴゴ
...NOW, THEN...
THERE CERTAINLY WERE A LOT OF THEM...
...BUT THOSE SPELLS DIDN'T EVEN SLOW ME DOWN.
HALF-BREEDS.

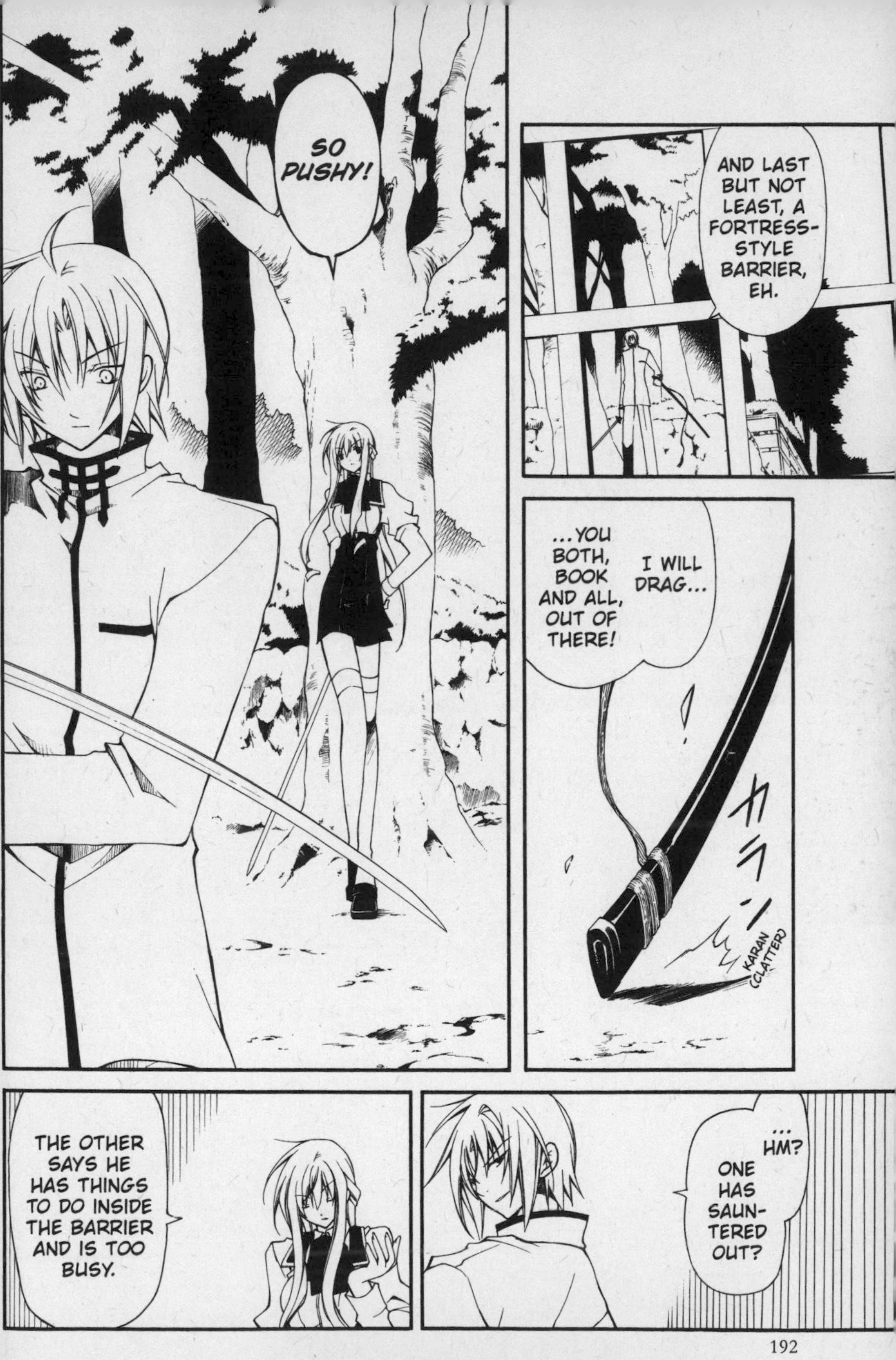
AND LAST BUT NOT LEAST, A FORTRESS-STYLE BARRIER, EH.
I WILL DRAG...
...YOU BOTH, BOOK AND ALL, OUT OF THERE!
KARAN (CLATTER)
SO PUSHY!
... HM? ONE HAS SAUNTERED OUT?
THE OTHER SAYS HE HAS THINGS TO DO INSIDE THE BARRIER AND IS TOO BUSY.

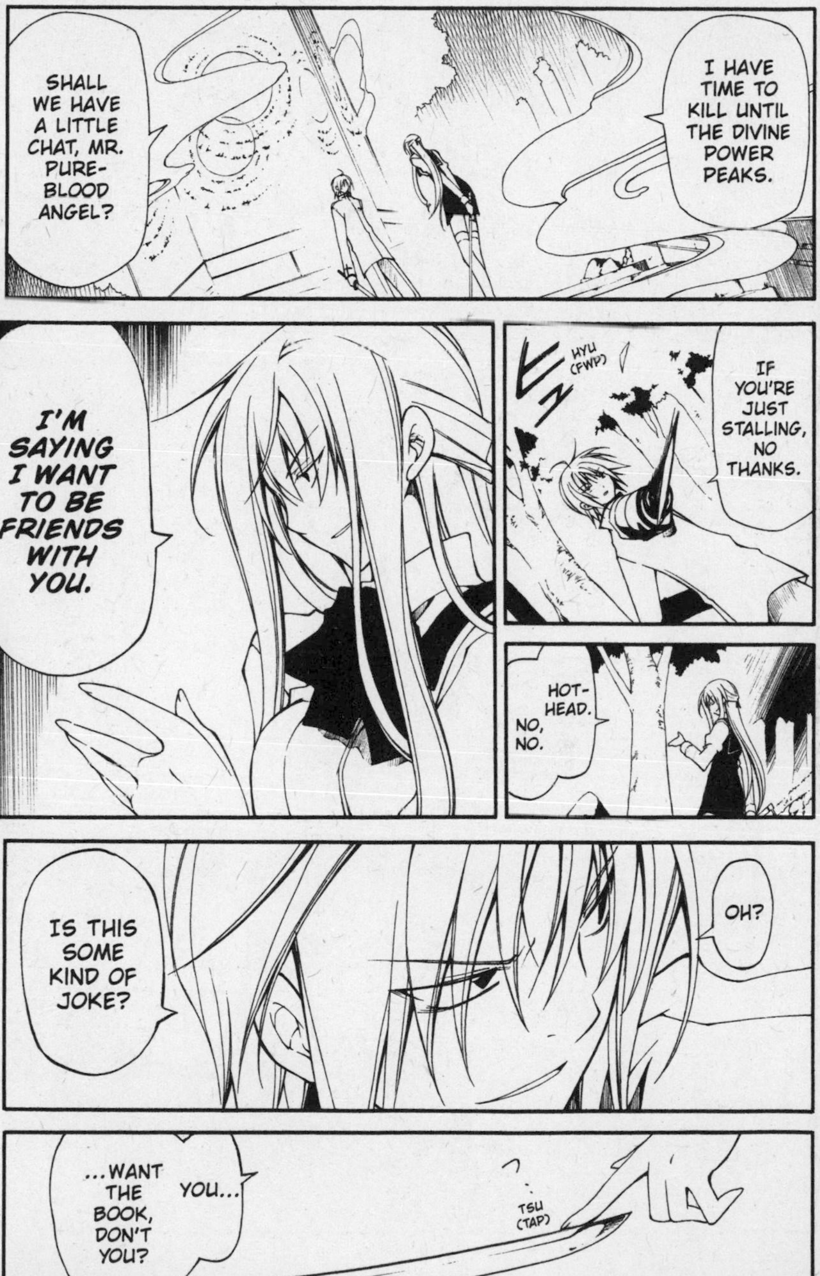
I HAVE TIME TO KILL UNTIL THE DIVINE POWER PEAKS.
SHALL WE HAVE A LITTLE CHAT, MR. PURE-BLOOD ANGEL?
IF YOU'RE JUST STALLING, NO THANKS.
HYU (FWP)
HOT-HEAD.
NO, NO.
I'M SAYING I WANT TO BE FRIENDS WITH YOU.
OH?
IS THIS SOME KIND OF JOKE?
TSU (TAP)
YOU...
...WANT THE BOOK, DON'T YOU?

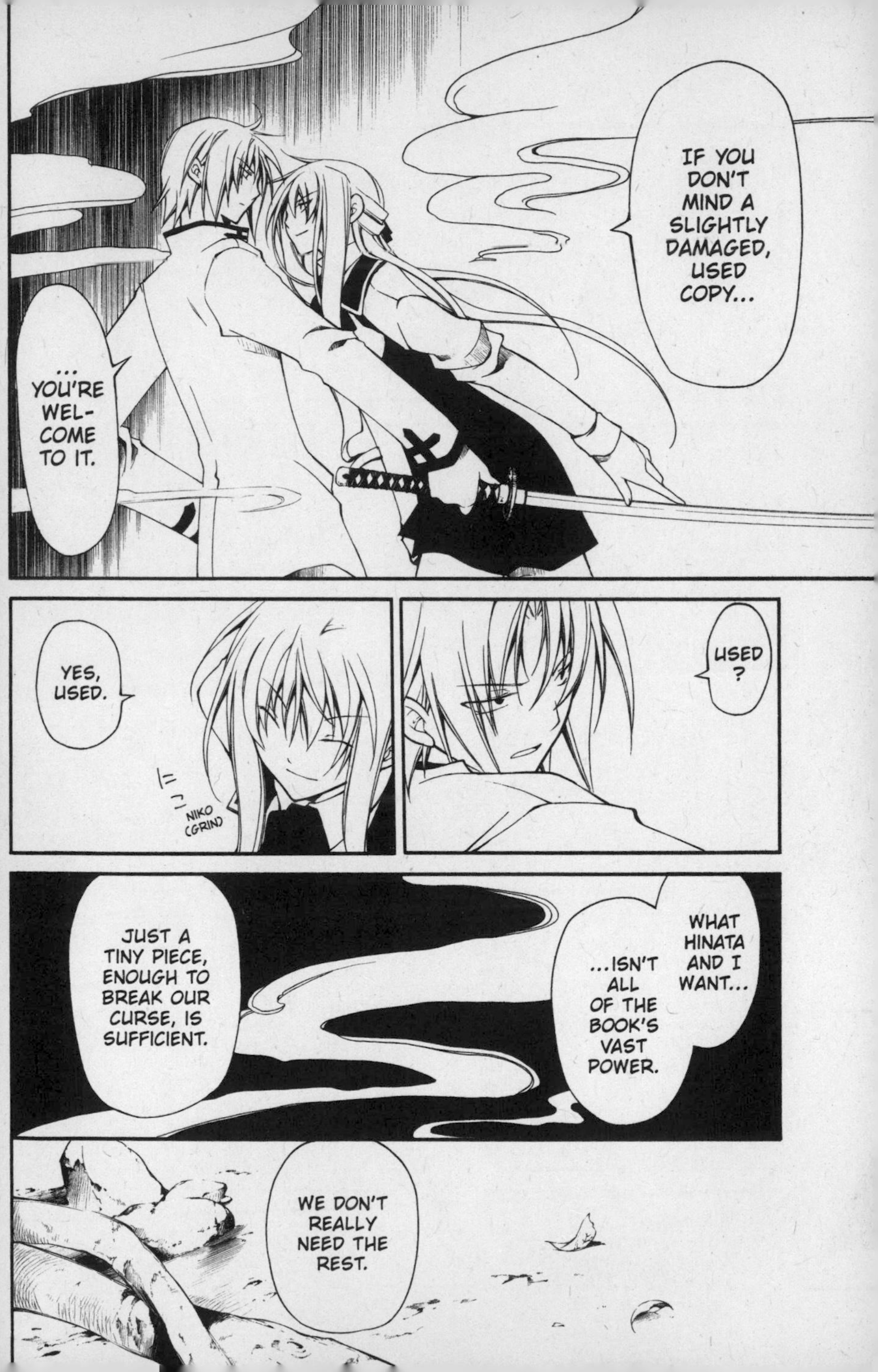
IF YOU DON'T MIND A SLIGHTLY DAMAGED, USED COPY...
...YOU'RE WEL-COME TO IT.
USED?
YES, USED.
NIKO (GRIN)
WHAT HINATA AND I WANT...
...ISN'T ALL OF THE BOOK'S VAST POWER.
JUST A TINY PIECE, ENOUGH TO BREAK OUR CURSE, IS SUFFICIENT.
WE DON'T REALLY NEED THE REST.

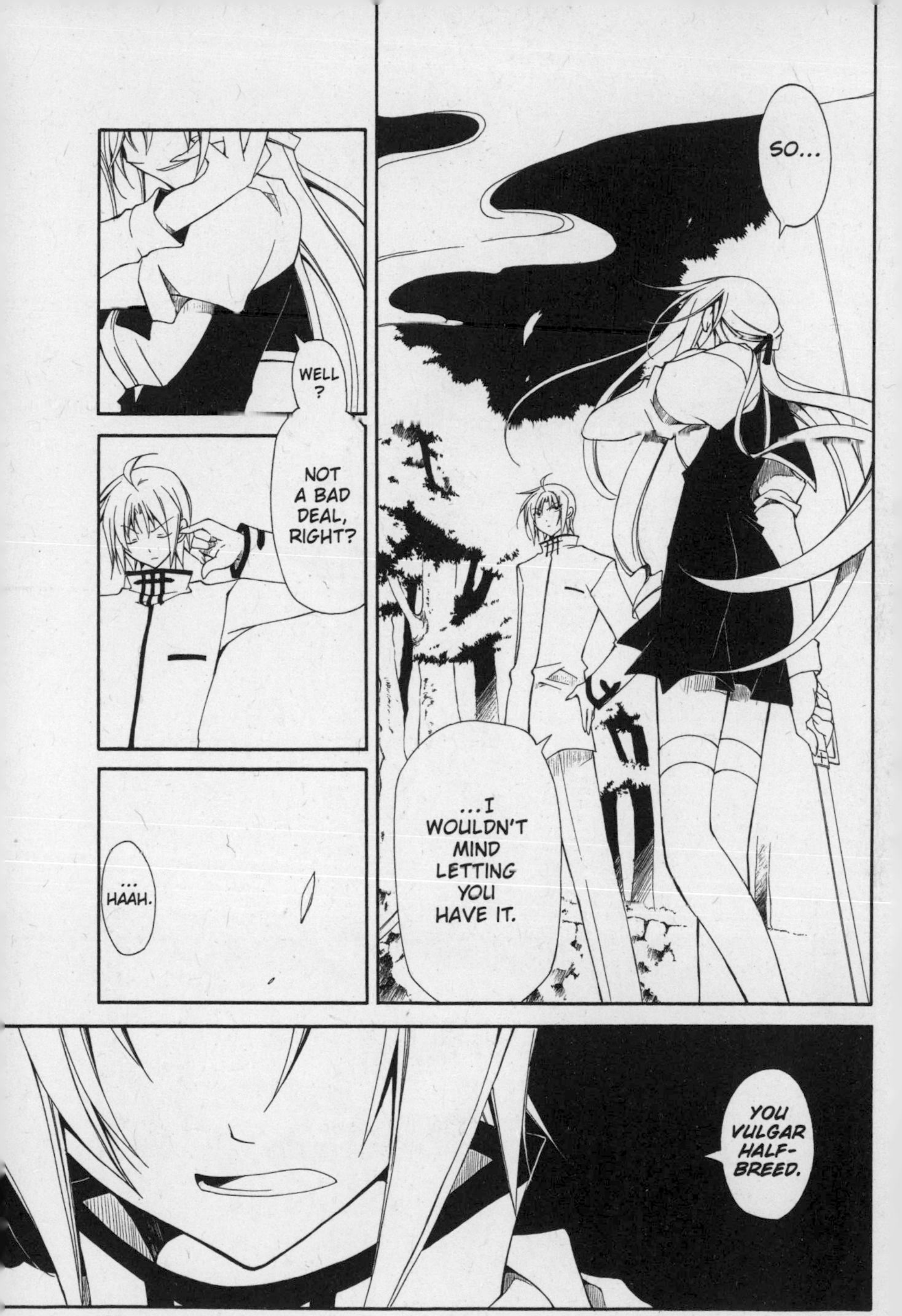
SO...
...I WOULDN'T MIND LETTING YOU HAVE IT.
WELL?
NOT A BAD DEAL, RIGHT?
...HAAH.
YOU VULGAR HALF-BREED.

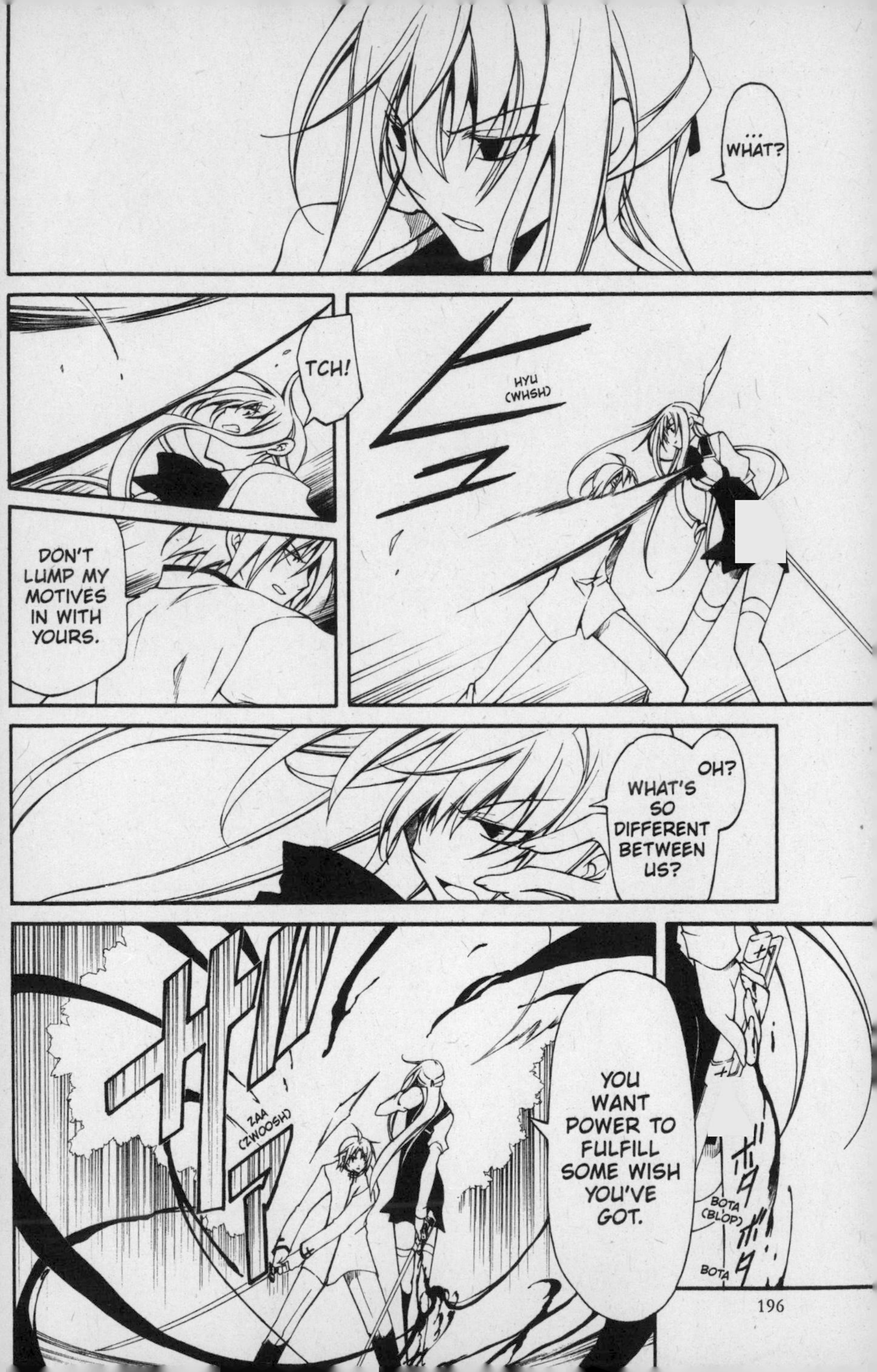
...WHAT?
HYU (WHSH)
TCH!
DON'T LUMP MY MOTIVES IN WITH YOURS.
OH? WHAT'S SO DIFFERENT BETWEEN US?
BOTA (BLOP)
BOTA
YOU WANT POWER TO FULFILL SOME WISH YOU'VE GOT.
ZAA (ZWOOSH)

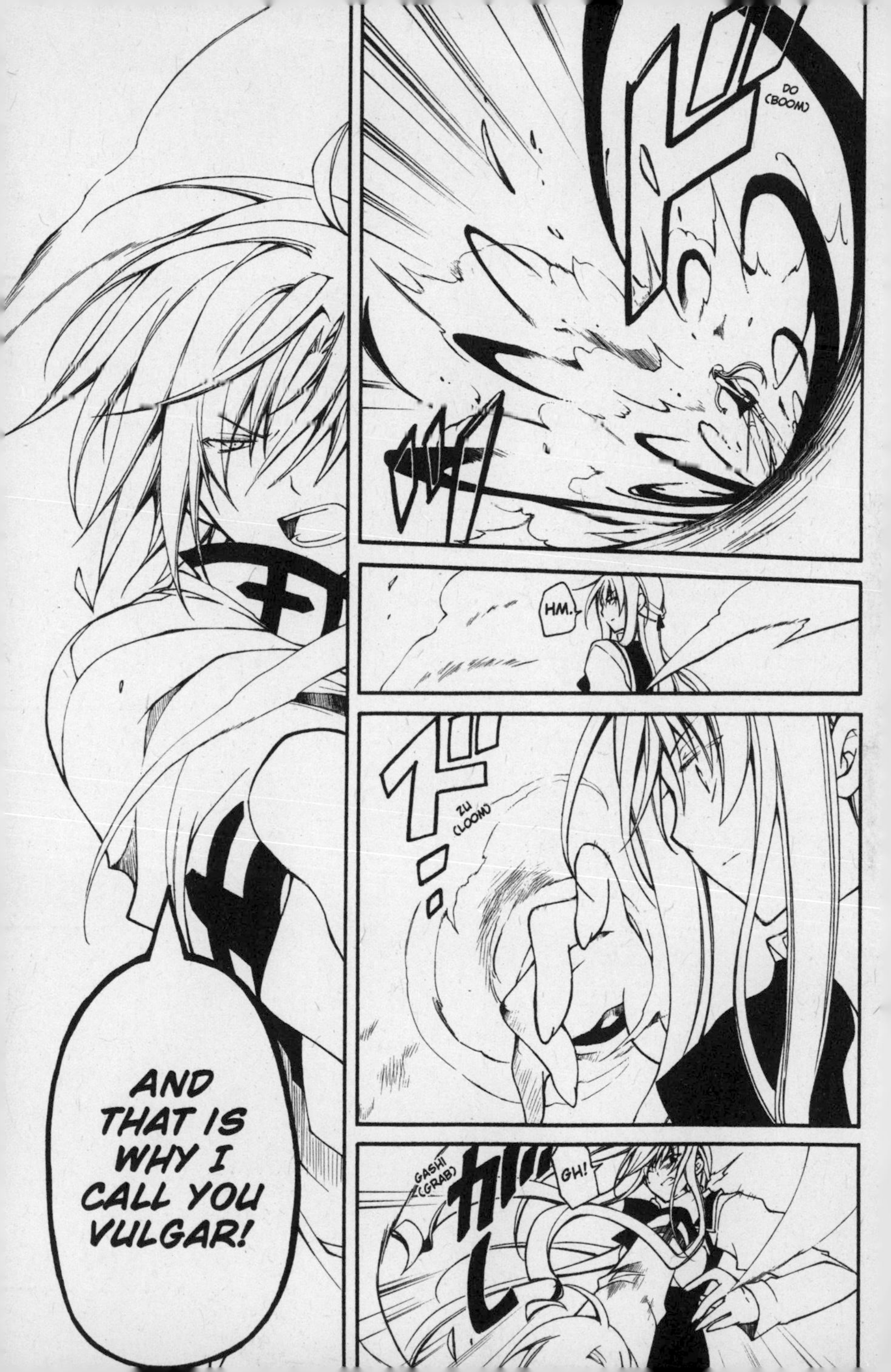
DO (BOOM)
HM.
ZU (LOOM)
GH!
GASHI (GRAB)
AND THAT IS WHY I CALL YOU VULGAR!

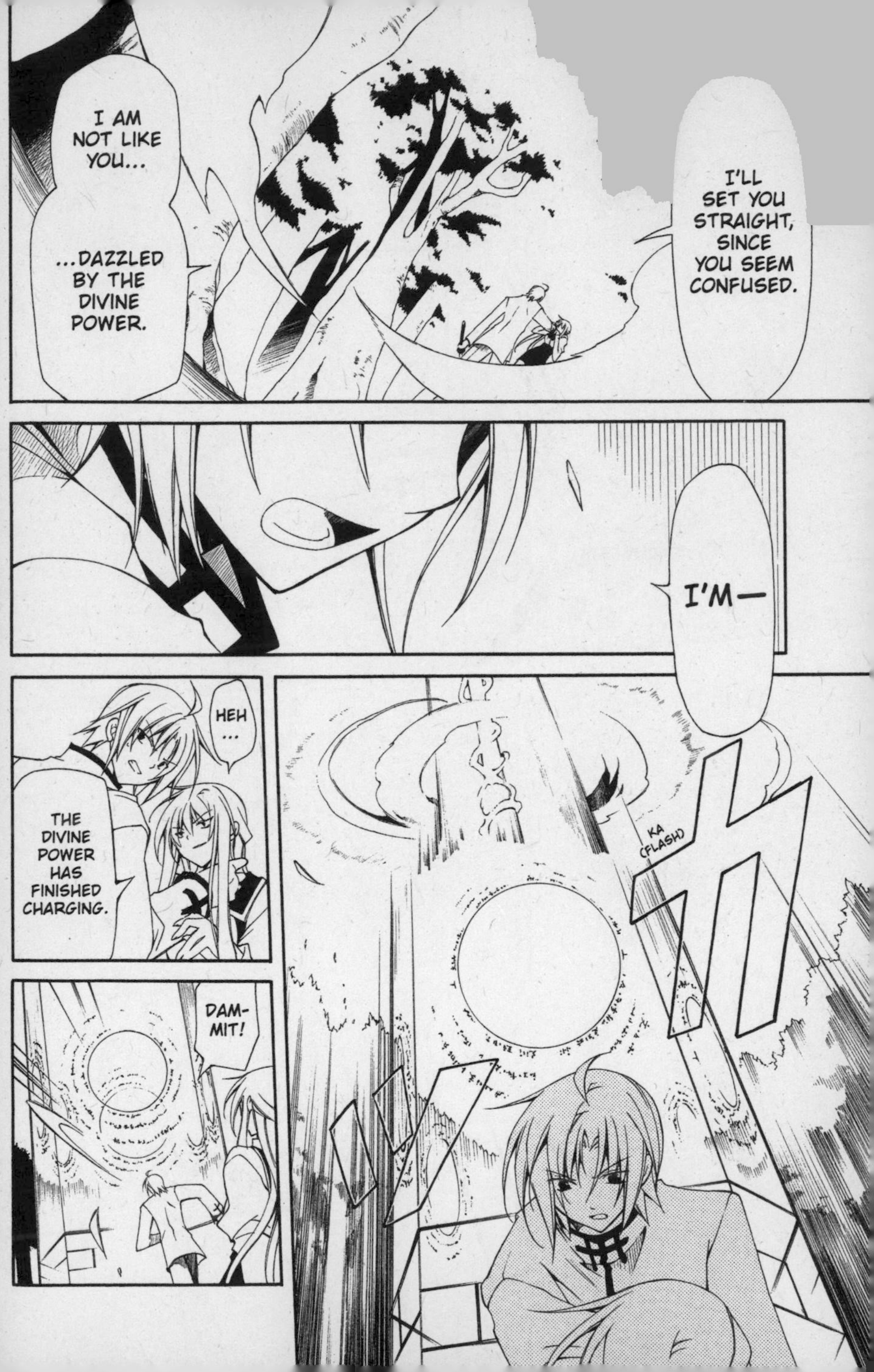
I'LL SET YOU STRAIGHT, SINCE YOU SEEM CONFUSED.
I AM NOT LIKE YOU...
...DAZZLED BY THE DIVINE POWER.
I'M—
KA (FLASH)
HEH ...
THE DIVINE POWER HAS FINISHED CHARGING.
DAM-MIT!

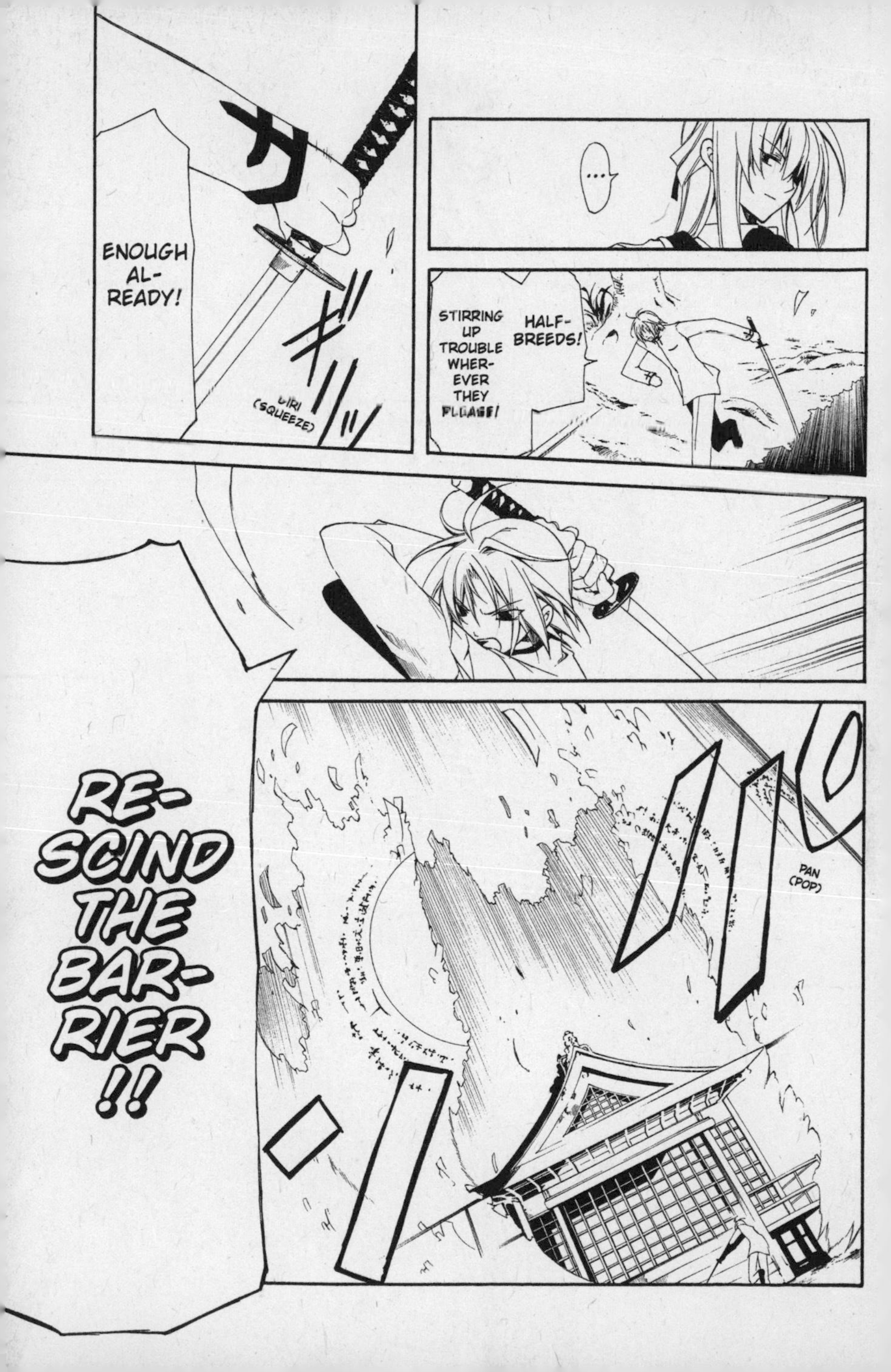

...
HALF-BREEDS!
STIRRING UP TROUBLE WHEREVER THEY PLEASE!
ENOUGH AL-READY!
GIRI (SQUEEZE)
PAN (POP)
RE-SCIND THE BAR-RIER!!

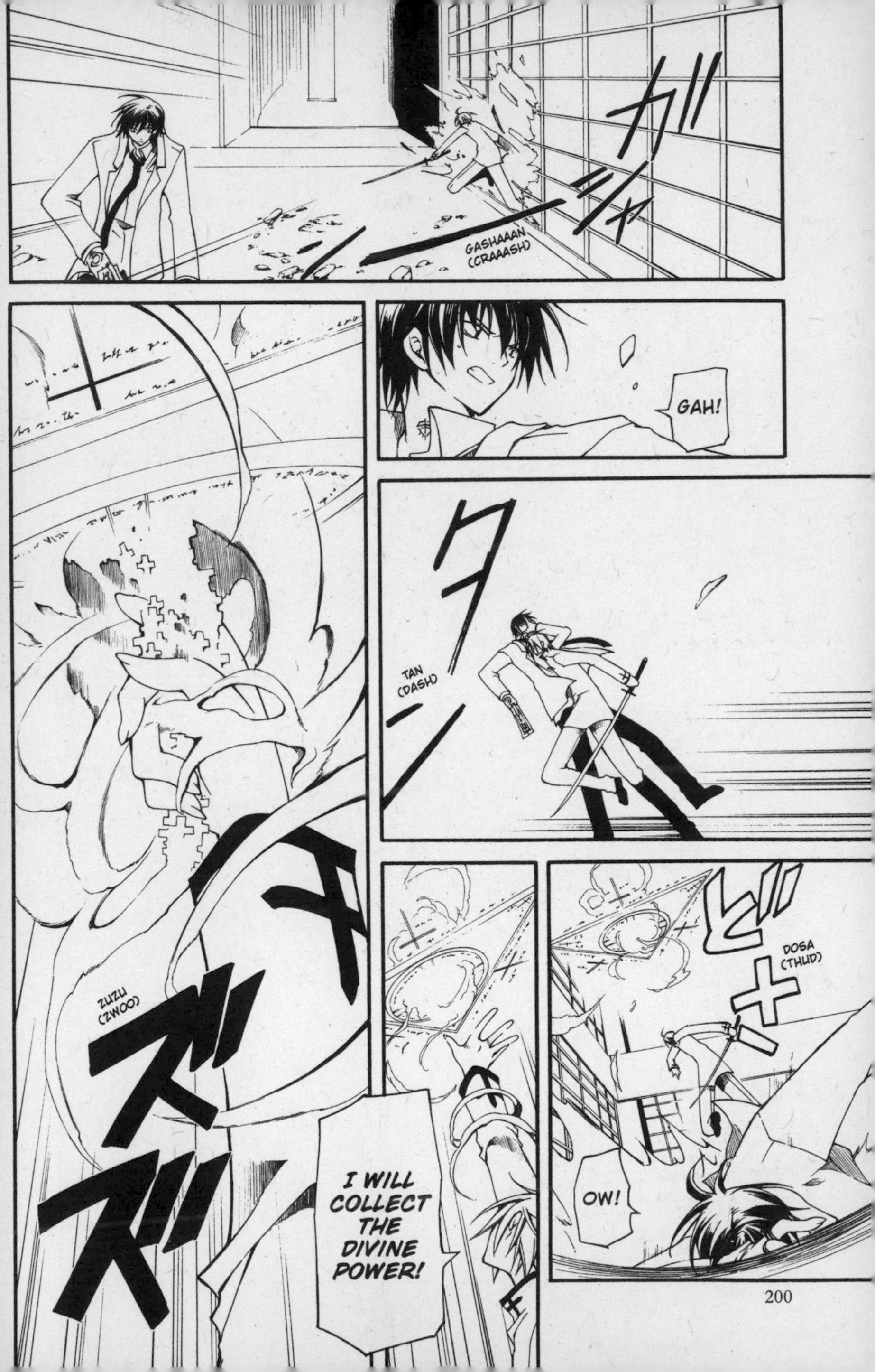
GASHAAAN (CRAAASH)
GAH!
TAN (DASH)
DOSA (THUD)
OW!
I WILL COLLECT THE DIVINE POWER!
ZUZU (ZWOO)

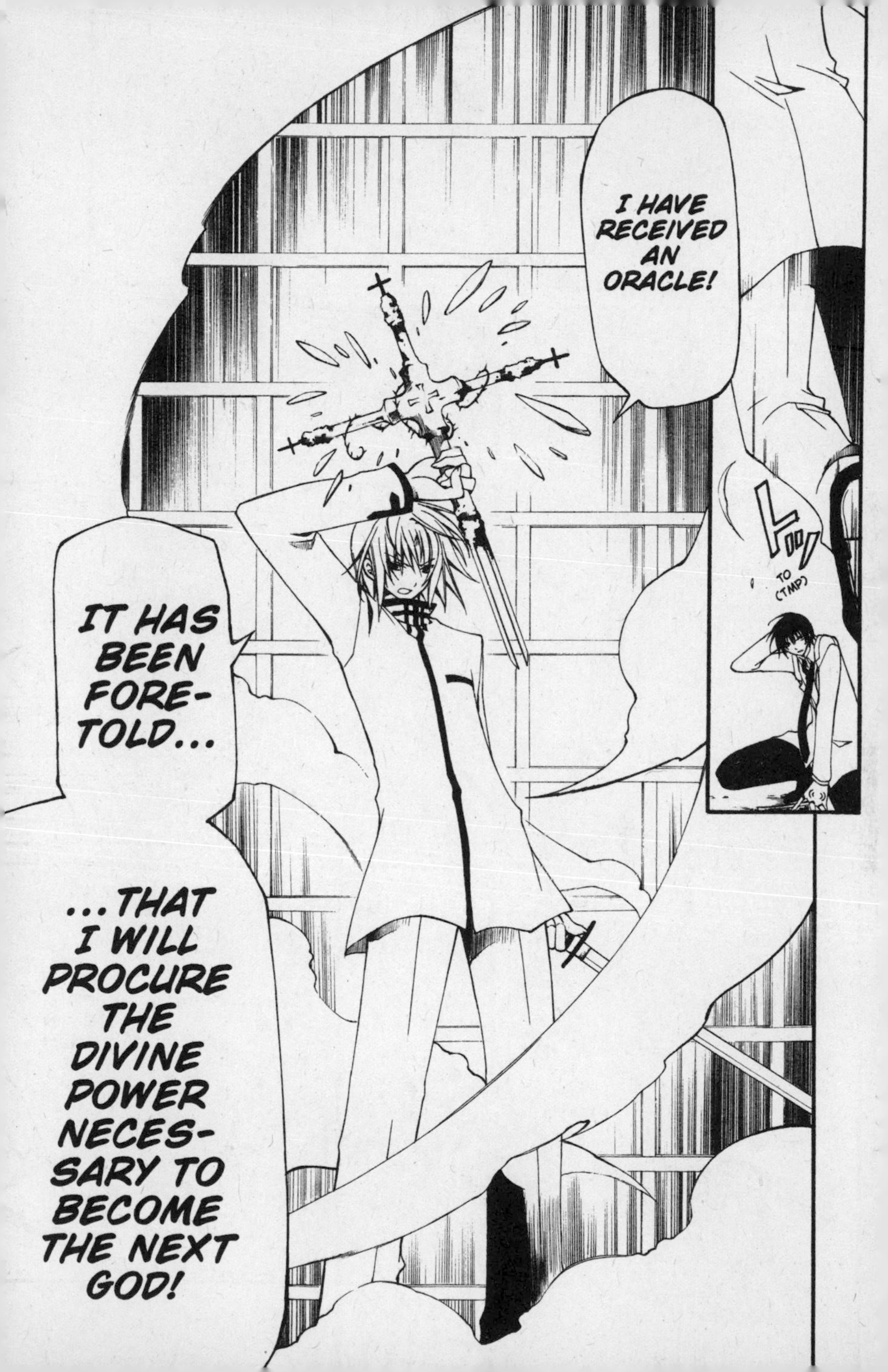
I HAVE RECEIVED AN ORACLE!
TO (TMP)
IT HAS BEEN FORE-TOLD...
...THAT I WILL PROCURE THE DIVINE POWER NECES-SARY TO BECOME THE NEXT GOD!

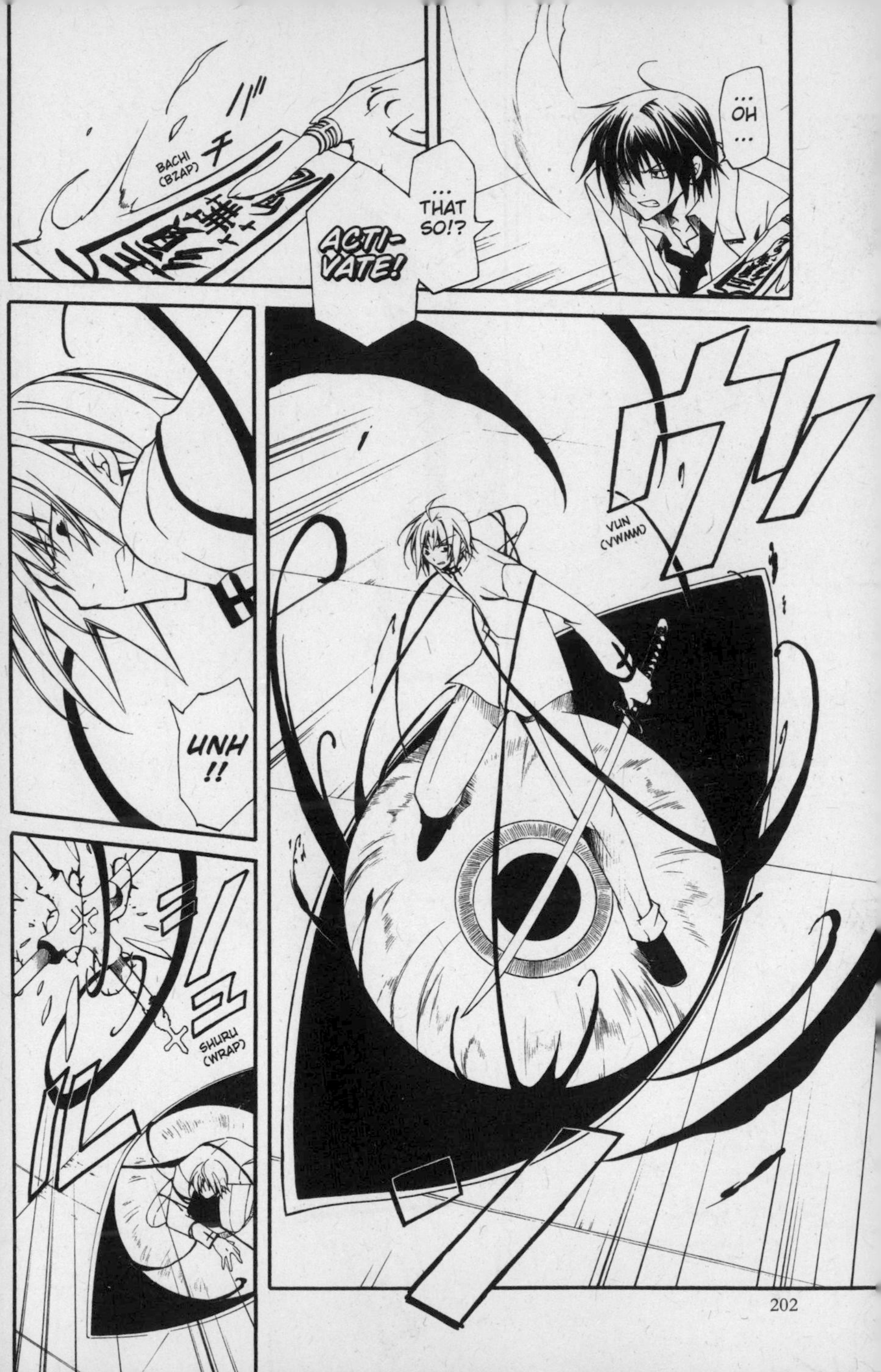

... OH ...
... THAT SO!?
BACHI (BZAP)
ACTI-VATE!
VUN (VWMM)
UNH !!
SHURU (WRAP)

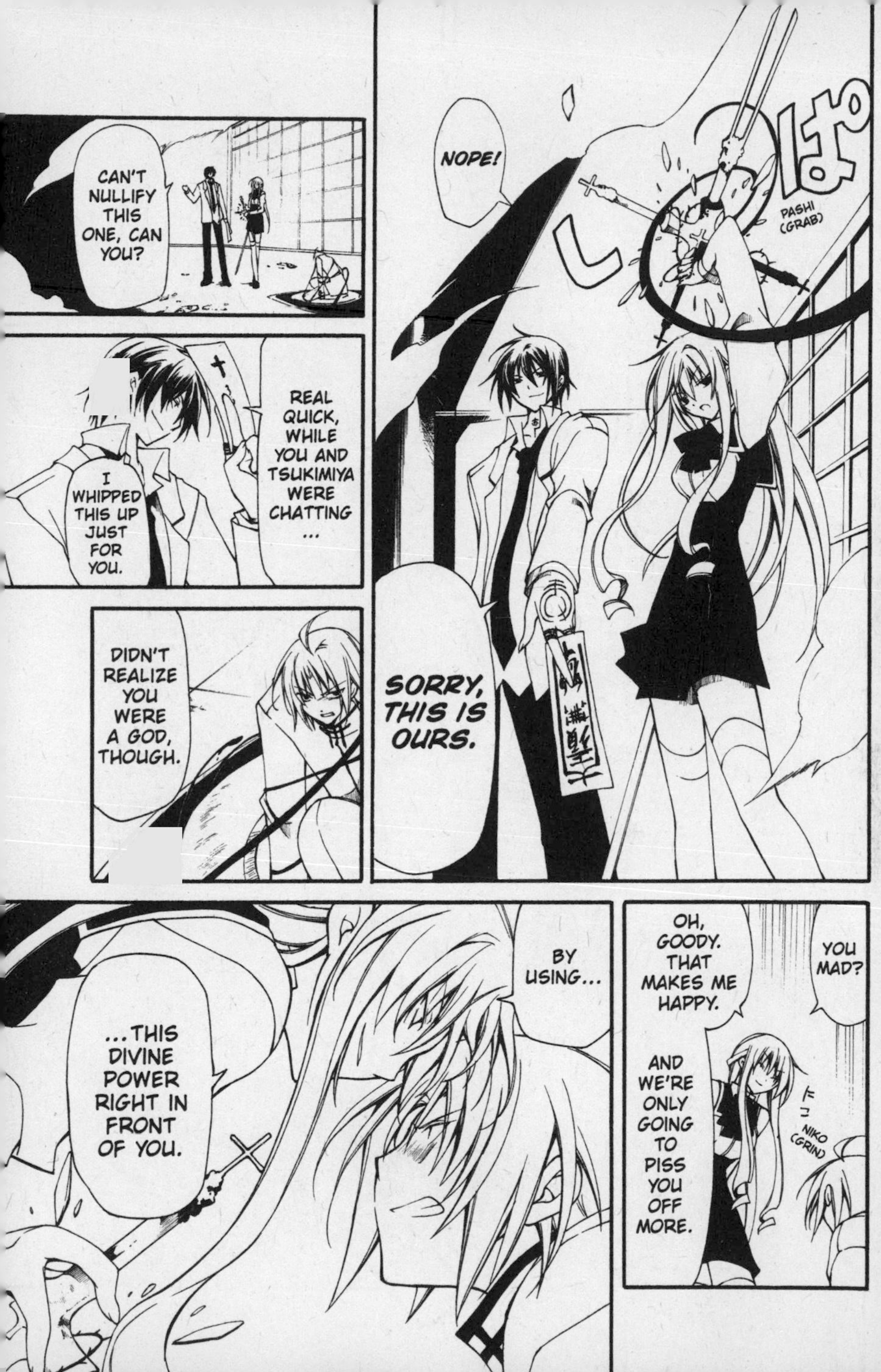
NOPE!
しぱ
PASHI (GRAB)
SORRY, THIS IS OURS.
CAN'T NULLIFY THIS ONE, CAN YOU?
REAL QUICK, WHILE YOU AND TSUKIMIYA WERE CHATTING...
I WHIPPED THIS UP JUST FOR YOU.
DIDN'T REALIZE YOU WERE A GOD, THOUGH.
YOU MAD?
OH, GOODY. THAT MAKES ME HAPPY.
AND WE'RE ONLY GOING TO PISS YOU OFF MORE.
ニコ
NIKO (GRIN)
BY USING...
...THIS DIVINE POWER RIGHT IN FRONT OF YOU.

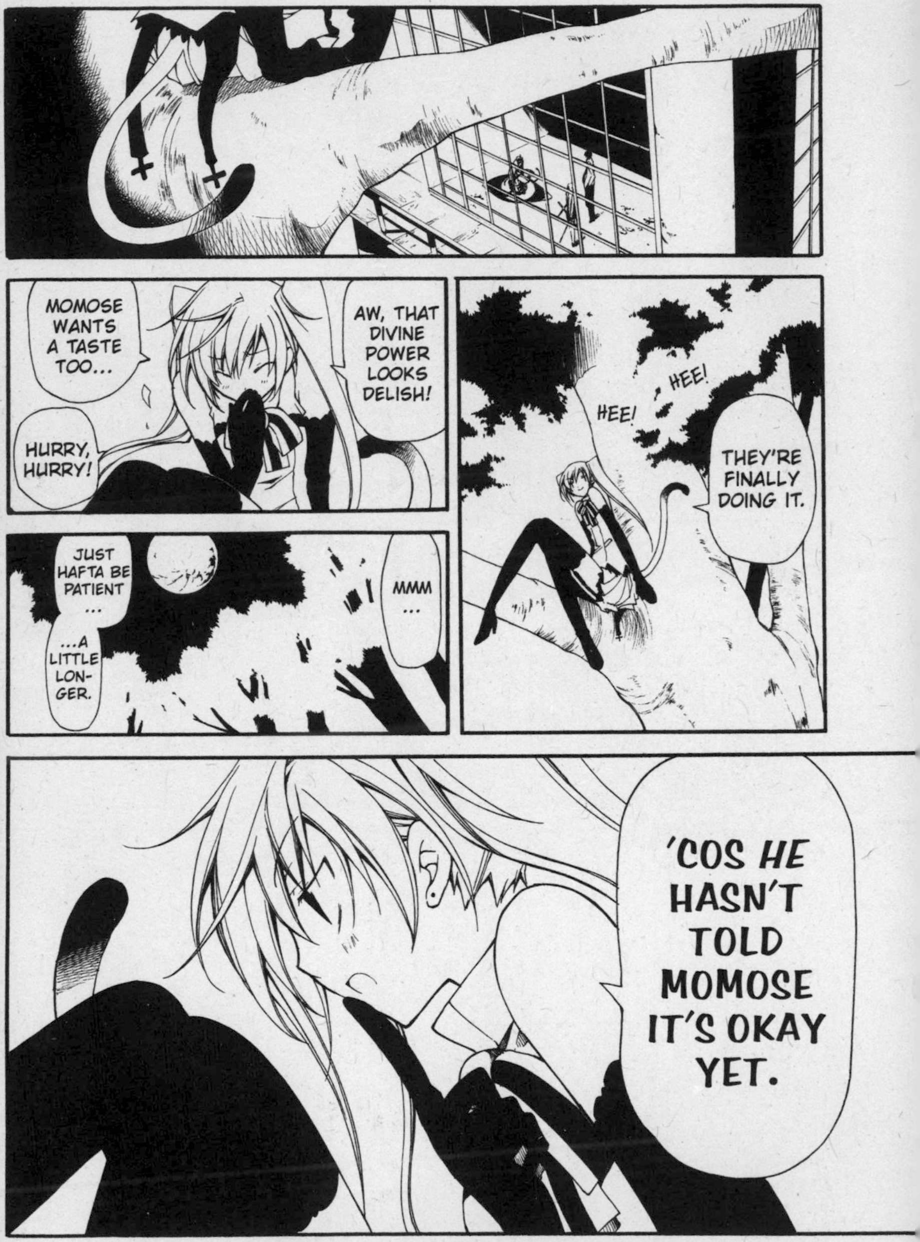
HEE!
HEE!
THEY'RE FINALLY DOING IT.
AW, THAT DIVINE POWER LOOKS DELISH!
MOMOSE WANTS A TASTE TOO...
HURRY, HURRY!
MMM...
JUST HAFTA BE PATIENT...
...A LITTLE LONGER.
'COS *HE* HASN'T TOLD MOMOSE IT'S OKAY YET.

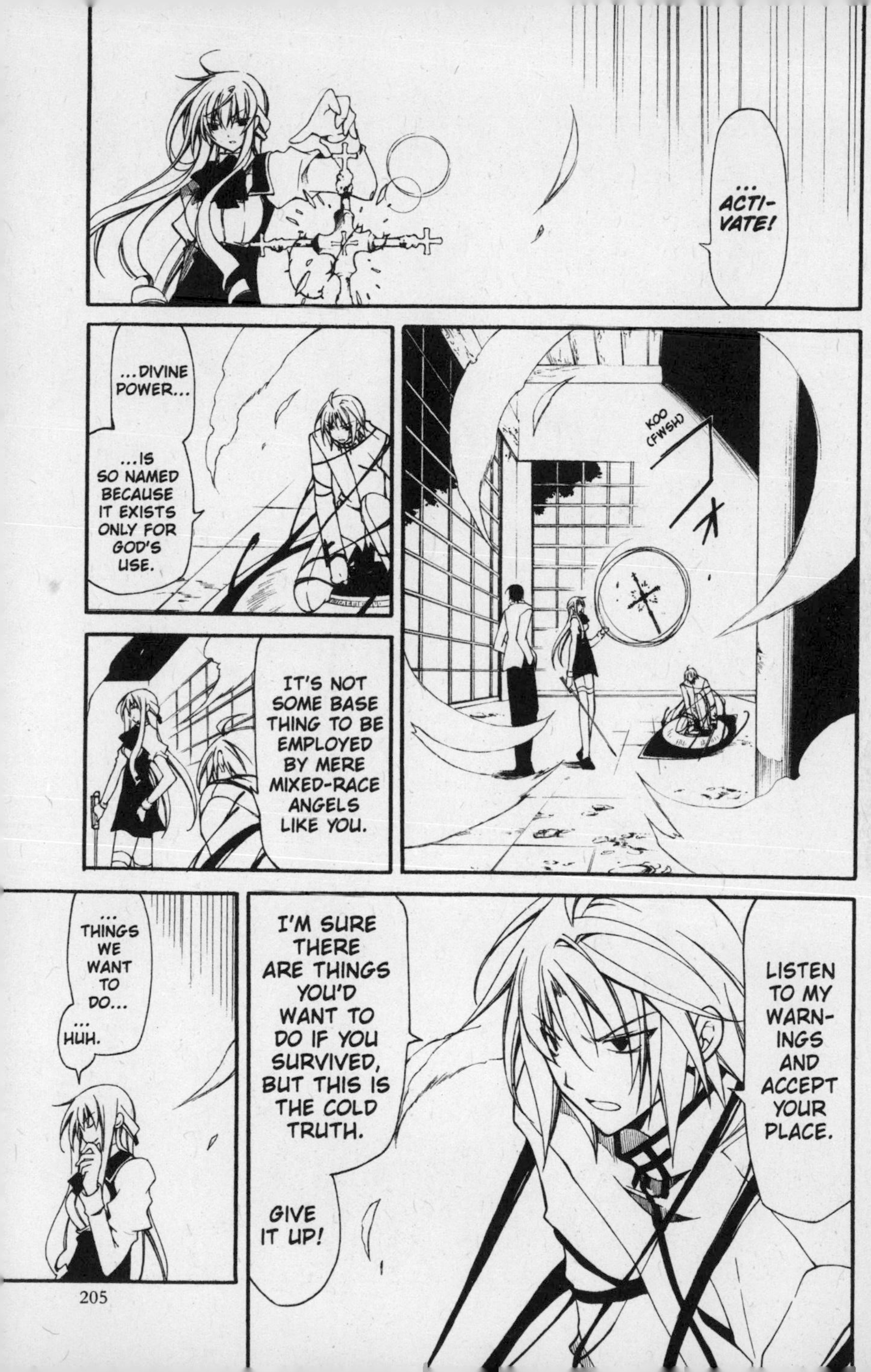
...ACTIVATE!
KOO (FWSH)
...DIVINE POWER...
...IS SO NAMED BECAUSE IT EXISTS ONLY FOR GOD'S USE.
IT'S NOT SOME BASE THING TO BE EMPLOYED BY MERE MIXED-RACE ANGELS LIKE YOU.
LISTEN TO MY WARNINGS AND ACCEPT YOUR PLACE.
I'M SURE THERE ARE THINGS YOU'D WANT TO DO IF YOU SURVIVED, BUT THIS IS THE COLD TRUTH.
GIVE IT UP!
...THINGS WE WANT TO DO... ...HUH.

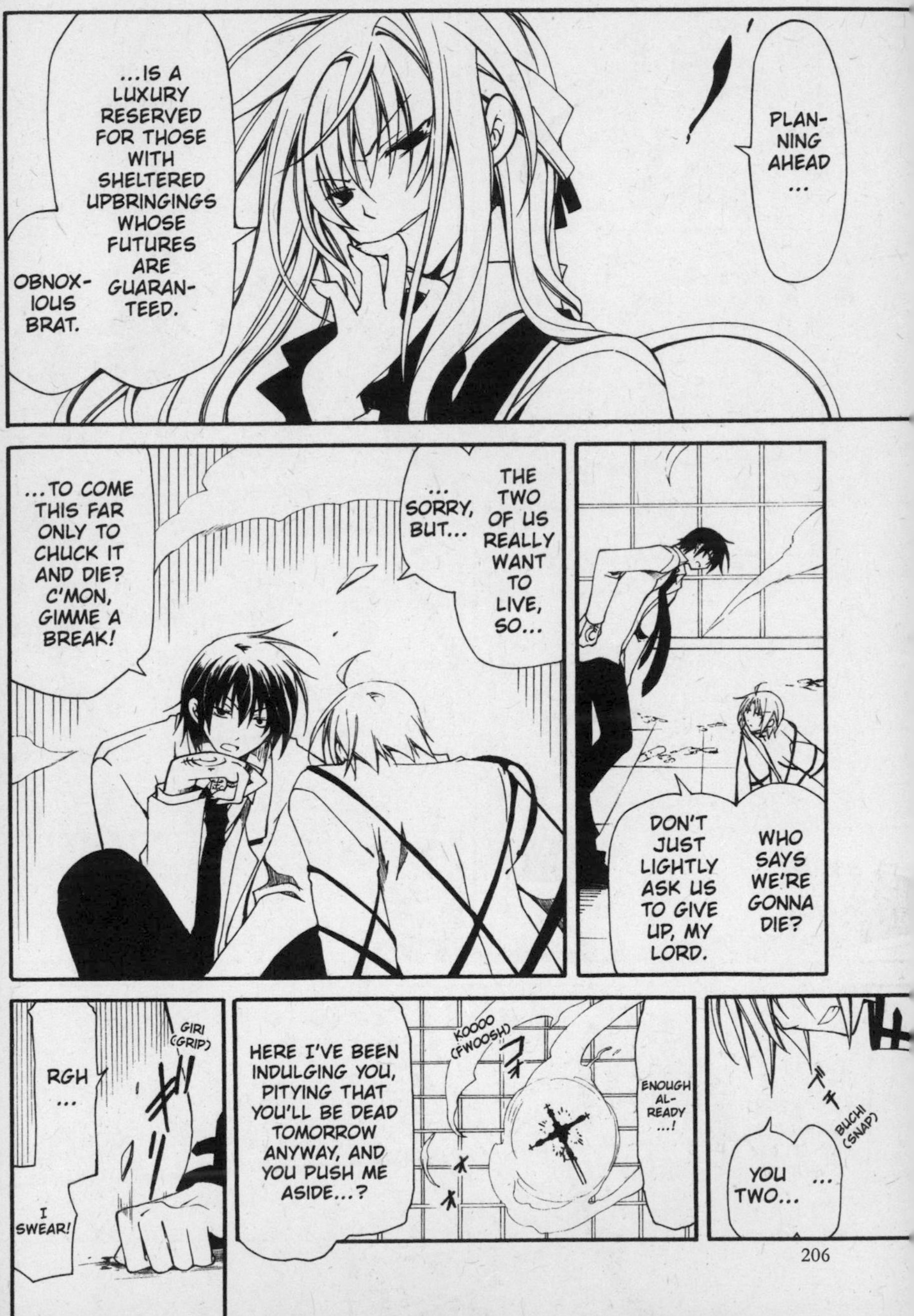
PLAN-NING AHEAD...
...IS A LUXURY RESERVED FOR THOSE WITH SHELTERED UPBRINGINGS WHOSE FUTURES ARE GUARAN-TEED.
OBNOX-IOUS BRAT.
WHO SAYS WE'RE GONNA DIE?
DON'T JUST LIGHTLY ASK US TO GIVE UP, MY LORD.
THE TWO OF US REALLY WANT TO LIVE, SO...
...SORRY, BUT...
...TO COME THIS FAR ONLY TO CHUCK IT AND DIE? C'MON, GIMME A BREAK!
BUCHI (SNAP)
...
YOU TWO...
KOOOO (FWOOSH)
ENOUGH AL-READY...!
HERE I'VE BEEN INDULGING YOU, PITYING THAT YOU'LL BE DEAD TOMORROW ANYWAY, AND YOU PUSH ME ASIDE...?
GIRI (GRIP)
RGH...
I SWEAR!

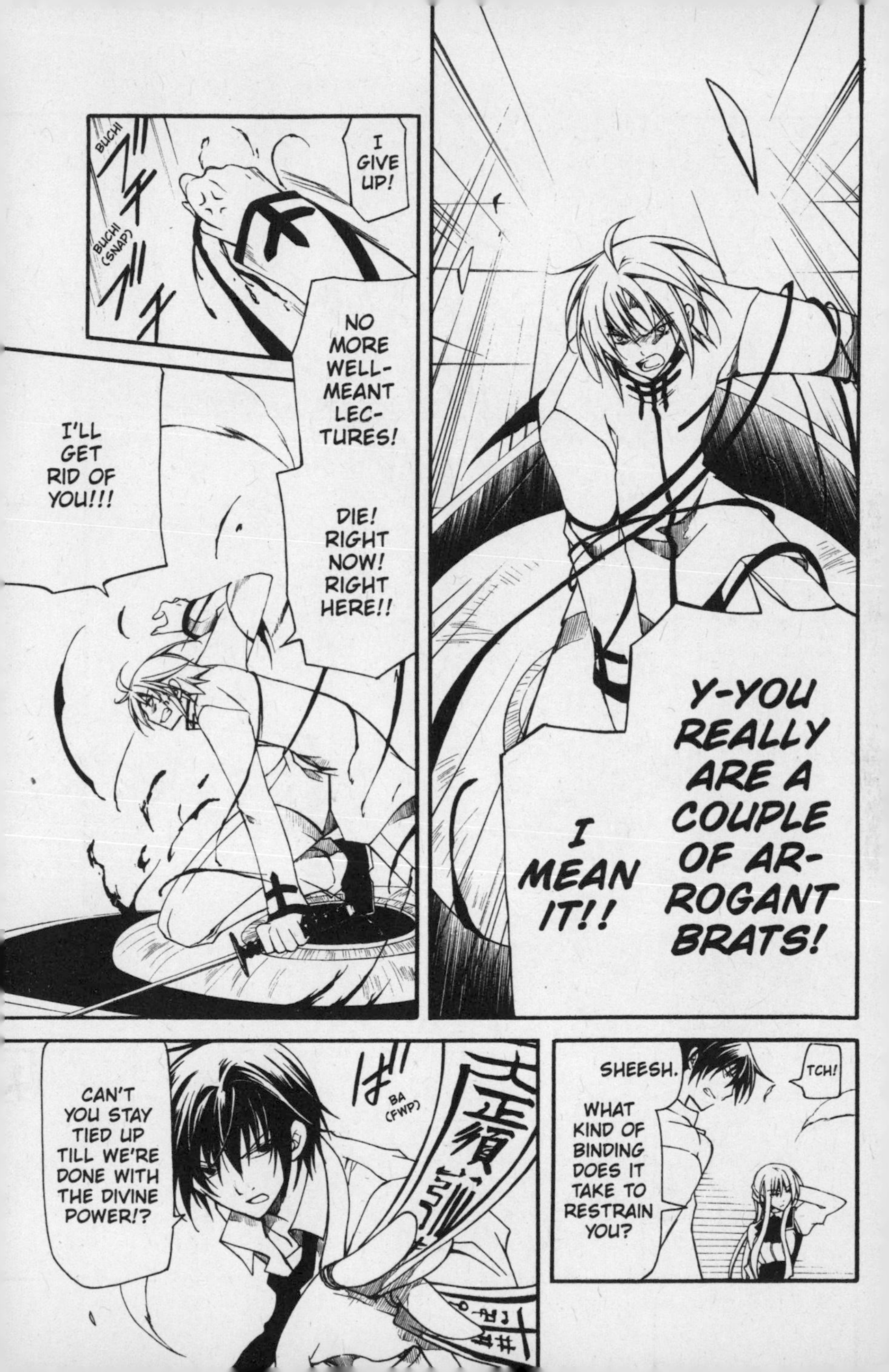
Y-YOU REALLY ARE A COUPLE OF AR-ROGANT BRATS!
I MEAN IT!!
I GIVE UP!
BUCHI
BUCHI (SNAP)
NO MORE WELL-MEANT LEC-TURES!
I'LL GET RID OF YOU!!!
DIE! RIGHT NOW! RIGHT HERE!!
SHEESH.
TCH!
WHAT KIND OF BINDING DOES IT TAKE TO RESTRAIN YOU?
BA (FWP)
CAN'T YOU STAY TIED UP TILL WE'RE DONE WITH THE DIVINE POWER!?

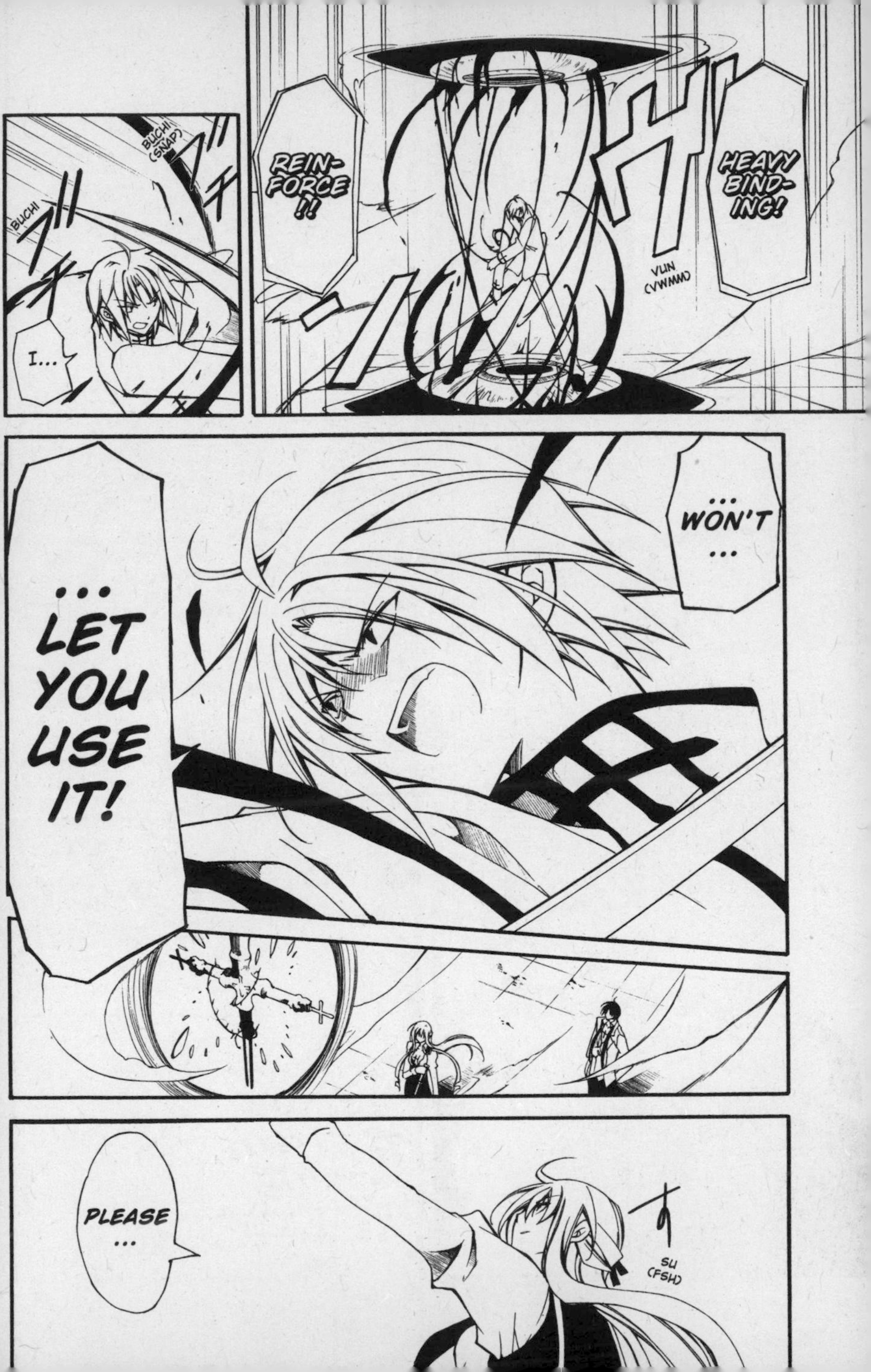
HEAVY BINDING!
VUN (VWMM)
REIN-FORCE!!
BUCHI (SNAP)
BUCHI
I...
... WON'T ...
... LET YOU USE IT!
SU (FSH)
PLEASE ...

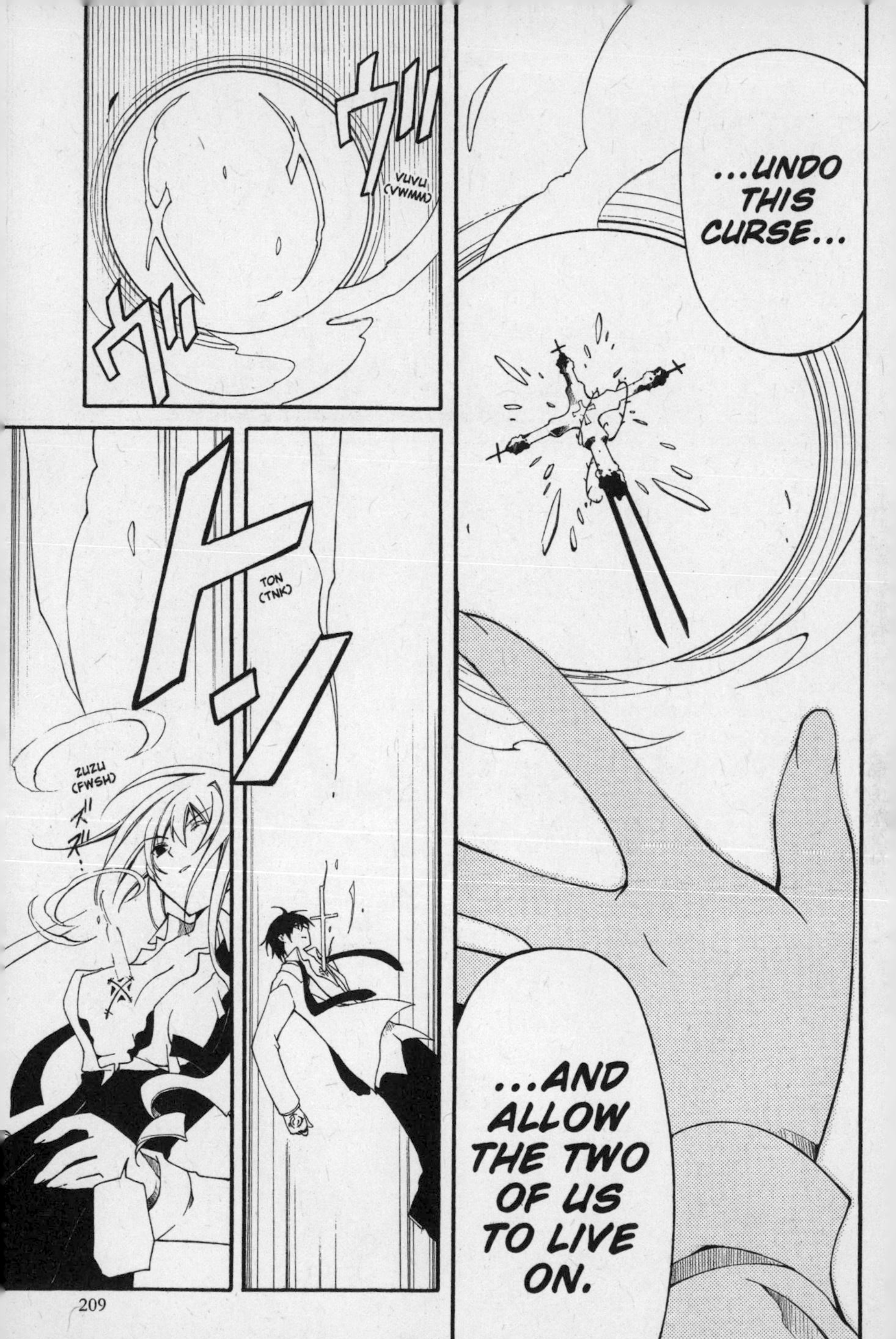
...UNDO THIS CURSE...
...AND ALLOW THE TWO OF US TO LIVE ON.
VUVU (VWMM)
TON (TNK)
ZUZU (FWSH)

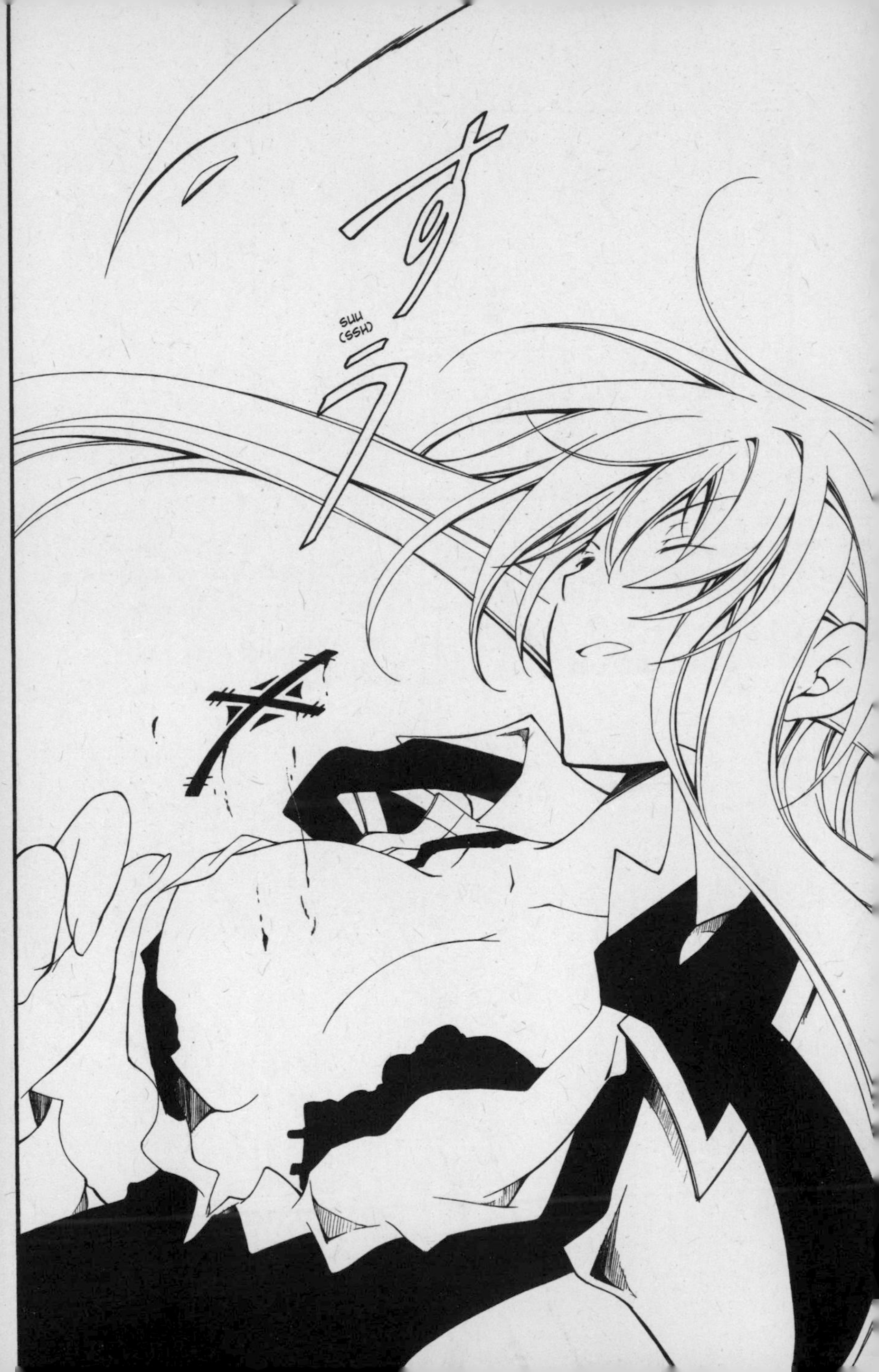
SUU
(SSH)

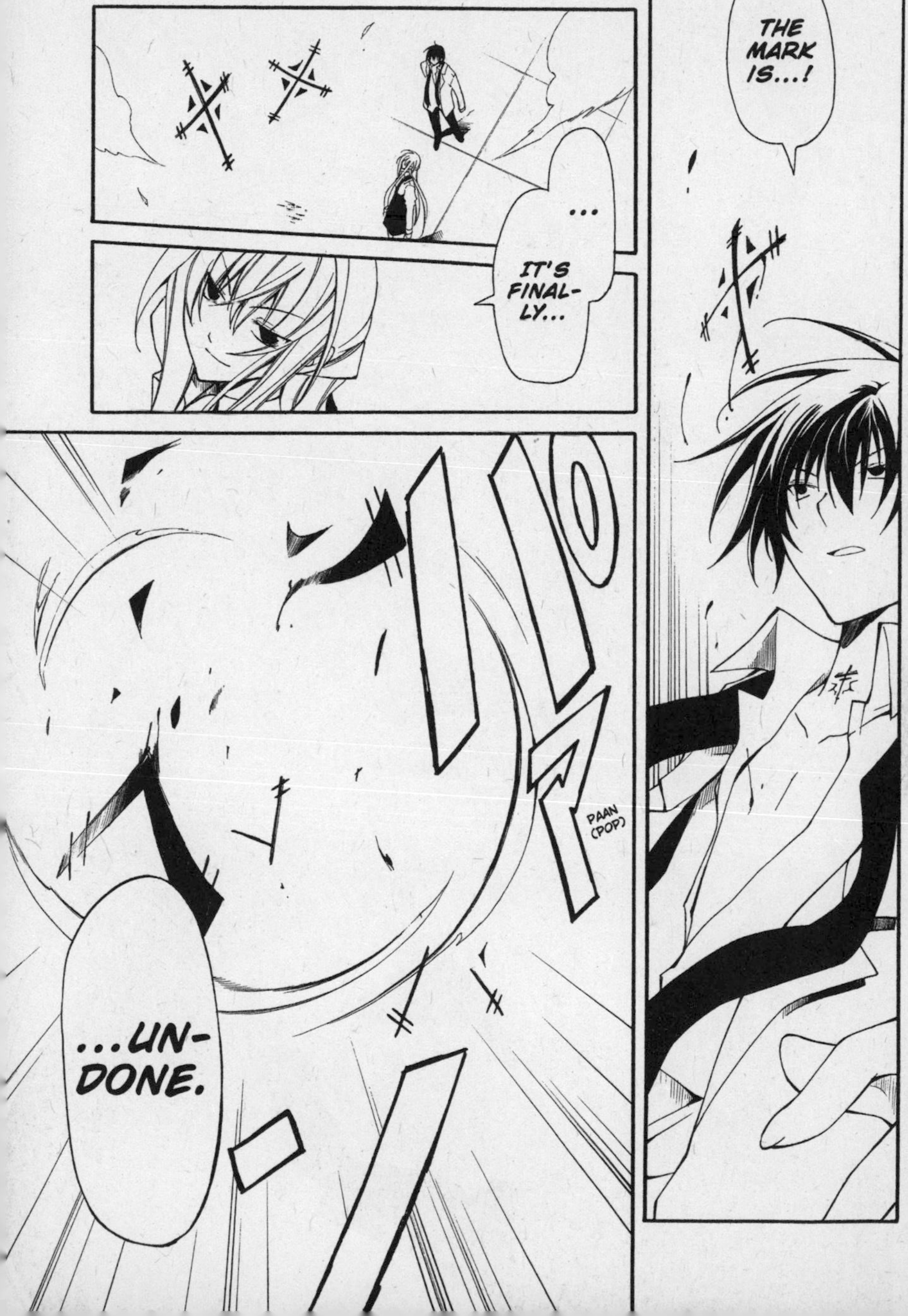
THE MARK IS...!
...
IT'S FINAL-LY...
PAAN (POP)
...UN-DONE.

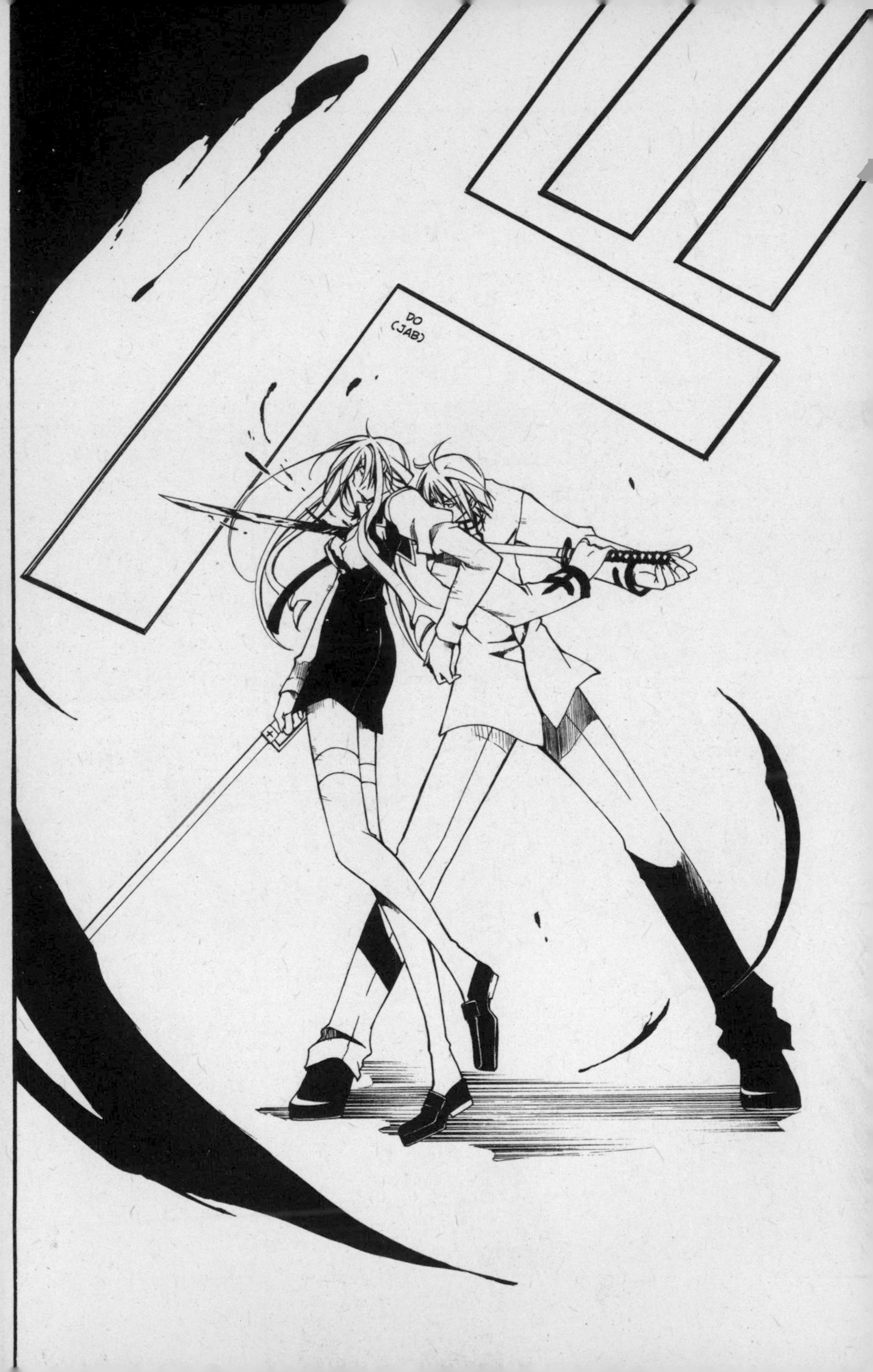
DO
(JAB)

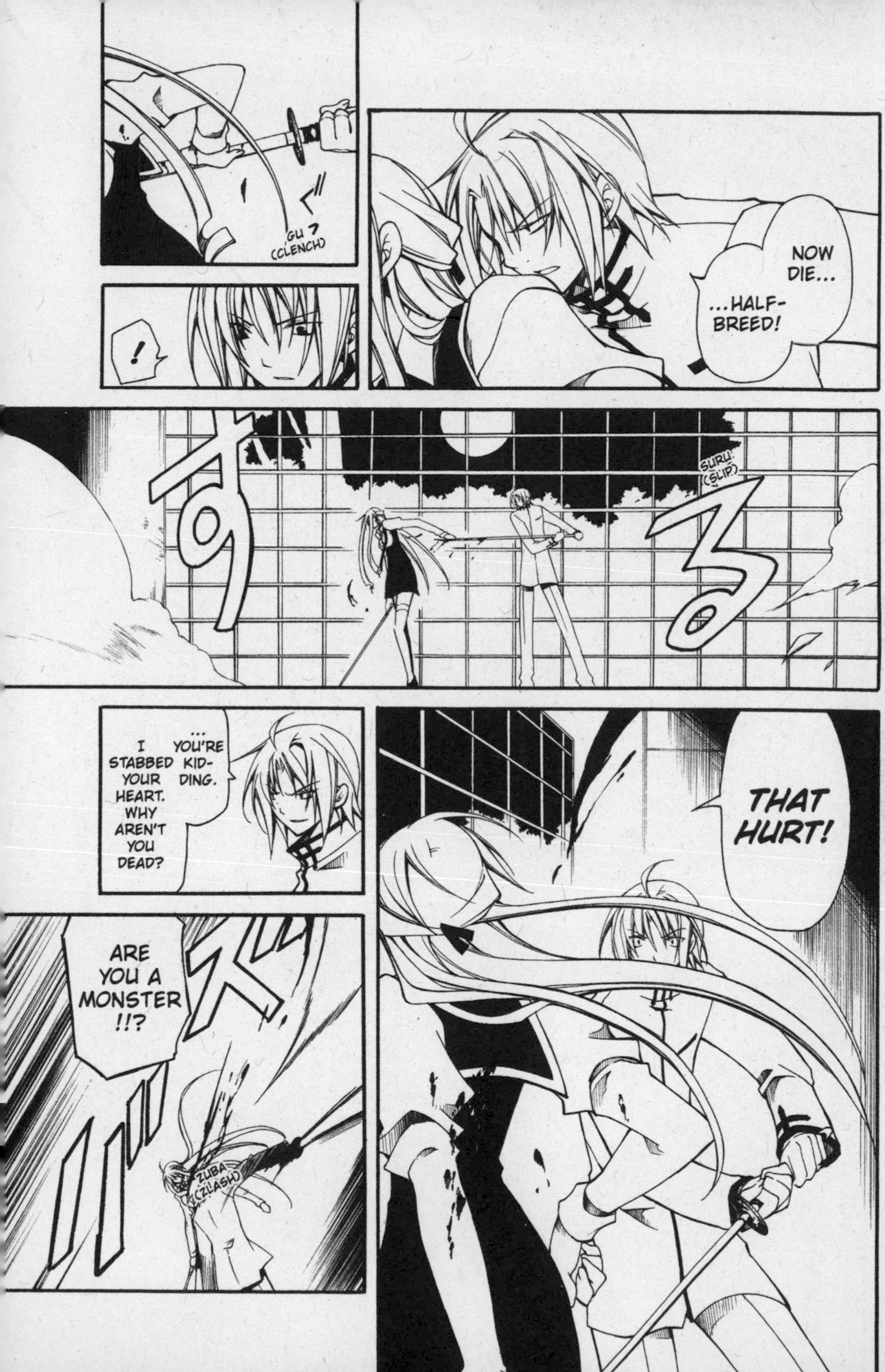
NOW DIE...
...HALF-BREED!
GU (CLENCH)
!
SURU (SLIP)
する
THAT HURT!
...YOU'RE KIDDING.
I STABBED YOUR HEART. WHY AREN'T YOU DEAD?
ARE YOU A MONSTER!!?
ZUBA (ZLASH)

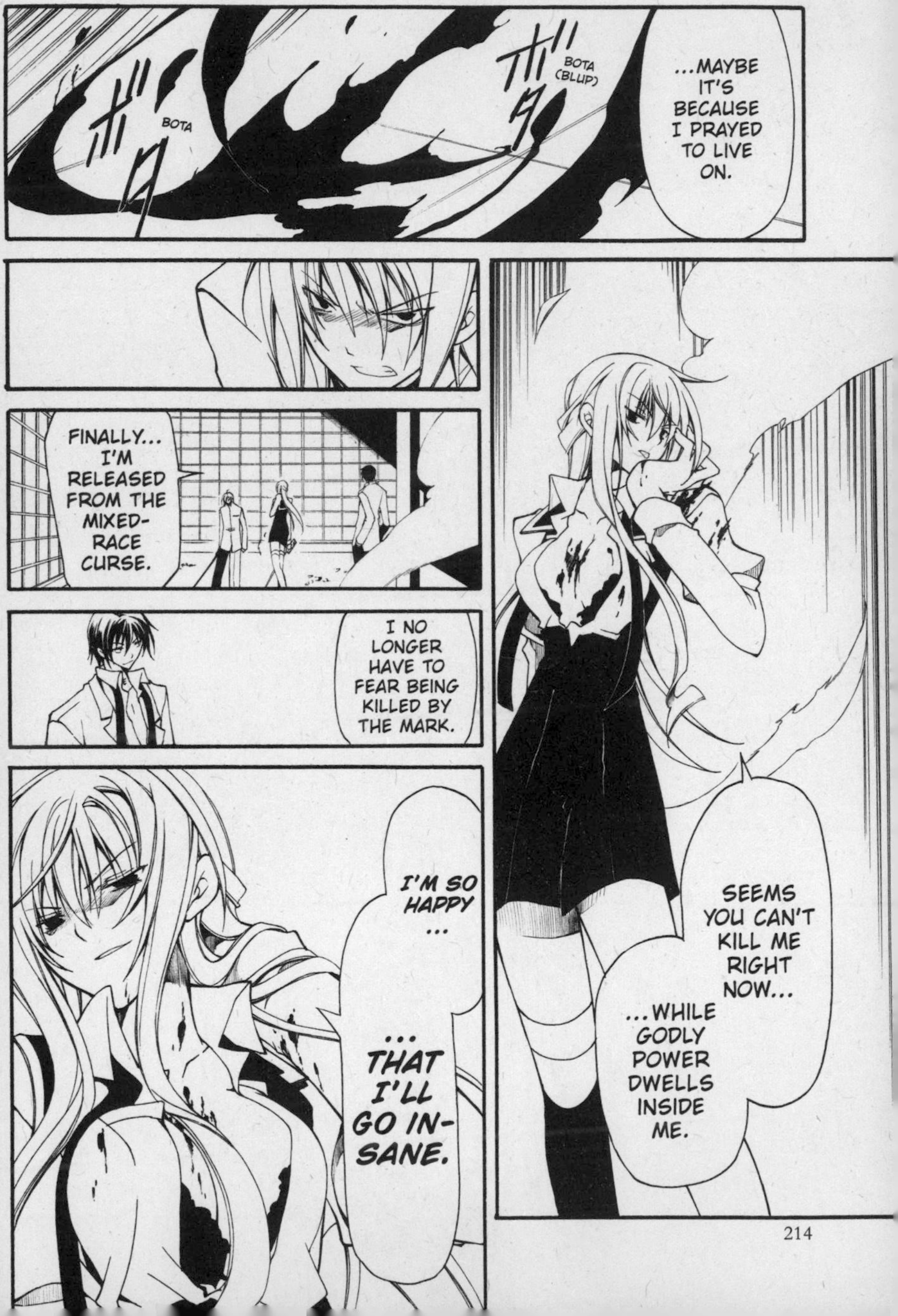
...MAYBE IT'S BECAUSE I PRAYED TO LIVE ON.
BOTA (BLUP)
BOTA
SEEMS YOU CAN'T KILL ME RIGHT NOW...
...WHILE GODLY POWER DWELLS INSIDE ME.
FINALLY... I'M RELEASED FROM THE MIXED-RACE CURSE.
I NO LONGER HAVE TO FEAR BEING KILLED BY THE MARK.
I'M SO HAPPY ...
... THAT I'LL GO IN-SANE.

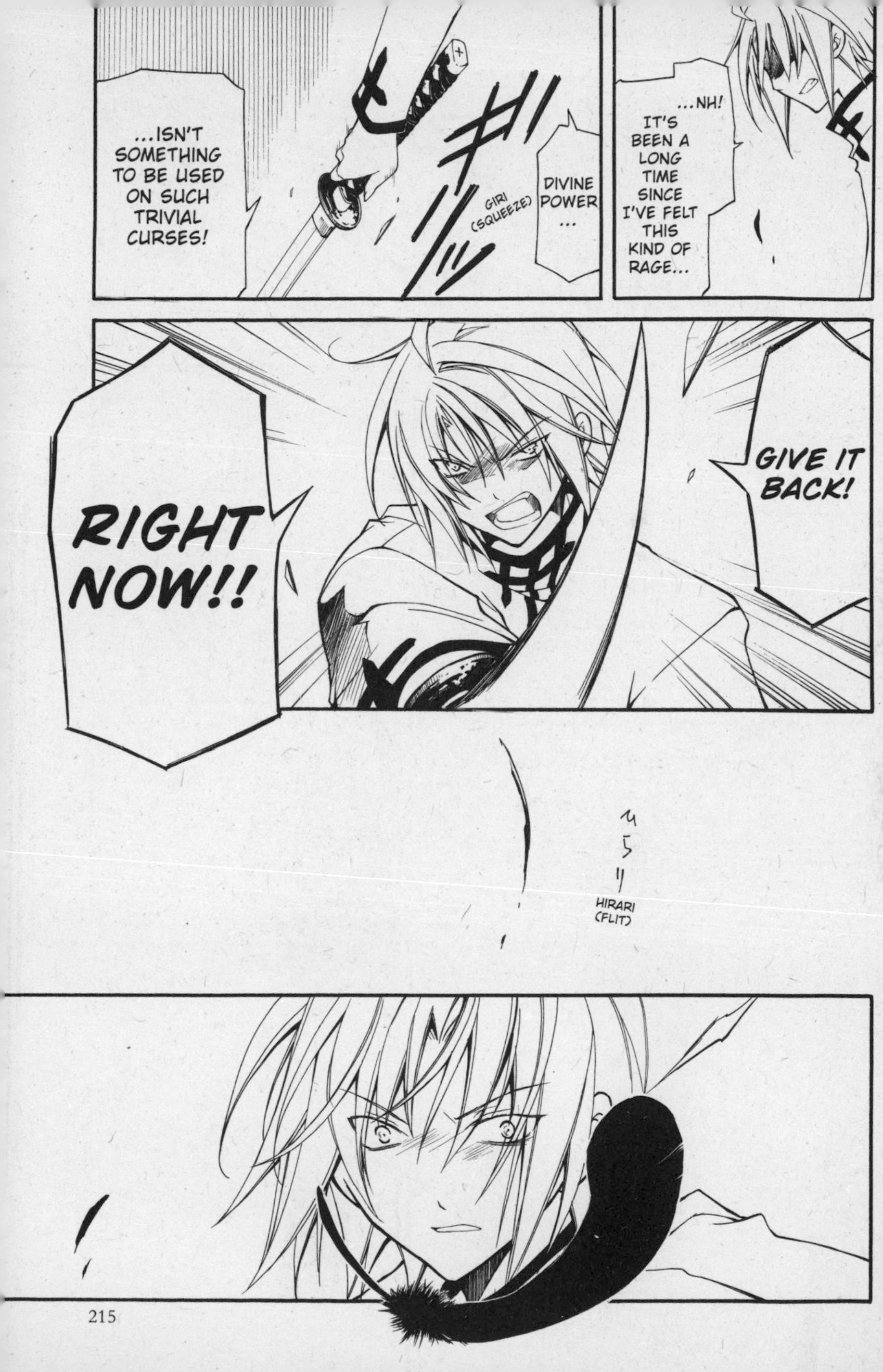
...NH!
IT'S BEEN A LONG TIME SINCE I'VE FELT THIS KIND OF RAGE...
DIVINE POWER ...
GIRI (SQUEEZE)
...ISN'T SOMETHING TO BE USED ON SUCH TRIVIAL CURSES!
GIVE IT BACK!
RIGHT NOW!!
ひらり
HIRARI (FLIT)

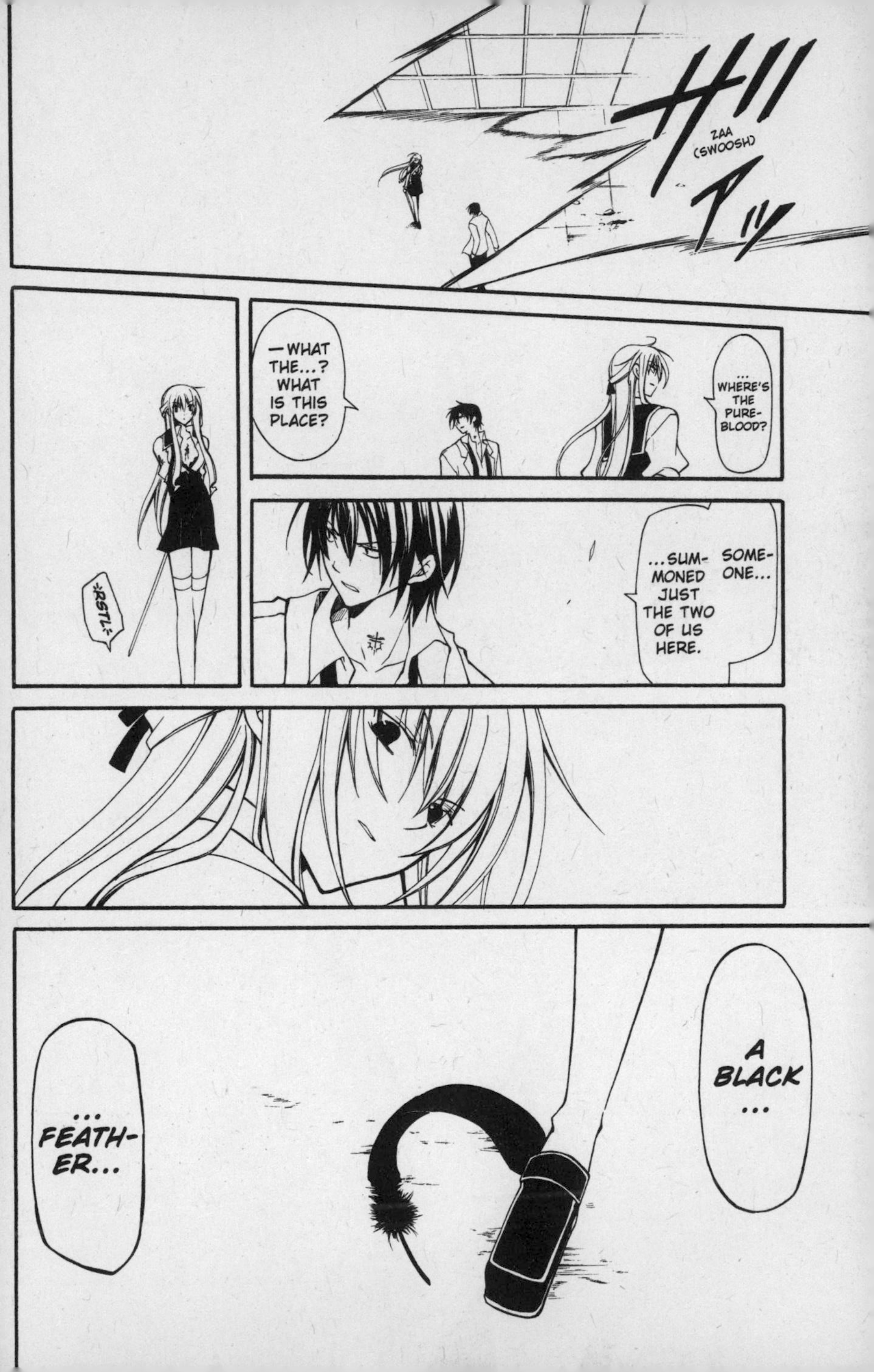
ZAA (SWOOSH)
... WHERE'S THE PURE-BLOOD?
—WHAT THE...? WHAT IS THIS PLACE?
SOME-ONE...
...SUM-MONED JUST THE TWO OF US HERE.
RSTL
A BLACK ...
... FEATH-ER...

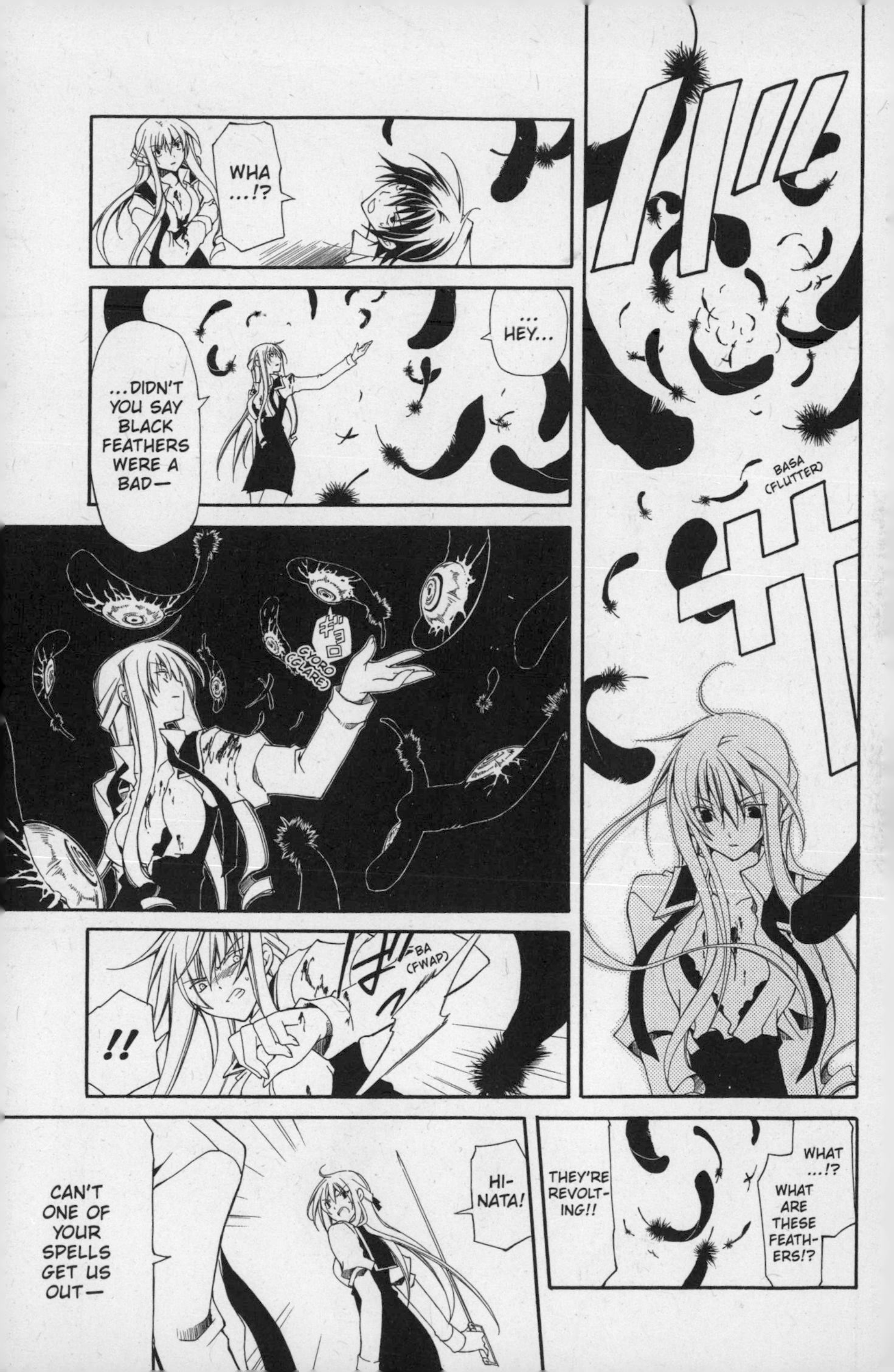
BASA (FLUTTER)
WHA ...!?
... HEY...
...DIDN'T YOU SAY BLACK FEATHERS WERE A BAD—
ギョロ
GYORO (GLARE)
BA (FWAP)
!!
WHAT ...!?
WHAT ARE THESE FEATHERS!?
THEY'RE REVOLTING!!
HI-NATA!
CAN'T ONE OF YOUR SPELLS GET US OUT—

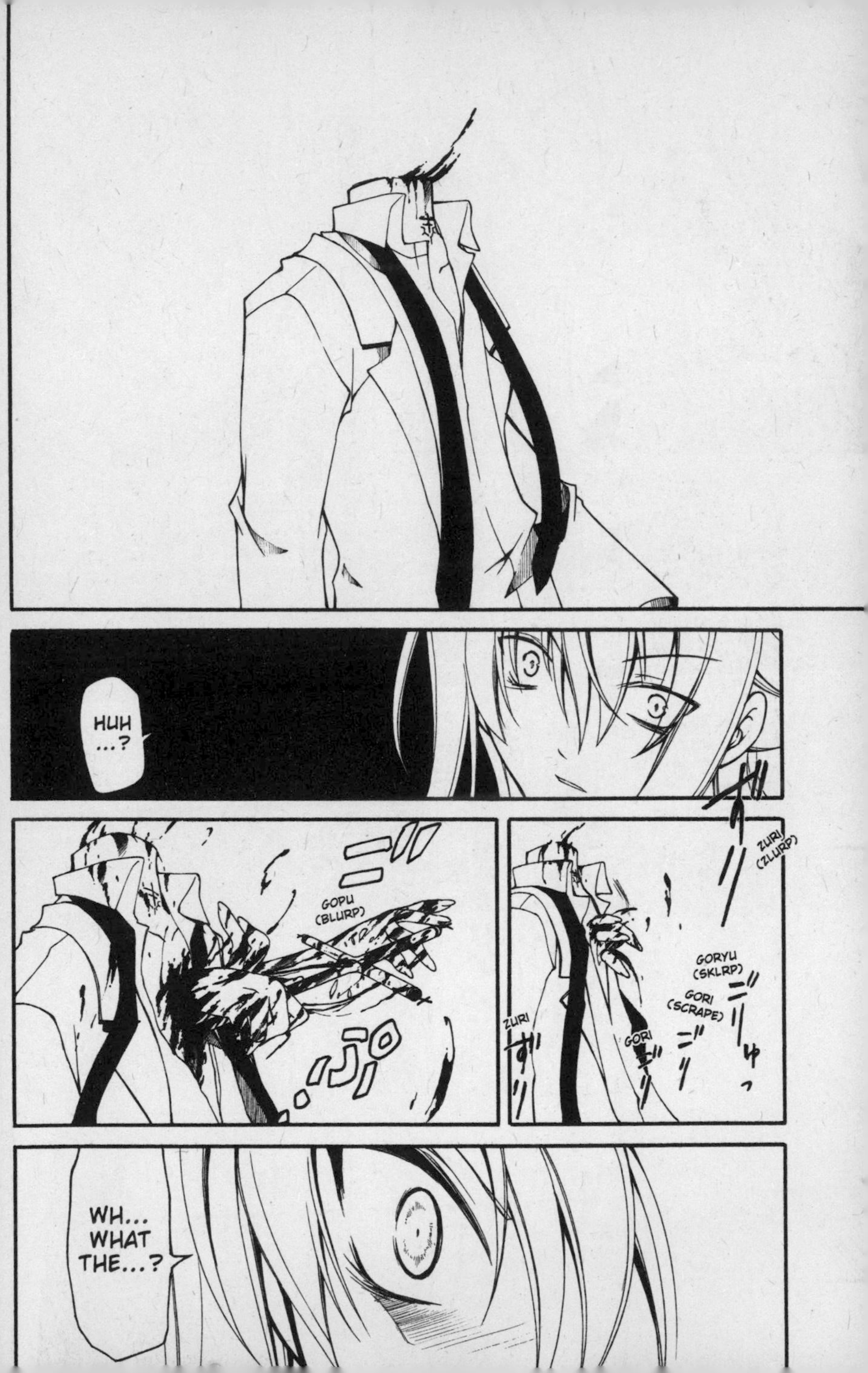
HUH ...?
ZURI (ZLURP)
GORYU (SKLRP)
GORI (SCRAPE)
GORI
ZURI
GOPU (BLURP)
WH... WHAT THE...?

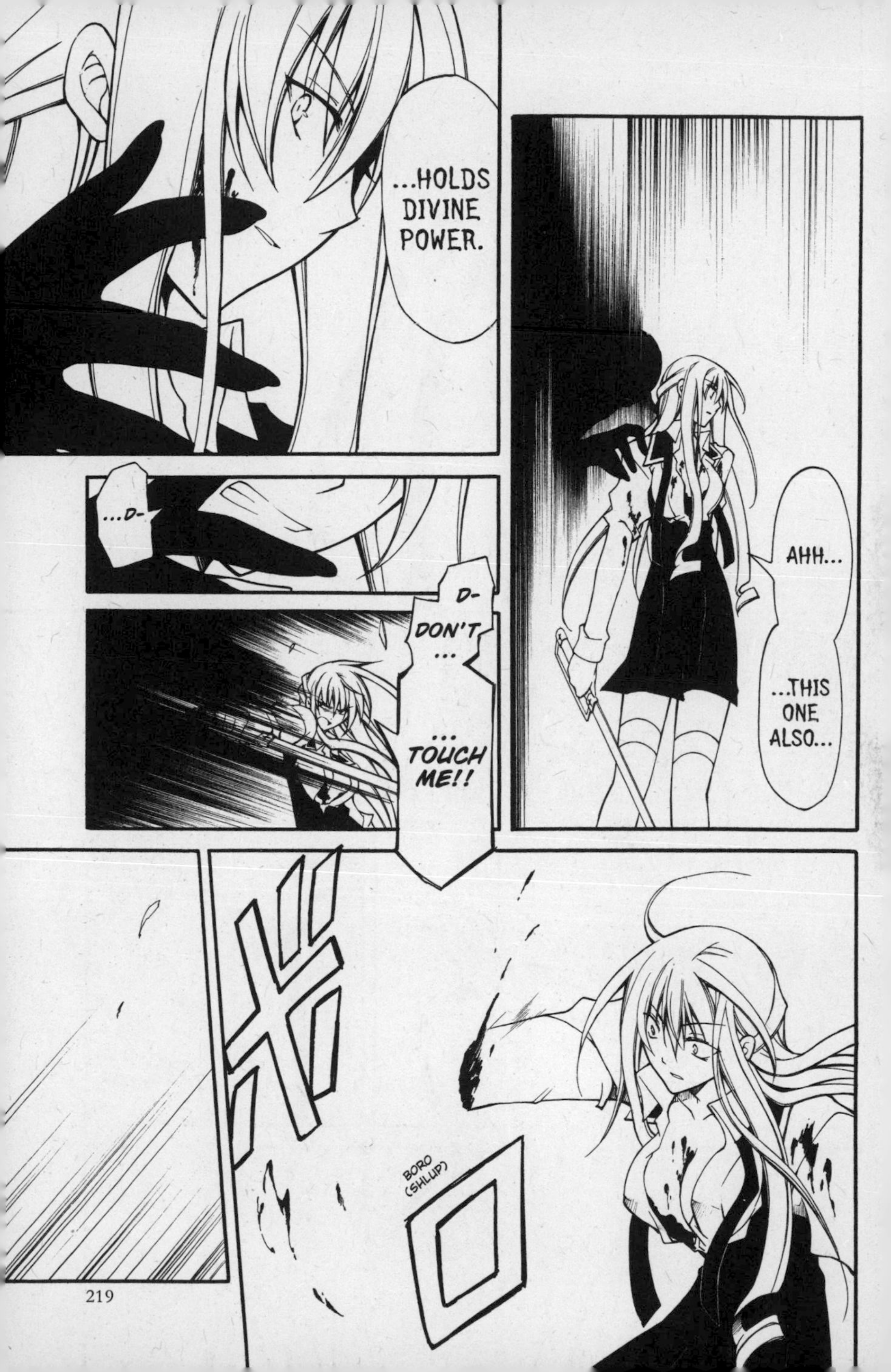
...HOLDS DIVINE POWER.
AHH...
...THIS ONE ALSO...
...D-
D-DON'T...
...TOUCH ME!!
BORO (SHLUP)

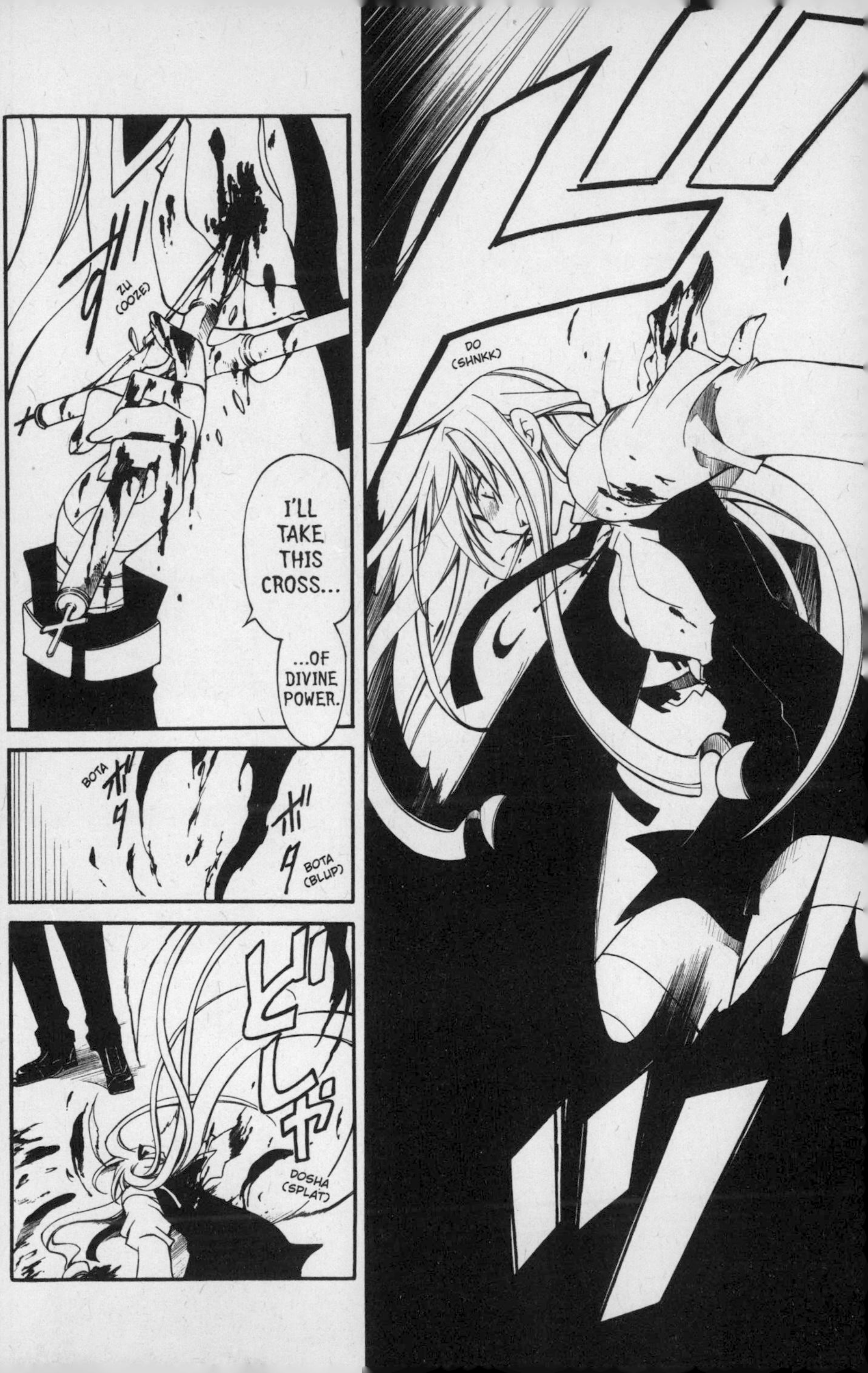
DO (SHNKK)
ZU (OOZE)
I'LL TAKE THIS CROSS...
...OF DIVINE POWER.
BOTA
BOTA (BLUP)
DOSHA (SPLAT)

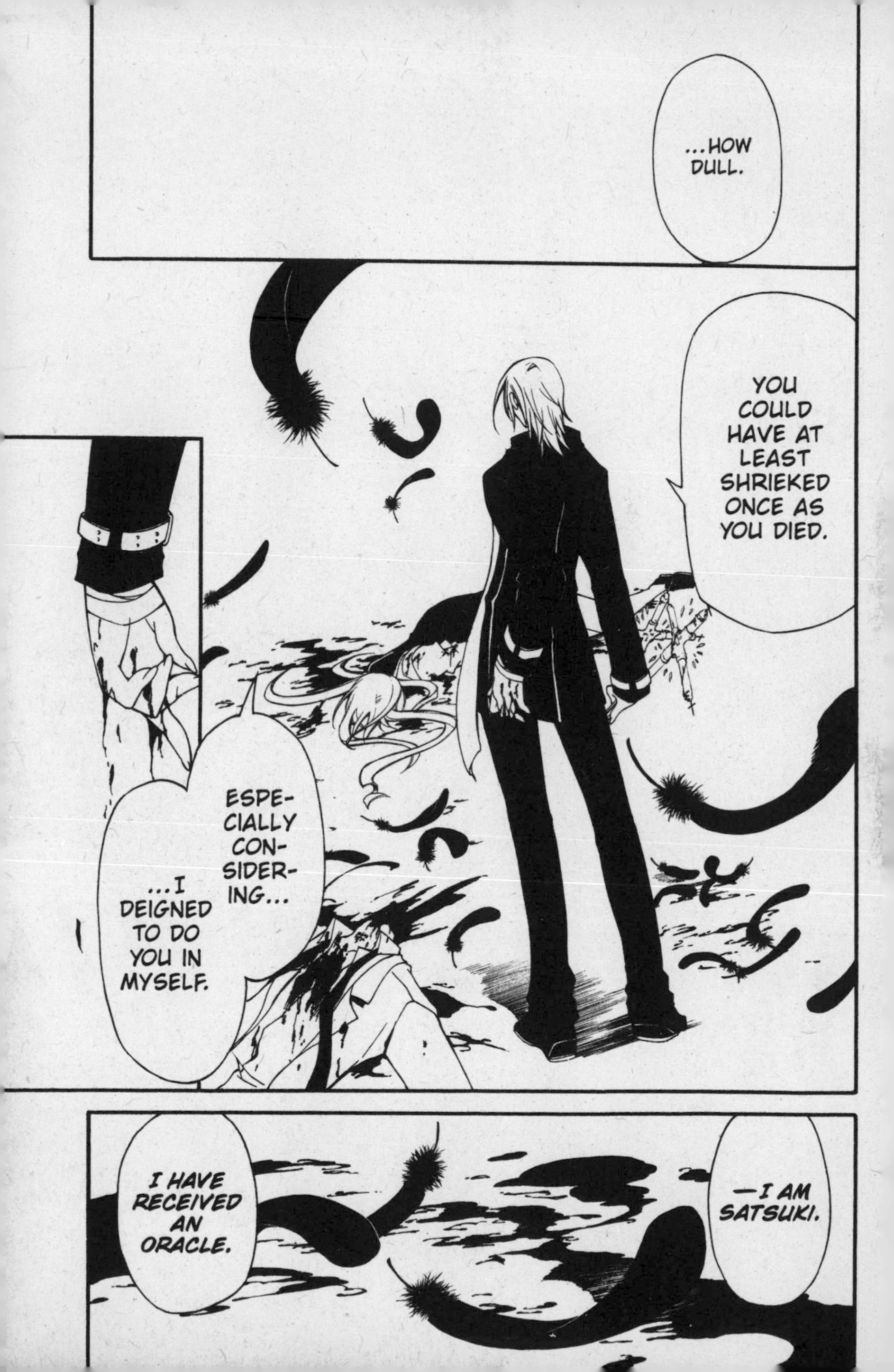
...HOW DULL.
YOU COULD HAVE AT LEAST SHRIEKED ONCE AS YOU DIED.
ESPECIALLY CONSIDERING...
...I DEIGNED TO DO YOU IN MYSELF.
—I AM SATSUKI.
I HAVE RECEIVED AN ORACLE.

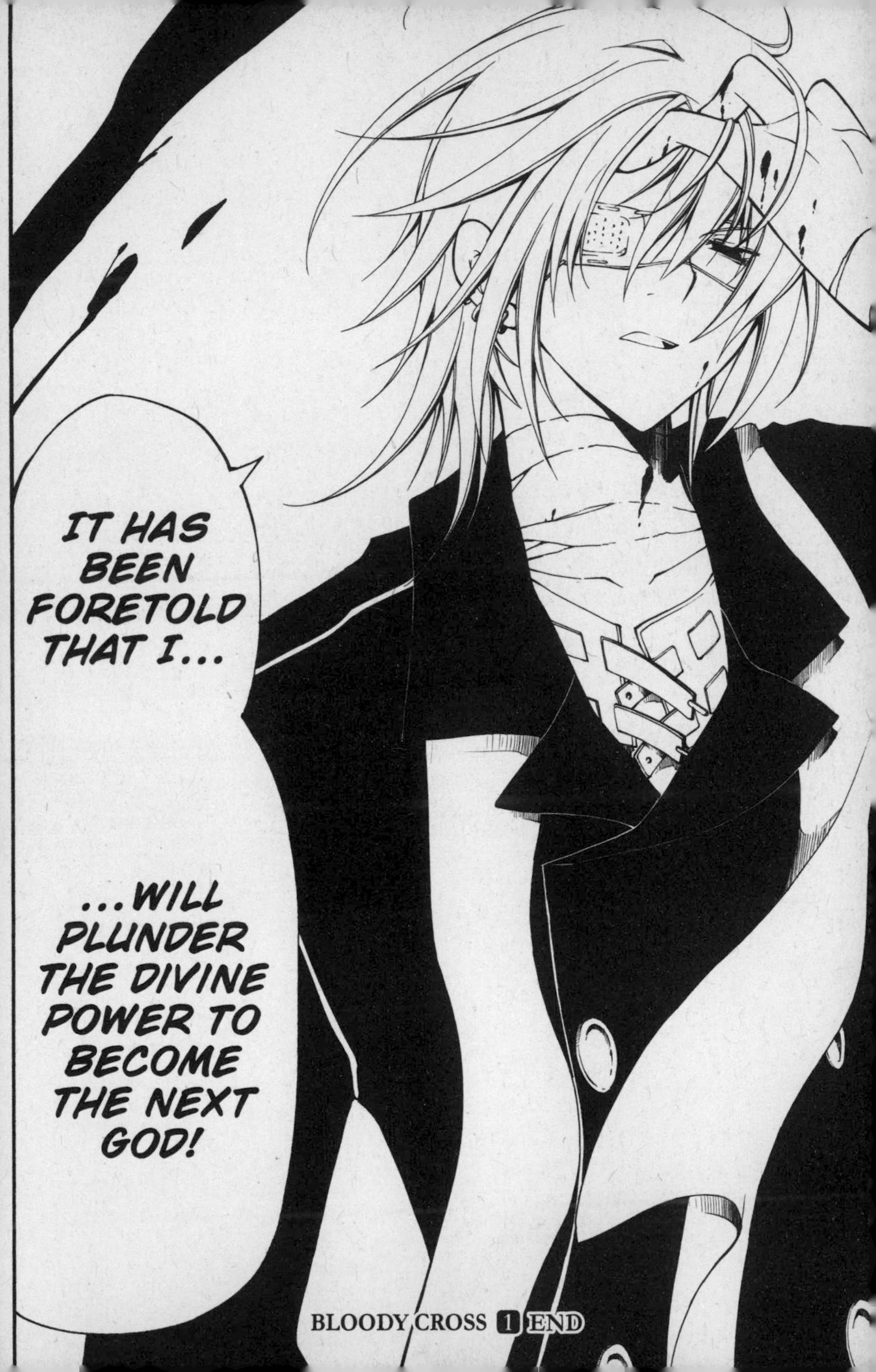
IT HAS BEEN FORETOLD THAT I...
...WILL PLUNDER THE DIVINE POWER TO BECOME THE NEXT GOD!

BLOODY CROSS 1 END

BLOODY CROSS

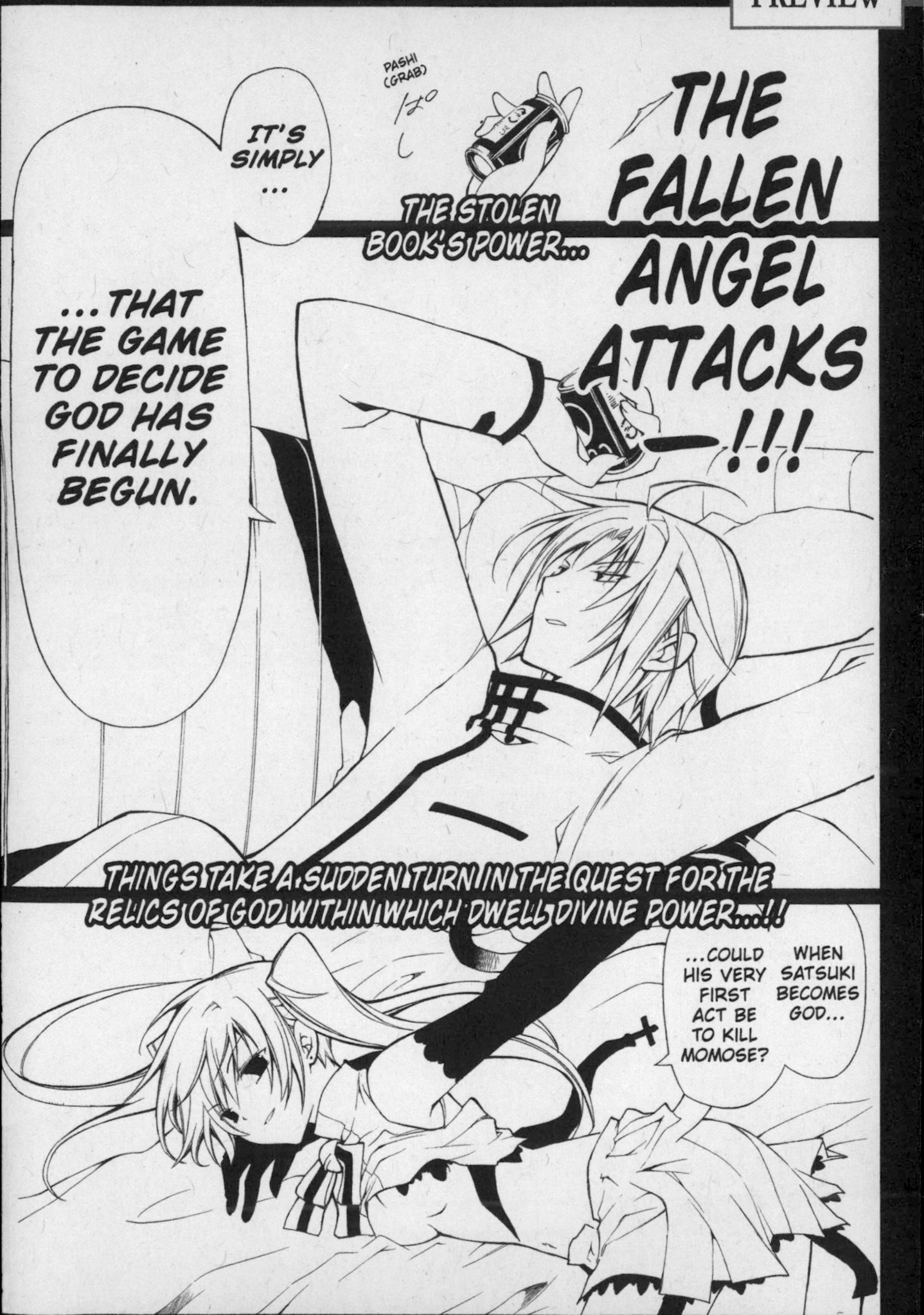
THE FALLEN ANGEL ATTACKS—!!!
PASHI (GRAB)
ぱし
IT'S SIMPLY...
...THAT THE GAME TO DECIDE GOD HAS FINALLY BEGUN.
THE STOLEN BOOK'S POWER...
THINGS TAKE A SUDDEN TURN IN THE QUEST FOR THE RELICS OF GOD WITHIN WHICH DWELL DIVINE POWER...!!
WHEN SATSUKI BECOMES GOD...
...COULD HIS VERY FIRST ACT BE TO KILL MOMOSE?

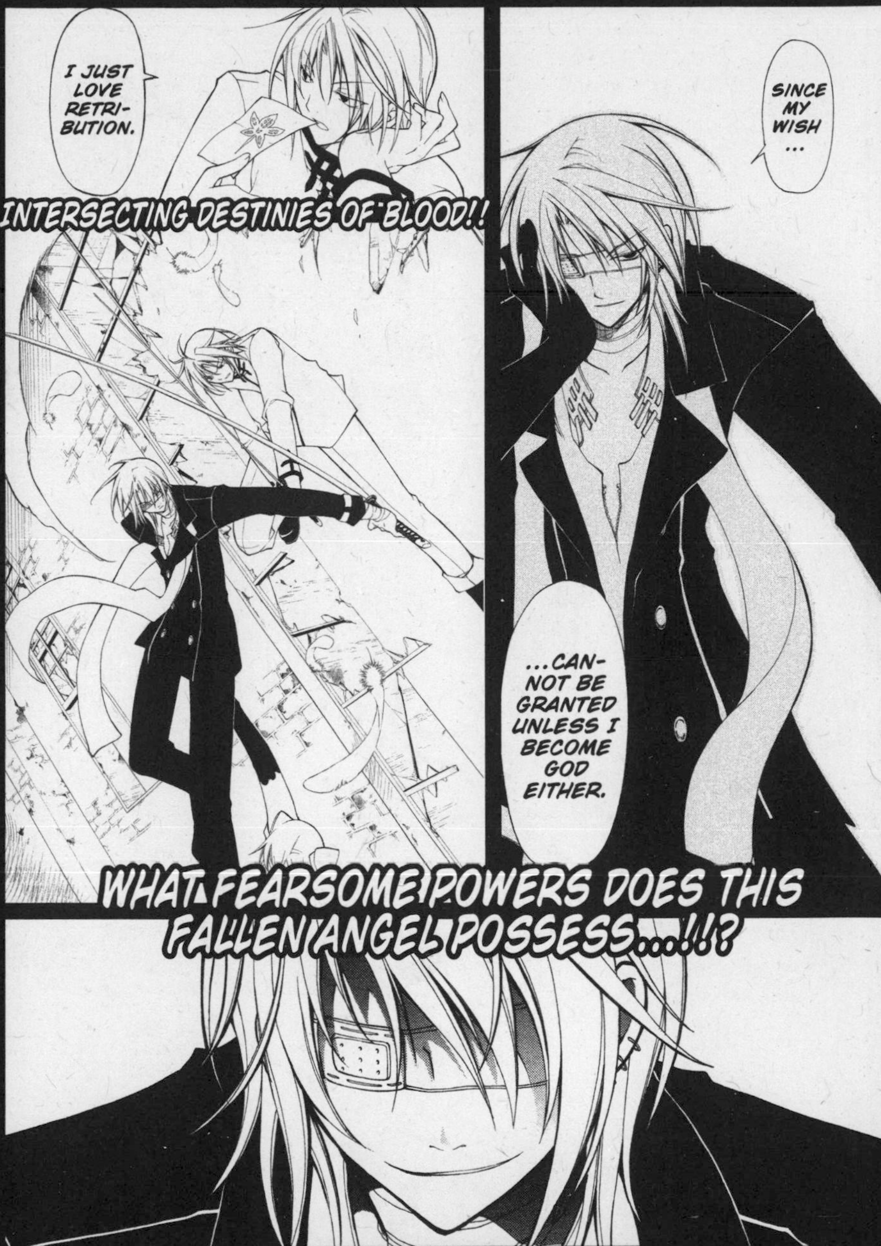
SINCE MY WISH...
...CAN-NOT BE GRANTED UNLESS I BECOME GOD EITHER.
I JUST LOVE RETRI-BUTION.
INTERSECTING DESTINIES OF BLOOD!!
WHAT FEARSOME POWERS DOES THIS FALLEN ANGEL POSSESS...!!?

To be Continued in BLOODY CROSS Vol. 2!!

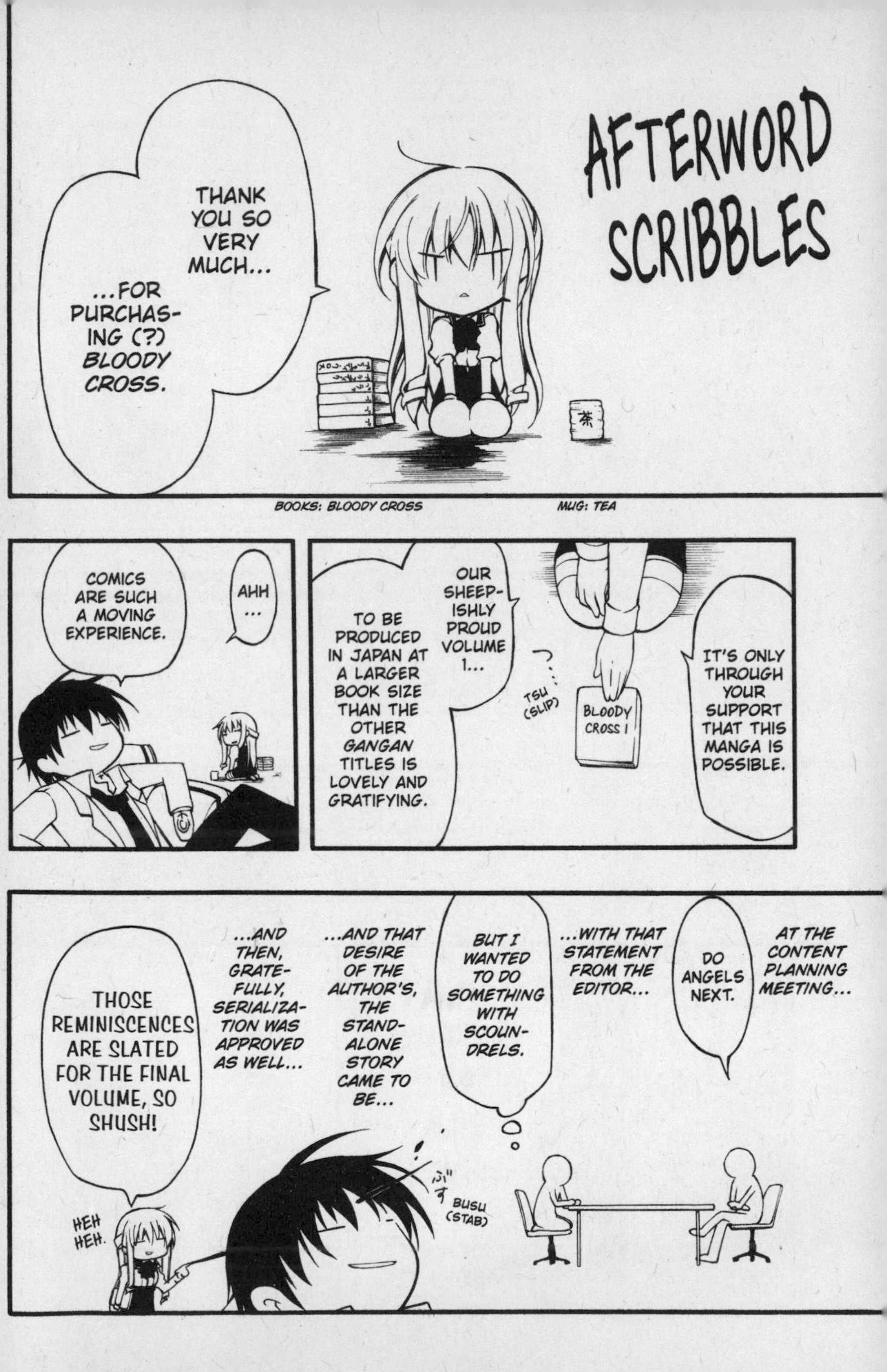
AFTERWORD SCRIBBLES
THANK YOU SO VERY MUCH...
...FOR PURCHASING (?) BLOODY CROSS.
茶
BOOKS: BLOODY CROSS
MUG: TEA
IT'S ONLY THROUGH YOUR SUPPORT THAT THIS MANGA IS POSSIBLE.
TSU (SLIP)
BLOODY CROSS 1
OUR SHEEPISHLY PROUD VOLUME 1...
TO BE PRODUCED IN JAPAN AT A LARGER BOOK SIZE THAN THE OTHER GANGAN TITLES IS LOVELY AND GRATIFYING.
AHH...
COMICS ARE SUCH A MOVING EXPERIENCE.
AT THE CONTENT PLANNING MEETING...
DO ANGELS NEXT.
...WITH THAT STATEMENT FROM THE EDITOR...
BUT I WANTED TO DO SOMETHING WITH SCOUNDRELS.
...AND THAT DESIRE OF THE AUTHOR'S, THE STANDALONE STORY CAME TO BE...
...AND THEN, GRATEFULLY, SERIALIZATION WAS APPROVED AS WELL...
ぶす BUSU (STAB)
THOSE REMINISCENCES ARE SLATED FOR THE FINAL VOLUME, SO SHUSH!
HEH HEH.

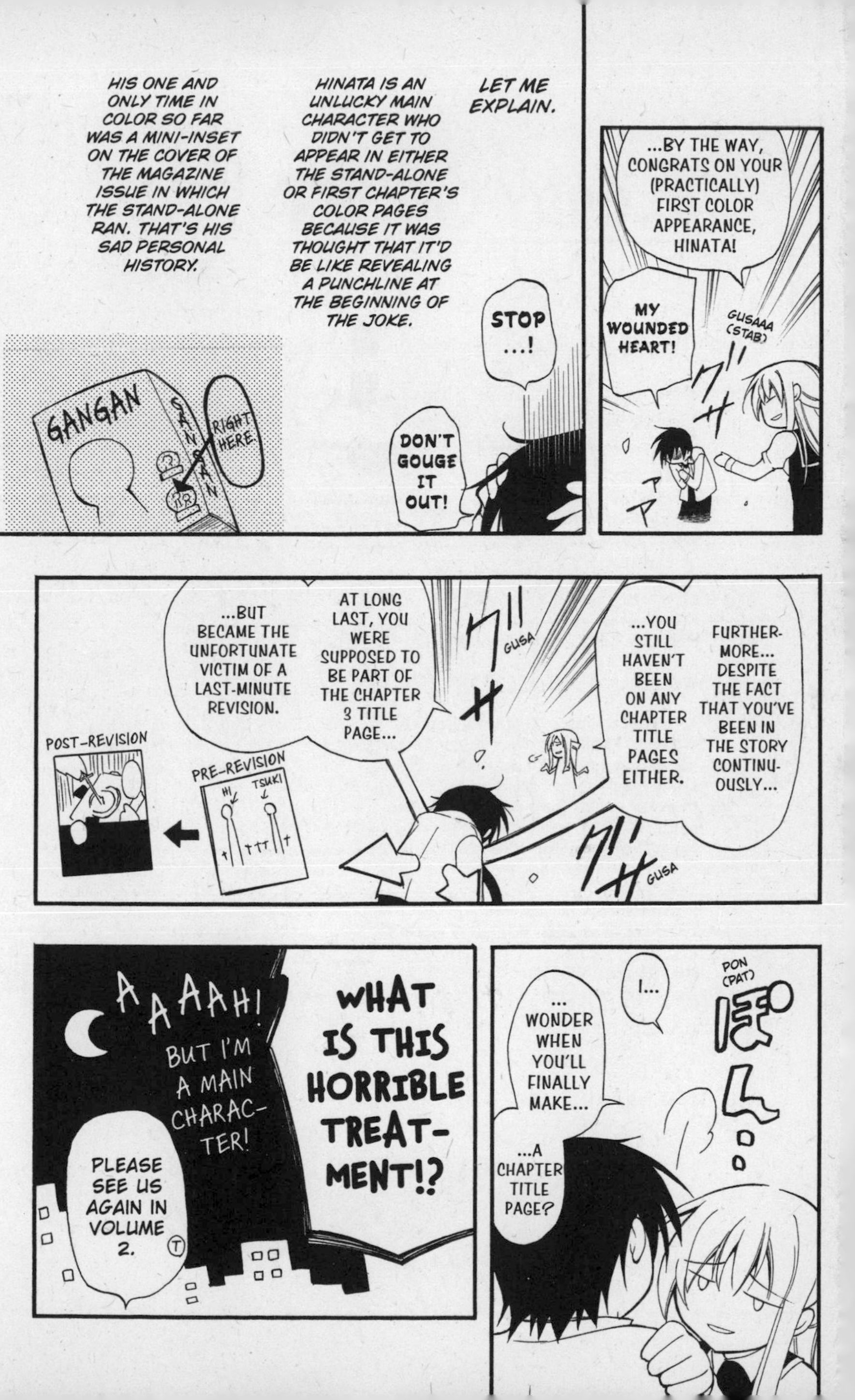
...BY THE WAY, CONGRATS ON YOUR (PRACTICALLY) FIRST COLOR APPEARANCE, HINATA!
GUSAAA (STAB)
MY WOUNDED HEART!
LET ME EXPLAIN.
STOP ...!
HINATA IS AN UNLUCKY MAIN CHARACTER WHO DIDN'T GET TO APPEAR IN EITHER THE STAND-ALONE OR FIRST CHAPTER'S COLOR PAGES BECAUSE IT WAS THOUGHT THAT IT'D BE LIKE REVEALING A PUNCHLINE AT THE BEGINNING OF THE JOKE.
DON'T GOUGE IT OUT!
HIS ONE AND ONLY TIME IN COLOR SO FAR WAS A MINI-INSET ON THE COVER OF THE MAGAZINE ISSUE IN WHICH THE STAND-ALONE RAN. THAT'S HIS SAD PERSONAL HISTORY.
GANGAN
RIGHT HERE.
FURTHERMORE... DESPITE THE FACT THAT YOU'VE BEEN IN THE STORY CONTINUOUSLY...
...YOU STILL HAVEN'T BEEN ON ANY CHAPTER TITLE PAGES EITHER.
GUSA
AT LONG LAST, YOU WERE SUPPOSED TO BE PART OF THE CHAPTER 3 TITLE PAGE...
...BUT BECAME THE UNFORTUNATE VICTIM OF A LAST-MINUTE REVISION.
GUSA
PRE-REVISION
HI
TSUKI
POST-REVISION
PON (PAT)
I...
...WONDER WHEN YOU'LL FINALLY MAKE...
...A CHAPTER TITLE PAGE?
WHAT IS THIS HORRIBLE TREATMENT!?
AAAAHI
BUT I'M A MAIN CHARACTER!
PLEASE SEE US AGAIN IN VOLUME 2.

BLOODY CROSS ❶

SHIWO KOMEYAMA

Translation: Mari Morimoto • Lettering: Abigail Blackman

BLOODY CROSS Vol. 1 © 2009 Shiwo Komeyama / SQUARE ENIX CO., LTD. All rights reserved. First published in Japan in 2009 by SQUARE ENIX CO., LTD. English translation rights arranged with SQUARE ENIX CO., LTD. and Hachette Book Group through Tuttle-Mori Agency, Inc., Tokyo.

Translation © 2013 by SQUARE ENIX CO., LTD.

Yen Press
Hachette Book Group
237 Park Avenue, New York, NY 10017

www.HachetteBookGroup.com
www.YenPress.com

Yen Press is an imprint of Hachette Book Group, Inc. The Yen Press name and logo are trademarks of Hachette Book Group, Inc.

First Yen Press Edition: December 2013

ISBN: 978-0-316-32238-6

10 9 8 7 6 5 4 3 2 1

BVG

Printed in the United States of America